**ENGLAND®
RUGBY**

ENGLAND

THE OFFICIAL
RUGBY FOOTBALL UNION HISTORY

ENGLAND ®
RUGBY

ENGLAND

THE OFFICIAL
RUGBY FOOTBALL UNION HISTORY

Virgin BOOKS

Publishers' Acknowledgements

The Publishers would like to thank the following for their help and enthusiasm during the production of this book:

Jed Smith, Ross Hamilton, Matt Sandell, Richard Hewson and Anne-Laure Delorme at the Museum of Rugby, Twickenham; Timothy Collings and everyone at Collings Sport; Jane Barron at the Rugby Football Union; Sean McAuliffe, Frazer Hughes and Anna Hatjoullis at CPLG; Natalie Jones at Getty Images and Emily Lewis at Empics.

This edition published in Great Britain in 2004 by

Virgin Books Ltd
Thames Wharf Studios
Rainville Road
London
W6 9HA

First published in hardback in 1999

Copyright © Rugby Football Union 1999, 2004
Licensed by Copyright Promotions Licensing Group

A catalogue record for the book is available from the British Library

ISBN: 1 85227 210 4

Design by Alchemedia
Printed and bound in Slovenia

Picture credits

© **Museum of Rugby, Twickenham**: 9, 11, 12, 13, 15, 17, 18, 21 (both), 22, 23, 25, 27, 29 (both), 30, 31, 32 (both), 33, 34, 34-5, 35, 36 (bottom), 39, 40, 40-1, 41 (both), 42 (all), 43 (both), 44 (both), 47 (bottom)

© **Getty Images**: 1, 2, 6, 7, 73 (bottom left), 76, 78, 79, 80, 81, 85, 87 (bottom left), 88, 91 (both), 97, 101, 103, 104, 107, 108, 109, 113, 114, 115, 116, 117 (both), 118, 119, 121, 123, 124, 125, 126-7, 128, 129, 130, 131, 133 (both), 134-5, 136, 137, 138, 139, 140, 141, 144, 145 (both), 146, 148 (both), 150 (both), 152 (both), 154, 156, 158, 161, 162, 166, 167

© **Empics**: 36 (top), 37, 47 (top), 48, 49 (top), 52 (right), 53, 55, 56 (top), 57 (top), 58, 62 (top), 65 (top left and right), 65 (top right), 67 (top), 73 (bottom right), 74, 75, 82, 86, 87 (top left), 92, 93, 94, 98, 99, 105, 106, 110, 111, 112, 153, 155, 157, 159, 160, 163, 164, 165

ENGLAND
RUGBY

Contents

ENGLAND RUGBY

Foreword

I'M delighted to write this foreword and in doing so I want to pay tribute to all the players and the management who have helped England develop into a much stronger and more consistent side over the past four years. I also want to thank all the fans for their continued and invaluable support, which has been so important to the squad, never more so than in Australia last October and November.

Our record of 45 wins and seven defeats since we lost to South Africa in the quarter final of the 1999 Rugby World Cup is one of which I know all England fans are proud.

Understandably, people will focus on our victory in Australia last year and regard it as the pinnacle of England's success on rugby's world stage. To date it has been. To get to that level, however, took a great deal of time, effort and skill from all concerned and for their commitment I will always be grateful.

We are now approaching the next stage of England's development as we aim to defend the Webb Ellis trophy in 2007, in France, and it promises to be an exciting period for rugby in this country.

As we found in the 2004 RBS Six Nations Championship we now face the facts of losing a number of international players through retirement, including Martin Johnson and Jason Leonard. They have all been fantastic ambassadors for the game on and off the field but now changes are inevitably being made.

On the surface it may appear that many players are experiencing the international environment for the first time; a number, including Olly Barkley, have been working with the squad for the past two to three years and have learnt and benefited from the experience.

I am now looking forward to continuing the productive working partnership we have with the Zurich Premiership clubs to help develop the international careers of some very talented players.

I hope you enjoy the book. It highlights not just recent history but the achievements of an England squad who have recorded many memorable moments since the first international was played in 1871.

These include twelve Grand Slams, 34 Championships and 23 Triple Crowns. There have been some fantastic characters in English rugby history from Wavell Wakefield in the 1920s through to Bill Beaumont in the 1980s.

The mantra in the modern game is 'never look back', and in terms of preparing a team, you can't afford do that because it's always about the next game. But it is totally appropriate, at other times, to look back at the great achievements of previous England sides and enjoy the history that surrounds them.

All the key facts and personalities are included in this comprehensive and enjoyable book. It is a fitting tribute to all the players who have had the privilege of wearing the white jersey.

Happy reading.

Best wishes

Sir Clive Woodward

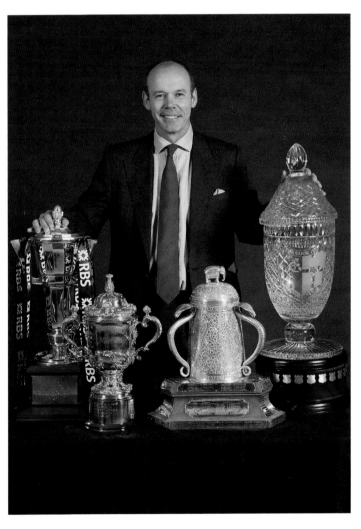

**ENGLAND
RUGBY**

And did those feet in ancient time
Walk upon England's mountains green?
And was the holy Lamb of God
On England's pleasant pastures seen?
And did the countenance divine
Shine forth upon our clouded hills?
And was Jerusalem builded here
Among those dark satanic mills?

Bring. me my bow of burning gold!
Bring me my arrows of desire!
Bring me my spear! Oh clouds, unfold!
Bring me my chariot of fire!
I will not cease from mental fight,
Nor shall my sword sleep in my hand,
Till we have built Jerusalem
In England's green and pleasant land.

'Jerusalem', William Blake

I see you stand like greyhounds in the slips,
Straining upon the start. The game's afoot.
Follow your spirit; and upon this charge
Cry, 'God for Harry, England, and Saint George!'

Henry V Act III, Scene I

1871-1909

In the beginning

IT IS ALMOST IMPOSSIBLE TO CONTEMPLATE THE ORIGINS OF RUGBY
FOOTBALL WITHOUT MENTIONING THE MYTH OF WILLIAM WEBB ELLIS, THE
SIXTEEN-YEAR-OLD CREDITED WITH INVENTING THE GAME WE RECOGNISE
TODAY. ACCORDING TO THE POPULAR LEGEND, WHILE PLAYING IN A
SCHOOL FOOTBALL MATCH IN 1823 MASTER WEBB ELLIS CAUGHT THE BALL
– THAT HE PICKED IT UP IS A COMMON MISCONCEPTION – AND RAN WITH IT,
THEREBY FASHIONING A FUNDAMENTALLY NEW SPORT.

IN 1895 a stone plaque was erected on Rugby School's wall in honour of his deed. Its inscription reads: 'This stone commemorates the exploit of William Webb Ellis, who with a fine disregard for the rules of football as played in his time, first took the ball in his arms and ran with it, thus originating the distinctive feature of the rugby game. AD 1823'.

One problem with this wonderfully romantic version of events is that for centuries games closely resembling rugby football were played in these isles, and all, in one form or another, have involved moving with the ball in hand. As early as circa 30 BC there are accounts of the ancient Romans playing *harpastum*, a game with many similarities to the football codes that were to follow, and it is likely that their conquering armies introduced this pastime to Britain, and that it was a forerunner of regional games such as 'camp-ball' and 'hurling to goales'.

Throughout the Middle Ages games of 'mob football', traditionally played by indeterminate numbers on Shrove Tuesday in open countryside, were so widespread that they were banned by a succession of English monarchs. Richard II (king from 1377 until 1399), Henry V (1413–22) and Edward IV (1461–83) issued proclamations prohibiting football for fear that the men were neglecting the archery practice imperative to national defence. The early contests were extremely rowdy and often degenerated into violent free-for-alls resulting in serious injury and property damage.

In 1533, the Mayor of Chester, Henry Gee, replaced the Shrovetide festival match with various athletic events, and in 1608 a similar fate befell Manchester. Along with Chester, the game has been longest established in Derby (hence the term 'local derby'), and myth has it that the first such encounter was held in AD 217 to celebrate the slaughter of a cohort of Roman troops.

The sport was not staged in any organised form until the nineteenth century when pupils at Britain's public schools began to arrange matches during their leisure time. The rules were devised by the senior boys, without the intervention of masters, and were constantly updated by mutual consent. By the 1820s, their games already comprised many of the characteristics of modern rugby. The exact role played by the precocious Ellis in this development was minimal at best and certainly did not herald a new sport; nor did he suddenly transform a game played on the floor to one played in the hand. The real innovators of the day were those boys at Eton and the like who insisted on keeping the ball at their feet. Although there is no evidence to substantiate the famous story, it is not impossible that Ellis was the first person to attempt the manoeuvre at his particular seat of learning.

In the early 1800s opportunities to run with the ball at Rugby School were extremely limited. Matches involved the entire school population – approaching 400 in 1816 – and were played on a relatively small pitch. Although the shrouds of time will forever conceal the full truth of the matter, we do know that by the end of the 1830s 'running in' had become an accepted, if rarely practised, element of matches at Rugby School. Despite the fact that Webb Ellis' role in the development of the game has been exaggerated, if not invented, in 1987 the inaugural World Cup trophy was named in his honour.

The game continued to thrive, and the most illuminating description of its progress up to and during the 1840s can be read in the evocative *Tom Brown's Schooldays*. A seminal work written by Thomas Hughes and first published in 1857, it recounts the author's own experiences at Rugby School through the eyes of his fictional hero, Tom Brown. As captain of rugby football, Hughes had a comprehensive knowledge of his subject, and his attention to detail provides a fascinating insight into how

little rugby has changed in over 150 years. He describes the traditional H-shaped goal posts and how the object of the game was to score goals by either place- or drop-kicking the ball between the posts and above the crossbar. Any player touching down beyond the opposition's goal line would carefully punt the ball to a team-mate, whose 'fair catch' or mark would provide him with the opportunity to 'try at goal', the precursor of today's converted try. Games were played with an oval-shaped ball, and scrummages and line-outs were already well established. Laws to govern 'off your side' were even in use, and in the novel, when Tom Brown asks if he can play in a match on his first day at school he is informed that he will be a month learning the rules.

The original word-of-mouth method of instructing new pupils was becoming increasingly impractical, and in 1845 three senior boys, one the son of the late headmaster Dr Thomas Arnold, produced the first official Rugby School laws. 'Running in', was permitted, provided the player did not pick up the ball, as was 'hacking' – basically kicking an opponent, but only below the knee. (The latter's inclusion would have profound consequences, and would be responsible for the split with soccer [association football].)

In all, 37 laws were recorded, including those for a 'fair catch', knock-on and drop-out. Some, particularly those concerning offside, endure virtually unchanged to this day. Law 31 – 'no body may wear cap or jersey without leave from the head of house' – applied directly to another school innovation, that of awarding caps. These were bestowed only on those

players of sufficient ability to participate, or 'follow up', in the main game, to distinguish them from the remaining minions who were required to act as goalkeepers behind the goal line.

As former pupils joined universities and entered teaching posts, so Rugby's codified game spread throughout the realm. Businessmen, the military and the clergy introduced it to the colonies, and by 1875 rugby football had reached almost every corner of the British Empire.

The claim of Guy's Hospital, London, that they were formed in 1843, made them the first official rugby club. The first in Ireland was founded at Trinity College, Dublin eleven years later, and three years after that, in 1857, Scotland gave rise to Edinburgh Academicals. Scholars of Blackheath Preparatory School are claimed to have founded the 'Club', in 1858, and their match with Richmond in 1867 – or according to some sources as early as 1863 – is the game's oldest surviving club fixture.

Within a twenty-year period from the 1850s a great number of teams emerged; few, however, could agree on which laws to follow. In 1839, Old Rugbeian Arthur Pell tried to establish a side at Cambridge University, only to be thwarted by familiar disputes over the interpretation of the disparate rules. Cambridge University drew up the Cambridge Rules in 1848, which would

Left The English line-up for the very first rugby union international, against Scotland in Edinburgh on 27 March 1871
Right The jersey worn by J H Clayton during the 1871 match, together with his cap, on display at the Museum of Rugby at Twickenham

subsequently form the basis of the Football Association's laws, and in 1857 Sheffield also devised their own code, outlawing the regulations laid down at Rugby twelve years before. In 1862, both Blackheath and Charterhouse School contrived their own equally varied guidelines. University students from divergent backgrounds would habitually disagree on which version of the sport they should adopt. Old Rugbeians and former pupils of the schools influenced by Rugby would invariably insist on playing the game according to their traditions, while those educated at other public schools balked at the idea of running with the ball or being hacked. Their preference was for a pastime played almost entirely on the floor.

For some, the choice was purely a matter of environment: the hacking advocated at Rugby was dangerous enough on grass, but when practised on paving or cobblestones it could be positively lethal, and certain institutions therefore embraced the less precarious dribbling game. To exacerbate the peculiarities between teams, different-shaped balls were being used. In 1851 a 'Rugby School football', made from a pig's bladder by the renowned ball manufacturer James Gilbert, was displayed at the International Exhibition in London. Though it would become even more so in later years, it was already oval-shaped, in contrast to the round balls which other schools favoured.

Despite their seemingly incongruous disparities, football and Rugby football were still considered to be basically the same

sport. It does not appear to have occurred to players or officials that two vastly differing games had evolved and, in October 1863, a conference was convened with the specific intention of resolving the numerous anomalies and creating a single, national football code. In the first instance the majority of the distinctive features of the game developed at Rugby were recognised in draft legislation. Hacking, tripping, holding, running with and handling the ball were all included – until, that is, delegates began to voice strenuous objections. Blackheath vigorously defended the faith, but the die was cast, and on 8 December 1863, following six further meetings, a general consensus was finally reached: handling the ball was prohibited and, more disturbingly for the rugby fraternity, so was hacking. Blackheath stepped down, and the remaining clubs founded the Football Association (FA), agreeing to a game consisting of eleven players per side. (In one of the supreme ironies, three years later Blackheath and Richmond agreed to abolish hacking, and by the close of the decade it was also banned at Rugby.) Thus rugby and football went their separate ways, and just over seven years later, on 26 January 1871, 32 representatives of 21 rugby clubs gathered at the Pall Mall restaurant in Cockspur Street, London and founded the Rugby Football Union (RFU), the sport's first national governing body. Algernon Rutter was elected as the inaugural RFU president, and a committee was installed to formulate a set of laws based on those codified at Rugby.

Prior to this, England and Scotland had met in two unofficial matches played under the auspices of the Football Association. The Scottish teams mainly comprised London-based players, and a total of five soccer 'friendlies' were contested before the FA secretary and Old Harrovian Charles Alcock could organise a full football international, in 1872. The first of these five games resulted in a goalless draw, and after England had won the second 1–0, several of Scotland's leading clubs challenged their southern counterparts to a rugby match. In an open letter published in the *Scotsman* and *Bell's Life* in December 1870, they stated that as the majority of their foremost teams followed the rugby code, they would relish the opportunity of testing themselves against the English in a more familiar game. They requested a twenty-a-side contest, standard for the time, played in either Edinburgh or Glasgow on any convenient date during the current season. The newly contrived RFU accepted the challenge, and on 27 March 1871 Raeburn Place, Edinburgh staged not only the first rugby international, but also the first official meeting between two countries at any sport. While Scotland arranged trial matches in order to finalise their strongest team, England had less time to prepare, and consequently several key players were unavailable. Ten of their side were former pupils of Rugby School, and one of these, future RFU president Frederick Stokes, was nominated captain.

In these early years teams contained thirteen or fourteen forwards, and play tended to congregate around mass scrummages and rucks which could last for several minutes.

FOUNDER MEMBERS OF THE RUGBY FOOTBALL UNION

Addison	Law
Belsize Park	Marlborough Nomads
Blackheath	Mohicans
Clapham Rovers	Queen's House
Civil Service	Ravenscourt Park
Flamingoes Gipsies	Richmond
Guy's Hospital	St Paul's School
Harlequins	Wellington College
King's College	West Kent
Lausanne	Wimbledon Hornets

The upright forwards attempted to kick the ball through the opposing ranks, and when it did emerge it would often do so accidentally. The convention of 'heeling' out was not developed until scrum sizes were later reduced, and the sparse possession that did come the way of the backs was generally kicked to gain ground or to drop goals. Although running the ball back at the opposition was also growing in popularity, passing from hand was still an unfamiliar concept. Indeed, in some areas it was considered poor form for a player to offload the ball before being tackled.

Initially, matches were decided by the number of goals kicked - tries would later be taken into account in the event of a tie – and Scotland won the opening contest by a goal, i.e. a converted

try, and a try to a solitary English try scored by Reginald Birkett. (In 1879, Birkett became the first of only three individuals to represent England at both rugby and football, keeping goal in a 5–4 victory over Scotland, and the following season playing in the Clapham Rovers team that beat Oxford University in the FA Cup final.) The Scottish pushover try, from which Cross struck their match-winning kick, was a controversial affair. Instead of putting the ball to the floor, as the law required, and then driving over the English line, the Scots pushed their entire scrum into goal before grounding the ball.

Even so, in excess of 4,000 spectators ensured that the event was a great success, and in February 1872 the Kennington Oval, also the venue for the first football and cricket internationals played in England, hosted the rematch. The narrow confines of the Raeburn place pitch, just 55 yards wide, were thought in part to have contributed to the English defeat, and on the expanse of the Oval restitution was made in full. The home side won by a goal, a drop goal and two tries to a drop goal. A year later the annual fixture was permanently established, and in Glasgow the two nations played out the first international draw. Finney looked to have broken the deadlock for England, but his kick from a mark flew so high above the uprights the umpires were unable to judge whether or not it dissected them, and the game ended goalless.

Before the 1873 match, the principal Caledonian teams had formed the Scottish Football Union, which was subsequently renamed the Scottish Rugby Union in 1924. In Ireland, however, the creation of a controlling body was less straightforward. In the space of a month the Dublin-based clubs launched the Irish Football Union, and the men of Ulster the Northern Football

Union. For their international debut, against England at the Oval in February 1875, the Irish selected from both unions and many of their players had never actually met prior to kick-off. Despite this rather obvious handicap, they limited the English to two tries, one of which Pearson converted, and a drop goal scored by the double Oxford Blue Edward Nash. On 13 December 1875, a return match was arranged at Rathmines, the home of Leinster Cricket Club. Again the Irish acquitted themselves well and again Pearson kicked the winning goal for England, after having failed to convert an earlier try by Clark. By the end of the decade the two independent unions had amalgamated, and an all-Ireland rugby team has prevailed to this day.

While the English were winning in Dublin, Oxford University were defeating their peers at Cambridge in the first Varsity match to be contested between teams of fifteen players. The attacking advantages of playing a game with reduced numbers were indisputable, and clubs across the country quickly adopted the revolutionary new style. Standard formations began to appear, with most sides favouring ten forwards, two half-backs, two full-backs and one three-quarter back. In the only common variation of this, an additional forward would occasionally replace one of the full-backs. At the Oval in February 1877 England beat Ireland in the first fifteen-a-side international and both countries employed a 9–2–2–2 formation. These positions remained more or less unaltered until 1881, at which time Scotland introduced a third three-quarters against the Irish in Belfast, once more at the expense of a full-back.

Between 1871 and 1878 England and Scotland played eight internationals and England narrowly led the series 3–2. When the teams assembled for the ninth game at Raeburn Place in March 1879, the Calcutta Cup was at stake for the first time. The magnificent trophy, forged by Indian craftsmen from melted-down silver rupees, was presented to the RFU president Arthur Guillemard in 1878 by the former captain and treasurer of the defunct Calcutta Football Cup. The club had been founded in 1874 to promote the game in India, but polo and billiards proved the more popular activities on the subcontinent and within three years the dwindling membership recognised that there was not sufficient interest to sustain a rugby team. They therefore very generously agreed that, in order to achieve 'some lasting good for the cause of Rugby Football', their assets at closure would be spent on the creation of a trophy to be awarded to the winners of an annual challenge competition. The RFU declined to accept the trophy as a rugby equivalent to the new and very popular FA Cup in soccer and so the annual England versus Scotland fixture was considered the most appropriate. Ever since the two countries have contested the Calcutta Cup with much distinction and, it must be said, a certain amount of animosity, a great deal of which surfaced during the 1880s.

Chiefly due to the economic climate, few of the population were privileged enough to send their sons to public school or university, so rugby took longer to establish in Wales than the rest of Britain. Neath, Wales's first senior club, was formed in 1871, and ten years later Wales were awarded an international against England at Blackheath. The experienced English, unbeaten since 1877, were far too strong for the Welsh novices, winning by seven goals, one drop goal and six tries to nil. England did not

exceed this total of thirteen tries until Holland were put to the sword 110–0 in 1998. On that day, Jeremy Guscott and Neil Back helped themselves to half of England's sixteen touchdowns, but in 1881 George Burton and Harry Vassall were the cardinal beneficiaries of the philanthropic Welsh defence: Vassall scored a hat-trick, and Burton went one better with four. Captain Lennie Stokes, brother of former skipper Frederick, kicked six conversions, and Robert Hunt became the first player to register a try, a conversion and a drop goal in the same match. Applying the modern system of scoring, England won that game 82–0. Determined that they would never again suffer such a humiliating defeat, three weeks later the eleven senior teams in Wales gathered at the Castle Hotel in Neath and formed the Welsh Rugby Union.

After their decisive victory, England gave the fixture a miss the following year, and the next encounter fell in the 1882–83 season, generally accepted as the first season in which the four home nations contested the International Championship, even though an official championship did not exist for more than a century. The newspapers were primarily responsible for the publication of points tables, and the terms 'Grand Slam', 'Triple Crown' and 'wooden spoon' were coined by the press (although the latter term originated at Cambridge University, where it was applied to the student with the lowest mark in the mathematical tripos). Indeed,

until 1993, when the competition was finally ratified and the title decided on points difference, no trophy was even awarded. Who says the game's administrators were reluctant innovators?!

Officially endorsed or not, the tournament has always aroused great passion, and the first in 1883 produced a nail-biting climax. England commenced their campaign with an assured six-try win over a much-improved Wales in Swansea, and then beat the Irish at Whalley Range, Manchester. Gregory Wade, with a debut hat-trick against Wales, and Wilfred Bolton scored in each game. Scotland also won their first two fixtures, and their match against England in Edinburgh would later be viewed as the championship decider. England, without a victory in six attempts on Scottish soil, took the lead through an unconverted try from one of their halves, Alan Rotherham. Reid then equalised for the home side after the interval, but MacLagan missed the goal and the game looked like ending in another draw – the two teams had already shared five – when Bolton scored his third try of the season. Though their accomplishment would only be acknowledged retrospectively, England had won the first International Championship and Triple Crown. The fact that there was no fixture arranged between Ireland and Wales does not appear to have been deemed relevant, as both had lost their two matches.

They did meet a year later, though, and for the first time all four countries played each other in one season. England, applying the tactical passing game pioneered by Harry Vassall at Oxford University, successfully defended their title, and in the process again won the Triple Crown. For the second year in a row the forward Edward Temple Gurdon marshalled the side. His overall record as captain was eight wins and a draw in nine matches. From 1878 to 1886 he made a record sixteen international appearances with just the one loss, while his brother and Richmond team-mate Charles Gurdon won fourteen caps during the same period, with the pair playing together on ten occasions.

After the contention surrounding the legality of Scotland's winning try in the inaugural game of 1871, disputes were a prevalent feature of international matches. Each country's varied interpretations of the game's laws were rarely in harmony, and England's second consecutive championship, clinched with victory against Scotland in 1884, produced the most famous and consequential altercation of them all. The result of the incident was six years of antagonism, a great deal of lasting resentment and ultimately an independent governing body.

Scotland were leading the season's vital end game by a try to nil when one of their own players flicked the ball back with his hand. Moments later England overturned possession and Richard Kindersley scored an equalising try. The Scots construed the knock-back as a knock-on and argued, spuriously according to the English, that as they had committed an earlier offence, play should have been stopped before Kindersley was able to score. England, on the other hand, maintained that no knock-on had taken place and that even if it had it would not be ethical to permit a team to benefit from its own infringement. The referee, the former Ireland captain George Scriven, allowed the try to stand and, after the players had stood quarrelling for ten minutes, the game resumed with Wilfred Bolton kicking the match- and championship-winning goal. Scotland refused to accept the referee's ruling, and England declined their request to put the matter to arbitration. In the ensuing stalemate the two countries did not play each other the following season, and England had to content themselves with victories over Wales and Ireland.

The fixture was resumed in 1886, England and Scotland sharing the championship with two wins and a draw, but by this stage Ireland and Wales were embroiled in their own dispute. To help resolve this, and to adjudicate on future disagreements, the Irish proposed the formation of an international panel comprising members of all four home nations. While the RFU agreed in principle, they were clearly concerned that this would affect their position as the game's senior ruling body, and eventually opted not to join, leaving Ireland, Scotland and Wales as the three founding members of the International Rugby Football Board (IRFB, later renamed the IRB in 1998).

Despite England's reticence, a full programme of matches was completed in 1887. After drawing the opener with Wales, England had a winning sequence of thirteen championship fixtures broken when Ireland defeated them for the first time, and concluded a fruitless season with another draw against Scotland. Having failed to win a single game they shared the wooden spoon with Ireland. At the end of the year the RFU were again invited to join the International Board, and when they declined all three home unions agreed that matches with England would be suspended until they could be persuaded to reconsider. It was no idle threat, and the English did not play their next championship game until 1890.

Their one international fixture in the intervening years came in 1889 against the New Zealand Natives, a predominantly Maori team undertaking the longest tour of all time. In eighteen months they played 107 matches, 74 of them in Britain (the remainder were played in Australia and New Zealand). England had never previously faced overseas opposition and their victory was unremarkable save for Frank Evershed's try, scored when most of the players had stopped to allow Andrew Stoddart to change his torn shorts! Stoddart won ten caps at three-quarters for England and went on to captain his country at rugby and cricket. He made his rugby debut in 1885 against Wales, and three years later opened the batting against Australia in the first of sixteen Test matches. While still in Australia he assumed the captaincy of the British Isles maiden tour when Bob Seddon drowned in a sculling accident.

POINTS-SCORING SYSTEMS

Period	Try	Con	DG	PG	GM
1891–92 to 1892–93	2	3	4	3	4
1893–94 to 1904–05	3	2	4	3	4
1905–06 to 1947–48	3	2	4	3	3
1948–49 to 1970–71	3	2	3	3	3
1971–72 to 1976–77	4	2	3	3	3
1977–78 to 1991–92	4	2	3	3	–
1992–93 to present	5	2	3	3	–

ENGLAND

IRELAND.

February 9th, 1907.

W. C. WILSON,
(Eastern Counties).

E. J. JACKETT,
(Cornwall).

G. LEATHER,
(Lancashire).

C. H. SHAW,
(Midlands).

R. JAGO,
(Devon).

J. G. MILTON,
(Cornwall).

J. GREEN, (Capt.)
(Yorkshire).

L. A. N. SLOCOCK,
(Lancashire).

T. S. KELLY,
(Devon).

H. M. IMRIE,
(Durham).

S. G. WILLIAMS,
(Devon).

J. PETERS,
(Devon).

A. S. PICKERING,
(Yorkshire).

H. E. SHEWRING,
(Somerset).

W. MILLS,
(Devon).

Above A comprehensive 22–0 victory at Leicester on 30 January 1909 maintained England's unbeaten record over the French

By 1890 the International Board and the RFU had come to accept that little could be gained from prolonging England's banishment, and both factions were willing to make concessions. The RFU had always reasoned that as they governed by far the largest union they should have a greater say in the game's administration and development. Astonishingly, the other nations acceded to this supposition and England joined the IRB with six seats, compared to two each for Ireland, Scotland and Wales. In essence they would still control the sport, having the power to veto any overtures not to their liking. To restructure the balance of power, England relinquished two of these seats in 1911, and a further two in 1948 (when Australia, New Zealand and South Africa were accepted as members). Initially each of the southern hemisphere nations was granted one vote, only receiving a second ten years later. In 1978 France was the last of the eight senior countries allocated two seats on the IRB's executive council. Argentina, Canada, Italy and Japan have since been admitted, all with a single representation, as has the regional body FIRA-AER.

In February 1890, England returned to championship competition, losing to Wales for the first time before beating Scotland and Ireland for a share of the title. Within weeks Lord Kingsburgh, the Lord Justice Clerk, and the president of the Football Association, Major Marindin, the men belatedly asked to mediate on the cataclysmic Anglo-Scottish dispute of 1884, found conclusively in England's favour. The contentious try would stand, and England were officially declared winners.

The augmented IRB was now solely responsible for amendments to the laws of international rugby – in time the club game would also come under their dominion – and one of their first acts was to establish a uniform points-scoring system. The RFU had tried to introduce a similar procedure in 1886, but their recommendations – three points for a goal and one for an unconverted try – were not universally accepted and values differed from country to country. According to the IRB, from 1891 a try was worth one point, a conversion two, a goal from a mark and a drop goal three, and a penalty goal two.

The following season an extra point was added to every method of scoring, and in 1894 the value of a try was increased to three and a conversion reduced to two.

Penalties had existed since 1882, but until the law changes of 1891 it was not permissible to score from one directly. The great Welsh full-back Billy Bancroft was the first player to land a penalty goal, scoring with a drop-kick, as opposed to a place-kick, to win a match against England in 1893. Two years later Fred Byrne despatched England's first in a defeat at the hands of Scotland. While it is difficult to imagine a game unfettered by penalties, for many years they were a comparatively rare feature of play. England converted just eleven in 85 internationals prior to the First World War, and did not score another against Scotland until 1936. A far cry from today's Calcutta Cup matches.

If penalties would one day dictate the way the game was played, another advancement, the advent of a fourth three-quarter, had a more immediate effect. Coventry were the first to play the extra back, and their system was refined at Cardiff under captain Frank Hancock. Wales experimented with the formation against Scotland in 1886, Hancock's last international, before adopting it permanently in the early 1890s. The previously indistinguishable half-backs started to specialise in either the scrum half position or as outside-halves, more commonly known as fly-halves. The forwards, now eight in number, also began to occupy specific positions, and the 'first up, first down' method of scrummaging evolved into the 3–2–3 formation, and eventually the conventional 3–4–1 system. Only the All Blacks deviated significantly, playing a seven-man pack in a 2–3–2 configuration. The extra man, the wing forward or rover, was responsible for the put-in, enabling the scrum half to collect a quick heel and instantly release his backs. New Zealand were still using this strategy until the IRB introduced a mandatory three-man front row in 1932, principally to negate the disruptive role of the wing forward.

Two seasons after their international reintroduction, England won a third Triple Crown without conceding a single point. Wales were beaten 17–0, Ireland 7–0 and Scotland 5–0, a remarkable accomplishment still unequalled in the championship's history. With individuals of the quality of Richard Lockwood, Samuel Woods, Frank Evershed and William Bromet, England's immediate future seemed assured, but one very dark cloud would soon appear on the horizon: the controversial practice of recompensing players for an unpaid absence from work, otherwise known as 'broken time' payments.

Notwithstanding its inception in the exclusive realm of England's most expensive schools, rugby began to attract a large following in traditional working-class areas. Men who had to toil for a living could ill afford to lose several days' pay each month playing and travelling to and from matches, and it was for these players that 'broken time' payments were intended.

The game's Victorian forebears took a less sympathetic view, maintaining that rugby should be enjoyed as a healthy recreation and that payments of any kind were unacceptable and would surely represent the thin end of the wedge. On the last part they were probably right. Matches now attracted large attendances and a share of the spectators' entrance money was finding its way into the players' pockets. Clubs in the north of England made no secret of the fact that their members were being reimbursed for loss of earnings, and some clubs were patently going further, offering financial inducements to entice players from other teams.

This plainly contravened the game's amateur code, and the matter came to a head in September 1893 at the RFU's annual general meeting. The motion 'That players be allowed compensation for bona-fide loss of time' was defeated by 282 votes to 136. Of the dissenting ballots, 120 were cast by proxy on the back of some Machiavellian-style canvassing by RFU members. Tumultuous applause greeted the result, but two years later the cheering had a somewhat hollow resonance when 22 of the strongest Yorkshire and Lancashire clubs resigned from the English Rugby Union to form the Northern Football Union. Many others were to follow them. In 1906, they switched to a thirteen-man game and, in 1922, took the name the Northern Rugby League, dropping the 'Northern' in 1980. Taking into account American Football (gridiron), Canadian Football, Gaelic Football and Australian Rules Football, the last invented by Old Rugbeians Henry Colden Harrison and Thomas Wills, seven very distinct sports had emerged from little more than a mass brawl first played on the green pastures of England's public schools.

The split was to prove incredibly damaging to English rugby. In ten years 237 of the 481 clubs affiliated to the RFU had defected, taking with them the cream of the England side. An entire generation of players was lost to the amateur game, and the effect on the national team's results was quite catastrophic. From 1871 to 1895 England won 34 and drew nine of their 54 matches, including ten consecutive victories between 1882 and 1886. In the next twelve seasons they were to win just ten of 40 games. The same team that convincingly claimed the International Championship in 1892 did not do so again until 1910, and in five of nine seasons England collected the wooden spoon having lost all three championship fixtures. In 1905 the far-sighted 'Originals', the first New Zealand side to tour the British Isles, inflicted a painful five-try drubbing, and only the fledgling French were beaten with any regularity. Wales and Scotland made the most of England's downfall, dominating the championship for the opening decade of the twentieth century and respectively winning five and three Triple Crowns.

The stringent legislation drafted by the RFU in 1895, finally convincing the Roses clubs to go it alone, further tightened the amateur laws. Professionalism of any kind was outlawed, and even the act of taking the field alongside a known professional was enough to see a player forfeit his amateur status. Accordingly, working men gravitated towards either association football or rugby league, and the union game in England became clearly defined as an élitist sport played by the wealthy. When the Welsh Rugby Union magnanimously donated a house to their distinguished back Arthur Gould, purchased from the proceeds of a testimonial fund, they were immediately accused of 'a professional act'. England, anxious to preserve their lucrative club matches against Welsh opposition, for once wisely looked the other way, but Ireland and Scotland refused to play Wales in their 1897 fixtures, and the Scots continued the protest in 1898. Happily, these were the last major boycotts to undermine the championship for more than 30 years.

Golden Age

IN JANUARY 1901 THE UNITED KINGDOM'S LONGEST-REIGNING
MONARCH, QUEEN VICTORIA, DIED. SHE HAD PRESIDED OVER THE
NATION FOR ALMOST 64 YEARS, AND AS A MARK OF RESPECT ENGLAND
AND IRELAND WORE BLACK ARM-BANDS FOR THEIR MEETING IN
DUBLIN A FORTNIGHT LATER. ON THE ACCESSION OF EDWARD VII,
THE FUTURE KING GEORGE V WAS INVESTED PRINCE OF WALES.

THROUGHOUT his sovereignty, from 1910 until 1936, George remained a staunch patron of English rugby and regularly attended matches. By the time of his visit to Richmond in 1909, to watch the annual Calcutta Cup fixture, there were tentative indications that England were beginning to emerge from the depths to which they had plummeted following the mass exodus of northern clubs. During the previous four seasons the national selection committee, probably more by luck than judgment given their past inconsistencies, had unearthed several genuine talents, each of whom would play an indispensable role in their country's revival.

The astute half-back Adrian Stoop, the earliest player to clearly define the scrum and fly-half positions, made his debut against Scotland in 1905, and twelve months later, against the same opposition, future captains Robert Dibble and John Birkett won their first caps. In the same year Alfred Kewney, fetchingly nicknamed 'Kicking Ginger', came into the side, and England played France and South Africa for the first time. The French were beaten 35–8 at the Parc des Princes. Wing Arthur Hudson, only playing because Thomas Simpson was not able to travel to Paris, scored four of England's nine tries. At Crystal Palace 40,000 spectators watched the 3–3 draw with the Springboks, Frederick Brooks equalising the tourists' early score in his one international appearance. In the return match against France in 1907 England again produced a nine-try display, 'Daniel' Lambert scoring five on his debut to equal George Lindsay's world record for Scotland against Wales in 1887. (Eighty-two years later another Englishman, Rory Underwood, scored five tries, against Fiji, and the record was finally broken in the 1995 World Cup when Marc Ellis claimed six in New Zealand's 145–17 routing of Japan.) In addition to Lambert's nap hand, Birkett scored the first of ten senior tries, and added four more in

1908. He was unavailable in 1909, missing both the inaugural meeting with Australia and England's 100th international match, against Wales in Cardiff. Both were lost, but in the next game the ebullient centre-cum-wing Ronnie Poulton gave notice of his massive potential by creating several tries for his team-mates in a 22–0 victory over the French. While they were never actually deployed in unison, Stoop, Birkett, Poulton and, to a lesser extent, Lambert were all major contributors to the rejuvenation of the English rose.

Unlike their rivals, who either had grounds or would alternate between two or three designated venues, England were without a permanent home. International fixtures were staged at a succession of miscellaneous clubs across the country. In 1906 the RFU decided to end this itinerant existence and began the search for a suitable site to base the national team. One of their committee members, William Williams, a former Harlequins player and Middlesex leg-break bowler, nominated ten acres of market garden in the London suburb of Twickenham, and it was subsequently purchased in 1907 for the princely sum of £5,572, twelve shillings and sixpence. Affectionately christened 'Billy Williams' cabbage patch', Twickenham staged its first game in October 1909, Harlequins beating Richmond 14–10, and three months later England entertained Wales in the International Championship.

Having accumulated six championship titles and five Triple Crowns in a decade, Wales were irrefutably the best side in Britain. They had not lost to England since 1898, and of the eleven ensuing encounters could boast ten wins and a draw. For the home side William Johnston at full-back, a position he would eventually make his own, wing Frederick Chapman and the flanker 'Cherry' Pillman were all making their first appearances, with Poulton on the opposite wing and Birkett at centre. Fly-half

Adrian Stoop, who had last played in the corresponding fixture of 1907, returned as captain, and within seconds of the start created a decisive opening try, running the kick-off back into the Welsh half before combining with Solomon and Birkett to put Chapman away. England never surrendered their lead and went on to record a famous 11–6 victory, Chapman landing a penalty goal and converting a splendid solo effort from Solomon. From this propitious inception, Twickenham would gradually develop into something of an English fortress. Of the 28 wins England have recorded against the southern hemisphere giants Australia, New Zealand and South Africa, nineteen were achieved at headquarters, and in all England have won 144 and drawn 23 of Twickenham's 223 home fixtures.

One of these draws came in the next game of the 1910 International Championship against Ireland, an anti-climactic affair of few thrills and no points. Though France had previously encountered three of the Home Union teams in a single season, they had not been included in the International Championship until Scotland granted them a match in 1910. They lost the first two games, and were then beaten 11–3 by an English side now containing Norman Wodehouse, John Riton and Arthur Hudson, whose four-try burst destroyed the French in 1906, and who scored two more in his last appearance. Percy Lawrie replaced the Gloucester wing and centre Frank Stoop followed his older sibling Adrian into the side for the final game of the season against Scotland. After a ten-match break John Birkett resumed the captaincy, and commemorated the event with two tries in a victory as impressive as it was unexpected. England had captured a first championship for eighteen years, and the first-ever Five Nations crown.

They were unable to defend their title in 1911, losing narrowly away to Wales and Ireland, but significant progress

continued in other areas. Only one change was made to the team all year, and 'Bruno' Brown, an Australian studying at Oxford University, was admirably acquainted with the front row. Daniel Lambert also produced one of the greatest individual performances of all time when he scored 22 of England's 37 points against France at Twickenham. With two tries, five conversions and two penalty goals, Lambert surpassed his own

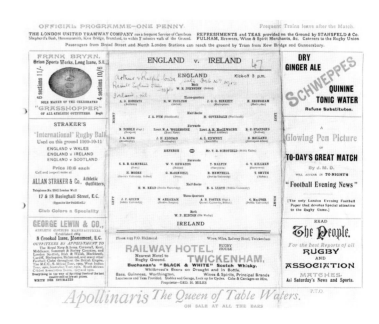

English record of fifteen, set against France in 1907 with the aid of five tries. (Incredibly, the record would stand for 79 years until Simon Hodgkinson registered 23 points in a 51–0 annihilation of Argentina in 1990.) In the wake of their victory over England, Wales went on to win all four championship matches to accomplish the first Grand Slam, an expression originally used to denote the winning of thirteen tricks in a game of bridge, and first applied in a rugby context by *The Times* in 1957.

Welsh hopes of retaining the title in 1912 disappeared at Twickenham, and by the time England faced Scotland in Edinburgh the likelihood was that they would immediately emulate Wales. They had not conceded a point in winning two matches, the second against Ireland, while Scotland were bottom of the pile with two defeats. In a rigorous battle the English overcame the early loss of King with broken ribs and a three-point deficit, only to throw the game away in the closing minutes, Usher seizing on a wayward pass to finish the simplest of tries and send the visitors home empty-handed. England derived some consolation by recovering to beat France, Birkett scoring in his last international, but ultimately had to settle for a share of the championship with Ireland.

Their aspirations were better served the following year thanks in no small part to the inclusion of two of the finest players ever to grace an England jersey. In the first game of the season, against the inbound South Africans, the irrepressible fly-half 'Dave' Davies and the doyen of English rugby Cyril Lowe made their international debuts. For six seasons Davies was acknowledged as the fulcrum of the side – later forming a legendary half-back partnership with Cyril Kershaw – and Lowe the rapier. The diminutive wing scored eighteen tries in 25 consecutive appearances. Another wing, the overlooked and largely forgotten

Vince Coates, also played his first game against the Springboks, and although he was scandalously discarded after one season, Coates actually made a more substantial impression than either Davies or Lowe.

In point of fact none of the newcomers instantly prospered, and it was left to the sublime Ronnie Poulton to confound the powerful South Africans with two twinkling, swerving runs. From the first he scored a magical try, and the second, reputedly of even greater daring, was stopped an agonising yard short of the line. For all Poulton's enterprise, England were unable to contain the huge atypical Springbok pack and went down 9–3. A creditable result, considering the tourists' 38–0 demolition of Ireland, and the selectors obviously concurred as they dropped only two of the team for the imminent encounter with Wales at the Arms Park. Coates was given a second opportunity, and he and Cherry Pillman scored the tries in a 12–0 victory, England's first on Welsh territory for eighteen years. The pair continued their scoring spree during easy wins over France and Ireland, Coates claiming five tries and Pillman three.

Defeat at the hands of Scotland in the penultimate fixture of 1912 had deprived England of the supreme prize, but on this occasion they scraped home 3–0 in a drab and error-strewn game, the strength and determination of Bruno Brown carrying him across the line under close attention from the Scottish backs. Captain Norman Wodehouse had led his country to a memorable and unique Grand Slam, his side scoring thirteen tries without reply. Coates, who would, perversely, never play again,

Wales	France	Ireland	Scotland
18.01.1913	25.01.1913	08.02.1913	15.03.1913
Cardiff Arms Park	Twickenham	Lansdowne Road	Twickenham
12–0	20–0	15–4	3–0
W R Johnston	W R Johnston	W R Johnston	W R Johnston
C N Lowe	C N Lowe	C N Lowe	C N Lowe
F E Steinthal	F E Steinthal	A J Dingle	F N Tarr
R W Poulton	R W Poulton	R W Poulton	R W Poulton
V H M Coates	V H M Coates	V H M Coates	V H M Coates
W J A Davies	W J A Davies	W J A Davies	W J A Davies
W I Cheesman	W I Cheesman	W I Cheesman	F E Oakeley
J A S Ritson	J A S Ritson	J A S Ritson	J A S Ritson
J A King	J A King	J A King	J A King
J E Greenwood	J E Greenwood	J E Greenwood	J E Greenwood
G Ward	G Ward	A E Kitching	L G Brown
L G Brown	L G Brown	L G Brown	N A Wodehouse*
N A Wodehouse*	N A Wodehouse*	N A Wodehouse*	S Smart
C H Pillman	C H Pillman	C H Pillman	C H Pillman
S Smart	S Smart	S Smart	G Ward

Points Scorers	**Points Scorers**	**Points Scorers**	**Points Scorers**
R W Poulton – 4	V H M Coates – 9	V H M Coates – 6	L G Brown – 3
V H M Coates – 3	C H Pillman – 6	C H Pillman – 3	
C H Pillman – 3	R W Poulton – 3	J A S Ritson – 3	
J E Greenwood – 2	J E Greenwood – 2	J E Greenwood – 3	

contributed six and Pillman four. Their almost impregnable defence conceded a meagre four points, a drop goal from the Irish fly-half Dicky Lloyd, the lowest number in Five Nations history. Twelve players appeared in every match, and the next season five of them – full-back William Johnston, wing Cyril Lowe, centre Ronnie Poulton, and the forwards Bruno Brown and Sidney Smart – again played in all four games as England went on to win back-to-back Grand Slams.

Ronnie Poulton assumed the captaincy in 1914 and very nearly began his tragically brief reign with a defeat against Wales at Twickenham. Entering the final ten minutes England trailed 9–5 when the Welsh centre, Watt, spilt the ball and the industrious Pillman pounced to score his seventh international try. The recalled Hartlepool Rovers wing Frederick Chapman nonchalantly converted, and Poulton's side resisted fierce Welsh pressure to win 10–9. Cyril Lowe, six matches without a try, finally broke his duck in England's subsequent meeting with Ireland at Twickenham. King George V and the Liberal Prime Minister Herbert Asquith were two of the more esteemed members of a 40,000-strong crowd that saw Lowe score twice in a 17–12 victory. Dave Davies, with a spectacular individual effort, Alan Roberts and Cherry Pillman all traversed the Irish

Right During the last season before war broke out, Ronnie Poulton's England defeated the Irish 17–12 at Twickenham on St Valentine's Day 1914 on their way to a second consecutive Grand Slam

Wales	**Ireland**	**Scotland**	**France**
17.01.1914	14.02.1914	21.03.1914	13.04.1914
Twickenham	Twickenham	Inverleith	Stade Colombes
10–9	17–12	16–15	39–13
W R Johnston	W R Johnston	W R Johnston	W R Johnston
C N Lowe	C N Lowe	C N Lowe	C N Lowe
F E Chapman	F E Chapman	J H D Watson	J H D Watson
R W Poulton*	R W Poulton*	R W Poulton*	R W Poulton*
J H D Watson	A D Roberts	A J Dingle	A J Dingle
F M Taylor	W J A Davies	W J A Davies	W J A Davies
G W Wood	F E Oakeley	F E Oakeley	F E Oakeley
A G Bull	H C Harrison	H C Harrison	H C Harrison
A F Maynard	A F Maynard	A F Maynard	A R V Sykes
J E Greenwood	A L Harrison	J E Greenwood	J E Greenwood
L G Brown	L G Brown	L G Brown	L G Brown
J Brunton	J Brunton	J Brunton	A L Harrison
S Smart	S Smart	S Smart	S Smart
C H Pillman	C H Pillman	C H Pillman	R L Pillman
G Ward	G Ward	G Ward	F le S Stone

Points Scorers	**Points Scorers**	**Points Scorers**	**Points Scorers**
F E Chapman – 4	C N Lowe – 6	C N Lowe – 9	J E Greenwood – 12
L G Brown – 3	W J A Davies – 3	H C Harrison – 4	R W Poulton – 12
C H Pillman – 3	C H Pillman – 3	R W Poulton – 3	N Lowe – 9
	A D Roberts – 3		W J A Davies – 3
	F E Chapman – 2		J H D Watson – 3

line, the latter for his eighth try, a record for an English forward until Neil Back scored his ninth try against the USA in 1999. Having discovered a taste for try-scoring, Lowe's appetite grew ever more voracious, and his initial brace was followed by hat-tricks against Scotland and France. The Scots were beaten 16–15, but the dramatic victory was marred by the broken leg sustained by Pillman, an injury which ended his international career. Captain Ronnie Poulton also scored in Edinburgh, and his four tries in the 39–13 defeat of France eclipsed even Lowe. A year later, Poulton lay dead in Ploegsteert Wood on the Western Front, killed by a sniper's bullet.

Poulton was one of 111 rugby union internationals killed in the Great War, 26 of them English. Percy Kendall, Francis Tarr and Alexander Todd fell at Ypres in the Flanders mud, and John King and Alfred Maynard perished at Field Marshal Haig's Battle of the Somme shooting gallery, one of the bloodiest and most senseless offensives in the history of warfare. Twenty thousand British troops were cut down on day one, for the sake of about as much ground as a half-decent full-back could gain from the annual Varsity match kick-off.

Arthur Harrison was awarded a posthumous Victoria Cross for his part in the blocking of Zeebrugge harbour on 23 April

1918, St George's Day. George Dobbs, three times mentioned in dispatches and a recipient of the Légion d'Honneur for his part in the struggle for the Belgium town of Mons, died of wounds inflicted at Poperinghe. Daniel Lambert, five-try protagonist against the French in 1907, was killed at Loos; heartbreakingly, his son was born two months later. Cherry Pillman, a lieutenant in the Dragoon Guards, survived the entire shebang, but brother Robert, his replacement in the final Grand Slam match of 1914, died at Armentières. Another one-cap wonder, Charles Wilson, a professional soldier and Boer War veteran, met his end on the banks of the river Aisne, 45 days after Britain's declaration of war. Arthur Dingle's body was never recovered from Suvla Bay on the Gallipoli peninsula, and the only telegram his family received read MISSING PRESUMED KILLED. The mother of the Stoop brothers, Adrian and Frank, was more fortunate: her sons were wounded in Mesopotamia, now Iraq, and both lived to tell the tale. Leonard Haigh and Reg Schwarz had less luck: Haigh was killed in training, and Schwarz died of influenza a week after the Armistice. Dave Davies emerged unscathed from duty with the Grand Fleet aboard HMS *Iron Duke*, and Cyril Lowe, now

Right Lest we forget. The Great War claimed many England internationals

literally a flying wing, downed nine enemy aircraft while serving with the Royal Flying Corps. One of the most extraordinary stories surrounds the former England captain Edgar Mobbs who, refused a commission due to his age, enlisted his own private corps which included many rugby players, and was slain punting a rugby ball into battle! Foolhardy no doubt, but it must have taken a particular kind of nerve to charge enemy machinegun posts with the aid of an inflated piece of leather. The Mobbs Memorial Match is still contested to commemorate his courage.

In the abhorrent conflict of the 'war to end all wars' the youth of a nation was sacrificed on the killing fields of Europe. Young men from every walk of life died side by side, and rugby suffered its fair share of grief. Almost 50 Scottish, Welsh and Irish internationals were killed, and hundreds of British rugby clubs lost thousands of players. Even those fortunate enough to survive the hostilities had their careers severely truncated. When England

resumed international competition in 1920, only four pre-war players were included in the team to face Wales at Swansea: Cyril Lowe, 'Jenny' Greenwood, Sidney Smart and Harry Coverdale. Greenwood was awarded the captaincy for the season after being persuaded to postpone his imminent retirement plans. England were well beaten by an equally inexperienced Welsh team, and few of the eleven new caps would remain in the side beyond the end of the season. The two notable exceptions were Wavell Wakefield and Cyril Kershaw.

A versatile second- or back-row exponent with great tactical acumen, Wakefield radically updated the function of the then still predominantly static pack. He developed forward play in the loose and at the line-out, and also conceived the use of forwards in defensive positions. Very much in the manner of Cherry Pillman, the first wing forward, or flanker, to cultivate a fast break from the scrum, Wakefield used the blindside to harry the opposition scrum half, and the openside and number eight to support the fly-half. Leading by example, he captained his country in thirteen of 31 appearances, a record not overtaken until another lock, Bill Beaumont, secured the post in the early 1980s.

The half-back partnership record set by scrum half Cyril Kershaw and fly-half Dave Davies would take even longer to transcend. The pair first played together for the Grand Fleet in 1919, and a few months later were reunited for England's victory against France at Twickenham. It was Davies who ensured the duo got off to a winning start, marking his return to the side with England's only try in a hard-fought victory. France had led for much of the first half, and most bystanders agreed that this was the most proficient Gallic team to date, a theory borne out by three championship wins in a twelve-month period, compared to just one pre-war victory over the Scots. Over the next four seasons Davies and Kershaw combined in fourteen internationals, all of which were won save an 11–11 home draw with France. In 1991 Rob Andrew and Richard Hill finally bettered their appearance record, but no combination has ever come close to matching the wins-to-games ratio attained by the Royal Navy men.

THE SOLDIER

If I should die, think only this of me;
That there's some corner of a foreign field
That is for ever England. There shall be
In that rich earth a richer dust concealed;
A dust whom England bore, shaped, and made aware,
Gave, once, her flowers to love, her ways to roam
A body of England's, breathing English air,
Washed by the rivers, blest by the aura of home

And think, this heart, all evil shed away,
A pulse in the eternal mind, no less
Gives somewhere back the thoughts by England given;
Her sights and sounds; dreams happy as her day;
And laughter, learnt of friends; and gentleness,
In hearts at peace, under an English heaven.

Rupert Brooke 1887–1915, educated and 'capped' at Rugby School

THIRD GRAND SLAM – 1921

Wales	Ireland	Scotland	France
15.01.1921	12.02.1921	19.03.1921	28.03.1921
Twickenham	Twickenham	Inverleith	Stade Colombes
18–3	15–0	18–0	10–6
B S Cumberlege	B S Cumberlege	B S Cumberlege	B S Cumberlege
C N Lowe	C N Lowe	C N Lowe	C N Lowe
E D G Hammett	E D G Hammett	A M Smallwood	L J Corbett
E Myers	E Myers	E D G Hammett	E D G Hammett
A M Smallwood	A M Smallwood	Q E M A King	A M Smallwood
W J A Davies*	W J A Davies*	W J A Davies*	W J A Davies*
C A Kershaw	C A Kershaw	C A Kershaw	C A Kershaw
R Edwards	R Edwards	R Edwards	R Edwards
E R Gardner	E R Gardner	E R Gardner	T Woods
L G Brown	L G Brown	L G Brown	L G Brown
F W Mellish	F W Mellish	T Woods	W W Wakefield
T Woods	T Woods	R Cove-Smith	R Cove-Smith
A E Blakiston	A E Blakiston	A E Blakiston	G S Conway
A T Voyce	A T Voyce	A T Voyce	A T Voyce
W W Wakefield	W W Wakefield	W W Wakefield	A F Blakiston

Points Scorers	Points Scorers	Points Scorers	Points Scorers
A M Smallwood – 6	C N Lowe – 7	E D G Hammett – 6	E D G Hammett – 4
W J A Davies – 4	A Blakiston – 3	L G Brown – 3	A E Blakiston – 3
C A Kershaw – 3	L G Brown – 3	R Edwards – 3	C N Lowe – 3
C N Lowe – 3	B S Cumberlege – 2	Q E M A King – 3	
E D G Hammett – 2		T Woods – 3	

The Cambridge Blues Alistair Smallwood and Geoffrey Conway were awarded the first of their respective fourteen and twenty caps in that Twickenham match against France, and for the last two games of the season England's selectors shuffled the pack, coming up with a full house. In the Bradford centre Edward Myers and the forwards Tom Voyce and Arthur Blakiston, who with Wavell Wakefield would form one of the strongest back rows in world rugby, they had discovered three more members of a team poised to make history. The new-look England concluded the 1920 season with confident victories over Ireland and Scotland, Cyril Lowe opening his post-war account with a try in each game, and their late rally resulted in a three-way championship tie.

In 1921 they improved still further to win the first of an unprecedented hat-trick of Grand Slams in four years. In the season in which the RFU were celebrating their Golden Jubilee and Dave Davies was named captain, England could hardly put a foot wrong. At Twickenham Wales were repaid in kind for the previous year's fourteen-point defeat, and an unchanged team quelled Ireland's initial ardour to win 15–0. Another of Wakefield's inestimable pack, the lock Ronnie Cove-Smith, made his debut against Scotland in Edinburgh. He would play 29 times for his country, the last seven as skipper. A home defeat by France

Above England go down by the considerable margin of 28–6 at Cardiff on 21 January 1922

Wales	Ireland	Scotland	France
20.01.1923	10.02.1923	17.03.1923	02.04.1923
Twickenham	Leicester	Inverleith	Stade Colombes
7–3	23–5	8–6	12–3
F Gilbert	F Gilbert	T E Holliday	T E Holliday
C N Lowe	C N Lowe	C N Lowe	C N Lowe
E Myers	E Myers	E Myers	E Myers
L J Corbett	L J Corbett	H M Locke	H M Locke
A M Smallwood	A M Smallwood	A M Smallwood	A M Smallwood
W J A Davies*	W J A Davies*	W J A Davies*	W J A Davies*
C A Kershaw	C A Kershaw	C A Kershaw	C A Kershaw
E R Gardner	E R Gardner	E R Gardner	E R Gardner
R Edwards	F W Sanders	F W Sanders	F W Sanders
W G E Luddington	W G E Luddington	W G E Luddington	W G E Luddington
W W Wakefield	W W Wakefield	W W Wakefield	W W Wakefield
R Cove-Smith	R Cove-Smith	R Cove-Smith	R Cove-Smith
H L Price	H L Price	A F Blakiston	A F Blakiston
A T Voyce	A T Voyce	A T Voyce	A T Voyce
G S Conway	G S Conway	G S Conway	G S Conway

Points Scorers	Points Scorers	Points Scorers	Points Scorers
A M Smallwood – 4	G S Conway – 4	A M Smallwood – 3	W J A Davies – 4
H L Price – 3	W J A Davies – 4	A T Voyce – 3	G S Conway – 3
	L J Corbett – 3	W G E Luddington – 2	W W Wakefield – 3
	C N Lowe – 3		W G E Luddington – 2
	H L Price – 3		
	A M Smallwood –3		
	A T Voyce – 3		

and a loss in Dublin had left Scotland reeling, and though they held out stoically for twenty minutes, England were always in control. The 18–0 victory was their highest over the Scots since the introduction of points-scoring. The Blackheath and Army centre King scored a debut try on what also happened to be his last appearance. He was replaced by Leonard Corbett for England's next game against France in Paris. After their marvellous result in Scotland, the French needed to win to maintain a realistic hope of sharing their first Five Nations title. At half-time they trailed 10–3 before staging so spirited a fightback that England were relieved to escape with a nervy 10–6 victory and a third Grand Slam.

Their chances of repeating the feat in 1922 were washed away by a week of uninterrupted rain and a waterlogged Cardiff Arms Park pitch. The entire English team, without their captain Davies, failed to come to terms with the atrocious conditions, while the Welsh quickly adapted and ran in eight tries in a 28–6 massacre. The French, too, came perilously close to causing an upset at Twickenham. Only a last-minute Tom Voyce try and conversion from Harold Day salvaged an 11–11 draw, the first between the two countries.

Whereas the elements contributed to England's Arms Park demise, in the 1923 Twickenham return they played a major part in a slender English victory, the fierce wind holding up Wakefield's kick-off for Price to catch and attempt a drop goal. He missed, but instead of the ball clearing the dead-ball line, as the Welsh expected, the wind kept it in play and Price chased through to score.

The try was timed at approximately ten seconds, and was executed without the opposition having touched the ball. An uncommon occurrence, and England's winning score was similarly bizarre, Frederick Chapman, loitering on the left wing towards the halfway line, dropping a goal from an almost impossibly acute angle.

Above right Captain Dave Davies introduces King George V to his English side before the clash with Wales st Twickenham on 20 January 1923. The Welsh were just edged out 7–3 and England won their fourth Grand Slam. Another was to follow in 1924

Right The English/Welsh line-up for the Centenary Match against Ireland/Scotland at Rugby School in 1923

Above Wavell Wakefield's first match as captain was the game against Wales on 19 January 1924

In an endeavour to introduce international rugby to the provinces, Welford Road, Leicester was chosen as the venue for the meeting with Ireland. A lower than anticipated crowd of 20,000 witnessed Cyril Lowe score his last try, and England win as easily as the 23–5 scoreline suggests. In comparison to Twickenham, which was regularly attracting twice as many spectators, the attendance was disappointing, and the RFU did not sanction another home fixture away from HQ until Wembley hosted a Test against Canada in 1992.

Wing Eric Liddell was in the Scottish team for a contest which would, to all intents and purposes, decide the Five Nations title. The Scots had won their three championship games and could settle the issue in front of their own supporters, while England still had to play France. In an extremely tight affair both teams crafted two tries, but the visitors prevailed purely as a result of Chapman's conversion. (This, incidentally, was their last game at Inverleith. When England next visited Edinburgh it was to play at the new Murrayfield stadium.) And so on to the Stade Colombes in Paris, where England duly completed a fourth Grand Slam in six seasons, winning a scrappy match with a nine-point burst in the dying minutes. The educated left foot of Dave Davies, captain for the eleventh time, dropped a goal, and heir-apparent

Wavell Wakefield scored his second senior try. A year later, in the same stadium, Eric Liddell and Harold Abrahams, the athletes immortalised in the film *Chariots of Fire*, won their Olympic gold medals.

Cyril Lowe, Dave Davies and Cyril Kershaw made their last international appearances in this match against France. Kershaw, who also fenced for Great Britain at the 1924 Olympics, played sixteen times for his country, and Lowe 25, including all sixteen of England's Grand Slam matches. His record of eighteen tries endured until another RAF man, Rory Underwood, scored against Ireland in 1990. Davies missed one Grand Slam game, the single-point victory over Wales in 1914, and retired without losing a championship fixture. Of his 22 caps, twenty were won and one drawn, the only blemish to a near-perfect career record being a debut defeat by the South Africans in 1913. It was not quite the end of an era, though. In the November of 1923 Davies and Kershaw combined again for a special match held at Rugby School to commemorate the epoch-making deed of William Webb Ellis and the sport's

Wales
19.01.1924
Swansea
17–9

B S Chantrill
H C Catcheside
L J Corbett
H M Locke
H P Jacob
E Myers
A T Young

R Edwards
A Robson
R Cove-Smith
W G E Luddington
G S Conway
A F Blakiston
A T Voyce
W W Wakefield*

Points Scorers
H C Catcheside – 6
H PJacob – 3
H M Locke – 3
E Myers – 3
G S Conway – 2

Ireland
09.02.1924
Belfast
14–3

B S Chantrill
H C Catcheside
L J Corbett
H P Jacob
R H Hamilton-Wickes
E Myers
A T Young

C K T Faithfull
A Robson
R Cove-Smith
W G E Luddington
G S Conway
A F Blakiston
A T Voyce
W W Wakefield*

Points Scorers
H C Catcheside – 6
L J Corbett – 3
R H Hamilton-Wickes – 3
G S Conway – 2

France
23.02.1924
Twickenham
19–7

B S Chantrill
H C Catcheside
L J Corbett
H M Locke
H P Jacob
E Myers
A T Young

R Edwards
A Robson
R Cove-Smith
W G E Luddington
G S Conway
A F Blakiston
A T Voyce
W W Wakefield*

Points Scorers
H P Jacob – 9
G S Conway – 4
H C Catcheside – 3
A T Young – 3

Scotland
15.03.1924
Twickenham
19–0

B S Chantrill
H C Catcheside
L J Corbett
H M Locke
H P Jacob
E Myers
A T Young

R Edwards
A Robson
R Cove-Smith
W G E Luddington
G S Conway
A F Blakiston
A T Voyce
W W Wakefield*

Points Scorers
E Myers – 7
G S Conway – 6
H C Catcheside – 3
W W Wakefield – 3

Left Twenty years after the first match between the two countries, New Zealand recorded another success over England with a 17–11 victory at Twickenham on 3 January 1925

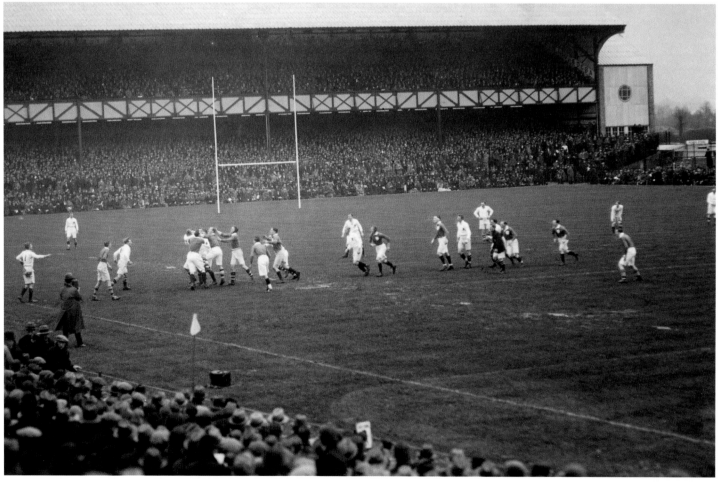

Opposite above The mud-splattered English players celebrate their 17–9 victory in Swansea
Opposite below A line-out during the Five Nations 6–6 draw with Ireland at Twickenham in February 1925
Above Action from England's closely contested 13–11 defeat of France at the Stade Colombes in Paris on 13 April 1925

centenary. The amalgamated team of England and Wales beat the Scots and Irish 21–16.

Bearing in mind the departure of three of the team's more distinguished players, England's 1924 Grand Slam was all the more laudable. They scored seventeen tries, their second-highest tally in Five Nations competition, and won every game by at least an eight-point margin. Lowe and Kershaw were replaced by two new caps, Carston Catcheside on the wing and Arthur Young at scrum half, and Edward Myers moved from centre to fly-half, to fill the not inconsiderable void left by Davies. In Wakefield's first match as captain, England beat Wales 17–9 in Swansea. Catcheside scored a brace of tries, and added another two in the 14–3 defeat of Ireland. Left-wing Herbert Jacob also scored a try on debut against Wales, and at Twickenham completed a hat-trick in a 19–7 win over France. Catcheside was again on the mark, and when he scored

against Scotland he became the first player to register a try in every match of a championship season. England were now eleven games unbeaten, and their fifth Grand Slam also produced a seventh Five Nations title in eight years. Since the defeat of Scotland in 1911 they had won a remarkable 29 out of 34 internationals.

In the long term it would not be feasible to sustain such impeccable standards. The team was ageing, and by the end of 1925 the cracks were already beginning to show. Sam Tucker, the recipient of a single cap three years earlier, was 29 when he was recalled to the side against New Zealand, and would play until he was 35. The All Blacks were touring the British Isles for the first time in twenty years, and 60,000 enthusiastic spectators crowded into Twickenham to watch the side dubbed the 'Invincibles'. After ten minutes of an ill-natured skirmish, the New Zealand forward Cyril Brownlie secured his own indelible, though decidedly dubious, entry in the record books by becoming the first player to be sent off in 54 years of international rugby. His expulsion, for deliberately kicking an opponent, made no appreciable difference to the outcome: even with fourteen men, the All Blacks won 17–11.

England reacted to a first loss in almost three years by extending their undefeated championship record to thirteen

matches. Edward, Prince of Wales, was present at Twickenham for the win over his principality, but the prospects of a third Grand Slam in a row were scuppered on Valentine's Day by Ireland, England frittering away a six-point lead in a tame draw. The Scottish team, containing the entire Oxford University three-quarter line, succeeded England as Five Nations champions and also brought to an end their long unbeaten run. On one joyous day 80,000 euphoric Scottish fans celebrated the opening of their new Murrayfield stadium, a 14–11 defeat of England and their country's first Grand Slam.

The next two years were lean ones for the English. Scotland and Ireland each won six of their eight Five Nations matches, while England engineered just three victories in the same period. In 1926 they lost a first championship match at Twickenham, going down 17–9 to Scotland, and a year later lost to France, again for the first time. Leonard Corbett had replaced the ubiquitous Wakefield as captain for the 1927 season, and they both bade a mournful adieu against the French. Blakiston, Voyce and Conway, who together with

Above left Wavell Wakefield talks with King George V before the 11–0 defeat of France at Twickenham on 27 February 1926
Above The Irish team emerges from the Twickenham tunnel. This clash was won by England 8–6

Wakefield were pivotal members of the vanguard pack, had also departed, and of the 1924 Grand Slam side only lock Ronnie Cove-Smith and scrum half Arthur Young remained. In 1928, having previously led the British Isles in South Africa, Cove-Smith was handed the captaincy, and responded by guiding England to one final hurrah.

As the only state side in Australia, the opening game of the season against New South Wales was regarded as an international fixture, and caps were awarded to the England players. A large number of reference books thus view England's subsequent victory as their first over the Wallabies. Strictly speaking, this is not the case; Eric Evans' team was the first to conquer a truly representative Australian outfit in the notorious battle of 1958. The 1928 Waratahs were of a more cordial disposition, and the Twickenham faithful were treated to an entertaining 18–11 home win. Harlequins fly-half Henri Laird, England's youngest cap at eighteen years and 134 days, took his first-half opportunity minutes after missing a drop goal attempt, and was joined on the score sheet by the veteran hooker Sam Tucker, the Waterloo flanker Joe Periton and wing William Taylor.

Above right An expectant Twickenham crowd before the match against Ireland on 12 February 1927
Right Five Nations action from England's 18–8 victory over france in February 1928

Above A French attack is broken down by the corner flag during the England v. France game in 1928

Left The Governor General of Ireland is introduced to the England team at half-time during the match against Ireland at Lansdowne Road

Fourteen of the successful England side travelled to Swansea for the game against Wales, Jerry Hanley replacing the unavailable Periton. For most of the match Cove-Smith's men were forced to absorb intense pressure. The Welsh won the forward struggle and enough ball to beat two teams, only to concede a sloppy try totally against the run of play. Their captain, Rowe Harding, lost his footing and Taylor effortlessly rounded the full-back, Rees, to score.

Inside ten minutes Laird had added a breakaway second and, critically, James Richardson converted both. Wales had a try scrubbed out for offside and continued to lay siege to the English line. They did cross twice, but could only convert the second and lost 10–8.

In Dublin, Richardson came to the rescue when Ireland scored the first tries on a mire of a Lansdowne Road pitch. The driving

Wales	Ireland	France	Scotland
21.01.1928	11.02.1928	25.02.1928	17.03.1928
Swansea	Lansdowne Road	Twickenham	Twickenham
10–8	7–6	18–8	6–0
K A Sellar	K A Sellar	K A Sellar	T W Brown
W J Taylor	W J Taylor	W J Taylor	W J Taylor
C D Aarvold	C D Aarvold	C D Aarvold	C D Aarvold
J V Richardson	J V Richardson	J V Richardson	J V Richardson
Sir T G Devitt	G V Palmer	G V Palmer	G V Palmer
H C C Laird	H C C Laird	H C C Laird	H C C Laird
A T Young	A T Young	A T Young	A T Young
E Stanbury	E Stanbury	E Stanbury	R H W Sparks
J S Tucker	J S Tucker	J S Tucker	J S Tucker
R Cove-Smith*	R H W Sparks	R H W Sparks	E Stanbury
D Turquand-Young	K J Stark	K J Stark	K J Stark
K J Stark	R Cove-Smith*	R Cove-Smith*	R Cove-Smith*
T M Lawson	J Hanley	J Hanley	J Hanley
J Hanley	H G Periton	H G Periton	H G Periton
T J Coulson	F D Prentice	F D Prentice	F D Prentice

Points Scorers	**Points Scorers**	**Points Scorers**	**Points Scorers**
J V Richardson – 4	J V Richardson – 7	G V Palmer – 6	J Hanley – 3
H C C Laird – 3		H G Periton – 6	H C C Laird – 3
W J Taylor – 3		J V Richardson – 6	

rain and raging gale made it virtually impossible to string two passes together, and an hour into the game Ireland led a lottery 6–0. After good work from the forwards, Richardson reduced the deficit with a try from close quarters, before inexplicably slicing an elementary conversion wide of the posts. Undeterred, England took the game to the wire, and Richardson atoned in full by dropping the winning goal in the final seconds. Joe Periton returned in the Ireland victory, and against France he and the Richmond wing, Godfrey Palmer, shared England's four tries. Richardson added six of the eight supplementary points, and France again failed to register a win at headquarters.

The English vintage of 1928 certainly suffered in comparison to the great pre-war teams, or those of the early twenties. They played with less flair and possessed fewer individual talents, yet they were on the verge of achieving a feat that had eluded all those fine sides. No English fifteen had ever beaten a touring team and won the Grand Slam in the same season, and Cove-Smith's men were one match away from doing just that. Their final match against Scotland produced a typically gritty performance. The forwards controlled the game, and a try in each half by the teenager Laird and the flanker Hanley won it 6–0. England's sixth Grand Slam in eleven seasons. Halcyon days indeed, but they would not return for 29 years – and then only for the briefest of moments.

Below The England team poses before the match against Scotland at Twickenham in 1928. Captain Ronald Cove-Smith is seated fifth from the left in the front row

The storm clouds gather

FOR VARIOUS REASONS, SIX OF THE 1928 GRAND SLAM SIDE DID NOT PLAY AGAIN, AND ONLY FOUR PROLONGED THEIR CAREERS BEYOND THE 1930 SEASON. WHILE IN GENERAL THE ENGLAND TEAM REMAINED COMPETITIVE THROUGHOUT THE THIRTIES, THEY WERE ALSO INCONSISTENT, FAILING TO WIN THREE MATCHES IN A ROW UNTIL 1934, AND ONLY DOING SO AGAIN IN 1937.

LEGENDS of the ilk of Davies, Kershaw, Lowe and Wakefield were never likely to be superseded simultaneously, and Joe Periton, capped against Wales in 1925, was the last individual before the Second World War to make twenty international appearances. The dearth of players of commensurate ability would impede England's development until the rise of their third great team towards the end of the 1950s.

By winning 14–13 in 1931, France consigned England to their first wooden spoon of the Five Nations era. It was a bittersweet occasion for the French, who were about to undergo seven years of exile for violating rugby's sacrosanct amateur laws. Their club sides first contested an official club championship in 1892, in complete contradiction of the philosophy exhorted by the British unions, who did not believe that organised competition was healthy and would endorse only matches of the friendly variety. For some years the diametrically opposed parties co-existed in a state of disquiet. Scotland declined to fulfill the country's 1914 fixture because of the unpleasant nature of the previous year's Parc des Princes crowd, and the French were repeatedly refused representation on the International Board.

This simmering unease persisted until it became blindingly obvious that the top teams in France were paying players and had established a rudimentary transfer system – they were even advertising for players in regional British newspapers. Consequently the four home unions warned the French Federation that, unless they were able to bring their clubs into line, all future engagements would be suspended indefinitely. The ultimatum was carried out in 1931 after twelve French teams, who preferred not to be hampered by the restrictions imposed by other countries, resigned from their federation and formed their own union. Though they abruptly rejoined, for several seasons

the home unions remained unconvinced that the French were doing enough to put their house in order, and their Five Nations isolation continued. Their readmission, earmarked for the 1939–40 season but postponed by war, had more to do with the expedient nurturing of an ally than any change of policy by the French. They did concede that individuals remunerated for playing would be banned, while still enjoying a thriving club competition eventually adopted by the British and Irish.

In January 1932, the same season in which the home nations began the ostracism of France, South Africa arrived at Twickenham for the penultimate international of their second tour of Britain. Adjudged the best in the world, they overpowered England with a side featuring the full-back Gerry Brand and the tactical kicking connoisseur and Captain Bennie Osler. Osler, the man credited with inventing ten-man rugby, punted for touch so often he would have made Rob Andrew look like the Barry John of fly-halves, and the South Africans attracted the same criticism levelled at England in the 1990s. Their immense forwards recycled an abundance of possession, but rather than using it in a constructive way the Springboks interminably worked the touchlines to gain territory. As it did for England years later, this attritional strategy worked wonders for the 1930s South Africans, who beat New Zealand 2–1 in a three-match series, twice won rubbers against Australia and completed a whitewash of British Test teams on their 1932 tour.

With players permitted to kick directly to touch from anywhere on the field, barely a modicum of skill was required to imitate the Boks, and over the years the proliferation in kicking created a monotonous, prosaic game. The match between Scotland and Wales at Murrayfield in 1965, for instance, contained 111 lineouts, one every 43 seconds. Five years later the International Board acted to reverse the trend by introducing the southern hemisphere regulation permitting the ball to be kicked into touch on the full only from within each team's 25-yard line. At first the move worked, opening up the game and increasing the attacking intent of the full-backs and fly-halves, but as players became more adept in the art of grub-kicking for touch and a plethora of penalties was utilised to the same end, so the intense scrummaging and set-piece game took hold. The Lions led the way in 1974, beating South Africa with basically eight forwards plus their half-backs, and for almost two decades the majority of international sides applied variations of the same ten-man theme.

Three of the England side beaten by these influential South Africans survived the selectors' increasingly eccentric whims, and played against Wales in the opening championship game of 1934. Ronald Gerrard, Gordon Gregory and John Hodgson joined seven new caps, including Peter Cranmer at centre and the South African-born full-back 'Tuppy' Owen-Smith, against one of the most inexperienced Welsh line-ups to set foot on the Cardiff Arms Park pitch. Thirteen of the team were formerly uncapped, and England made them look very ordinary with a 9–0 victory. Graham Meikle scored the first two tries of his short career, and Bernard Gadney took over as captain. Meikle added another try in Dublin, where an unchanged England came from behind to beat Ireland 13–3. They also trailed in the Triple Crown decider with Scotland at Twickenham, Shaw putting the Scots ahead, only for Meikle to equalise with his fourth try in three matches. Lu Booth won the game and the championship for England with a fine individual try in the last ten minutes.

Gadney was still in charge when New Zealand returned to Twickenham in January 1936. The Prince of Wales, shortly to be crowned King Edward VIII, was among a crowd of 72,000, all of whom would depart acclaiming another prince, Prince Alexander Obolensky. The son of a serving Tsarist cavalry officer, Obolensky – or 'Obo' to his team-mates – was born in St Petersburg at the height of the Great War. A nineteen-year-old student at Oxford University, he won two Varsity Blues, and on his debut against the All Blacks was the catalyst in a memorable English victory. Peter Cranmer supplied the pass for the first of his two tries, Obolensky collecting the ball from within his own half before setting off down the touchline. His prodigious speed took him outside and beyond the despairing New Zealand full-back to score in the right-hand corner. An outstanding try, but almost pedestrian compared to his second. Again Obolensky received the ball on the right, only this time rather than run at the converging defence he cut inside and made for the left wing, circumventing the disconcerted All Blacks cover for a peerless score. England went into the interval leading by six points, and soon after Cranmer extended the advantage with a drop goal. The final word was left to Hal Sever, winning his first cap on Obolensky's opposite wing. On any other day Sever's burst to the line would have grabbed the headlines, and while he never quite received the acclaim afforded to the young Russian, he sustained a longer and more successful career.

Three months after leading England to this 13–0 victory, their first over New Zealand, Obolensky settled as a naturalised British citizen. In that one match he attained the pinnacle of an evanescent career, and represented his country on only three more

Below This huge Twickenham crowd witnessed a 0–0 draw against Scotland in March 1930

occasions without adding to his two tries. An RAF pilot officer, he died in a training accident in March 1940, the first England international to lose his life in the Second World War.

Hal Sever fulfilled his potential in Tuppy Owen-Smith's Triple Crown-winning team of 1937. Sever dispensed the winning score in every match, beginning at Twickenham with a drop goal to beat Wales 4–3. On the same stage against Ireland, he snatched a sensational late try as England fought back from 8–3 down to win 9–8, and again worked the miracle at Murrayfield with the

second touchdown in a 6–3 victory over Scotland. The Scots had their revenge in 1938, winning a pulsating encounter 21–16. This game was the first to be televised, eleven years after the inaugural BBC radio commentary of the England versus Wales international, and has always been referred to as 'Wilson Shaw's match', after the Scottish captain twice outstripped the English defence for unforgettable tries.

In the summer of 1938 the British Isles toured South Africa for a three-match series. Lions tours to the southern hemisphere

nations have been a traditional feature of international rugby since a privately arranged team visited Australia and New Zealand in 1888. A further six excursions followed before the RFU organised an official squad to visit South Africa in 1910. In the early days, tour parties mainly comprised uncapped players, and it was not until 1899 that individuals from all four home countries were invited to participate. The first Lions rubber – no Test matches were played on the original trip – was contested against South Africa in 1891, the visitors winning 3–0, and the first series defeat was inflicted by the same country twelve years later. Historically, the Lions have enjoyed their greatest success in Australia, winning every Test series except two – in 1930 and 2001 – a massive disparity when compared to their results in New Zealand (one victory in ten rubbers) and South Africa (two wins this century).

While the number of players a country has selected for the Lions is always a good indication of their current standing in the

Above The Irish narrowly won this 1931 Twickenham match 6–5
Above right B H Black converts a try but Scotland still won 28–19 in Edinburgh on 21 March 1931
Right J H van der Westhuizen of South Africa is tackled by England's C C Tanner during the South African's 7–0 victory at Twickenham in January 1932

Left Prime Minister Ramsay MacDonald (left) contemplates England's Twickenham clash with Scotland in March 1932

game, it can never be entirely accurate due to the politicking and horse-trading involved in pacifying every nation. In 1950, the Home Unions Tour Committee replaced the RFU as tour selectors, and naturally members were inclined to state a case for the inclusion of as many of their compatriots as possible. Their mollifying concessions usually resulted in the selection of at least a handful of inferior and undeserving players, to the general detriment of the team. Only three Englishmen were included in the 1950 squad to New Zealand and Australia compared with the 22 – eighteen original selections and four replacements – sent to South Africa in 1997; four years before that, eleven England internationals played in the Second and Third Tests against New Zealand.

The imposing Welsh teams of the 1970s yielded arguably the two greatest British Isles sides. Inspired by the half-backs Barry John and Gareth Edwards, full-back J P R Williams and three-quarter Gerald Davies, the 1971 Lions beat New Zealand 2–1 in a four-match series. This first and, to date, only victory over the All Blacks was followed in 1974 by a 3–0 thrashing of South Africa. J J Williams scored a record four tries in this infamous series,

Below High-spirited Scottish fans couldn't prevent a 16–3 defeat at the hands of the Auld Enemy at Twickenham in 1932
Right An English try against Scotland is ruled out by the referee, 1932

remembered for the violent collective response induced by the war cry 'Ninety-nine!', the Lions' rallying code whenever a fight broke out anywhere on the field. The number of brawls witnessed were legion, and on one conspicuous occasion J P R Williams ran, by conservative estimates, a full 50 metres to partake in a mêlée on the half-way line. The Irish lock Willie John McBride played in every match of both these rubbers, and holds the record for the highest number of Lions appearances with seventeen between 1962 and 1974. Scrum half Dickie Jeeps holds the record for an Englishman with thirteen caps, and Scotland's Gavin Hastings the points-scoring record: 66 in six tests.

In September 1938 the Lions won the third Test against South Africa, having already lost the first two, and hence the series. In the month the British tourists sailed home, the Third Reich stood poised to invade Czechoslovakia and Prime Minister Neville Chamberlain returned from his Munich meeting with the German Chancellor Adolf Hitler. As Chamberlain espoused 'Peace for our time' and waved his slip of paper – to some an Anglo-German peace accord, to the Czechs a flag of surrender – Hitler was preparing the Blitzkrieg that would lay waste to the heart of mainland Europe. Within a year the tanks that rolled into Prague were heading towards Warsaw, and Britain was at war.

The conflict was to cost millions of lives, and again many of England's rugby internationals would perish. The captain of the first Grand Slam side, Norman Wodehouse, drowned commanding an Atlantic convoy. The 54-year-old Wodehouse was recalled from the retirement list, having previously served in World War One. Ronald Gerrard, a member of the Triple Crown-winning team of 1934 and recipient of the Distinguished Service

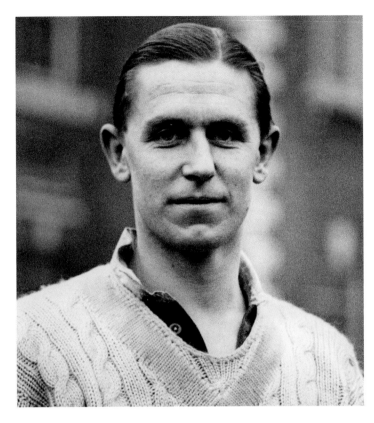

declined to follow suit – and the French were welcomed back into the international fold. Oxford and Cambridge met biannually in the Varsity match, and large crowds flocked to see the Red Cross and Service internationals.

By 6 June 1944 and the D-Day landings in Normandy, the tide had irrevocably turned against the Nazi war machine. Inside eleven months Britain and her allies were celebrating V E Day, and the bloodiest conflict in humanity came to an end with the surrender of Japan in August 1945. A series of Victory Internationals was arranged for the first post-war season and, in 1947, after a hiatus lasting the best part of a decade, the Five Nations Championship finally resumed.

Left C D Aarvold captained England seven times
Below D W Burland kicks for goal during England's 17–6 defeat of Ireland at Twickenham on 11 February 1933

Order, was killed by Rommel's 15th Armoured Division in Libya, and naval chaplain Chris Tanner, a try-scorer against Scotland in 1931, died of exhaustion when his cruiser, HMS *Fiji*, was sunk by German dive-bombers during the bombardment of Crete. He died rescuing men in the water, and was posthumously awarded the Albert Medal. Other sports suffered just as dearly. The England Test match cricketer Hedley Verity, a captain in the Green Howards, died in a prisoner-of-war camp of wounds sustained during an 8th Army battle in Sicily.

Sport in general played an enormous part in restoring some semblance of normality to the country, and most rugby clubs tried to maintain fixtures. The RFU revoked the ban on professionals to allow servicemen to participate in games while on leave – though unaccountably the Scottish Rugby Union

ENGLAND
versus
SCOTLAND

At TWICKENHAM

Saturday, 17th March 1934

Kick-off 3 p.m.

Left England won this Four Nations match 6–3
Below Prince Alexander Obolensky scored two memorable tries in the 1936 triumph over the mighty New Zealand
Bottom This English team became the first to beat New Zealand, recording a remarkable 13–0 victory at Twickenham on 4 January 1936

LIONS TOURS AND TEST RESULTS

Year	Opposition	P	W	D	L	Series
1888	Australia	–	–	–	–	–
	New Zealand	–	–	–	–	–
1891	South Africa	3	3	0	0	3–0
1896	South Africa	4	3	0	1	3–1
1899	Australia	4	3	0	1	3–1
1903	South Africa	3	0	2	1	0–1
1904	Australia	3	3	0	0	3–0
	New Zealand	1	0	0	1	0–1
1908	Australia	–	–	–	–	–
	New Zealand	3	0	1	2	0–2
1910	South Africa	3	1	0	2	1–2
1924	South Africa	4	0	1	3	0–3
1930	New Zealand	4	1	0	3	1–3
	Australia	1	0	0	1	0–1
1938	South Africa	3	1	0	2	1–2
1950	New Zealand	4	0	1	3	0–3
	Australia	2	2	0	0	2–0
1955	South Africa	4	2	0	2	2–2
1959	Australia	2	2	0	0	2–0
	New Zealand	4	1	0	3	1–3
1962	South Africa	4	0	1	3	0–3
1966	Australia	2	2	0	0	2–0
	New Zealand	4	0	0	4	0–4
1968	South Africa	4	0	1	3	0–3
1971	Australia	–	–	–	–	–
	New Zealand	4	2	1	1	2–1
1974	South Africa	4	3	1	0	3–0
1977	New Zealand	4	1	0	3	1–3
1980	South Africa	4	1	0	3	1–3
1983	New Zealand	4	0	0	4	0–4
1989	Australia	3	2	0	1	2–1
1993	New Zealand	3	1	0	2	1–2
1997	South Africa	3	2	0	1	2–1
2001	Australia	3	1	0	2	1–2
		98	**37**	**9**	**52**	

1947–1962

Second coming

OF THE SIX TEAMS PARTICIPATING IN THE VICTORY MATCHES – THE FOUR HOME UNION NATIONS, FRANCE AND A TOURING KIWI PARTY OF 8TH ARMY SOLDIERS – ONLY THE FRENCH BESTOWED CAPS ON THEIR RANK AND FILE. NEW ZEALAND AND AUSTRALIA THUS DISPUTED THE FIRST FULL PEACETIME INTERNATIONAL, AND ENGLAND RETURNED TO COMPETITION AT THE ARMS PARK IN JANUARY 1947.

THE cousins Dick Guest and Jack Heaton, and the Richmond fly-half, Tommy Kemp, all at one stage added to their pre-war appearances, Guest at the earliest possible opportunity in a line-up against Wales containing fourteen players making their debuts and eight students. Flanker Mickey Steele-Bodger, like Kemp a future RFU president, was among a contingent of five Oxbridge players in addition to three from St Mary's Hospital. A timely drop goal by prospective captain Nim Hall, who began his long, punctuated career in the number ten jersey and finished it at full-back, settled the game for an England side that went on to win three of four championship matches and share the Five Nations title with Wales. This feat was not repeated for five relatively unproductive seasons, as the national side amassed just four victories in their next sixteen championship games and finished bottom of the table in both 1948 and 1950.

By way of consolation, their meagre run was made to look positively bountiful in comparison to Scotland's abject results. From their one-point reverse against Ireland in February 1951 to the 15–0 defeat by France in January 1955, Scotland lost seventeen matches in a row and were whitewashed in the Five Nations every year from 1952 to 1954. The 44–0 obliteration at the hands of South Africa during this period was their largest margin of defeat until the Springboks caned them again, 68–10 at Murrayfield in 1997.

In each of Scotland's three wooden spoon seasons a resurgent England fell one win shy of the Grand Slam. An 8–6 defeat by eventual champions Wales cost them the title in 1952. Number eight Alec Lewis had a would-be last-gasp winner ruled out for offside, and the Wasps wing Ted Woodward scored the first of his six international tries. Against Scotland, the erstwhile captain John Kendall-Carpenter, another player destined for the RFU presidency, and the perennial hooker Eric Evans also recorded

maiden tries, and England completed the term with a pair of three-point victories over Ireland and France.

Having formerly disposed of Wales, Gaelic fortitude denied England the utmost accolade in 1953. In a close contest at Lansdowne Road two evenly matched sides drew 9–9. Ireland led until skipper Nim Hall rescued his team with an opportune penalty goal. The evasive centre Jeff Butterfield answered his international call by scoring one try and creating another in the ensuing 11–0 victory over France. An unselfish player with an immaculate pass, Butterfield accrued 28 consecutive caps for his country and four more for the British Lions. He scored again in his next match as the easy pickings in the face of a fragile Scottish defence reaped six English tries and a first outright Five Nations title since 1937.

Several senior players elected to retire during the close season, and the team to face Wales in the first all-ticket encounter at Twickenham in 1954 contained six new caps. Four changes were made to the pack, and Bob Stirling replaced the dropped Hall as captain. Despite two tries from Ted Woodward, England laboured to subdue a Welsh side hindered by a catalogue of injuries. With 80 minutes on the watch and the scores level, Tug Wilson and Kendall-Carpenter carved an opening for Chris Winn to pull the proverbial iron out of the fire. A first-class cricketer with two centuries under his belt, Winn also received a niggling injury in the nail-biting victory. Obliged to sit out the next two fixtures – a defeat by the touring All Blacks and a win over Ireland – he returned in Edinburgh where England beat Scotland to take a twelfth Triple Crown and extend their undefeated championship run to ten matches.

Jean Prat, whose immense contribution to the French game earned him the apt sobriquet 'Monsieur Rugby', had recently conducted his country's first victory over the All Blacks.

Above The teams line up for the National Anthem before the England v. Scotland match on 15 March 1947

Outplayed at every phase, Prat seized France's one genuine opportunity and six weeks later steered them to a first share of the championship with five points in the 11–3 victory over England. Prat dropped a goal and converted a try by his brother Maurice as France, England and Wales all tied with three wins apiece. Tug Wilson scored four tries in the last three games of the season, and seven of the side vanquished in Paris never played again. RAF World War Two veteran Bob Stirling won eighteen caps in the England front row and John Kendall-Carpenter 23 at the rear of the pack. In addition to his RFU duty, the former Oxford captain served as chairman of the International Rugby Board and also chaired the 1987 World Cup organising committee.

Ten new players were invited to test their mettle in 1955, but only one, the prop George Hastings, was able to command anything approaching a regular berth. The rest failed either to shine or gel and England slumped from first to fourth position in the championship table. After the final match against Scotland, paradoxically the one victory of the season, another eight players were jettisoned and the selectors scuttled off to search for a new drawing board or a larger hat. Eschewing all accepted logic, their deliberations, whether by sound intuition or blind panic, prompted the introduction of another ten caps for the 1956 curtain-raiser with Wales, eight of whom would play in every match of the following season's Grand Slam.

Six years after failing to make the grade in an England trial, scrum half Dickie Jeeps partnered the Welsh stand-off Cliff Morgan in all four Test matches of the Lions' 1955 tour of South Africa. By virtue of his rave reviews he went on to make 37

international outings, 24 for England and thirteen for the British Isles. The wing three-quarters Peter Jackson and Peter Thompson scored a combined total of eleven tries in 37 England games. The inimitable Jackson, whose languid gait deceived a host of opposition defences, reckoned six and two more for the Lions against New Zealand in 1959. An individualist touched by genius, his second try left four All Blacks groping at thin air and

Above Ireland won this Five Nations battle by the closest of margins, 11–10

inspired the British visitors to only their second victory on Kiwi soil. Of the forwards the Oxbridge and Harlequins locks John Currie and David Marques formed a long-standing second-row union. The pair made 22 consecutive appearances until illness accounted for Currie prior to the 1961 fixture with Wales. Prop Ron Jacobs played 29 times, twice as captain, a positional record exceeded by Fran Cotton and subsequently Jason Leonard. Flanker Peter Robbins, a contemporary of Currie's at Oxford, won nineteen caps, three more than the Waterloo number eight Ned Ashcroft. Of the two that failed to create a lasting impression against Wales, Dennis Allison lingered for three years without ever establishing himself at full-back, and fly-half Mike Smith, better known as M J K to cricket enthusiasts, was not selected again. He did, however, score more than 2,000 runs and three centuries in a Test match career spanning fifteen years and 50 matches.

The injection of so much quality evoked a palpable upturn in English fortunes, and though Wales won 8–3, the result itself was irrelevant. With hooker Eric Evans, prop Hastings and the centres Jeff Butterfield, Lewis Cannell and Phil Davies added to the mix, the selectors had inadvertently stumbled upon the best England side since the 1920s. They lost just one of the next seventeen games, and in four seasons won three championship titles, commencing in 1957 with a first Grand Slam for 29 years.

For the opening match of the 1957 campaign, against Wales in Cardiff, Dennis Allison was selected at full-back in what had become something of a problem position. Until Don Rutherford

and John Willcox were given prolonged runs, England cast their net far and wide in the search for a suitable full-back, employing seventeen in the first 56 post-war internationals. By playing seven times, Allison fared better than the rest, and it was his cleanly struck left-foot penalty goal that beat Wales 3–0. Surplus to requirements for the remainder of the season, Allison made his final two appearances in 1958.

At Lansdowne Road his place was taken by Robert Challis, the first international to kick penalties to touch with a place-kick rather than a punt. After losing Peter Thompson with a rib injury, Ned Ashcroft moved out of the pack to bolster the defence, and Peter Jackson conjured one of his 'special' tries, running from half-way and, in full flight, chipping the transfixed Irish cover to gather and score. Challis added a penalty, and the centre Lewis Cannell ended a ten-year, nineteen-game career in a 6–0 win.

England returned to Twickenham for the final two matches of the season. In the first, against a French side destined for the wooden spoon, Phil Davies was recalled to partner Jeff Butterfield, and Jackson scored twice down his right wing. When the visitors did briefly threaten, captain Eric Evans doggedly chased a loose bouncing ball to complete an 11–5 victory.

Four years after her coronation, the young Queen Elizabeth was at headquarters to watch England land the fourth leg of

Above England's Squire Wilkins (right) kicks the ball on in the course of the Five Nations match against France in 1953

Right England recorded an 11–0 success over the French, 1953

their seventh Grand Slam by beating Scotland 16–3. Butterfield put Davies away for his only international try, and in the second half flanker Reg Higgins created a score for Thompson before breaking three Scottish tackles to claim the third. Challis converted two of the tries and kicked a penalty in by far England's best performance of the season.

Substantially the same side made a positive defence of their title in 1958. A 3–3 draw with Wales precluded any possibility of another Grand Slam, but wins over Ireland and France and a second draw against Scotland were sufficient to retain the Five Nations Championship. Moreover, England recorded a dramatic first victory against a bona fide Australian touring team. In a pernicious contest, full-back John Hetherington, playing his first game, suffered concussion and Jeff Butterfield was knocked out four times. When an Australian stamped on Peter Thompson, the disquiet among the crowd gave way to full-fledged booing, previously unheard of at Twickenham. After 30 minutes Phil Horrocks-Taylor retired injured and Butterfield moved to fly-half. Flanker Peter Bobbins stepped into the middle and England played the rest of the game with fourteen men and a seven-man pack. Twice behind, a visibly groggy Hetherington wobbled over a penalty goal to square the match, and in an absorbing finale Peter Jackson scored a thrilling winner. Hugging his right wing, Jackson gained a yard by handing off Phelps before feinting outside the full-back Curley and heading for the line. Phelps recovered, but at the very moment he flung himself into a saving tackle Jackson made a desperate leap for the corner to seal a 9–6 England victory.

It was a momentous win for skipper Eric Evans, and at the end of the season, after a draw with Scotland, he retired. England's first great hooker, Evans made 30 appearances for his country, one

RUGBY FOOTBALL UNION

ENGLAND
v
FRANCE

TWICKENHAM
SATURDAY 28th FEBRUARY
1953
ONE SHILLING

short of Wavell Wakefield's total, and captained the side on thirteen occasions to equal the record established by Wakefield and Nim Hall. Later, Dickie Jeeps and John Pullin would also lead England thirteen times, and the inauspicious tally was eventually exceeded by Bill Beaumont in 1981 and subsequently by Will Carling.

Fifty years after entering the competition, France won their first outright Five Nations Championship in 1959. England, unbeaten for 33 months, slipped up 5–0 in Cardiff, and Jeff Butterfield, Peter Thompson and Ned Ashcroft finished their international careers, along with five others, in a 3–3 draw with Scotland at Twickenham.

Butterfield had captained the side throughout the season, and in 1960 Dickie Jeeps began his three-year tenure with a 14–6 win over Wales. Wing Jim Roberts scored two tries on his debut, and the fly-half Richard Sharp and Mike Weston were also among the seven new caps who contributed to England's highest score against the Welsh since 1924. Sharp, a British Lion and Oxford Blue, won fourteen caps, the last, after a premature retirement and four-year absence, against Australia in 1967. Weston made the first 24 of his 29 appearances at centre before ending his career in Sharps stand-off position. Omitted from the national side for two years,

Left I King dribbles the ball clear during England's 14–3 victory over the Irish on 13 February 1954
Below left England's D L Sanders is grasped firmly by Irishman J A O'Meara, 1954
Below English players pounce on W O Williams during Wales's 3–0 victory over the English at Cardiff on 22 January 1955

he eventually retired in 1968 as England's most capped back. Both players made a big impact in their first season. Sharp dropped a goal in the 8–5 defeat of Ireland, and Weston scored his side's only try in a 3–3 draw with defending champions France. With Scotland beaten 21–12 in Edinburgh, England won the Triple Crown, their last for twenty years, and shared the Five Nations honours with France.

For some unfathomable reason, the best wing in the land, Peter Jackson, played no part in England's success and was largely overlooked until 1963. Recalled to an inexperienced team – Dickie Jeeps, John Currie and Peter Robbins had retired – his explosive

Above left Eire President Sean O'Kelly meets the England team before the 6–8 draw in Dublin in 1953

Above Dejected Englishmen leave the Twickenham pitch, tails firmly between their legs, 1956

run created the opening try in a 13–6 victory over Wales in Cardiff, England's last at the Arms Park until 1991. Penalties settled their next two encounters. On a bemired and almost unplayable Lansdowne Road surface, Ireland missed three in a scoreless draw, and at Twickenham the Oxford University full-back John Willcox landed a brace to beat France 6–5. The boot of Willcox was also instrumental in England recovering from an early eight-point deficit in Peter Jackson's farewell appearance against Scotland. Lock Nick Drake-Lee initiated the comeback with a try converted by Willcox, and just after the interval captain Richard Sharp bamboozled the Scottish defence by thrice feinting to pass wide and each time breaking inside, eventually to score by the post. Willcox added the extra two points, and in winning 10–8 England regained the Five Nations title and extended their unbeaten run against the Scots to thirteen matches, ten of them victories.

The advent and growth of air travel in the 1960s impelled a spate of short overseas tours by the Home Union teams. Scotland were the first to partake, visiting South Africa in 1960, and three years later European champions England embarked on a brief Antipodean sojourn. Expected to play a trio of Test matches, two with the All Blacks and one against Australia, in the space of eleven days England predictably lost the lot and returned home licking wounds that would take the best part of three decades to heal.

Left Welsh supporters present their captain with a giant leek at Twickenham. R H Williams' Wales team lost 14–6 to England in this 1960 fixture

Below England scrum half Dickie Jeeps feeds the ball to his backs with a flying leap in this match against South Africa on 7 January 1961

Right England's Bev Risman makes inroads into the Welsh defence at Cardiff, 21 January 1961. Wales won 6–3

SEVENTH GRAND SLAM – 1957

Wales	Ireland	France	Scotland
19.01.1957	09.02.1957	23.02.1957	16.03.1957
Cardiff Arms Park	Lansdowne Road	Twickenham	Twickenham
3–0	6–0	9–5	16–3
D F Allison	R Challis	R Challis	R Challis
P B Jackson	P B Jackson	P B Jackson	P B Jackson
J Butterfield	J Butterfield	J Butterfield	J Butterfield
L B Cannell	L B Cannell	W P C Davies	W P C Davies
P H Thompson	P H Thompson	P H Thompson	P H Thompson
R M Bartlett	R M Bartlett	R M Bartlett	R M Bartlett
R E G Jeeps	R E G Jeeps	R E G Jeeps	R E G Jeeps
C R Jacobs	C R Jacobs	C R Jacobs	C R Jacobs
E Evans*	E Evans*	E Evans*	E Evans*
G W D Hastings	G W D Hastings	G W D Hastings	G W D Hastings
J D Currie	J D Currie	J D Currie	J D Currie
R W D Marques	R W D Marques	R W D Marques	R W D Marques
P G D Robbins	P G D Robbins	P G D Robbins	P G D Robbins
R Higgins	R Higgins	R Higgins	R Higgins
A Ashcroft	A Ashcroft	A Ashcroft	A Ashcroft

Points Scorers	**Points Scorers**	**Points Scorers**	**Points Scorers**
D F Allison – 3	R Challis – 3	P B Jackson – 6	R Challis – 7
	P B Jackson – 3	E Evans – 3	W P C Davies – 3
			R Higgins – 3
			P H Thompson – 3

1963-1987

The wilderness years

THE LUNATIC SCHEDULE INFLICTED ON THE 1963 TOURISTS WAS ONLY
PARTIALLY RESPONSIBLE FOR THEIR THREE TEST MATCH DEFEATS.
THE CELEBRATED ENGLAND SIDE OF THE LATE FIFTIES HAD ALL BUT
DISPERSED, AND THE BALANCE OF INTERNATIONAL POWER, HELD BY
THE SOUTHERN HEMISPHERE NATIONS ON THE WORLD STAGE,
WAS INEXORABLY SHIFTING IN EUROPE.

DOMESTICALLY, the Welsh and the French took their turn in the sun, between them winning or sharing fourteen of the next fifteen Five Nations titles. The decade, though, belonged to New Zealand.

Within seven months of twice beating England at home, Wilson Whineray's 1963–64 touring All Blacks were altogether too quick in thought and deed for their Twickenham opposition. They won 14–0, and only a scoreless draw with Scotland prevented them from completing a full set of victories over the four Home Union countries. From the 3–0 whitewash of France in 1961 to the defeat of Wales in 1969, New Zealand won 34 and drew two of 38 matches. Their two defeats, one each by South Africa and Australia, were sustained in victorious rubbers. They won ten consecutive series, and in 1966 beat the best of Britain and Ireland 4–0.

Under the management of Charles Saxton and the shrewd tactical eye of coach Fred Allen, Brian Lochore's oft-eulogised 1967 side revolutionised the game. At a time when the boot was very much to the fore and forwards dominated the pitch, Saxton introduced the concept of total rugby: fifteen players supporting each other at every phase in a fast, attacking and above all handling-based game. After years of practising and refining the ten-man attritional system pioneered by South Africa, the All Blacks' progressive approach wowed spectators and nonplussed defences across the globe. Continuing a run originated by their 1965 side, they won seventeen successive Test matches, a world record later emulated by South Africa.

The 1967 tourists, containing the bellicose second-row legend Colin Meads, beat all three British teams, as well as France, and were only denied a Grand Slam when an outbreak of foot and mouth disease prevented them from traveling to Ireland. In the victory over Scotland, Mead's misdemeanours finally caught up

with the staunchly patriotic lock when he became the second player – after another All Black, Cyril Brownlie – to be dismissed in an international, ironically for one of his less aggressive offences. For all his belligerence, or maybe because of it, Meads was viewed as a god in his homeland, and it was no coincidence that the All Blacks' first series defeat for a decade, against South Africa in 1970, followed the intentional breaking of his arm in a provincial match.

Of the three home countries to succumb in 1967, England put up the least resistance. Within 30 minutes New Zealand had scored eighteen points, and would certainly have won by more than 23–11 had they not eased off considerably in the second half. The result was indicative of England's lowly standing in the international pecking order. Although the doldrums were sporadically interspersed with the odd implausible victory, the late 1960s and 1970s were primarily bleak years for a moribund national team.

The statistics alone make dismal reading. From the defeat at the hands of the All Blacks in 1963 until immediately prior to what transpired to be the false dawn of the 1980 Grand Slam, England won just 23 of 81 fixtures, losing on a formerly inconceivable 50 occasions. Their only Five Nations title came in the quintuple tie of 1973, when every country won their two home matches, and even then, had the competition followed today's format and been decided on points difference, England would have actually finished last. They collected six wooden spoons, were twice beaten in all four games of a championship campaign and lost a record seven consecutive matches between March 1971 and March 1972.

In addition to a haphazard, almost senseless selection policy, the complete absence of any playing infrastructure frustrated England's immediate ambitions and hindered their long-term development. In

Above Ireland's Willie John McBride (centre) turns to feed his backs after winning the line-out ball against England in February 1964

the southern hemisphere the step up to international level was facilitated by strong provincial rugby, but in England, the County Championship aside, players were reared on a staple diet of meaningless friendly fixtures. Somewhat akin to today's politically correct school governors, the powers that be were not willing disciples of competitive rugby, be it at club or international level. Instead they held an innate belief that any form of competition would instantly topple the ivory towers of amateurism.

While the 1972 introduction of a national knockout tournament, originally the John Player Cup, was a step in the right direction, at the time it was not enormously effective. The RFU president and former England scrum half Dickie Jeeps did attempt reform, inaugurating a divisional championship that ran intermittently from 1977 to 1985, and then continuously until it was disbanded in 1995. In terms of showcasing young talent the championship was a qualified success, but it was nowhere near sufficient and players still stepped into the international arena completely unprepared for what lay ahead.

The 1980 Grand Slam masked many of the system's inherent deficiencies and postponed for five years the creation of a league involving club sides. Merit tables were conceived in 1985 and the Courage League introduced for the 1987–88 season. This was then supplanted by a new sponsor and the Allied Dunbar Premiership in 1997 which has since become the Zurich Premiership. Meanwhile, the County Championship, first awarded by common consent to unbeaten Yorkshire in 1889, was downgraded in 1994 to the exclusion of players from the top two

Above Budge Rogers captained England seven times in the 1960s, winning a total of 34 caps

Below English captain John Willcox talks to new cap R Rowell at training in 1964

divisions of the Courage League. Pointedly, the long overdue organisation of a club competition, coupled with the stability that manager Geoff Cooke brought to team selection, would coincide with England's phoenix-like ascent to the heights of the world game from the late 1980s onwards.

In his autobiography, *Thanks to Rugby*, Bill Beaumont, one of the most admired and respected England Captains, laid the blame for his country's alarming demise squarely on the shoulders of the national selectors, ever so succinctly referring to the regional trials, where team-mates would meet barely an hour before kick-off, as 'organised chaos' and highlighting the need for the type of approach later adopted by Cooke. Instead of which, caps were tossed about like confetti and endowed on those who by rights should never have donned an England jersey. Indifferent to individual form, the selectors appeared equally oblivious to the need for continuity, and a single reverse would often result in the summary dismissal of any number of established internationals. With such alacrity did England discard and recall their players that they named only five unchanged teams in the entire decade of the 1970s and were never able to field the same side three games in a row. Given the constant chopping and changing, it was a wonder any matches were won.

However, some talent did survive the selectors' foibles, and against all the odds produced the occasional gem to lift the gloom. No one present at Twickenham will ever forget England's miraculous escape when trailing by three points to Scotland in 1965. Entering the fourth minute of time added on by the Welsh referee, a weak clearance by Mike Weston was seized upon by the Scottish wing Dave Whyte. Held up on the 25-yard line, Whyte lost possession and Weston was on hand to find Andy Hancock with a simple pass. As the Northampton wing took the first strides of his eternal run there did not appear to be any prospect of him scoring, but by the time he cleared half-way and evaded an almost token lunge by full-back Stewart Wilson, the Scottish cover was encouragingly thin. Head erect and gasping for air, Hancock made straight for the corner, despairingly pursued by centre Ian Laughland. Exhausted, he collapsed over the line at the very moment Laughland timed his unavailing tackle. Making only his second appearance, Hancock's 90-yard effort was the longest solo try seen at Twickenham until Dan Luger raced almost 100 metres against South Africa in November 2001, and though Don Rutherford missed the conversion, England drew 3–3. Hancock's reward for his heroics? A year-long wait for a third cap against France in Paris, where a torn hamstring limited his effectiveness and any hopes of being picked again. *C'est la vie.*

Injury-time was kinder still to England on their 1967 visit to Lansdowne Road. This time Colin McFadyean underlined the importance of playing to the final whistle when a misplaced Irish pass ricocheted off his knee and presented an unimpeded run at goal. The try and subsequent conversion from full-back Roger Hosen transformed a certain 3–3 draw into a fortuitous 8–3 victory. England made a habit of snatching games at the death that season. Losing 14–13 to Scotland at Twickenham, they preserved a 21-year unbeaten home record against the Scots with fourteen points in a riveting six-minute finale. Switched from wing to centre, McFadyean scored two of his team's four tries in a 27–14 win.

Above England's Philip Judd chases the loose ball after team-mate Bob Hearn was tackled by France's Christian Carrere in 1967

Right England and Ireland played out a 9–9 draw in this 1968 Five Nations meeting

Imitating the initiative pioneered in the southern hemisphere, Wales were the first of the Home Union countries to acknowledge the need for a national coach. They appointed the former Ebbw Vale back-row forward David Nash, whose maiden challenge ended in an 11–11 draw at Twickenham in 1968. Leading 11–3, defensive errors cost England a deserved victory, and within a few months Nash resigned. On his debut, fullback Bob Hiller converted Brian Redwood's try, and over the next four seasons scored a record 138 points in nineteen international outings. After receiving a first cap in 1966, hooker John Pullin returned for the second of 42 appearances. Pullin would eventually become England's most capped player, overtaking the mark established in 1969 by Bedford's loyal wing forward Budge Rogers. In an unexpected 22–8 victory over Five Nations champions France, Rogers passed Wavell Wakefield's 42-year-old record of 31 caps, and his final tally of 34 stood until 1974.

Two weeks before the France game, David Duckham scored a try on his debut against Ireland. An incisive centre or wing, Duckham played 36 times for his country and the last three Tests

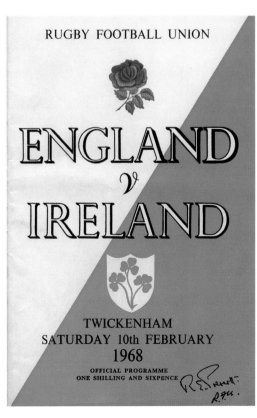

RUGBY FOOTBALL UNION

ENGLAND v IRELAND

TWICKENHAM
SATURDAY 10th FEBRUARY
1968
OFFICIAL PROGRAMME
ONE SHILLING AND SIXPENCE

of the Lions' victorious 1971 series in New Zealand. For seven years his flamboyance illuminated many a grey England performance, and until Rory Underwood redefined the art of scoring, only Cyril Lowe exceeded Duckham's total of ten tries.

His initial season was also the one in which the International Rugby Board ruled that replacements would be permitted for injured players. Scotland were the first side to take advantage of the new legislation, bringing Ian McCrae on for scrum half Gordon Connell against France in January 1969. Three months later England had occasion to call on their first substitute when the Moseley wing Keith Fielding damaged an ankle in the 8–3 win over Scotland, and was replaced by Tim Dalton. Dalton was not selected again and so joined Ireland's founder member Colin Grimshaw in the already burgeoning club of players to have represented their country without starting a match.

England implemented their own innovation for the 1969–70 season, assembling a squad of 30 players on a monthly basis under the tutelage of coach and selector Don White. In the short term the measure appeared to produce positive dividends. At the sixth time of asking England recorded a first win over South Africa before two towering Bob Hiller drop goals and a Roger Shackleton try beat Ireland 9–3 at Twickenham. Alas, the revival was short-lived, and a 13–3 lead against a Welsh team including J P R Williams, John Dawes, Barry John and Gareth Edwards disintegrated into a 17–13 defeat. The year that began so buoyantly faded into a haze of mediocrity with heavy losses to Scotland, and particularly to France. The French scored six tries

in a sunny 35–13 Parisian romp, and from the Ireland game England scraped just one win in the next thirteen matches.

On a tour disrupted by anti-apartheid demonstrations, the Springboks drew two and lost two of their four Tests against the Home Union countries. At Twickenham, five days before Christmas 1969, a try apiece from the forwards Peter Larter and John Pullin retrieved an eight-point deficit in an 11–8 win for England. Universally condemned for their policy of racial segregation, the Boks did not revisit British shores until 1992. Although numerous governments declined to sever commercial ties and refused to implement trade embargoes, they were less reticent when it came to sport. South Africa soon found themselves cast as sporting pariahs, ostracised from almost every major international event. The one principal exception was rugby. England undertook official tours in 1972 and 1984, and when the All Blacks did likewise in 1976, 22 African nations boycotted the Montreal Olympic Games in protest at New Zealand's participation. In 1981 a reciprocal Springboks tour of New Zealand was marred by rioting, and to emphasise the double standards between sports, a year later England's rebel cricketers received three-year bans for their unauthorised trip.

The cause of the disparity was again amateurism. Rugby's administrators were mindful that in failing to maintain playing links they would eventually force Afrikaner companies to offer large financial incentives for teams, like the 1986 New Zealand Cavaliers, to participate in unofficial series. Hence the South African Rugby Union was never expelled from the International Board, and the sanctioned World XV that toured the country in 1989 received a small fortune for warding off professionalism! For all that, rugby did play a part in reforming South Africa's political system. Exclusion from the first two World Cups was almost too much for a fanatical sporting public to bear, and helped to highlight the urgent need for constitutional change.

With the Rugby Football Union going to great lengths to celebrate their centenary, the 1970–71 season was eagerly anticipated. Sadly, England's players and supporters were obliged to bask in past glories as the festivities coincided with the worst sequence of results in the nation's history. Open-side flanker Tony Neary was one of seven new caps who lost 22–6 to the eventual Grand Slam winners, Wales. An almost permanent fixture for the best part of a decade, Neary played 43 times for his country, one more than previous record holder John Pullin. Towards the end of an immense individual career, within a generally average team, his unstinting service was finally rewarded with a cap for the British Lions in the Fourth Test against New Zealand in 1977, and a Grand Slam in 1980.

Bob Hiller scored all 23 of England's points in their next two matches. He kicked three penalties in the 9–6 victory over Ireland, and converted his own try and landed three more place-kicks in a 14–14 draw with France. Dropped for the Welsh game, the full-back returned for his best season. He scored three of his team's paltry five tries, and in converting against the French became the first Englishman to pass 100 international points.

The prop Fran Cotton joined the front row for England's final Five Nations challenge, but even his huge physical bulk could not prevent Scotland from winning their first match at Twickenham since 1938. In addition to Tony Neary and the lock Nigel Horton, Cotton survived his country's darkest hour to participate in the brief 1980 revival, and also played seven Tests for the Lions – all four on the 'Ninety-nine' tour of South Africa and the remainder against the 1977 All Blacks.

England's wretched anniversary season concluded with two special centenary matches. In the first they were soundly thrashed 26–6 by Scotland in Edinburgh, and at Twickenham an assortment of world-class players from France and the southern hemisphere won 28–11. Assembled under the banner of an RFU President's Overseas XV, individuals of the ability of Colin Meads, Brian Lochore, Pierre Villepreux, Bryan Williams and Ian Kirkpatrick were always likely to be a shade too strong for a home side that did resist bravely until a fourth-quarter onslaught. Hiller again contributed all of England's points, and in the two games they scored one try and conceded eleven.

After a season in which they achieved one win in six outings, England's performances, confidence and results deteriorated still further in 1972. They lost all four championship fixtures to extend their sequence of consecutive defeats to seven. In the year that the value of a try was increased to four points, England benefited on only two occasions and scored just 36 points, one less than they conceded in the 37–12 loss to France. Even fortress Twickenham resembled a sand castle, kicked over by Ireland and Wales to leave the crestfallen landlords without a win at headquarters in six matches.

Although England could not possibly escape the wooden spoon, the Five Nations would forever remain unresolved as both Scotland and Wales, as a result of sectarian violence in Belfast,

Below Welsh lock M G Roberts gets the ball away to srum-half Gareth Edwards, January 1971

refused to travel to Ireland. Having won three matches, Wales declined the possibility of completing another Grand Slam, and the ill-starred Irish, with two away victories but no home opposition, were harshly deprived of an opportunity to accomplish what would have been only their second clean sweep.

Desperately chasing a positive result, the ever optimistic selectors doled out ten new caps, three of which settled on deserving heads. The giant Rosslyn Park number eight Andy Ripley made 24 England appearances and scored two tries before being jettisoned at his peak in 1976. An excellent all-round sportsman, he toured South Africa with the British Isles, and in 1980 won television's popular *Superstars* event. Fly-half Alan Old played sixteen times and scored 98 points. A useful cricketer with one first-class wicket for Warwickshire, his brother Chris appeared in 46 Test matches dismissing 143 batsmen. In February 1974, they represented their respective sports on the same day, Chris losing in the West Indies and Alan at Murrayfield. Unfortunately for prop Mike Burton, he will always be remembered as the first Englishman sent off in international rugby, receiving his marching orders in May 1975 for a late tackle on the Australian wing Doug Osborne. Another to suffer the vagaries of his country's selection

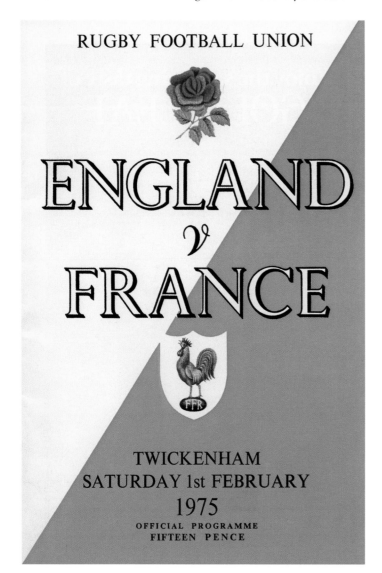

Above The French triumphed at Twickenham by a scoreline of 27–20

process, Burton was dropped three times and played only seventeen of 33 matches between debut and departure.

A tour of South Africa in the early summer of 1972, consisting of six provincial games and one Test match in eighteen days, did not initially appear to provide England with any realistic chance of ending their losing run. Even after they had won five and drawn one of six warm-up matches, nobody expected them to defeat a Springboks side unbeaten at home against British or Irish opposition. In all sports England are at their most dangerous when underestimated, and the response of John Pullin's players was typically bullish. Full-back Sam Doble kicked four penalties and converted Alan Morley's crucial second-half try, and a magnificent defensive line restricted South Africa to long-range kicks at goal. They were successful with only three, and in front of an increasingly disenchanted home crowd crashed 18–9. Worldwide, the result raised more than a few eyebrows. It wasn't until the summer of 1999 that the Welsh recorded their first win over South Africa, yet hapless England had beaten them twice, home and away, in two and a half years.

As immensely satisfying as the victory was, it did not suddenly transform a distinctly average English side into world-beaters, and consequently their supporters' inflated expectations were brought down to earth when New Zealand visited Twickenham in January 1973 and won 9–0. The 1972–73 All Blacks were an inconsistent and less talented squad than their 1967 predecessors. They won three of five Tests – a 10–10 draw in Ireland denied them a British Grand Slam – but were beaten by France and lost several regional contests. The last of these, against the Barbarians at the Arms Park, produced one of the best 40 minutes of rugby ever witnessed, and a try that will forever live in the memory of those fortunate enough to experience first-hand its sheer joy. Phil Bennett set the mood in front of his own posts, side-stepping as many black jerseys as you could count before unleashing a sumptuous, incisive, length-of-the-field move involving the exquisite handling skills of five players and culminating in John Bevan's dummy scissors for Gareth Edwards' stunning dive in the corner. At the temple of rugby, it was a try fit for the gods, and by half-time the Barbarians, featuring John Pullin, David Duckham and another ten of the 1971 victorious British Lions, led 17–0. Fatigue enabled the All Blacks to restore some credibility in a 23–11 defeat, but nobody trooping away from the Arms Park that January day doubted they were in the presence of genius.

For the English players on duty the transition to Five Nations competition must have been almost unendurable. Previously beaten in Cardiff, they traveled to Dublin and suffered a tenth defeat in eleven games. With the memory of the Scottish and Welsh boycott lingering, England did at least receive a rapturous welcome when they stepped out at Lansdowne Road. That, however, was as far as Irish appreciation extended, causing John Pullin to utter at the post-match dinner, 'We may not be much good, but at least we turn up.'

Two newcomers demonstrated sufficient ability in Dublin to find themselves randomly selected for the next few seasons. Roger Uttley, who would later coach England and the British Lions, made 23 appearances in the second or back row before retiring after the 1980 Grand Slam. He captained his country on five occasions and played in every Test of the 1974 Lions tour of South Africa, scoring an important try in the last. A strong and intelligent player, Steve Smith was England's most capped scrum half until Richard Hill took the field in the 1991 World Cup final. Also a national captain, his career spanned eleven seasons, during which he played 28 of 51 matches. Largely ignored by the selectors between March 1974 and November 1979, Smith joined the British Isles as a replacement on their 1980 and 1983 tours without securing a Test berth.

Both players were retained for the two remaining championship fixtures against France and Scotland at Twickenham. On Peter Squires' debut, David Duckham scored two tries to beat the French 14–6, and the dashing Harrogate wing scored himself in the 20–13 defeat of Scotland. Flanker Peter Dixon added two more, and Coventry's Geoff Evans registered his only international try as England at last put to rest their unenviable record of seven home games without a win.

Concerned by the possibility of civil insurgence, the RFU cancelled that summer's intended tour of Argentina and hastily arranged an alternative trip to Fiji and New Zealand for late August and September. England had not won three consecutive matches for fifteen years, and when they lost every provincial game in New Zealand – to Taranaki, Wellington and Canterbury – people were predicting, just as they had done in South Africa

the year before, an easy afternoon for the hosts. This, though, was not the All Blacks team of the sixties. In decline, they reverted to a ten-man game, and when England's pack refused to bend, their lack of options was critically exposed. After playing into a strong wind for the first half, the tourists overturned a four-point deficit with tries from the loosehead prop 'Stack' Stevens and Tony Neary. Their 16–10 victory remained the only English conquest on New Zealand soil until 2003.

Within two months of scoring the winner against the All Blacks, Tony Neary added his fourth England try in the 20–3 Twickenham defeat of Australia. Under the captaincy of John Pullin, a team incapable of mounting a credible challenge in Europe had vanquished all three of the southern hemisphere powers inside eighteen months, also winning four matches in succession for the first time since the Grand Slam season of 1957.

Despite having acquired the useful knack of beating the best teams in the world, domestically England continued to underachieve. In February 1974, in Edinburgh, Andy Irvine converted a last-minute penalty in Scotland's 16–14 win, and at Twickenham the home side trailed Ireland by twenty points before recovering slightly to lose 26–21. David Duckham's powerful run

Below Mike Rafter is tackled from both sides as England contest a Five Nations match in Paris in January 1978. France won 15–6

finished a super three-quarter move in the 12–12 draw with France, but the result was obscured by a tragic plane crash killing a number of England supporters on their way home from Paris. Among those to perish was the former Bedford prop Larry Webb, who played four times for his country in 1959. Already condemned to the championship wooden spoon, England completed their season in typically perverse fashion, beating Wales 16–14 at Twickenham. The Nottingham full-back Dusty Hare enjoyed an unforgettable debut in the only win over the Welsh between 1963 and 1980. Virtually disregarded for the next five years, Hare eventually made 25 international appearances, and his total of 240 points remained an English record until Jonathan Webb kicked two penalties and three conversions in the 1992 Grand Slam victory over Wales.

For the umpteenth time in a miserable decade, one decent result preceded a catalogue of ineptitude. England won an ignoble seven of their next 24 fixtures, and in 1976 lost every Five Nations match for the second time in five years. At the Arms Park in 1979 the careers of five players, most notably those of Peter Squires and full-back Alastair Hignell, were prematurely extinguished in a fearful 27–3 hammering by the Welsh.

Fortunately, the grass-roots production line of club rugby continued to breed individuals of the topmost quality. The quintessential English forward Bill Beaumont joined the fray against Ireland in 1975, and one game later hooker Peter Wheeler won the first of his 41 caps in a seven-point defeat at the hands of France. Both captained their country and appeared together in seven Tests for the British Isles. Mike Slemen's bristling moustache was introduced to the Twickenham public in the one-point Irish victory in 1976. The Liverpool and Lions wing scored eight tries in 31 matches, four of them against Scotland. Two members of the 1980 Grand Slam pack were awarded debuts in 1978. John Scott played 34 times and had the unusual distinction of captaining England and Cardiff. He concluded his career at lock having made 30 appearances at number eight, a record for the position since surpassed by Dean Richards. Lock Maurice Colclough won 33 international caps, eight of them for the British Lions. During their 1980 tour of South Africa he partnered Bill

Above England's Fran Cotton (second right) looks on open-mouthed as team-mate Dusty Hare (centre) dodges a tackle from New Zealand's David Loveridge (right, diving) in 1979.

Left The triumphant team of 1980, skippered by Bill Beaumont. This was England's first Grand Slam since 1957

EIGHTH GRAND SLAM – 1980

Ireland	**France**	**Wales**	**Scotland**
19.01.1980	02.02.1980	16.02.1980	15.03.1980
Twickenham	Parc des Princes	Twickenham	Murrayfield
24–9	17–13	9–8	30–18
W H Hare	W H Hare	W H Hare	W H Hare
J Carleton	J Carleton	J Carleton	J Carleton
A M Bond	C R Woodward	C R Woodward	C R Woodward
N J Preston	N J Preston	P W Dodge	P W Dodge
M A C Slemen	M A C Slemen	M A C Slemen	M A C Slemen
J P Horton	J P Horton	J P Horton	J P Horton
S J Smith	S J Smith	S J Smith	S J Smith
F E Cotton	F E Cotton	F E Cotton	F E Cotton
P J Wheeler	P J Wheeler	P J Wheeler	P J Wheeler
P J Blakeway	P J Blakeway	P J Blakeway	P J Blakeway
W B Beaumont*	W B Beaumont*	W B Beaumont*	W B Beaumont*
N E Horton	M J Colclough	M J Colclough	M J Colclough
R M Uttley	R M Uttley	R M Uttley	R M Uttley
A Neary	A Neary	A Neary	A Neary
J P Scott	J P Scott	J P Scott	J P Scott

Replacement		**Replacement**	
C R Woodward (13)		M Rafter (6)	

Points Scorers	**Points Scorers**	**Points Scorers**	**Points Scorers**
W H Hare – 12	J P Horton – 6	W H Hare – 9	J Carleton – 12
J P Scott – 4	J Carleton – 4		W H Hare – 10
M A C Slemen – 4	N J Preston – 4		M A C Slemen – 4
S J Smith – 4	W H Hare – 3		S J Smith – 4

Beaumont in all four Tests, and scored England's winning try against the All Blacks in 1983. Centre Paul Dodge and fly-half John Horton also came into the side in 1978, and a year later the 7–7 Calcutta Cup draw included prop Gareth Pearce.

Quite apart from the intolerable results, another worrying development in the seventies was the bad nature that began to mar encounters between England and the other home nations. As Celtic parochialism intensified, matches involving Wales, and later Scotland, were often played in a genuinely unpleasant climate. Considering the subsequent hostility, Phil Bennett's rabble-rousing prior to England's 1977 game in Cardiff was actually one of the more moderate and amusing team-talks: 'Look what these bastards have done to Wales. They've taken our coal, our water, our steel. They buy our houses and they only live in them for a fortnight every twelve months. What have they given us? Absolutely nothing. We've been exploited, raped, controlled and punished by the English – and that's who you are playing this afternoon.'

Arrogance is always the heinous crime laid at the English door, yet no British team was ever as arrogant, possibly with some justification, as the great Welsh side captained by none other than Phil Bennett. Globally, the Springboks of the late 1990s took self-confidence to previously unexplored heights, at times showing an almost manifest contempt for their opposition. After their 1995 World Cup triumph the South African rugby president Louis Luyt boasted to guests at the post-match banquet that given the opportunity his compatriots would also have lifted the trophy in 1987 and 1991!

Although Anglophobes can muster a wealth of legitimate historical and political grievances, as Scotland have discovered, you can only use ancient resentment to your advantage for so long. The Welsh still act as if defending Harlech Castle against 'Saxon tyrants', and the unbridled tartan antipathy extends well beyond an annual grudge match. When England faced Australia in the 1991 World Cup final the Scotland squad, beaten on home soil by England in the semi-final, attended the Twickenham showpiece bedecked in green and gold. A joke, perhaps, but had Brian Moore attempted such a witticism the howls of outrage north of the border would have echoed long and loud.

Twickenham international, the Northern Division had played a ten-man game to such purpose that they beat New Zealand 21–9. Flankers Roger Uttley and Tony Neary destroyed the tourists in the loose, and the discarded England flyhalf Alan Old produced a brilliant display of positional kicking. When the North did deign to interject some width, their backs made merry in the acres of space left unmanned by an overextended All Blacks defence. The half-backs Steve Smith and Old scored a try apiece, and the Sale centre Tony Bond grabbed two in front of an enthralled Orley crowd.

For obvious reasons coach Mike Davis intended to employ the same tactics at Twickenham, but England selected the wrong

Below Steve Smith made 28 international appearances between 1793 and 1983

In some respects the obsessive Celtic desire to better their colonial oppressors translates into a deep-rooted lack of ambition. At no time during the previous century did England possess the best rugby team in the world. They produced sides capable of beating the best, but never consistently and never in the same dominant manner as New Zealand or South Africa. They did not therefore represent the standard to which other nations should have aspired, and while Scotland and Wales remained content to recite from Max Boyce's whimsical song book, 'He'll not ask how you played the game, but ... whether you beat England!', they would never fulfill the destinies that their fine traditions warranted. One of the most ill-tempered British games was contested between England and Wales in 1980, when Bill Beaumont's side had the temerity to suggest they were no longer prepared to roll over before the Welsh and might instead beat them to that year's championship.

After the previous season's shambles in Cardiff, the chairman of selectors Sandy Sanders was replaced by Budge Rogers, and Mike Davis succeeded Peter Colston as coach. Once England's record cap holder, Rogers brought a certain pragmatism to the post, consulting frequently with Captain Beaumont and introducing a steadfast approach to team selection. He did, though, make one inexplicable faux pas in his first match against the touring All Blacks on 24 November 1979. A week before the

Above England's Peter Wheeler (right) helps to keep the Scotland forwards at bay as team-mate Stephen Boyle (centre) feeds scrum half Steve Smith (left)

Below An all-action Rory Underwood makes a dive pass during the victory over Ireland at Twickenham on 18 February 1984

Above right Mike Slemen leaps highest against the All Blacks, November 1983. England prevailed 15–9

team for the task. Mike Rafter was preferred to Roger Uttley on the openside, and Les Cusworth won his first cap in the fly-half position that should have been occupied by Alan Old. Cusworth had never partnered Smith before and his running style was totally unsuited to the kicking role obligatory in ten-man rugby. The upshot was a listless 10–9 England defeat and a chastening afternoon for Cusworth, precipitating an eternal and unmerited association with an ineffectual performance. In nine seasons, the Leicester devotee represented his country just twelve times and endured a two-year wait for his second appearance.

The frustration of having squandered a rare opportunity to beat the All Blacks was taken out on Ireland in the first championship match of 1980. Budge Rogers rectified his earlier mistake, although possibly not in the eyes of Alan Old or Les Cusworth, by selecting the 29-year-old Phil Blakeway at tight-head and switching Fran Cotton to the loosehead berth. Two years after breaking his neck, Blakeway excelled on his debut and England stormed to a 24–9 victory. In response to three penalty goals from the Irish kicking sensation Ollie Campbell, full-back Dusty Hare landed his own two penalties and also converted tries by Steve Smith, Mike Slemen and John Scott. The one downside in a consummate exhibition was the broken leg sustained by Tony Bond. Replaced by the current national coach Clive Woodward, Bond played only once more for England, in a single-point loss to Ireland in 1982.

Excluding Woodward, who retained his position, only one alteration was made to the team that flew to Paris to face France: Maurice Colclough, having missed the Irish encounter with injury, was restored to the second row in place of Nigel Horton. England had not won on the 'wrong' side of the Channel for sixteen years, and after two minutes the French went ahead through their blond-haired captain, Jean-Pierre Rives. They also finished much the stronger, but in between England amassed an unassailable lead with a pair of John Horton drop goals and two tries. Nick Preston, ignoring the inside scissors by Mike Slemen, broke two weak tackles for the first, and Steve Smith's subtle dummy created sufficient space for John Carleton's right-hand corner acrobatics. Neither had previously scored at international level, and while Carleton remained an ever-present for four years, the indisposed Preston withdrew from the next squad, never to return, and was replaced by Paul Dodge.

And so to Twickenham and the almost preordained abrasive showdown with Wales. Both sides were unbeaten, and for two weeks the press eagerly fanned the flames, using a Welsh steel strike to stoke the growing enmity between the downtrodden, barefooted Celtic martyrs and their tyrannical English masters. Conveniently overlooking the fact that England had defeated Wales on only one occasion in the last sixteen years, they lit the touchpaper and retreated to a safe distance to recount, with great surprise and righteous indignation, the brutality that followed.

As was always likely to be the case, the pre-match hostility erupted on the pitch, and after one heated confrontation too many the Irish referee, David Burnett, called upon both captains to restrain their teams, warning that the next player to commit a serious offence would have first use of the showers. A few minutes later, Paul Ringer was dismissed for what, over the years, has been euphemistically described as a late tackle on John Horton; in reality, Ringer made no attempt to play the ball. His rush of blood deprived Wales of a victory and, far more harrowingly from the Welsh perspective, presented England with the third leg of their Grand Slam. Even reduced to fourteen men, Wales should have won. They scored the game's two tries, Gareth Davies missed half a dozen kicks at goal, and they were still

Above The scoreboard tells the story of England's 15–24 Five Nations defeat by Wales at Twickenham, March 1984

Below England's front row for the game against Wales on 17 March 1984 – Phil Blakeway, Peter Wheeler and Paul Rendall

ahead in injury-time when Terry Holmes was caught on the wrong side of a ruck. From the right-hand touchline Dusty Hare carefully stroked home his third penalty, and the exultant Twickenham crowd rose to applaud a 9–8 victory. To top a proud day for Bill Beaumont, that evening he was invited to lead the British Isles on their impending tour of South Africa.

With three wins under their belt, a highly motivated England team arrived at Murrayfield pursuing a first Grand Slam since 1957, and a first Triple Crown since 1960. From the start they played like champions, scoring three tries and building a 16–0 lead within half an hour. Clive Woodward was at his mesmerising best, tormenting a static Scottish defence and manufacturing openings gleefully accepted by the two wings, John Carleton and Mike Slemen. Steve Smith's perfectly timed retrieval from the base of a driving scrum handed Carleton his second try of the match, and the scrum half himself added the fourth, applying the finishing burst to an awesome move involving twelve players. Between Scottish tries, a speculative kick from Paul Dodge fell ideally for Carleton to complete a 30–18 win. Herbert Jacob had been the last Englishman to score a hat-trick, against France in 1924, and no English side had previously totalled 30 points against Scotland. Tony Neary surpassed John Pullin's national record of 42 caps, and Bill Beaumont equalled the record for most appearances as captain, jointly held by Wavell Wakefield, Nim Hall, Eric Evans, Dickie Jeeps and Pullin.

For the team's senior members, the 1980 season was the culmination of years of honest endeavour and perseverance. The battle-scarred foot soldiers Peter Wheeler, Fran Cotton, Roger Uttley, Neary and Beaumont had experienced the depressing lows of the mid-seventies, and together, for one isolated season, they scaled the peaks of European rugby. Rarely has any group of players been more worthy of their success, and seldom can that success have been so fleeting. Within two years, half of England's superlative pack was no longer available, and by 1983 the Grand Slam was

Above The England team prior to the Test match against Australia which took place on 3 November 1984

already beginning to resemble a mirage in a desert of inadequacy. Roger Uttley and Tony Neary retired after the 1980 Murrayfield win, and in Cardiff, during the first game of the very next season, a torn hamstring curtailed Fran Cotton's international involvement.

In January 1982, Bill Beaumont captained England against Scotland in the Calcutta Cup at Murrayfield. With four minutes of injury-time played and the visitors leading 9–6, the match is generally remembered for the soaring penalty goal struck from inside his own half by Andy Irvine, to rescue his country with a 9–9 draw. Two weeks later the occasion assumed a far greater significance when a stray knee in the County Championship final between Lancashire and the North Midlands ended Beaumont's career. Advised by experts that another blow to the head could result in brain damage, the big-hearted lock retired, and with him disappeared English hopes of repeating their 1980 success in the near future. An integral part of his team's engine room and an inspirational captain, at 29 Beaumont was one of a rare breed of players for whom the word 'irreplaceable' was entirely apt. In the four seasons following his retirement, England won only seven of their 27 fixtures, and were twice beaten by a record margin: on the 1985 tour of New Zealand they conceded six tries and lost the second Test 42–15, and the 36–3 reverse sustained at Murrayfield in February 1986 remains their heaviest defeat against Scotland.

A month after this ordeal in Edinburgh, Maurice Colclough closed one chapter of English rugby when he became the last member of the 1980 side to stand down. Captain Steve Smith had been shunted aside in 1983, and a further seven players had either retired or been dropped during 1984. Peter Wheeler and Clive Woodward finished their international careers at Twickenham with a 24–15 defeat at the hands of Wales, and Dusty Hare, John Horton and John Scott made their final bows on an ill-conceived and ill-fated tour of South Africa (both Tests were lost, and the trip attracted considerable political rancour).

Bidding to replenish England's ageing team, and at the same time arrest their shocking slide, a procession of national selectors

Left Les Cusworth drop-kicks for goal, 1984

tackled the predicament in an immutable manner. That is to say, they threw as many new caps at the situation as humanly possible and then continually dropped and reselected the same players. In five years, eight of England's next Grand Slam-winning side were discovered, yet few would feel secure in their positions until Geoff Cooke took charge in 1987.

A rapidly deteriorating pack was bolstered in 1982 by the introduction of flanker Peter Winterbottom, and Rory Underwood, in a direct swap for Mike Slemen, made his debut on the wing against Ireland in 1984. Regrettably, the RAF fighter pilot spent his formative years either shivering on the wing waiting forlornly for a useful ball, or attempting to throw himself in front of rampaging opposition backs. In his first seventeen internationals Underwood scored two tries; in his next 68 matches he touched down 47 times. Bath's Richard Hill, a scrum half equivalent in quality to Steve Smith, also joined the fray in 1984, for the South Africa jaunt in May and June, and in February 1985 the names of fly-half Rob Andrew and lock Wade Dooley appeared on the teamsheet for the inaugural meeting with Romania. Still ensconced in a Cambridge education, Andrew scored two drop goals and eighteen points, a record for a player

Below Rory Underwood and Rob Andrew pose for the photographer before Andrew makes his debut in a 22-15 defeat of Romania in January 1985
Below right This particular Calcutta Cup contest ended in a closely-fought 10-7 victory for England

on his debut. One match later the Gloucester back row specialist Mike Teague appeared as a second-half replacement in a 9–9 draw with France. Andrew kicked a last-minute penalty, and the French wasted a golden opportunity when their wing Patrick Esteve, challenged by Richard Harding, dropped the ball beyond England's goal line. Visually an unlikely crowd-pleaser, Dean Richards established himself in the hearts of every England supporter by grounding two pushover tries on his first appearance for the national side, against Ireland in 1986. Often doubted by coaches and managers alike, the gargantuan Leicester forward won a world record 53 caps at number eight, six of them for the Lions.

Another Herculean figure, Brian Moore, joined the side for the last Five Nations fixture prior to the 1987 World Cup, against Scotland at Twickenham. He received his call when Richard Hill, Wade Dooley, Gareth Chilcott and rival hooker Graham Dawe were suspended for their part in a savage clash at Cardiff Arms Park. Determined that his team was no longer going to be intimidated in the Welsh heartland, Captain Hill delivered one of the most vitriolic pre-match orations ever heard in an English dressing room. Presumably the Welsh Captain, Pickering, was doing much the same in the home dressing room, because when the bell went – sorry, the match kicked off – both sets of forwards stood toe to toe knocking the living daylights out of each other. Dooley, preferring to be hung for a sheep than a lamb, broke Phil Davies's cheekbone, and had the Scottish

RUGBY FOOTBALL UNION

THE

Calcutta Cup

ENGLAND
V
SCOTLAND

TWICKENHAM
SATURDAY 16th MARCH

Above Wade Dooley prepares to take off as England just edge past Ireland 25–20, March 1986

referee, Ray Megson, been in a less charitable mood, the game – incidentally, won 19–12 by Wales – could easily have ended twelve-a-side. While the one-match bans imposed by the RFU were appropriate, their unilateral stance was undermined by the Welsh refusal to take any action against their own players. Charged with inciting the fracas, Richard Hill was stripped of the captaincy and missed England's only championship victory of the season, a 21–12 win over Scotland. He was succeeded as captain by the Wakefield wing Mike Harrison, who retained the position for the inaugural World Cup, jointly hosted by Australia and New Zealand.

In Britain's conservative establishments reaction to the new competition was mixed. Many failed to appreciate the event's long-term implications, expressing a discernible lack of interest for what was seen to be a fatuous enterprise, the more perceptive realising that a global tournament attracting saturation media coverage – 600 million people watched the final between France and New Zealand – and enormous corporate sponsorship was bound to have an adverse effect on amateurism. For this very reason, the Home Union element within the International Board had for years rejected southern hemisphere calls to institute a world championship. Although the first competition was a comparatively low-key affair, the traditionalist's reservations were well founded. Rugby was abruptly propelled into the commercial world and it was only a question of time before the players demanded a share of the huge sums changing hands.

No qualifying matches were organised for the 1987 event; instead, sixteen nations were invited to participate, each being seeded into groups according to ability. England, managed by selector Mike Weston and coached by Martin Green, joined Australia, Japan and the United States in Pool One.

With two teams from each group qualifying for the quarter-finals, an opening 19–6 defeat in Sydney at the hands of Australia was not overly damaging. Mike Harrison scored the first try of the match, and at 6–6 his side remained in contention until undone by the New Zealand official. Australian wing David Campese was awarded a try without actually grounding the ball, and England, who had already lost the services of concussed full-back Marcus Rose, were unable to respond to the setback.

After receiving his first cap as an injury replacement for Rose, Jonathan Webb was included in the record 60–7 victory over the inventive but heavily outgunned Japanese minnows. Webb converted seven of England's ten tries, and Harrison completed a hat trick in thirteen minutes. Jamie Salmon, Kevin Simms and Nigel Redman registered their only international touchdowns, and Rory Underwood emerged from a two-year drought with a try in each half. A popular Captain, devoid of any pretensions, Harrison's purple patch continued when he scored his fifth try of the tournament in the final pool fixture against the United States. The forwards Peter Winterbottom and Wade Dooley also got in on the act as England won 34–6 to engineer an all-British quarter-final, with Wales.

In winning their three pool matches against Ireland, Canada and Tonga, the Welsh had collected so many injuries they were

Above Clive Woodward won 21 caps between 1980 and 1984 and then went on to become the England coach in 1997

compelled to recruit nineteen-year-old David Young from Australian grade rugby. Young walked straight into the side, and Bob Norster also played when clearly unfit. Concerned that bad blood might resurface to ruin the occasion, coach Martin Green ordered his players to refrain from physical confrontation. He need not have worried. England were so bereft of ideas that they lacked the imagination to throw a long pass, let alone a punch, and the only way the occasion could have been spoilt was if the referee had decided to play another twenty minutes. Although each team was as technically unsound as the other, the Welsh displayed greater desire and progressed to the semi-finals by eliminating an inexcusably poor English side 16–3.

The All Blacks were far less generous when confronted by a depleted team. They ruthlessly exploited Welsh deficiencies, winning 49–6 to reach a World Cup final to be staged in front of their own Auckland supporters. Wales, who had already done everything that had been asked of them, recovered exceptionally well to beat Australia 22–21 in the third-place play-off.

In keeping with New Zealand's previous contests, the Eden Park final was a dull, one-sided affair. The All Blacks were at their efficient best, and France had exhausted the *joie de vivre* that had manifested itself against Australia in the other semi-final, in which Serge Blanco had scored a majestic and thrilling winning try. Come the big day, they had nothing left, and the home side claimed an historic 29–9 victory. To underline their overall superiority, the New Zealanders scored 298 points and 43 tries in just six matches.

FIRST WORLD CUP – 1987

Australia	Japan	United States	Wales
23.05.1987	30.05.1987	03.06.1987	08.06.1987
Sydney	Sydney	Sydney	Brisbane
Pool One	Pool One	Pool One	Quarter-Final
Lost 19–6	Won 60–7	Won 34–6	Lost 16–3

Australia	Japan	United States	Wales
W M H Rose	J M Webb	J M Webb	J M Webb
M E Harrison*	M E Harrison*	M E Harrison*	M E Harrison*
K G Simins	K G Simins	F J Clough	K G Simins
J L B Salmon	J L B Salmon	J L B Salmon	J L B Salmon
R Underwood	R Underwood	M D Bailey	R Underwood
P N Williams	P N Williams	C R Andrew	P N Williams
R M Harding	R M Harding	R J Hill	R M Harding
P A G Rendall	P A G Rendall	G J Chilcott	P A G Rendall
B C Moore	B C Moore	R G R Dawe	B C Moore
G S Pearce	G J Chilcott	G S Pearce	G S Pearce
W A Dooley	N C Redman	W A Dooley	W A Dooley
N C Redman	S Bainbridge	S Bainbridge	N C Redman
P J Winterbottom	P J Winterbottom	P J Winterbottom	P J Winterbottom
G W Rees	G W Rees	G W Rees	G W Rees
D Richards	D Richards	D Richards	D Richards

Replacement
J M Webb (15)

Replacements
F J Clough (13)
C R Andrew (10)

Replacement
G J Chilcott (1)

Points Scorers
M E Harrison – 4
J M Webb – 2

Points Scorers
J M Webb – 20
M E Harrison – 12
R Underwood – 8
N C Redman – 4
G W Rees – 4
D Richards – 4
J L B Salmon – 4
K G Simms – 4

Points Scorers
J M Webb – 18
P J Winterbottom – 8
W A Dooley – 4
M E Harrison – 4

Points Scorers
J M Webb – 3

The glory years

DESPITE OVERSEEING ENGLAND'S DISAPPOINTING WORLD CUP CAMPAIGN, CHAIRMAN OF SELECTORS MIKE WESTON WAS OFFERED AND ACCEPTED THE NEW POST OF ENGLAND MANAGER. HOWEVER, HIS TENURE WAS BRIEF AS THE RFU FELT UNABLE TO ACCEDE TO HIS REQUEST TO RETAIN MARTIN GREEN – WHOSE SERVICES AS COACH HAD ALREADY BEEN DISPENSED WITH – AS A SELECTOR, AND WESTON DULY RESIGNED.

HE was replaced by Geoff Cooke, who had previously coached Bradford, Yorkshire and the North. From the outset Cooke's byword was continuity, and he immediately set about reducing the national selection panel from seven to three: himself, new coach Roger Uttley and divisional selector John Elliott.

For his first match in charge, against France in Paris on 16 January 1988, Cooke introduced three new caps: flanker Mick Skinner, tighthead prop Jeff Probyn and a 22-year-old reading Psychology at Durham University by the name of Will Carling. Though it was to be the start of a partnership which would steer England to their greatest triumphs for 70 years, whether Cooke conceived such a vision when he first selected Carling is uncertain. He was undoubtedly a player of tremendous potential, but two other centres – Simon Halliday and John Buckton – were ahead in the pecking order, and if either had been fit it is a matter of record that the young prodigy would not have played.

As it was, Carling was given his opportunity and England turned in a terrific display, losing by just one point to a French try in the dying minutes. In fact, if it had not been for two crucial mistakes England would have recorded a most unlikely victory. Ironically, Carling was responsible for the first when, with a two-man overlap and a stretched French defence, he mistimed his pass and a certain try went begging. Unfazed, England pressed on and led 9–6 with two minutes remaining when captain Mike Harrison attempted to collect a hopeful kick from Andrieu. He would have done better to fall on the loose ball, and could only watch in horror as the French number eight Laurent Rodriguez hacked on to score the decisive try.

England may have lost, but their performance was encouraging, and certain players greatly enhanced their international reputations. In the scrum, hooker Brian Moore took several balls against the head and had his most effective

international to date, and Wade Dooley was a colossus in the lineout. The back row of Skinner, Peter Winterbottom and Dean Richards produced an outstanding display of controlled aggression, and were well complemented by the rest of the pack.

If Cooke had unearthed the nucleus of a good side, it rapidly became apparent that he had no instant remedy for England's age-old problem of inconsistency, as the courageous effort in Paris was followed by a Twickenham mauling at the hands of Wales. The new manager's honeymoon period was now officially over, and the critics were taking aim when England prepared for their next match in Edinburgh. Aware that only a victory would keep his detractors at bay, Cooke made changes: Mike Harrison, Kevin Simms and Les Cusworth were all permanently discarded. Rob Andrew was restored at fly-half in place of Cusworth, and half-back partner Nigel Melville resumed the captaincy. As is so often the case in matches against Scotland, the game itself was a dour encounter which England won 9–6, thanks to two penalties from Jon Webb and a drop goal from Andrew. Amid much post-match bad feeling both sides accused each other of killing the game, and while it is certainly true that England did not allow Scotland to play, they did little more than employ the same tactics the Scots had used so successfully on numerous occasions.

Although England's victory silenced some sceptics, the manner of it did not allay the fears of others, and, if Ireland were to win the final championship match of the season, England would share the wooden spoon with Scotland. At half-time the portents did not look good: Captain Melville was carried off with a dislocated ankle which was to end his international career, and Ireland led by three points to nil. England had now gone four and a half matches without crossing their opponents' goal line, but with so much talent the straining floodgates were inevitably breached in the second half and Geoff Cooke's brave new order unleashed a veritable feast of attacking rugby which totally overwhelmed the bewildered Irish. In 40 minutes England scored 35 unanswered points, including six tries. Chris Oti, playing in only his second international, became the first Englishman to score a Five Nations hat-trick since John Carleton in 1980, and England's points total was their largest in the championship since France were beaten 37–0 in 1911. If it is perhaps an exaggeration to suggest that the England three-quarters saw more of the ball in this one match than they had done in the previous five years, it certainly felt like it, and the relief among the players was as tangible as it was throughout the crowd. Each of the tries was treated with unfettered jubilation, and for the first time the

strains of 'Swing Low, Sweet Chariot' reverberated around Twickenham.

This victory over Ireland proved to be something of a watershed in English rugby history. All but the sternest of Geoff Cooke's critics conceded that he was leading England in the right direction, and his position was further strengthened a month later when England again beat Ireland in a special match to celebrate the Dublin millennium. They had now won three consecutive games for the first time in eight years, and would face the impending summer tour of Australia and Fiji with renewed optimism.

In Bob Dwyer, Australia too had a new coach and were also in the process of rebuilding for the 1991 World Cup. They met England on the back of a series defeat in Argentina and were by no means the world-class outfit they would later become. Nevertheless, with players of the calibre of David Campese, Michael Lynagh and Nick Farr Jones they were still good enough to win both Test matches against a vastly disappointing English side. In the first, Rory Underwood and John Bentley (who went on to play rugby league for Great Britain before returning to union) scored breakaway tries to give the visitors an unexpected 13–3 lead. Underwood almost added another, but Australia rallied, Lynagh kicked six penalties and they eventually won 22–16. After this narrow escape, they outplayed England in the second Test, and their 28–8 victory was far more conclusive. Total ignominy at least was avoided when Fiji were beaten in Suva, but in truth it was a laboured victory with the backs wasting much of the ball presented to them by the hard-working forwards.

That there were certain mitigating factors would have been of scant consolation to the England management. Will Carling had missed the opening Test to take his university exams, and fellow centre Simon Halliday had returned home shortly before Carling's arrival. There were also problems with team spirit, most of which involved Nigel Melville's replacement as captain, Bedford's John Orwin. Orwin was not a natural choice to lead England; he had few of the prerequisite skills and his brusque manner did little to

Left Geoff Cooke took over the England reins in 1988 and guided the team to a World Cup final and two Grand Slams
Below England's Jonathan Webb is tackled by Australia's Michael Lynagh, watched by team-mate Wade Dooley (right), in 1988

endear him to the rest of the players. His lack of fitness was also a concern, and following the defeats by Australia it was obvious that a new skipper would have to be appointed in time for the 1989 Five Nations Championship. Several names were mentioned, including Rob Andrew, who was considered by many to be the ideal candidate. Geoff Cooke, however, felt that Andrew was not sufficiently on top of his own game to be burdened with further responsibility, and thus startled the entire rugby community by naming Will Carling as the fifth England captain in eight matches.

Even with hindsight it seems a remarkable and inspired decision. Carling had just seven caps; he was the youngest member of the squad and had yet to win the respect of the senior players. He would need to undertake a rapid learning curve, and in the short term at least would live or die by his own performances. His first opportunity to do either arrived on 5 November 1988 when England entertained Australia at Twickenham. It is a date that Carling and English rugby fans will no doubt always remember, as England turned on the style to win 28–19. The backs were devastating. Rory Underwood scored a fine brace of tries, and Dewi Morris, making his debut at scrum half, and Simon Halliday both touched down. Two other players enjoyed rather mixed debuts: 30-year-old Paul Ackford was drafted into the second row in place of Owin and gave the type of immense display for which he would become renowned, while Harlequins' graceful winger Andrew Harriman, as if to illustrate fate's fickle hand, knocked-on five yards from an undefended goal line and never played for England again.

An auspicious beginning for Carling, but the euphoria did not last long, as Scotland, ably demonstrating the tactics they so vehemently objected to during the teams' preceding clash, completely stifled England to snatch a 12–12 draw in the opening Five Nations match of 1989. Carling's men had only themselves to blame: Rob Andrew and Jon Webb converted four of eleven kicks at goal, and Webb was also guilty of spilling the garryowen from which John Jeffrey scored the game's one try. Under many former regimes such a result would have instigated an apoplexy

of axe-wielding, but Geoff Cooke did not panic and instead named an unchanged team to face Ireland a fortnight later. The strategy was the correct one. England won comfortably, and went on to beat France 11–0 at Twickenham. With two wins and a draw, they travelled to Wales knowing that victory would secure a first Five Nations title for nine years. If you say it quickly it sounds easy enough, but no England team had prevailed in Cardiff since 1963, and the Arms Park hoodoo struck yet again as Wales won 12–9.

If England's inconsistencies were a source of frustration to Cooke, he would have been pleased that he had been able to bring a greater degree of continuity to team selection. In his second season just sixteen players were used in four championship matches, and this number would have been reduced by one if concussion had not accounted for Jeff Probyn during the Ireland international. He also had the satisfaction of watching two further pieces of his jigsaw fall into place during the closing match of the season as both Jeremy Guscott and Simon Hodgkinson produced superb debut performances against Romania in Bucharest. Guscott, displaying his trademark change of pace and silken running style, helped himself to three tries in the absence of injured centre Will Carling, and in Hodgkinson, England at last discovered a reliable goal-kicking full-back. In all, he scored nineteen points, and his eight conversions broke Jon Webb's England record of seven. Not that they were the only players to excel as a strong Romanian side that had recently beaten Wales in Cardiff were hammered 58–3. The forwards were dynamic, and secured enough possession for England to score nine tries, including four by Chris Oti to complete a second hat-trick in six internationals.

The summer's rugby was dominated by the British Isles tour of Australia to play a three-match series. With Rob Andrew summoned to replace the injured Paul Dean, eleven Englishmen

were selected to represent the Lions and four of them played in the opening Test. Australia won with ease, and by the second game eight of the England team were named in the starting line-up. The Lions knew they had to win to square the series, and did so in convincing fashion with tries from Gavin Hastings and Jeremy Guscott. In the deciding match Australia led a tense encounter 12–9 until the gifted but unpredictable David Campese committed a schoolboy error in front of his own goal line from which Ieuan Evans scored. It was to prove a costly mistake. The British Isles won by a single point to record their first series victory since the legendary 'Ninety-nine' tour of South Africa in 1974.

With so many English players involved in the Lions' success, confidence was high when Fiji visited Twickenham in November 1989, and the host nation matched their previous points total against Romania by beating an ill-disciplined team 58–23. It was a red-letter day for flying wing Rory Underwood as he became only the third player, behind George Lindsay for Scotland against Wales in 1887 and Daniel Lambert for England against France in

1907, to score five tries in an international match. After an absence of two years Richard Hill returned to the side at scrum half, and Will Carling and Jeremy Guscott launched their enduring centre three-quarters alliance. Even taking into account the quality of the opposition, England's win was impressive. They scored ten tries and played with an assurance that would bode well for the coming Five Nations Championship.

The opening fixture was against Ireland who, after a difficult start, were swept aside by a sixteen-point rampage in the final ten minutes. Four tries were scored without reply, and Rory Underwood passed another milestone when he touched down for the nineteenth time to exceed the English try-scoring record established by Cyril Lowe in 1923. From here England went from strength to strength, playing the type of exhilarating, expansive

Wales	Scotland	Ireland	France
19.01.1991	16.02.1991	02.03.1991	16.03.1991
Cardiff Arms Park	Twickenham	Lansdowne Road	Twickenham
25–6	21–12	16–7	21–19
S D Hodgkinson	S D Hodgkinson	S D Hodgkinson	S D Hodgkinson
N J Heslop	N J Heslop	N J Heslop	N J Heslop
W D C Carling*	W D C Carling*	W D C Carling*	W D C Carling*
J C Guscott	J C Guscott	J C Guscott	J C Guscott
R Underwood	R Underwood	R Underwood	R Underwood
C R Andrew	C R Andrew	C R Andrew	C R Andrew
R J Hill	R J Hill	R J Hill	R J Hill
J Leonard	J Leonard	J Leonard	J Leonard
B C Moore	B C Moore	B C Moore	B C Moore
J A Probyn	J A Probyn	J A Probyn	J A Probyn
P J Ackford	P J Ackford	P J Ackford	P J Ackford
W A Dooley	W A Dooley	W A Dooley	W A Dooley
M C Teague	M C Teague	M C Teague	M C Teague
P J Winterbottom	P J Winterbottom	P J Winterbottom	P J Winterbottom
D Richards	D Richards	D Richards	D Richards

Points Scorers

Wales	Scotland	Ireland	France
S D Hodgkinson – 21	S D Hodgkinson – 17	S D Hodgkinson – 8	S D Hodgkinson–14
M C Teague – 4	N J Heslop – 4	M C Teague – 4	R Underwood–4
		R Underwood – 4	C R Andrew–3

rugby their supporters could only formerly dream about. France were beaten 26–7, their highest-ever defeat at the Parc des Princes, and if the Welsh once held fears for those wearing the red rose they no longer lingered as they in turn were thrashed 34–6. England were simply irresistible, and in the process of winning five consecutive matches had scored 199 points and 30 tries. Only Scotland stood between them and the Grand Slam. By a strange coincidence the Scots had also won their three championship games, and the two sides met at Murrayfield on 17 March 1990 for the inaugural Grand Slam decider between British teams.

It was dubbed the match of the century, and in a media frenzy sports and news editors alike clamoured for every conceivable story. England were odds-on favourites, the Scots had struggled to overcome the same opposition England had beaten so emphatically, and the southern press continually referred to the massive gulf in class between the teams. Indeed, Scotland were given little chance. Their supporters interpreted the pre-match hype as another example of a deep-rooted colonial arrogance and a strong anti-English feeling began to emerge. To make matters worse, the Conservative government of the day was extremely unpopular north of the border, and the England team that arrived in Edinburgh to play a game of rugby, albeit an important one, did so amid a sea of Scottish nationalism. Instead of being viewed as amateur sportsmen they were perceived more as marauding invaders attempting to further subjugate the Celtic brethren. It was, of course, utter nonsense, but it made for good copy and ensured that the 106th Anglo-Scottish confrontation would be played in a unique and electrifying atmosphere.

Given the prize at stake the actual match was never likely to be a classic, and so it proved. England had not played for a month and found it difficult to establish any rhythm, and the Scots tackled like demons to prevent them from doing so. Both sides conceded penalties, but whereas the Scottish kicked theirs to take an early lead, England, seeking to deny the Scots possession, elected to run on several occasions. It was not a successful strategy, and though Guscott did score following a superb move by the backs, they were always chasing the game. At the interval the home side led 9–4, and when 21-year-old Tony Stanger scored his sixth international try, the writing – writ large in blue, no doubt – was on the wall. To their eternal credit the English heads did not fall and they tried desperately to claw their way back, but the Scots defended heroically, and when the final whistle blew the hugely partisan crowd erupted in delight. For England, abject despair; for Scotland, joy unconfined. That Scotland thoroughly deserved their moment is undeniable, but it is equally true to suggest that they would have relished it less if they had been able to forecast the heavy price they would later pay for their victory.

Above Jeff Probyn has clearly received close attention in Suva as England chalk up a rather less than comfortable 28–12 win over Fiji in July 1991

Ensuing England teams, striving to eradicate the disconsolate memories of 1990, allowed Scottish patriotism and fervour to count for little.

After a physically and mentally demanding season, England's players badly needed a break, and the decision to send a touring team to Argentina in the height of the British summer was not a sensible one. Manager Geoff Cooke expressed his own concerns, and it was no surprise when a large number of senior players decided to remain at home with their families. With so many regulars absent four new caps were introduced, including loosehead prop Jason Leonard, who was to miss just one of England's next 56 matches and go on to hold the England record for the greatest number of caps and the world record of 114 England caps. Simon Hodgkinson continued his outstanding form with 26 points in the two Tests, but it was not a successful trip and the series was drawn 1–1.

With Argentina making a reciprocal tour of the British Isles in the autumn of 1990, England faced the same opposition in their next match. They were, however, now fresh and at full strength, and the Argentines were trounced 51–0. The prolific Rory Underwood scored three of the seven tries, and Simon Hodgkinson broke Daniel Lambert's English points scoring record with 23. Lambert had accumulated 22 against France in 1911, and Hodgkinson surpassed his mark with seven conversions and three penalty goals.

As pleasing as the result was, the English treated the match merely as preparation for their next authentic challenge: the 1991 Five Nations Championship. They were acutely aware that for all their stylish rugby they had won nothing, and there was a ruthless determination that the Edinburgh nightmare would not be repeated. They would have to wait to exorcise their Scottish ghosts, but with the first game of the season being played in

Wales they did have an immediate opportunity finally to lay to rest their Cardiff Arms Park jinx. It was 28 years to the day that England had last won there, and they made three changes, plus some positional modifications, to the team beaten at Murrayfield. Nigel Heslop was preferred to Simon Halliday on the wing, and Jason Leonard came into the front row at the expense of Paul Rendall. In the back row, flanker Peter Winterbottom was switched to open-side in place of Mick Skinner, and Mike Teague replaced Winterbottom at blind-side. Dean Richards returned at number eight.

The changes were well made, as England employed a no-risk policy using their forwards' power to grind the Welsh into submission. As a tactic it was neither attractive nor instantly successful, but gradually England established some control and Mike Teague rolled off the pack and across the line to score the only try. Both sides at times were undisciplined and gave away a succession of penalties. Fortunately for England, Paul Thorburn missed all but one of his, and in contrast Simon Hodgkinson kicked seven to set a world record. England coasted home 25–6. Not only had they won in Cardiff for the first time since 1963, they had also recorded their highest ever score at the Welsh citadel.

Not surprisingly, they were unchanged for the next match versus Scotland and took to the field at Twickenham with the sole purpose of avenging their irksome 1990 defeat. It did not matter how it was accomplished, just as long as when they left the pitch it was to cheers and not jeers. England again relied heavily on their forwards, and they and half-backs Richard Hill and Rob Andrew kept Scotland pinned in their own half for most of the match. As in Cardiff Hodgkinson kicked his penalties and Nigel Heslop scored a peach of a try somewhat out of place in a stilted game.

Half of a Grand Slam had been completed, and England journeyed to Lansdowne Road in search of the Triple Crown. It was to be a titanic contest as the strength of the English forwards was met head-on by the Irish, who defended stoutly. The two teams changed ends with the score at 3–3, but early in the second half England fell behind when Simon Geoghegan evaded Rory Underwood to touch down in the corner, and they still trailed with seven minutes remaining. Shades of Murrayfield, only this time England were not to be denied. More outstanding forward play freed Underwood to thread his way through the Irish defence, and Mike Teague's injury-time try clinched a 16–7 win and the Triple Crown. It was a first palpable success for Geoff Cooke, Will Carling and an England team on its knees when Cooke took up the managerial reins. Success was sweet, but it was never going to be enough. In successive Five Nations campaigns England had approached their final fixture aware that a win would secure the championship. They had lost both games and could not afford to do so again.

On this occasion, France would present the possible stumbling block, for they too were hunting the Grand Slam. After a sluggish start to the year French form had improved beyond measure, and in their previous outing they had demonstrated all of their Gallic flair in beating Wales 36–3. They continued in similar vein at Twickenham, scoring one of the all-time great tries, a classic counterattacking effort which began under their own posts and finished with Philippe Saint-Andre touching down a crossfield kick from Didier Camberabero. It was truly breathtaking, and would have deflated lesser teams, but England rose to the challenge and launched their own brand of fluent, attacking rugby. Their backs played with width and pace and the forwards retained the ball for long periods, starving the French of quality possession. A Rob Andrew drop goal pulled England level, and Rory Underwood scored his by now almost obligatory try to take them into a lead they were not to lose. In the dying seconds, with the French desperate to keep the ball alive, Franck Mesnel scored another wonderful try, but it was too late: England had won 21–19. After so many barren years the home supporters were ecstatic. In an impromptu display of emotion they engulfed their heroes and chaired them from the field. The players too were overjoyed. Their doughty performances had been constantly criticised by those who did not understand that sometimes the end result can justify the means. The year before they had galloped naively down the entertainment road only to be lambasted for their enterprise when mugged in Scotland. This year had been about learning how to win. Winning in style would come later.

In July 1991 the players that had given so much throughout an exacting season should have been at home enjoying a well-deserved rest. Unfortunately their management decreed that with the World Cup looming they needed exposure to southern hemisphere rugby, and arranged a tour of Fiji and Australia. With confidence already stratospheric, the decision to send an England team that had not played for three months 10,000 miles to face one of the strongest sides in international rugby can at best be described as counterproductive. After losing three of their four warm-up matches – to New South Wales, Queensland and Fiji B – a 28–12 win in the Fiji Test was at least encouraging. Martin Bayfield made his debut in place of the injured Wade Dooley, and Rob Andrew scored his first try. Australia on a hard, fast Sydney pitch were an altogether different proposition, and England's World Cup preparations surely cannot have been assisted by a record 40–15 defeat. Far more significant than the result was the ease with which the powerful and mobile Australian pack dominated the English forwards, the ramifications of which would be seen at Twickenham three months later.

The excitement that embraced the build-up to the second World Cup was far in excess of anything witnessed in 1987. Rugby was now a high-profile sport, and as such it attracted intense media coverage. Due primarily to the regeneration of the national team, the popularity of the game in England had also increased and would reach unparalleled levels as the drama of the World Cup began to unfold. Australia and New Zealand were favourites, and many also believed that the unpredictable flair of the French might see them improve on their runners-up spot of 1987. As in 1987, sixteen teams would take part, and the only new faces were Western Samoa in place of Tonga, whom Japan

Below Jeff Probyn, Brian Moore and Jason Leonard – England's formidable front row during the 1991 World Cup

had eliminated in the Asian/Pacific qualifying competition. The teams were again divided into four preliminary groups of four, with the top two in each pool progressing to the quarter-finals.

England were drawn in Pool One with defending champions New Zealand, Italy and the United States. Although this presented a straightforward path to the next stage, the importance of the game against the All Blacks could not be over-emphasised as the losers would almost certainly have to travel to Paris to play France in the quarter-final. Conscious that this would be far from ideal, England made just two changes to the team that played in all four Grand Slam matches. Jon Webb replaced the unfortunate Simon Hodgkinson at full-back, and winger Chris Oti was preferred to Nigel Heslop. After their

considerable efforts in the Five Nations the pack was unchanged, and it was on them that England hoped to build a winning platform against New Zealand.

That, at least, was the theory; that it never materialised had more to do with a subdued England performance than any imposing display by their famous opposition. Perhaps it was the weight of expectation, or maybe they too succumbed to the inferiority complex that can consume teams faced with those black jerseys. Whatever the reason England did not perform, and New Zealand completed a comparatively untroubled 18–12 victory.

So France beckoned, but before the English could formulate another triumph beside the Seine they would first have to overcome World Cup minnows Italy and the USA. In actuality, both matches were routinely won. Italy came and went in a game notable only for the 37 penalties they conceded. Jon Webb kicked four of them and the same number of conversions to beat, by one, Simon Hodgkinson's record of 23 points in an England international. For the last group match against the USA several fringe players were given a run-out, including Hodgkinson, Gareth Pearce and Gary Rees, all of whom, it would later transpire, were making their final England appearances. They had served their country well, and one felt particularly sorry for the perennially undervalued Hodgkinson, who had scored 60 points in the recent Five Nations season to shatter Dusty Hare's previous championship record of 44. In his last match he signed off with seventeen more to hoist his career tally to 203. In the same game Will Carling captained England for the 22nd time to overtake Bill Beaumont's total, and he celebrated with one of five tries in a 37–9 victory.

Most of the teams that were expected to reach the quarter-finals did, with the exception of Wales, who lost to the Samoans at Cardiff Arms Park. Canada also did well to make the last eight by beating Fiji and Romania. As the Welsh headed forlornly back across the Severn, England braced themselves for another bruising engagement with the French. Flanker Mick Skinner was selected for his extra aggression in place of Dean Richards, and Mike Teague was moved to number eight. The decision was incredibly hard on Richards, who had never let England down, but by the final whistle it would be vindicated as Skinner's competitive qualities turned the match. Not that it initially appeared they would need to, as the French completely lost their heads and indiscriminately attacked their opposite number. Even the incomparable Serge Blanco indulged, and by the time some semblance of order had been restored England had kicked two penalties and led by six points. When Jeremy Guscott broke and put Rory Underwood in, the game looked over, but the French countered and the score was 10–10 when Skinner provided for many the abiding memory of the entire World Cup. England were defending a five-yard scrum when the burly French number eight Marc Cecillon ran off the pack towards the English line, only to be met full-on by Skinner, who proceeded to hit him with such force that man and ball were displaced several yards. With the destruction of Cecillon came the evaporation of French hopes, and England won 19–10. On the same day Scotland beat Western Samoa, and would now face their Auld Enemy in the semi-final at Murrayfield.

After the epic victory in Paris, England knew that Scotland would present just as rigorous an examination, and the squad made the short journey to Edinburgh for the first time since their nadir of 1990. If the press interest had then seemed excessive, it was mild in comparison to the 1991 version which applied every imaginable national stereotype to fuel the animosity between the two countries. In many ways this was more than a rugby match, it was a matter of national pride, and as the kick-off approached the air crackled with ill feeling. Not an ideal environment for the playing of attractive rugby, and the

quality did suffer as the tension increased. The English forwards promptly assumed control, but had nothing to show for their dominance. After 30 minutes Scotland led 6–0. Their advantage was reduced late in the first half, and after the interval parity was restored when Jon Webb eased home a second penalty goal. The pressure was unbearable; neither team could begin to contemplate defeat and no risks were taken. As frequently happens in such a situation, it was a mistake that effectively settled the match. Well into the last quarter, and with the scores tied at 6–6, Gavin Hastings missed an easy penalty in front of the posts. The crowd and Hastings were stunned, and his aberration would ultimately cost Scotland a place in the World Cup final. If the miss lifted England, it was not immediately apparent, and the match was heading towards extra-time when they finally made their superiority tell. The forwards produced another surging drive and front the resulting scrum Rob Andrew dropped the match-winning goal. England won 9–6, and the defeat of 1990 was all but expunged.

In the other semi-final, Australia dealt effortlessly with their own historic antagonists, New Zealand. David Campese and Tim Horan scored the tries in a game almost as noteworthy for who did not take part. Michael Jones, one of rugby's best openside flankers

Above Teague's relief at the final whistle is clear for all to see as England edge out the Scots 9–6 to progress to the final

and a member of New Zealand's 1987 World Cup-winning team, declined to play because the match was held on a Sunday, and he would not compromise his religious beliefs. In an often cynical sporting world it was a commendable stand by Jones, who also missed the quarter-final for the same reason, but it was also an expensive one as the All Blacks were eliminated and Jones was excluded for the 1995 competition.

Whether his presence would in actual fact have made any difference is debatable. Australia were the far superior team, and England would have to play exceedingly well to be crowned world champions. To date, manager Geoff Cooke and his willing

lieutenants, coach Roger Uttley and Captain Will Carling, had constructed England's achievements on the strength of their forward play and the expert touch kicking of Rob Andrew. These tactics, though sound and fabulously successful, were not pretty, and the disapproval that surfaced during the 1991 Five Nations Championship reached a crescendo as the final approached. Australian David Campese, whose speed of tongue was almost as quick as his wing play, declared that England were too negative to

New Zealand
03.10.1991
Twickenham
Pool One
Lost 18–12

J M Webb
R Underwood
W D C Carling*
J C Guscott
C Oti
C R Andrew
R J Hill

J Leonard
B C Moore
J A Probyn
P J Ackford
W A Dooley
M C Teague
P J Winterbottom
D Richards

Points Scorers
J M Webb – 9
C R Andrew – 3

Italy
08.10.1991
Twickenham
Pool One
Won 36–6

J M Webb
C Oti
W D C Carling*
J C Guscott
R Underwood
C R Andrew
R J Hill

J Leonard
B C Moore
J A Probyn
P J Ackford
N C Redman
M C Teague
P J Winterbottom
D Richards

Replacement
P A G Rendall

Points Scorers
J M Webb – 24
J C Guscott – 8
R Underwood – 4

United States
11.10.1991
Twickenham
Pool One
Won 37–9

S D Hodgkinson
N J Heslop
W D C Carling*
S J Halliday
R Underwood
C R Andrew
R J Hill

J Leonard
C J Olver
G S Pearce
W A Dooley
N C Redman
M G Skinner
G W Rees
D Richards

Points Scorers
S D Hodgkinson – 17
R Underwood – 8
W D C Carling – 4
N J Heslop – 4
M G Skinner – 4

France
19.10.1991
Parc des Princes
Quarter-Final
Won 19–10

J M Webb
N J Heslop
W D C Carling*
J C Guscott
R Underwood
C R Andrew
R J Hill

J Leonard
B C Moore
J A Probyn
P J Ackford
W A Dooley
M G Skinner
P J Winterbottom
M C Teague

Points Scorers
J M Webb – 11
W D C Carling – 4
R Underwood – 4

Scotland
26.10.1991
Murrayfield
Semi-Final
Won 9–6

J M Webb
S J Halliday
W D C Carling*
J C Guscott
R Underwood
C R Andrew
R J Hill

J Leonard
B C Moore
J A Probyn
P J Ackford
W A Dooley
M G Skinner
P J Winterbottom
M C Teague

Points Scorers
J M Webb – 6
C R Andrew – 3

Australia
02.11.1991
Twickenham
Final
Lost 12–6

J M Webb
S J Halliday
W D C Carling*
J C Guscott
R Underwood
C R Andrew
R J Hill

J Leonard
B C Moore
J A Probyn
P J Ackford
W A Dooley
M G Skinner
P J Winterbottom
M C Teague

Points Scorers
J M Webb – 6

have any chance of winning, and his sentiments echoed those already expressed by many. Until now, such dissenting voices had easily been ignored, but with the most important match in their history just days away, it was decided that England would forsake their attritional game and attack Australia with expansive, open rugby. This sudden switch did rather smack of desperation – after all, an identical strategy had been employed for a year to great effect, but if Cooke and co were guilty of wilting under the intense media pressure only they will know. It is more likely that the England hierarchy, and most of the back division, were concerned that their pack would not be able to exact the same influence against Australia as they had against European teams. Memories drifted back to the recent Test in Sydney where more or less the same forwards had been severely mauled. No matter that it was a vastly under-prepared team that had faced Australia, in a one-off encounter, on basically a meaningless tour. England had lost, and to avoid doing so again had to pursue a different approach.

As it happened, the English pack made light of their manager's doubts. They matched Australia in every department and recycled a great deal of ball, only to watch the backs adopt a running game that would have made a Fijian Sevens side shudder. Instead of patiently probing the Australian lines, they played with an abandon bordering on irresponsibility, throwing the ball to all and sundry but making little headway against a proficient Australian defensive line. The bare bones reflect that the tactical switch did not work; prop Tony Daly scored the only try, and Australia won 12–6. England had played some beautiful attacking rugby, but without sufficient time to hone specific routines their new-found style lacked penetration and Australia deserved to win. The newspapers and most of the country saw it as a glorious failure, but it was a failure nonetheless, and the players were left to rue what might have been.

As a competition, the 1991 World Cup was an unqualified success; viewing figures were high and the game reached a massive new audience. The revenue generated by television rights and sponsorship was also huge, and the players began to call for greater autonomy within their sport. In the November of 1990, the International Rugby Board had relaxed its draconian rules

TENTH GRAND SLAM – 1992

Scotland	Ireland	France	Wales
18.01.1992	01.02.1992	15.02.1992	07.03.1992
Murrayfield	Twickenham	Parc des Princes	Twickenham
25–7	38–9	31–13	24–0
J M Webb	J M Webb	J M Webb	J M Webb
S J Halliday	S J Halliday	S J Halliday	S J Halliday
W D C Carling*	W D C Carling*	W D C Carling*	W D C Carling*
J C Guscott	J C Guscott	J C Guscott	J C Guscott
R Underwood	R Underwood	R Underwood	R Underwood
C R Andrew	C R Andrew	C R Andrew	C R Andrew
C D Morris	C D Morris	C D Morris	C D Morris
J Leonard	J Leonard	J Leonard	J Leonard
B C Moore	B C Moore	B C Moore	B C Moore
J A Probyn	J A Probyn	J A Probyn	J A Probyn
M C Bayfield	M C Bayfield	M C Bayfield	M C Bayfield
W A Dooley	W A Dooley	W A Dooley	W A Dooley
M G Skinner	M G Skinner	M G Skinner	M G Skinner
P J Winterbottom	P J Winterbottom	P J Winterbottom	P J Winterbottom
T A K Rodber	T A K Rodber	D Richards	D Richards

Replacement		**Replacement**	**Replacement**
D Richards (8)		D Pears (10)	N J Heslop (13)

Points Scorers	**Points Scorers**	**Points Scorers**	**Points Scorers**
J M Webb – 14	J M Webb – 22	J M Webb – 19	J M Webb – 12
C D Morris – 4	J C Guscott – 4	C D Morris – 4	W D C Carling – 4
R Underwood – 4	S J Halliday – 4	R Underwood – 4	W A Dooley – 4
J C Guscott – 3	C D Morris – 4	penalty try – 4	M G Skinner – 4
	R Underwood – 4		

regarding amateurism and the players, as a consequence, were free to benefit financially from non-rugby-related ventures. Different governing boards interpreted these fairly vague new rules in a variety of ways. Some, particularly in the southern hemisphere, took the liberal approach and allowed their representatives plenty of scope with regard to the definition of 'rugby-related'; others, wishing to preserve the status quo and the amateur ethic, took the hard-line view and made it difficult for their athletes to earn even modest sums.

Although there had for some years been a disparity in the status of players throughout the world, certain countries even providing well-paid coaching posts for their stars, the differences were now far more pronounced and caused a degree of disharmony and resentment. To some extent this had surfaced even before the World Cup, when the 1991 Five Nations Championship was contested against a backdrop of acrimony as the RFU rejected several commercial proposals made to the England squad. Not that the team, as they publicly stated, coveted payment for playing; they simply required an even field on which to do so and some recompense for the hours of dedication and commitment it took to sustain an international career. Standards in the sport had moved on, and family life and business interests suffered as the demands of the modern game reached exceptional levels. The world's élite were already professional in all but name, and it was only a matter of time before they were recognised as such and rewarded accordingly. The 1991 World Cup hastened this change, and if the purists had enjoyed its high drama, they would one day appreciate that it was to signify the beginning of the end of the amateur era.

For the time being, these were not immediate concerns. An uneasy truce existed among the players and officials, and Geoff Cooke was more interested in preparing his squad for the 1992 Five Nations Championship. Of the post-World Cup retirements the most conspicuous was lock Paul Ackford, who received his first cap at the age of 30 and retired at his peak three years later. After a prosperous four-year tenure, coach Roger Uttley also stepped down and was replaced by Dick Best. Cooke knew that his side was supreme in the northern hemisphere, but having lost three successive matches to Australia and New Zealand the team was far from the finished article, and would have to evolve to avoid being left behind in the world order. The tactics that had conquered Europe had served their purpose, and now England had to build on their World Cup final performance.

Below Rob Andrew strokes over another penalty and England register an 18–14 win in Paris, 5 March 1994

The nucleus of the team was retained, and it was not considered necessary to make wholesale changes for the annual clash with Scotland. The attacking flair of Orrell's Dewi Morris was preferred to Richard Hill at scrum half, and Northampton lock Martin Bayfield came in for Paul Ackford. In the absence of the physically exhausted Mike Teague, Tim Rodber was awarded his first cap at number eight, and Dean Richards had to content himself with a spot on the replacements bench. After an erratic start, during which the England pack conceded a pushover try, reducing hooker Brian Moore to speechless fury, two second-half penalties from Jon Webb calmed the nerves. Jeremy Guscott scored his first international drop goal to take England clear, and Dewi Morris sealed a 25–7 victory with a try towards the end.

The first hurdle had been comfortably negotiated, and against Ireland the running game attempted in the closing stages of the World Cup began to flourish. It was helped immeasurably by a Jon Webb try after 30 seconds, and though Ireland's fly-half Ralph Keyes levelled proceedings following an exquisite dummy, Brian Moore and Dewi Morris combined spectacularly for England's second try, and there was no way back for the men in green. Jon Webb finished the game as he started it with another touchdown, to become England's first full-back to score two tries in an international. If his goal kicking was not quite as dependable as Simon Hodgkinson's, he did provide an extra dimension in attack.

England had won their opening two matches, and the back division, playing with their customary verve and a new-found composure, had contributed all eight tries. The forwards too had played their part, but the towering presence of Dean Richards was missed in the back row and he returned for the match against France in Paris. The home side, who had not beaten England since 1988, started well and took the lead through a Sebastien Viars try. However, it was clear that they could not compete in the forwards and England quickly regained the initiative when a rolling scrum was collapsed on the goal line and

a penalty try awarded. Prior to the interval Webb scored his third try of the season, and the French rapier, so evident at Twickenham less than a year before, had been blunted. In the second period the already demoralised French fell further behind when two of their players comically collided and England collected the scraps to put Rory Underwood away for his 35th international try. France were now in total disarray and, as tends to occur when they are losing at home, the red mist rapidly descended. Irish referee Stephen Hilditch, in a remarkable act of courage in front of the partisan crowd, was forced to expel two of their number, and at the end of the game was popular enough to warrant his own police escort from the field.

England had done well to maintain their shape and discipline amid such absurdity, and now needed to overcome Wales at Twickenham to record another Grand Slam. As clear favourites, it was hoped they would also provide a fitting climax to an historic feat. They certainly tried, delighting the home fans with a succession of tap penalties, but the Welsh, in what amounted to a damage limitation exercise, resisted stubbornly and the Twickenham masses had to be satisfied with three tries and a 24–0 scoreline. Will Carling scored his sixth try as captain, outsprinting the Welsh defence to a high ball from Rob Andrew, and Mick Skinner, in his final appearance, registered the forwards' first score of the season. Appropriately, the last word was left to Wade Dooley, who celebrated his 50th cap with England's final touchdown of a magnificent campaign.

The players revelled in the acclaim. Not since the halcyon days of 1924 had England won back-to-back Grand Slams. In four championship matches they scored 118 points and fifteen tries. Rory Underwood, Dewi Morris and Jon Webb claimed three tries apiece, and Webb's 67 championship points ensured that Simon Hodgkinson's record of 60 had survived less than twelve months. In addition, he took his career tally to 246, six more than Dusty Hare's English record. Cooke's loyalty to his players had been amply rewarded, and if the 1991 Grand Slam had by necessity been laboured, the 1992 version was glorious by design.

Having played themselves to a standstill during the most demanding fourteen months in rugby history, not even the more zealous of the Marquis de Sade's followers would have expected England's players to tour in the summer of 1992. Instead, they were left to recharge their drained batteries and prepare for what could be their most momentous season yet. England had an ageing squad, and the dilemma for Geoff Cooke was whether to attempt to win an unprecedented third consecutive Grand Slam or dismantle his elderly team and begin rebuilding for the next World Cup. Before the 1993 Five Nations Championship England were scheduled to play Canada and South Africa. These were fundamentally warm-up matches, and would provide Cooke with an ideal opportunity to experiment. He usually favoured the same proven faces, but was not overly sentimental as his treatment of Dean Richards in the World Cup, and Richard Hill after it, had testified. In the end, an allegiance to his venerable old guard probably saw him fall between two stools and announce a familiar team with the addition of three new caps: Northampton's

Left Jason Leonard tries to keep cool on the Summer 1994 tour to South Africa

Above Victor Ubogu and Jason Leonard pose for the cameras after training local children in a South Africa Township, 1994
Below The indomitable Dean Richards takes a breather during the 31–10 Five Nations demolition of France at Twickenham, February 1995

Ian Hunter and Leicester's Tony Underwood were initiated on the wing – Tony had the distinction of succeeding his brother Rory, who had retired – and Bath's Victor Ubogu replaced Jeff Probyn at tight-head. John Olver was given a last game at hooker in place of Brian Moore.

As a result of building work at Twickenham, England's meeting with Canada on 17 October 1992 was the first rugby union international played at Wembley Stadium. If it was thought the evocative surroundings might inspire the hosts, they appeared to have the opposite effect. It was the Canadians who raised their game, and a below par England squeezed home 26–13. Five points were now awarded for a try and Ian Hunter scored two on his debut to guarantee inclusion in the squad to play South Africa a month later. Sadly for Hunter, he was injured while training with his club and had to withdraw. His departure did not cause too many headaches for the selectors as Rory Underwood ended one of the briefest retirements in sporting annals, lasting precisely one match, and duly joined his brother among the fifteen to face the Springboks. The Bath number eight Ben Clarke was also named for his first cap, and Brian Moore returned to the front row.

South Africa had only recently been readmitted to international sport following the disintegration of their apartheid system, and had not played in England since 1969. Their early results were mixed, but a drawn series in France was an indication that they would pose problems aplenty for England, and for 40 minutes they did. Tiaan Strauss scored from a line-out, and at one stage the Boks led a floundering home side 16–8. In the second half, England's superior fitness was telling as the Springboks struggled to maintain the breakneck pace of the contemporary game. Rob Andrew deftly exploited the resulting gaps with measured chip kicks touched down by Jeremy Guscott and Will Carling. Tony Underwood and Dewi Morris also scored, and England were good value for their 33–16 victory.

The second half against South Africa apart, England had not played well in their pre-championship matches and Geoff Cooke recalled prop Jeff Probyn at the prompting of his senior players. Ian Hunter also returned in place of Underwood the younger, and Martin Johnson made his debut when an eleventh-hour injury ruled out Wade Dooley. Cooke had evidently concluded that for this season at least his veterans would suffice, and England went in search of the elusive 'triple slam'.

Their grand ambitions should actually have been dealt a fatal blow by the French at Twickenham on 16 January 1993. In the first quarter, Jon Webb dropped a lofted ball on his goal line and Philippe Saint-Andre was on hand to score; minutes later Webb was again culpable when a towering kick was hoisted in-goal and Saint-Andre outjumped him for the second try. France were ahead 12–6, and an incoherent England team were in real danger of losing, until Webb was given the chance to redeem himself with an eminently kickable penalty. It did not appear to be his day when the ball struck the post, but Ian Hunter, showing remarkable awareness, collected the rebound and dived over for an opportunist try. To rub copious amounts of salt into the French wounds, Webb converted and England took the lead. It was a cruel blow to the visitors, and worse was to follow when Jean-Baptiste Lafond attempted a late drop goal only to watch in despair as the ball hit the same woodwork that had gifted England their try, and was safely cleared.

Above Rob Andrew, Tony Underwood and Jeremy Guscott celebrate the crushing win in Paris. The 1995 season brought England's eleventh Grand Slam success

If England had been the beneficiaries of outrageous fortune in beating France, they had exhausted their quota by the time they arrived in Cardiff to play Wales. This time Lady Luck deserted them and they left the Arms Park with their dreams of a third Grand Slam in tatters. Geoff Cooke had resisted the tabloids' vociferous calls to take an axe to his team, and his only change saw Martin Johnson give way to Wade Dooley. Despite an absence of luck, Webb again hit a post and Dewi Morris had a perfectly good try disallowed. England were leading 9–3 when flanker Emyr Lewis hacked the ball upfield beyond Rory Underwood. Not awake to the danger, Underwood slowly turned to retrieve it and Ieuan Evans was on him in a flash; he grubber-kicked forward and sprinted away to score. Neil Jenkins added the extra two points and Wales went into the break 10–9 ahead. England did not meekly lie down and accept their fate. For 40 second-half minutes wave upon wave of white shirts poured forward, but the Welsh defended magnificently. They covered every blade of grass and threw themselves into the tackle like men possessed. No addition was made to the first-half score, so a single lapse of concentration had cost England a chance to make history. The Welsh supporters celebrated deliriously. It was to be their one victory of the season, but to them it was the only one that really mattered.

Considering the importance of the occasion and the trauma of the result, not to mention the slating from the press, it came as something of a shock to discover that only two scapegoats were found for the Arms Park debacle. Three tries in as many matches were not enough to keep Ian Hunter in the team – Tony Underwood replaced him – and Bath fly-half Stuart Barnes, on the back of a substantial newspaper campaign, was recalled for the first time in five years at Rob Andrew's expense. The two men had been vying for the same position since they faced each other in the 1982 Varsity match, and Andrew had always dominated their private contest. He already had more than 50 caps to his name compared to the eight of his rival, four of which were earned as a replacement. Barnes, however, was a good player and was particularly adept at making destructive defence-splitting breaks. He was having an excellent season for Bath and there was talk of possible inclusion in the Lions squad to tour New Zealand that summer. One more eye-catching performance in a high-profile match could clinch it, and they did not come much bigger than England's next game, the 100th Calcutta Cup meeting with Scotland at Twickenham. The stage was set and Barnes did not disappoint; he had a hand in all three tries and his feint and run for Rory Underwood's score was world class. In fact, the entire back division played well and England produced their best rugby of the season. Both the Underwood boys, watched by a proud and very excited mum, scored tries and the 26–12 scoreline did not flatter.

Stuart Barnes had been the protagonist in a great victory, and there was much sage-like nodding of heads among the journalists who had called for his selection. For the first time the Five Nations title would be resolved on points difference, and now, the same voices confidently exclaimed, England could go on and win by stuffing Ireland. Unfortunately, the equations to calculate exactly how many points they needed to win by were rendered academic when the Irish decided they would rather not be stuffed and won 17–3. England fought hard, but had no answer to the guile of Ireland's fly-half Eric Elwood, and the score was a fair reflection of play.

The Stuart Barnes appreciation society dissipated as rapidly as it had formed and he was again consigned to the international wilderness. This time there would be no reprieve, and he ended his career with ten caps and a great deal of unfulfilled promise. There were sad farewells too for five of England's finest stalwarts: Wade Dooley, Jeff Probyn, Mike Teague, Jon Webb and Peter Winterbottom made their final appearances in the defeat at Lansdowne Road. Dooley, the second-row tank, played 55 times for his country, and Winterbottom, the man of granite and arguably the best English flanker of all time, 58. Surgeon Webb, quitting to concentrate on his medical career, won 33 caps and scored 296 points.

After England's worst Five Nations since 1988, Geoff Cooke was roundly castigated for his team's poor performances. It was suggested that his senior players were past their best and should have been replaced at the beginning of the season. Although this was partially true, in reality there were innumerable reasons for England's downfall, and the decline of individual players was barely perceptible. A more serious problem was the lack of appetite within the team. After so much success the players found it hard to motivate themselves, and the Welsh and Irish, and nearly the French, took full advantage. This should not in any way devalue either country's achievements: both played with skill and passion and their wins were well merited.

Another contributory factor was a nonsensical change in the game's laws. In their infinite wisdom the laws committee of the International Rugby Board, apparently in an effort to speed up play, dictated that the team taking the ball into a ruck or maul, i.e. the attacking team, would lose the put-in at the scrum if the ball were not recycled into the loose. This placed less emphasis on controlled forward play and allowed inferior teams to kill a move and regain possession. England's pack could no longer drive their opponents into oblivion and then expect to repeat the process at the ensuing scrum. The detrimental effects of the ruling were heightened by the age of the English forwards who, having spent their entire careers working on the inside, were slow to adapt to an unfamiliar style. After watching his team struggle against Canada, Geoff Cooke had tried to counteract the new laws. Ben Clarke's greater mobility in the open saw him selected at number eight, but to accommodate Clarke England were forced to drop the influential Dean Richards, whose strength and tenacity were essential in other areas. Rugby in general suffered too, as displaced forwards roamed the pitch congesting the midfield and limiting the space available for the backs to create try-scoring opportunities. Most neutral observers agreed that the experimentation had singularly failed to improve the game, and

called on the IRB to reverse their decision at the 1994 annual meeting. Instead they compounded it by abandoning the law change for the ruck but retaining it for the maul.

A record sixteen England players were selected for the British Isles 1993 tour of New Zealand, and at the same time the RFU sent an A team to Canada for a five-match tour. Before they left, five of the party were to take part in the inaugural World Cup Sevens at Murrayfield, a three-day tournament introduced following the enormous success of the Hong Kong Sevens. England's ten-man squad, captained by Andrew Harriman and coached by former fly-half Les Cusworth, included only two players with senior international experience: Tim Rodber had played at number eight against Scotland and Ireland in 1992, and Harriman had missed a gilt-edged chance on his debut against Australia and was never picked again. With a young team England were not expected to make a great impact on the event, and they did well to qualify for the semi-finals by beating South Africa and New Zealand. They did even better once there, completing a 21–7 victory against the Sevens specialists Fiji. In the final they faced a strong Australian side, and this time Harriman made no mistake. Inside the first minute he outflanked David Campese to score, and when Lawrence Dallaglio and Tim Rodber also went over, England were 21 points ahead. Australia did cut the deficit to four points, but England held on to become world champions. The competition may not have carried the same kudos as the 1991 World Cup, but it was nice all the same to see the English players lift the trophy in front of Campese. In all, Harriman scored twelve tries and Nick Beal kicked 70 points. Of the ten players to participate, eight would go on to win caps at senior level, including the future England skipper Lawrence Dallaglio.

Shortly after the Sevens success England's reserves embarked on their tour of Canada. No caps were awarded, and the two-match Test series was shared. As the rest of the party prepared to fly home, Martin Johnson boarded a New Zealand-bound plane to join the British Lions, called up as a replacement for Wade Dooley, taking the number of English players involved in the Lions junket to seventeen. When the original squad was announced there had been much consternation regarding its composition. England had lost in Cardiff and heavily in Dublin, yet only five Welshmen and two Irishmen were selected. If this was harsh on them it was just as true that at least one more England player should have been picked. The tighthead prop Jeff Probyn was left behind, but his rivals did not perform well, and loose-head Jason Leonard was drafted into the number three position for the last two Tests.

The tourists were managed by Geoff Cooke and coached by Scotland's Ian McGeechan, and the relatively inexperienced Scottish captain Gavin Hastings was chosen to skipper the side. It was widely anticipated that Will Carling would be given the honour, but full-back Hastings was in inspirational form and quickly won the respect of his players. His performance in the opening Test was characteristic: he kicked six penalties, and the Lions would surely have won but for two horrendous refereeing decisions. In the first half New Zealand's Frank Bunce was awarded a dubious try, and in the last few seconds, with the Lions leading 18–17, Dean Richards was penalised for a legitimate tackle on the same player. Grant Fox kicked the penalty, and the All Blacks won 20–17. No British Isles side had won a series in New Zealand after losing the First Test, and four changes were made for the second. A record eleven England players were included, and they manfully overcame the early setback of a converted All Blacks try to win 20–7. Rory Underwood sealed the victory with his only Lions try, sprinting down the touchline to score in the corner. The rubber was level, and as the players and supporters rejoiced there was the realisation that had it not been for poor refereeing they would have been celebrating the series. In the decider, the All Blacks finally stamped their authority on proceedings, erasing a ten-point deficit to win 30–13. In terms of results, then, the 1993 Lions were not successful. The Test series was controversially lost and so were six of thirteen fixtures. However, the mediocre dirt-trackers were responsible for the majority of these defeats and a number of players emerged with credit. The Welsh centre Scott Gibbs did extremely well to oust Carling from the Test side, and

Ben Clarke's uncompromising displays established him as one of the premier exponents of all-round back-row play in world rugby.

For the Lions' English contingent there was an instantaneous opportunity to rectify matters as New Zealand toured Great Britain at the beginning of the 1993–94 season. Due mainly to the large number of retirements nine changes were made to the team convincingly beaten in Dublin. Bath full-back Jonathan Callard and Bristol scrum half Kyran Bracken were given debuts, and Bath centre Phil de Glanville had a first start after two appearances as a replacement. De Glanville was called in for the injured Jeremy Guscott, who would miss the entire season with a pelvic problem. Rob Andrew usurped Stuart Barnes at fly-half, and Martin Johnson, Nigel Redman, Dean Richards, Tim Rodber and Victor Ubogu returned to the English pack.

New Zealand had started the tour in fine form, scoring 339 points and winning all ten of their opening fixtures. Sadly, their splendid rugby was slightly soured by some over-aggressive rucking. In one especially nasty incident against the South West

ELEVENTH GRAND SLAM – 1995

Ireland	France	Wales	Scotland
21.01.1995	04.02.1995	18.02.1995	18.03.1995
Lansdowne Road	Twickenham	Cardiff Arms Park	Twickenham
20–8	31–10	23–9	24–12
M J Catt	M J Catt	M J Catt	M J Catt
T Underwood	T Underwood	T Underwood	T Underwood
W D C Carling*	W D C Carling*	W D C Carling*	W D C Carling*
J C Guscott	J C Guscott	J C Guscott	J C Guscott
R Underwood	R Underwood	R Underwood	R Underwood
C R Andrew	C R Andrew	C R Andrew	C R Andrew
K P P Bracken	K P P Bracken	K P P Bracken	K P P Bracken
J Leonard	J Leonard	J Leonard	J Leonard
B C Moore	B C Moore	B C Moore	B C Moore
V E Ubogu	V E Ubogu	V E Ubogu	V E Ubogu
M O Johnson	M O Johnson	M O Johnson	M O Johnson
M C Bayfield	M C Bayfield	M C Bayfield	M C Bayfield
T A K Rodber	T A K Rodber	T A K Rodber	T A K Rodber
B B Clarke	B B Clarke	B B Clarke	B B Clarke
D Richards	D Richards	D Richards	D Richards
			Replacements
			S O Ojomoh (8)
			C D Morris (9t)
			G C Rowntree (1t)
Points Scorers	**Points Scorers**	**Points Scorers**	**Points Scorers**
C R Andrew – 5	C R Andrew – 16	R Underwood – 10	C R Andrew – 24
W D C Carling – 5	T Underwood – 10	C R Andrew – 8	
B B Clarke – 5	J C Guscott – 5	V E Ubogu – 5	
T Underwood – 5			t = temporary

Division, Phil de Glanville was badly raked and required fifteen stitches. A week prior to the England game, the All Blacks visited Murrayfield and beat the Scots 51–15. It was the first time in their history that Scotland had conceded 50 points, and twenty-year-old wing three-quarters Jeff Wilson scored a hat-trick of tries on his Test debut. He also added a conversion after the All Blacks goal-kicker Matthew Cooper was forced to depart with a groin injury. Business interests had already prevented legendary kicker Grant Fox from making the trip, and when Cooper did not recover in time to face England, his responsibilities were again entrusted to the fledgling Wilson. This was a massive request, even for the multi-talented Wilson, and seven days after the bouquets came the brickbats as he missed five of eight penalties and England won 15–9.

The new-look English pack was a revelation. Lock Nigel Redman, playing for the first time in two years, and only because Martin Bayfield was injured, gave the performance of his abbreviated career, and the back row of Rodber, Clarke and Richards overpowered their eminent opposition. All eight of the forwards took the game to the All Blacks, matching them tackle for tackle. Their heroics were consolidated by the skilled kicking and tactical *savoir-faire* of Rob Andrew. In one of his most effectual games, Andrew nursed the touchline with pinpoint accuracy and dropped his seventeenth international goal to take England six points clear. Jon Callard, on his debut the complete antithesis of Wilson, coolly slotted home four penalties to seal a first win against New Zealand for ten years. Although England were not able to score the tries their play warranted, they never relinquished control, and the All Blacks were fortunate to finish the match with fifteen players when their frustration boiled over and Jamie Joseph stamped on young Kyran Bracken's ankle in an off-the-ball incident.

The win was particularly satisfying for Geoff Cooke and Will Carling. Both had endured bitter disappointment during the recent British Isles tour and had now respectively managed and captained England to victory against all seven senior members of the International Rugby Board. The game was Carling's 36th as skipper, equalling the world record of Australian Nick Farr-Jones for the most appearances as a Test match captain.

The defeat of the All Blacks naturally confirmed England as favourites for the 1994 Five Nations, and only the French in Paris were given any hope of upsetting the odds. Cooke's team did not play on the opening championship weekend, and by the time they faced Scotland at Murrayfield on 5 February the Scots had already been thrashed 29–6 by Wales. England made three changes for what was expected to be one of their easier visits to Edinburgh, two of which were enforced by injuries to Dean Richards and Tim Rodber. Bath's John Hall and Leicester's Neil Back replaced them, and Martin Bayfield returned despite Nigel Redman's Herculean effort against the Kiwis. The changes did not initially appear to disrupt England, and in the first quarter only frantic Scottish defence denied them an early try. A score during this period of supremacy may well have signalled the end for Scotland, but as it was they grew in certitude and England began to fade. Rob Wainwright's try on the half-hour accentuated the transformation, and it seemed complete when Gregor Townsend dropped a goal in the final minute to give Scotland a

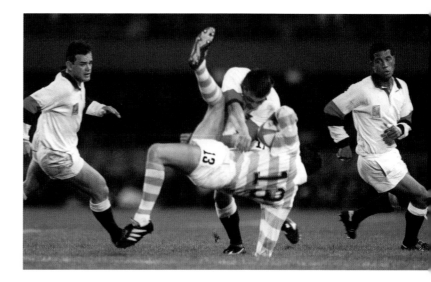

Above Will Carling and Jeremyy Guscott look on as Rory Underwood tackles Fransisco Garcia of Argentina

14–12 lead. Once again the spectre of 1990 loomed, and once again it was dispelled as England rallied and Jon Callard calmly sent over an injury-time penalty goal to silence the disbelieving Celtic hordes. The one-point defeat was cruel on Scotland, and Captain Gavin Hastings was inconsolable. The normally unflappable full-back had missed five penalties during the game and his post-match tears revealed the extent of his suffering. He would have felt even worse a fortnight later, when Ireland visited Twickenham and comprehensively exposed their hosts' shortcomings. England never looked capable of winning, or indeed scoring a try, and the escape act at Murrayfield proved to be more a postponement as Ireland won 13–12.

It was a first home defeat in twelve Five Nations matches, and a week later Geoff Cooke announced that he would be standing down at the end of the current campaign. He had arrived at this decision some months before, and it did not come, contrary to newspaper speculation, as a result of pressure from within the RFU. If Cooke was dismayed at only narrowly surviving an early-season vote of confidence, he engendered no response and instead cited tiredness as his reason for calling it a day. After six and a half years of unflagging commitment, under incessant media scrutiny, this was entirely understandable. England were due to tour South Africa in May and June, and had Cooke remained at the helm he would have been obliged to continue for another full year. As it was, his impending departure allowed sufficient time for a successor to prepare for the 1995 World Cup.

His last two matches were against France and Wales. He had commenced his management career with defeats against the same countries, and in an endeavour to avoid history repeating itself he discarded a third of the team beaten by the Irish. Ben Clarke, Ian Hunter, Dewi Morris and Nigel Redman were reintroduced, and Jon Callard, the match winner against New Zealand and Scotland, was dropped after failing with four kicks in the Ireland game. He was replaced by Harlequins full-back David Pears, and Rob Andrew was assigned the kicking duties. For some time Andrew's positional kicking at fly-half had been exemplary, but he was considered too inconsistent to be entrusted with the goal

kicking on a permanent basis. After the match in Paris this changed, and the former Cambridge man, nine years and 55 appearances since debut, embarked on the second and far more illustrious phase of his international career.

A lack of self-belief aside, the missing ingredient in England's unsatisfactory season had been their forwards' usual ability to control matches from the early stages. The mass retirements of 1993 and an injury to Dean Richards had undermined the pack's authority, and Cooke was compelled to experiment in a bid to restore cohesion. A number of different permutations were tried, but England remained unsettled until Ben Clarke and Nigel Redman returned against France. Their presence had a stabilising effect, and normal service was resumed as *Les Rosbifs*, as they were imaginatively nicknamed by the home supporters, took control and the French meekly gave way. Rob Andrew, positively thriving in his new role, dispatched five penalties and a drop goal to register all eighteen of England's points in a four-point victory. They had now gone five matches without a try, but, more consequentially, France were beaten for the seventh game in succession.

Events conspired to make Geoff Cooke's swansong as England manager a memorable occasion. The season after receiving the wooden spoon, Wales came to Twickenham on 19 March in search of the Grand Slam, and England knew that if they could

Above Ben Clarke jumps for the ball with Rolando Martin of Argentina

win by sixteen or more points they, and not the Welsh, would be crowned champions. If either side required any further incentive, the match was the 100th meeting between the two countries, and the Queen was in attendance to open the fabulous new East Stand and present the Five Nations trophy. The game was also a special one for Brian Moore, as he became only the fifth Englishman to win 50 caps for his country. Dean Richards had made a timely recovery from injury, and Cooke was finally able to select the same pack that had eclipsed New Zealand. The only other change saw Tony Underwood replace David Pears, and Ian Hunter switch to his preferred position at full-back.

For an hour the match was a terrific spectacle, and the Welsh were almost reduced to admiring onlookers as England went in search of the points needed to secure the title. Their first try of both the match and the season was well worth the wait as the backs at last loosened the shackles. Will Carling and Rob Andrew combined well to feed Phil de Glanville, and his turn of pace and consummate pass put Rory Underwood in beneath the posts. It was a majestic try befitting the royal presence, and early in the second half Tim Rodber plundered the Welsh line-out to add another. England led 15–3, and the title was there for the taking until former Olympic hurdler Nigel Walker produced a late touchdown to bestow on Wales the championship. Their skipper, Ieuan Evans, collected the spoils, but the day and the match belonged to England and to Cooke.

His team had provided a marvellous note on which to depart, and after such assiduous service Cooke undoubtedly deserved it. In less than seven years he had breathed new life into the corpse of English rugby and almost single-handedly turned a national embarrassment into one of the most successful teams in the world. He guided England to a World Cup final, delivered two Grand Slams, and only thirteen of 49 matches were lost. In Europe the same countries that once dismissed England as cannon fodder had now, much to their chagrin, grown accustomed to watching them win. At Twickenham, each of the three southern hemisphere powers was beaten, and if England were not yet on a par with these teams they had definitely narrowed the gap.

The hypercritical had frequently berated Cooke for his team's workmanlike approach, but more often than not these relatively isolated voices misjudged the mood of the nation. The English supporters have long memories, and when presented with images of Cardiff Arms Park in 1979 or Murrayfield in 1986 they would to a man, or woman, favour almost any of England's performances under Cooke. There was, of course, still plenty of room for improvement. England at times were very one-dimensional and found it difficult to overcome defensive formations, but it was still something of a fallacy to intimate that they were always dour and unimaginative. In 49 matches they scored 114 tries, hardly the record of a boring team.

Cooke was also criticised for picking the same faces regardless of form or age, though in truth he rarely had reason to regret the faith he placed in his players, and if on occasion he did show a little too much loyalty then it was still better than the previous practice of showing none at all. Fallible as he was – the tactical switch prior to the 1991 World Cup final may well have been a grievous error of judgement – the Geoff Cooke legacy was sound and his successor would have a tough act to follow.

The man the RFU chose to replace Cooke unquestionably had the pedigree to do so. In fifteen years Jack Rowell had transformed Bath into the most successful club side in the country, winning eight John Player Special/Pilkington Cups and five Courage League Championships, in the process establishing a reputation as an innovative coach with a commitment to expansive fifteen-man rugby. In his first move as manager he swapped Mike Slemen, brought in by Cooke to coach the backs, for Les Cusworth, and some months later Dick Best was dismissed to allow Rowell a dual management/coaching role. It was widely acknowledged that Rowell had inherited the foundations of a good team, but the game was developing rapidly, and if England were to keep apace they would have to do likewise.

The recent law changes had seen a dramatic variation in approach. Large mobile forwards, able to play with ball in hand, were very much the order of the day, and far greater integration was needed between the two divisions. The best teams in the world adapted quickly and were playing high-octane, 80-minute rugby. Rowell had eight matches to emulate them, and the first two would take place in one of the harshest rugby-playing environments on the planet.

England arrived in South Africa three weeks after African National Congress leader Nelson Mandela was inaugurated as president in the nation's first democratic elections. In the preceding months the country was beset by political and civil unrest, and a great number of people had died as a result. For some time doubts were expressed as to whether the tour should go ahead in such volatile surroundings, but any fears proved to be unfounded and the only problems England experienced were on the field. Several of the party had never before played at altitude, and on their first ascent to the high veldt, at Bloemfontein, England were beaten 22–11 by the Orange Free State. If the rarefied atmosphere was the cause of their lacklustre performance, the excuses were harder to come by when they returned to sea level and lost 21–6 to Natal in Durban. The unpalatable truth was that South Africa's provincial teams, assisted dramatically by the recently devised Super 10 competition, were already playing the type of rugby England aspired to. They performed at an astonishing pace, with few handling errors, and England's percentage game was made to look antiquated on the hard South African pitches. Four of the five warm-up matches before the First Test were lost – Transvaal

Below Physio Kevin Murphy, Dr Terry Crystall and Will Carling with the injured Dean Richard. England went on to beat Western Samoa 44–22 in this final pool game

and South Africa A also beat the tourists – and as the first match against the national side approached Martin Johnson was forced to return home with concussion.

Apart from having to replace Johnson, for whom Martin Bayfield came in, Jack Rowell made only one change to the Geoff Cooke team that had beaten Wales in March: Bristol's Paul Hull made his debut at full-back in a game the majority of neutrals expected the Springboks to win at a canter. Before the start both sides were introduced to President Mandela, and the Afrikaans crowd were in celebratory mood as they settled to watch the English whipping boys whipped. Fifteen minutes later they sat aghast and silent. England had produced one of the finest spells of rugby ever seen and led by twenty points. Ben Clarke and Rob Andrew scored the tries, and Andrew went on to become one of the few players to register all four possible scores in the same match. In addition to his touchdown he notched two conversions, five penalty goals and a drop goal for a new English record of 27 points. For Andrew it was a personal triumph, and for the team a collective one. They had utterly confounded their critics and won 32–15.

If England anticipated a backlash from the wounded South Africans, they did not have to wait long for its arrival. Three days after their Test victory, on 7 June, the second string met Eastern Province in Port Elizabeth. South Africa has always been a notoriously tough country to tour, not least because the southern hemisphere referees have traditionally taken a more lenient stance regarding certain infringements, particularly those in the line-out and at rucks. Rucking to the body in an attempt to uncover the ball is generally considered a legitimate practice, but raking to the head or with no possibility of recovering possession is another matter, and much of what transpires south of the equator would not be acceptable in Europe. The standard of refereeing on Jack Rowell's first tour was no exception. Several officials turned a blind eye to serious and violent foul play, and Jon Callard was fortunate not to be doing the same when the physical intimidation reached a peak in Port Elizabeth. In one of the most brutal matches ever played, Callard had his eye so badly cut by the boot of Elandre van der Bergh the wound needed 25 stitches. Salutary stuff, and the convivial ambience was not greatly improved when Tim Rodber responded to being repeatedly punched with a flurry of his own, and was dismissed. After Mike Burton in 1975, Rodber was only the second Englishman sent off playing for his country, and like Burton he escaped further punishment. England's disciplinary panel decided that considering the severe provocation the dismissal was sufficient, and the Green Howards officer was permitted to play in the final Test. Although it was probably not the right example to set – it allowed the South African authorities to ignore the disgraceful antics of their own players – it was hard not to concur with their ruling.

Newlands in Cape Town was the venue for the Second Test, and England would face the inevitable South African maelstrom without the injured Dean Richards. In light of the first meeting, and the scathing criticism heaped upon them, the Springboks' response was predictable. They greatly increased their physical presence and launched a ferocious and unremitting assault on the

Below Dewi Morris gets things moving during an enthralling World Cup quarter-final match against Australia, 10 June 1995

English lines. At half-time England had done exceptionally well to keep the score at 3–3, and with barely ten minutes remaining they were still in touch. Three points separated the sides until the door finally caved in and two tries and fifteen points buried the visitors 27–9. Honours were even. South Africa had saved face and England had gained a great deal of experience from an indispensable tour. The squad were accustomed to the altitude and high humidity, and had played in Durban, their base for the preliminary stages of the 1995 World Cup. More importantly, they had seen the standards required to win the World Cup and had even risen to them for fifteen unparalleled minutes.

When Jack Rowell was appointed manager his brief was to open up England's game, and he publicly stated that a change in attitude and style was required. On tour he had in the main watched and noted what his players were capable of, and at the beginning of the 1994–95 season the World Cup loomed and his work began in earnest. England had six games before the Webb Ellis trophy was contested for the third time: single Test matches against Romania and Canada, followed by the Five Nations Championship.

Romania were not likely to cause many problems at Twickenham, and Rowell made only minor adjustments to the fifteen beaten in Cape Town. For the first time in a year Jeremy Guscott was fit to renew his centre three-quarters partnership with Will Carling, who was winning his 50th cap, and Martin Johnson returned following his early departure from South Africa. After a five-month international break the players were on the rusty side, and at times it showed. Not all of the passes went to hand, and some of the backs lacked their usual fluidity, but 24 points from Rob Andrew, six tries and a 54–3 victory represented an acceptable start.

The attacking intentions evident, though infrequently fulfilled, against Romania came to fruition during the last 40 minutes of the next match with Canada. Dean Richards was back from injury and joined Tim Rodber and Ben Clarke to recreate the back-row triumvirate that had beaten New Zealand, Wales and South Africa. Kyran Bracken also returned, for Dewi Morris at scrum half, having withdrawn from England's summer tour in order to sit his law exams. The game was handsomely won, and the purist principles advocated by Jack Rowell were given their first unadulterated airing. His team played sensational, flowing rugby, and only a resolute Canadian defence kept the score to a close-to-respectable 60–19. Rob Andrew continued his incredible form with the boot, kicking six penalties to take England eighteen points ahead and then converting all six of their second-half tries. He did not miss a single attempt at goal, and his match total of 30 points surpassed his own English record of 27 and equalled the world record set by Didier Camberabero for France against Zimbabwe in the 1987 World Cup. Mike Catt, whose one previous appearance was as a replacement against Wales, came on at full-back for Paul Hull and took his chance with two tries. Similarly, Bracken substantially improved his own stock with a rounded performance and his first international score.

Catt's display impressed Rowell, and when England visited Dublin on 21 January for the opening Five Nations Championship game of 1995 he was included in the starting line-up. Paul Hull was the unfortunate player to give way in

what was to be the last team change prior to the World Cup encounter with Argentina. Having lost to Ireland in consecutive seasons, England had a score to settle, and after just a few minutes were given the best possible start when the Irish lost possession at their own throw and Andrew jinked through a gaping defence to put Will Carling over. Ben Clarke emerged from a rolling maul for another, and Tony Underwood put the game beyond doubt with a third in the second half. The conditions underfoot and the swirling wind were not conducive to good rugby, but the elements suited the intrepid English forwards and they won with plenty to spare.

While England were disposing of the Irish threat, France were doing the same at home against the Welsh, and the two nations' subsequent meeting at Twickenham was billed as Le Crunch. For one of the most disciplined French sides to visit these shores a more appropriate title would have been Le Damp Squib, as they left their passion in Paris and collectively failed to impress. True, they did score their customary length-of-the-field try, but it was an oasis in a desert of English domination. Tim Rodber, Ben Clarke and Victor Ubogu epitomised the new breed of forward and their bruising runs cut swathes through the French lines. The interplay between them and the backs was first-class. A clever dummy from Guscott ended a period of unrelenting pressure for the first try, and England would have added to Tony Underwood's second-half brace if France had not conceded penalties during some desperate last-ditch defending. Rob Andrew kicked four of them, and England made the journey to Cardiff Arms Park on the back of a 31–10 victory, their biggest over the French for 81 years.

If the graveyard of English dreams still held a degree of trepidation for Jack Rowell's men, it would have been tempered by the knowledge that the Welsh were without two of their best players, Scott Gibbs and Scott Quinnell, and had recently lost to a moderate French team. England's backs never reached the dizzy heights attained in their previous outing, but they rarely needed to as the forwards continued in identical fashion. Wales were pushed all over their hallowed turf, and three tries were forged from uncompromising drives. Victor Ubogu scored after a maul had surged a full twenty metres, and Rory Underwood made amends for the disastrous mistake of 1993 with his first two tries at the Welsh bastion. The second would have provided immeasurable pleasure as his momentum carried him and nemesis Ieuan Evans across the goal line. In the final quarter, England were handed a numerical advantage when the Welsh prop John Davies was needlessly dismissed for stamping, but they already led 18–6 and eventually won their fifth match of the season 23–9.

Meanwhile, Scotland were burying their own ghosts in Paris. Following twelve successive defeats in the French capital dating back to 1971, skipper Gavin Hastings completed a 23–21 victory with an excellent try on the stroke of full-time. England were not due to play again for a month, and two weeks after their win against the Welsh they watched Scotland beat the same opposition to manufacture the second Grand Slam showdown between the two countries in six years.

Five of the England team beaten at Murrayfield in 1990 – Carling, Guscott, Rory Underwood, Andrew and Moore – would start at Twickenham and four of the Scots – the Hastings brothers,

Chalmers and Milne – had also survived. Once again England were the overwhelming favourites. Before beating Canada in January, Scotland had gone nine games without a win while England had won eight of their last nine fixtures. Faced by superior opponents the Scots had little choice but to disrupt. They spent a great deal of the match offside, and the penalty count against them could easily have exceeded nineteen. As in the past, the English response was worrying. For long periods they camped in the Scottish half, but the Celts defended with great heart and the home team was not creative enough to break them down. They were, however, in complete control and Rob Andrew landed seven penalties and a drop goal to win the match 24–12 and become the first Englishman to score 300 international points. Captain Will Carling thus had the honour of leading his team to three Grand Slams, the first player of any nationality to do so.

Jack Rowell's grand design was underway, and seven victories in eight matches were ample testament to the significant strides made. At times there were glimpses of the total rugby preached by the former Bath supremo, but at others, notably against Wales and Scotland, England invariably reverted to type. When under pressure they adopted a cautious approach and relied on the strength and determination of their forwards. These are fine attributes in their own right, but they alone are not adequate to beat the likes of New Zealand or South Africa on a regular basis. In some respects Rowell's side fared similarly to those of his predecessor, Geoff Cooke. When faced with inferior teams, or quality teams cowed by the forwards, England were able to cut loose and play progressively. They were seldom as adventurous in tight situations, and found it hard to raise the tempo when Plan A failed. In the World Cup these limitations would be punished, and they had just nine weeks to master a system that was second nature in the southern hemisphere.

It was decided at the beginning of the season that in order to allow England's players to rest before the World Cup they would be available for only two Courage League matches during April. This move was not greeted with unrestrained joy by the clubs searching for honours, or to avoid relegation, but it did enable Rowell to keep his squad fresh for their coaching and training sessions at Marlow Rugby Club. The preparations were almost complete when, with less than a fortnight before the team's departure for South Africa, they were thrown into turmoil. A hastily convened RFU committee at London's East India Club announced that Will Carling, the longest serving captain in rugby union history, had been sacked following a disparaging remark made on a Channel Four documentary. In an unguarded moment he had referred to the 57 committee members as 'old farts'. The press orchestrated a full-blown public outcry and Carling's team-mates left the RFU in an untenable position by stating publicly that none was willing to replace their captain. Thankfully, three days later common sense prevailed and the RFU president Denis Easby accepted Carling's apology and reinstated him.

Free from the yoke of apartheid, the new democratic and multiracial society of South Africa, christened the 'Rainbow Nation', provided a vivid setting for the third World Cup. Of the 1991 nations three – Fiji, Zimbabwe and the United States – failed to qualify in 1995 and were replaced by the hosts, Tonga (who also participated in 1987) and the Ivory Coast. After a colourful opening ceremony in Cape Town the competition commenced with an exhilarating contest between South Africa and the defending champions, Australia. Spurred on by a fanatical home crowd, the Springboks hit the ground running and won 27–18. The match was of great relevance to England, who would in all probability meet the losers, David Campese et al, in the quarter-final.

Before the Wallabies could be tamed, Jack Rowell's men would need to subdue the Pumas, their first opponents in a testing pool including Western Samoa and Italy. Two changes were made to the team that edged Scotland for the Grand Slam, one enforced and one strategic: Bath's Steve Ojomoh came in at number eight for the injured Dean Richards, and scrum half Dewi Morris was preferred to Kyran Bracken. Argentina were known to be a durable but limited outfit: immediately prior to the World Cup they had toured Australia and conceded 83 points in losing two Test matches. England were therefore expected to win comfortably and confirm their pre-tournament status as one of the three favourites. Obviously, the Pumas had not read the same script, and they took an inexplicably out-of-sorts England to the brink of an embarrassing defeat. They possessed an outstanding set of forwards, and it was an edifying experience to witness Rowell's imperious pack treated with disdain in the scrummage. Luckily they were not as sophisticated in other areas. Their line-out presence was non-existent, and fly-half Lisandro Arbizu missed several attempts at goal. They also conceded penalties as if they were going out of fashion, and for the second game in a row Rob Andrew kicked all England's points. The 24–18 victory was far from convincing, and Argentina, who scored two second-half tries, would probably have won if not for a lack of tactical nous.

To compound a sorry performance, a late ankle injury to Will Carling prevented him from playing in the next match, against Italy. Phil de Glanville replaced Carling at centre, and Rob Andrew captained the side in his absence. Kyran Bracken was given another opportunity at scrum half and Leicester prop Graham Rowntree was included in the front row, with Jason Leonard switching to tight-head. Neil Back was selected for his extra pace at flanker, and Ben Clarke moved to his favoured position at number eight.

The Azzurri were no longer the poor relations of European rugby. Three weeks earlier they had played an Irish side nearing full strength and won 22–12. Against England they set out to prove it was no fluke, and their opening flourish was only subdued by a first-rate counterattacking try from Tony Underwood. Brother Rory added a second, and when Rob Andrew kicked his fifth penalty England led 27–10. At which point they collectively took their foot off the gas and coasted home. An Italian touchdown in injury time gave the 27–20 final score a deceptively close appearance, but England always looked certain to win. Even so, they were not impressive, and two matches against committed but modest teams had failed to reproduce anything like their Five Nations form. Manager Jack Rowell confessed that he was at a loss to explain why; the press had their own ideas and were busy writing the team off as sub-standard also-rans.

Not perhaps the most dispassionate, or accurate, of assessments, particularly as England had now won eight straight

Above Rob Andrew unleashes his last-gasp drop kick that clinched a 25–22 victory and sent England into the World Cup semi-finals, to face the might of the All Blacks

matches and had already qualified for the quarter-finals. Who they would meet there would depend on the outcome of the final pool match with Western Samoa. If England won they would face Australia in Cape Town; lose and it would be South Africa in Johannesburg. Rowell and right-hand man Les Cusworth were aware that either would present a substantial obstacle, and opted to rest key personnel. Their decision immediately ignited speculation that England would intentionally lose in order to play South Africa. Inane though the theory was – quite why anyone would want to face a strong host nation at an altitude of 6,000 feet was never explained – many subscribed to it until the second string walloped their South Seas opponents.

After missing matches with injury, Dean Richards and Will Carling were given run-outs in the Samoan game, and centre Phil de Glanville retained his place as Jeremy Guscott made way. Ian Hunter and Jonathan Callard played their first games under Rowell, and Dewi Morris again swapped with Kyran Bracken at scrum half. Gloucester lock Richard West made his debut, and

hooker Graham Dawe, who had won his fourth cap against the USA in the 1987 World Cup, was awarded a rather belated fifth almost eight years later. The fresh faces added a new impetus, and after just two minutes England led when Neil Back scored his first international try. Rory Underwood augmented the lead with his 44th, and by the interval a drop goal by Mike Catt and accurate place-kicking from Callard had taken England 21 points ahead. The Samoans came back in the second half, but England changed gears and another score by Underwood and a penalty try took them out of sight. In the closing stages, with half an eye turning towards the Australians, the pattern of the game was disrupted by a number of 'injuries'. In all, five replacements were used, and Bath's John Mallett (for Rowntree) and Wasps' Damian Hopley (for Carling) won their first caps after warming the bench. The combative Brian Moore, who had made no secret of

Above England's Tony Underwood fails to tackle New Zealand's Jonah Lomu in the 1995 World Cup semi-final

the fact that he did not want to be rested, found himself playing at flanker opposite that great blindside exponent ... Kyran Bracken! England's 44–22 win ensured a repeat of the 1991 clash with Australia, while Western Samoa would have to cope with the fervour surrounding hosts South Africa.

Ireland won the battle of the home unions by beating Wales 24–23. After finishing third in 1987, the Welsh had now failed to reach the quarter-finals in successive competitions. France handed Scotland the shortest of straws when they reversed the recent Five Nations result by winning 22–19 with a try deep into injury time. The French would play Ireland in the last eight, while Scotland could look forward to a match with the All Blacks. Scotland's captain, Gavin Hastings, did at least have the consolation of breaking the world record for most individual points in an international. In his country's 89–0 thrashing of Tonga, Hastings contributed 44 points with four tries, nine conversions and two penalty goals. Unfortunately for Hastings, nine days later Simon Culhane, on his debut, registered 45 – twenty conversions and a try – for New Zealand versus Japan. The All Blacks also surpassed the previous record for points in a match, winning 145–17 with 21 tries, six for Marc Ellis, setting yet another world best. Sadly, the exhilarating rugby and record-breaking performances were overshadowed by an horrific injury to Max Brito of the Ivory Coast. Brito was tragically paralysed by a seemingly innocuous tackle in the minnows' final pool match with Tonga. His plight sent shock waves through the rugby world, but did not deter the Samoans from indulging in some reckless high tackling in their

quarter-final with South Africa. The Boks won with four tries from their only black player, Chester Williams, and on the same day Ireland were sent packing by France.

In the first of the two remaining quarter-finals, England travelled to Cape Town hoping to avenge their 1991 final defeat. The match would also provide a perfect opportunity to silence the walking soapbox, David Campese. In his usual understated manner, the Australian wing had been rubbishing everything English – their style of play, chances of winning and even the abilities of captain Will Carling, whose muscular build was charmingly compared to a castrated bull. If his taunts were aimed at inducing a response, tactical or otherwise, on this occasion they did not. England would do their talking on the pitch.

For the first time since the Five Nations all first-choice players were available, and Jack Rowell named fourteen of the team that had beaten Scotland in March. The one exception was at scrum half, where Dewi Morris was deemed to have bettered Kyran Bracken in their personal joust. The back row of Tim Rodber, Ben Clarke and Dean Richards had played together in eight matches, and England had won them all. Against the much-vaunted Australians their record seemed destined to be stretched to nine as Carling's men made a mockery of both Campese's gibes and their early tournament form. Jeremy Guscott and Will Carling combined from their own 22-yard line to set Tony Underwood away for a try, and at half-time England were in the ascendant by thirteen points to six.

A short period of consolidation in the second half and they would have had at least one foot in the semi-final, but less than a minute after the restart England were caught cold. Michael Lynagh kicked over the top, and Damian Smith beat Mike Catt and Tony Underwood to level the scores at 13–13. Three penalty goals from Rob Andrew were equated by a trio from Lynagh and, as extra-time approached, the two teams could still not be separated. Campese screwed a drop goal attempt wide, and seconds later England forced a penalty which Mike Catt kicked from deep in his own half to the Australian ten-metre line. From the resulting throw and maul the English pack gained priceless ground; Dewi Morris fed Andrew who, without taking an upward glance, kicked a perfect drop goal from more than 40 metres. England's 25–22 victory was their first against Australia beyond British shores, and the seventh time that saviour Andrew had scored twenty points in an international. Now all that Jack Rowell had to ponder was how to counter their semi-final opponents, New Zealand, and particularly a giant wing called Jonah Lomu.

At the age of nineteen the youngest-ever All Black, Lomu, had played only two internationals prior to the competition and had hardly covered himself in glory in home defeats by the French. His reputation had been somewhat restored with a sensational campaign in the 1994 Hong Kong Sevens, and his 6ft 5in, nineteen-stone physique had already made a vast impression on the World Cup with two tries in the opening victory over Ireland. He was rested in the 128-point demolition of the Japanese, but returned with another touchdown in the 48–30 quarter-final win over Scotland. As would be the case in seven days' time, the result was never as close as this final margin of victory might suggest. Nevertheless, 30 points were fair reward for a brave Scottish effort, and it was heartening to see the thousands of travelling fans give Gavin Hastings a rousing farewell as he brought down the curtain on an illustrious career. The tartan talisman retired with 733 international points, at the time second only to Michael Lynagh's then world record of 911. This itself has now been

Below Tim Rodber, Brian Moore and Rory Underwood walk off after defeat by New Zealand

Argentina
27.05.1995
Durban
Pool Two
Won 24–18

M J Catt
T Underwood
W D C Carling*
J C Guscott
R Underwood
C R Andrew
C D Morris

J Leonard
B C Moore
V E Ubogu
M O Johnson
M C Bayfield
T A K Rodber
B B Clarke
S O Ojomoh

Replacements
P R de Glanville (13)
N A Back (8t)

Points Scorers
C R Andrew – 24

Italy
31.05.1995
Durban
Pool Two
Won 27–20

M J Catt
T Underwood
J C Guscott
P R de Glanville
R Underwood
C R Andrew*
K P P Bracken

G C Rowntree
B C Moore
J Leonard
M O Johnson
M C Bayfield
T A K Rodber
N A Back
B B Clarke

Points Scorers
C R Andrew – 17
R Underwood – 5
T Underwood – 5

Western Samoa
04.06.1995
Durban
Pool Two
Won 44–22

J E B Callard
I G Hunter
W D C Carling*
P R de Glanville
R Underwood
M J Catt
C D Morris

G C Rowntree
R G R Dawe
V E Ubogu
R I West
M O Johnson
S O Ojomoh
N A Back
D Richards

Replacements
J A Mallett (1)
T A K Rodber (7)
D P Hopley (13)
B C Moore (8)
K P P Bracken (7t)

Points Scorers
J E B Callard – 21
R Underwood – 10
N A Back – 5
M J Catt – 3
penalty try

Australia
10.06.1995
Cape Town
Quarter-Final
Won 25–22

M J Catt
T Underwood
W D C Carling*
J C Guscott
R Underwood
C R Andrew
C D Morris

J Leonard
B C Moore
V E Ubogu
M O Johnson
M C Bayfield
T A K Rodber
B B Clarke
D Richards

Replacement
S O Ojomoh (8t)

Points Scorers
C R Andrew – 20
T Underwood – 5

New Zealand
17.06.1995
Cape Town
Semi-Final
Lost 45–29

M J Catt
T Underwood
W D C Carling*
J C Guscott
R Underwood
C R Andrew
C D Morris

J Leonard
B C Moore
V E Ubogu
M O Johnson
M C Bayfield
T A K Rodber
B B Clarke
D Richards

Points Scorers
W D C Carling – 10
R Underwood – 10
C R Andrew – 9

France
22.06.1995
Pretoria
Third-Place Play-Off
Lost 19–9

M J Catt
I G Hunter
W D C Carling*
J C Guscott
R Underwood
C R Andrew
C D Morris

J Leonard
B C Moore
V E Ubogu
M O Johnson
M C Bayfield
T A K Rodber
B B Clarke
S O Ojomoh

Points Scorers
C R Andrew – 9

eclipsed by Neil Jenkins (1049 points for Wales and 41 with the Lions).

The Scottish performance would certainly have encouraged England. At times the All Blacks' defence appeared vulnerable, and if it had not been for some terrible lapses in concentration Scotland might have provided a much sterner test. England had won ten consecutive matches, and among the unchanged fifteen that faced the New Zealand haka there was an earnest belief that a second World Cup final was a realistic prospect. How long this belief lingered presumably rested on each player's individual level of optimism. The general consensus was that they were beaten after six minutes, by which point New Zealand led 12–0. Others were of the opinion that Lomu's try after 90 seconds, when he ran through Tony Underwood and over Mike Catt, effectively ended the contest. The latter is probably nearer the money. England simply withered in the face of the relentless All Blacks blitz, and at one stage trailed 35–3. Time after time their defence was found wanting, and poor Tony Underwood endured a torrid afternoon. When not being trampled by Lomu, he was being unceremoniously dumped to the ground by him, and it was difficult to escape the image of a Rottweiler shaking his favourite rag doll. Given the circumstances, many teams would have capitulated, but England played with an indomitable spirit and in the second half actually outscored New Zealand 26–20. Rory Underwood and Will Carling each scored two tries, and, if thanks only to the hopeless nature of the situation, the English enjoyed their best half of the competition. Though the damage was done and a Lazarus-type resurrection was never even a remote possibility, Carling and his team did emerge with some dignity.

The other semi-final between South Africa and France was a less straightforward affair. For the preceding 24 hours Durban had been the centre of a tropical deluge and the King's Park pitch was a quagmire before a ball was kicked. When the torrential rain returned shortly after the start, the match rapidly degenerated into a muddy farce, and both the playing conditions and final result were a travesty. South Africa eventually won 19–15, but how they escaped conceding a penalty try in the final minute, after collapsing two scrums on their goal line, only Welsh official Derek Bevan can elucidate. Not that the jubilant home fans cared. Their deities were heading for Johannesburg and a final showdown with New Zealand, while France and England decamped to the altitude of Pretoria for the third-place play-off.

It was purported to be a prestigious event with the winners automatically qualifying for the 1999 competition. For the English, however, mentally spent after the New Zealand drubbing, it was one game too far. With hindsight, Jack Rowell would have been wiser to rest a few of his jaded senior squad and select the reserves that had performed so admirably in the win against Western Samoa – players champing at the bit for another opportunity at the highest level. Instead, he reasoned, none too perceptively, that there was insufficient time to prepare new blood and made only two changes. Rather than subject Tony Underwood to further punishment, Ian Hunter came in on the wing, and an injury to Dean Richards necessitated Steve Ojomoh's inclusion at number eight. From the incipient exchanges it was plain that England were not at the races, and the French, who started almost as poorly, grew in confidence and capitalised on

Above Rory Underwood - RAF pilot and England's record try scorer

their opponents' deficiencies to win a dreadful game 19–9. It was England's first defeat by Les Bleus in nine matches, and the immense psychological advantage established during the previous eight victories had been squandered in one sub-standard performance. The repercussions of the dismal display would be felt as early as the next Five Nations Championship, and it would be almost four years before England were able to reassert their authority against their Gallic rivals. The defeat was particularly galling for that French agent provocateur Brian Moore, unwittingly playing the last international of a distinguished career.

The final between South Africa and the All Blacks was an absorbing affair, and what it lacked in enterprise it made up for in drama. With the score at 9–9 New Zealand's fly-half Andrew Mehrtens pushed a late drop goal attempt across the posts, and the two behemoths were still inextricably tied as the match entered extra-time. After a penalty goal apiece, Mehrten's opposite number, Joel Stransky, dropped his second goal of the game and South Africa somehow preserved their slender lead for the remaining eight minutes to win by three points. Captain François Pienaar received the Webb Ellis trophy from President Mandela, resplendent in a replica of Pienaar's number six jersey and Springbok cap, and the Rainbow Nation celebrated with typical exuberance. Just five years before, Mandela was still incarcerated on Robben Island and such scenes would have been unthinkable. The All Blacks were the tournament's outstanding team, but South Africa contained their phenomenon Jonah Lomu, and on the day were worthy victors.

1995-1999

The professional era

SOUTH AFRICA WERE THE THIRD OF THE SOUTHERN POWERS TO WIN THE
WORLD CUP, AND THE CHASM IN CLASS BETWEEN THE TWO HEMISPHERES
WAS NOW MORE MANIFEST THAN AT ANY OTHER STAGE SINCE THE
COMPETITION'S CONCEPTION IN 1987. IT WAS NO WONDER THAT ON THE
EVE OF THE FINAL, MEDIA BARON RUPERT MURDOCH CLOSED A
£360 MILLION TEN-YEAR BROADCASTING DEAL WITH THE AUSTRALIAN,
NEW ZEALAND AND SOUTH AFRICAN RUGBY UNIONS.

HIS News Corporation had negotiated exclusive rights to each country's provincial and international matches including a new home-and-away Tri-Nations series and an expanded Super 10 event now featuring twelve teams (retitled the Super 12). Both competitions were due to commence in 1996 and it was obvious that, given the massive influx of funds, the International Rugby Board would have to act or risk losing their leading players to a breakaway circuit. On 27 August 1995, almost exactly a hundred years after the union and league codes had gone their separate ways, the defining moment arrived: the IRB announced that all regulations pertaining to amateurism were to be abolished forthwith, and that the sport was now officially open.

The amateur ethos belonged to a bygone age when well-to-do young gentlemen played as a hobby while studying for their professional careers at university. They trained rarely and toured less, and would often step aside after one or two seasons. Rugby was now unrecognisable from that part-time cloistered world, as was its spiralling commercial appeal. For years professionalism had slowly eroded the principles of the game's founders. It had long been an open secret that several unions provided match fees, and at a domestic level the unenforceable laws were flouted even more blatantly. In addition to the surreptitiously sanctioned 'boot money' and inflated expense accounts, there were rumours of fictitious jobs and large win bonuses. As far back as the 1970s French club champions Béziers were paying their players a monthly salary, and the World XV that toured South Africa in 1989 received thousands of pounds for the privilege.

For some senior IRB members, namely the well-prepared southern hemisphere sides, the transition to the professional ranks was a seamless affair. Others, after years of entrenchment, were reluctant to assimilate a sport encompassing player contracts and transfer fees. The home unions squabbled incessantly over the income generated from television coverage of the Five Nations, and the RFU was embroiled in protracted disputes with the English clubs regarding the game's structure and availability of players for international duty. Four years later the machinations continued, but so did the rugby. Less than a week after the IRB edict the first professional international was staged at Ellis Park, in Johannesburg. Ironically, South Africa entertained Wales, a nation now languishing in the lower echelons of the world game after a generation of their most talented players were lost to the financial lure of rugby league. The newly crowned world champions easily won a bad-tempered match 40–11, and in November were welcomed to a revamped 75,000-capacity Twickenham for England's opening match of the 1995–96 season.

Prior to the World Cup, Brian Moore had declared his intention to retire, only to have second thoughts midway through the tournament. Unhappily for him and the English front row, Jack Rowell did not agree with his abrupt rethink and replaced Moore with the Bristol hooker Mark Regan. Rowell also needed to replace his half-back pairing of Dewi Morris and Rob Andrew. Morris, England's best player in South Africa, had decided to bail out at the top, and Andrew had accepted a lucrative contract from Sir John Hall to become the playing rugby development director of National Division Two side Newcastle. Kyran Bracken came back for Morris, and Mike Catt was switched from full-back to his club position of fly-half. Tony Underwood was injured and Jon Callard, Damian Hopley and Andy Robinson were all recalled, the latter after a six-year exile.

Kitch Christie had never tasted defeat as the Springbok coach, and his record was extended to fourteen wins in as many games when two tries from Chester Williams and another by Joost van der Westhuizen secured a 24–14 victory. It was the first time since 1988 that England had lost three consecutive matches, and the ten-point margin could have been far worse: Williams was denied a hat-trick by an error from referee Jim Fleming, and at-the-death replacement Phil de Glanville, on for Will Carling, gave the scoreline a faint air of respectability with his first international touchdown. In the aftermath of a disjointed and ineffective display, Callard and Robinson were permanently jettisoned and Bracken did not start another match for his country until a depleted squad toured Argentina in May 1997. Victor Ubogu was to wait even longer, winning his next cap from the bench against France in March 1999.

Another replacement, flanker Lawrence Dallaglio, made a better impression, and when England faced Western Samoa a month later Dallaglio remained in the side. Rowell also selected his third half-back combination in three games. The Northampton partnership of fly-half Paul Grayson and scrum half Matt Dawson had starred in the Midlands' 40–19 win over the Samoans, and both started their first internationals against the same opposition. Rowell's dalliance with Catt in the number ten jersey was deemed to have failed, and he was returned to full-back. Prop Graham Rowntree replaced Ubogu, and Jason Leonard was given the number three jersey. England again did not play well, but had some satisfaction in ending their three-match losing streak with a 27–9 victory. Grayson kicked five debut penalty goals to take England nine points clear, and second-half tries from Dallaglio and Rory Underwood made the game safe.

There was still no sign of the open fifteen-man game expounded by Rowell, and when England met France, who had recently shared a tough two-match series with New Zealand, in the opening Five Nations fixture on 20 January 1996, they did so as underdogs. Once more changes were made. Blindside Tim Rodber was surprisingly dropped in favour of Steve Ojomoh, and the Bath wing Jon Sleightholme was given a first outing in place of Damian Hopley. Rory Underwood came tantalisingly close to grounding a Mike Cart defence-splitting kick within seconds of the start, but that was as near as either side came to a try. The French, playing at home, were unexpectedly cautious and never looked like turning their supremacy into points. Thierry Lacroix kicked them into a 12–9 lead which Paul Grayson nullified with his second drop goal three minutes from time. At which juncture England could normally have expected French morale to evaporate. However, after their World Cup victory in the so-called meaningless match for third place, France at last believed they could win, and it was their young centre Thomas Castaignede who administered the *coup de grâce* with a drop goal in the final minute. The next day Castaignede celebrated his 21st birthday, while Jack Rowell deliberated a fourth defeat in five matches.

England had not played badly in Paris, but two weeks later, against Wales, who had not beaten anyone of note for a year. England were abysmal and still won 21–15. Tim Rodber had a decent enough game on his return to the back row, but the forwards were outplayed in the line-out and failed to support

each other as a unit. When they were able to distribute reasonable balls, the backs were profligate, none more so than Paul Grayson, who missed five kicks at goal. After falling behind to a Hemi Taylor score, Grayson gave England the lead when he converted Rory Underwood's final international try, and early in the third quarter Jeremy Guscott charged down a weak clearance to move them ahead. Penalties from Grayson extended the lead, but the Welsh played with gusto and their scrum half Robert Howley reduced the arrears with a well-taken try. The press were sharpening their pencils long before the players' apathy spread to the crowd, and the game finished in eerie silence. In one of the more benevolent articles the *Daily Telegraph* apologised to their readers for misleading them in reporting that England had intended to play an open game as per the World Cup.

In time-honoured tradition Jack Rowell, with his coaching assistants Les Cusworth and Mike Slemen, took three steps to alleviate the media censure. For the next match with Scotland he changed the team, threw away the coaching book entitled 'Expansive Rugby for Beginners' and then sent for trouble-shooter Dean Richards, who promptly located the nearest phone box and emerged wearing his tights and cape to save the day. To

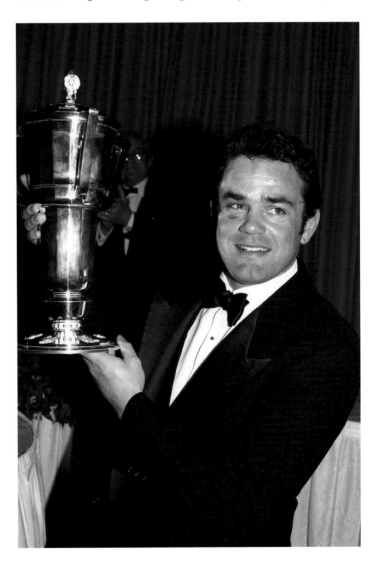

Above Will Carling proudly holds the Five Nations trophy following the 28-15 victory over Ireland at Twickenham, March 1996

accommodate Richards number eight Ben Clarke, again a victim of his own versatility, was switched to flanker and a bewildered Tim Rodber was dropped for the second time in three games. Bristol's Garath Archer made his debut at lock in place of Martin Bayfield, a casualty of the line-out failings.

In stark contrast the Scots, under new captain Rob Wainwright, had played positively in winning all three of their championship matches. For fifteen minutes they overran the French, and needed to beat the Sassenachs at Murrayfield for their first Grand Slam since 1990. For once the onus was on them to attack, but the robust English pack, superbly marshalled by Richards, smothered the play and dominated the game. When Scotland did try to move the ball they were enveloped in white jerseys and never looked capable of breaking the forwards' stranglehold. For their part England made no attempt to build on their authoritative performance, and Paul Grayson kicked the points in an 18–9 win. Pleasing as it was to deny the Scots the Grand Slam in front of their own supporters, the archaic up-the-jumper tactics were never going to appease the press, who placed the victory in the pyrrhic category.

As was the case when Geoff Cooke's team courted such controversy, the manager and his players could not have cared less, and for the meeting with Ireland at Twickenham Rowell named his first unchanged side of the season. Following his decision to step down as captain, Will Carling led England out for the final time, before his emotional farewell was abruptly curtailed by torn ankle ligaments. With Ireland leading 15–12 at half-time Carling's adieu appeared to be going awry on all fronts until the English tightened the game and the forwards took command. Paul Grayson scored six penalties, a third international drop goal and converted a Jon Sleightholme try for

a total of 23 points in a 28–15 victory. Moreover, Wales, who had lost their previous eight Five Nations matches, amazingly beat the French 16–15 to hand England the championship on points difference from Scotland. It was the fourth title of Carling's reign, and 44 of his world-record 59 captaincy appearances were won, with one draw against Scotland. As he limped up the Twickenham steps to collect the match trophy – the Five Nations version was still in Cardiff – the crowd saluted their hero with genuine appreciation and warmth.

Ostensibly England had salvaged their year with the Triple Crown and Jack Rowell's second championship in his two seasons in charge. Yet, in comparison to the sublime rugby being played in the Antipodes, they remained light years adrift, and Rowell's critical remarks on taking up office – he stated, a trifle obviously, that the two tries scored in the 1994 Five Nations were inadequate – returned with interest when his own team managed just three in 1996. Their often hapless performances were exacerbated by a capricious selection policy which saw 24 players used in six matches. The coach clearly had no idea of his best side, and his arbitrary decisions included the exclusion of scrum half Kyran Bracken, second choice in the World Cup to Dewi Morris, and the random selection of Tim Rodber, who was dropped twice without playing badly. In crisis, Rowell also recalled Dean Richards, and his virtuoso display against Scotland and Ireland, allied to a decisive penalty from Welsh fly-half Neil Jenkins against France, were instrumental in the England coach retaining his post. At a meeting in May 1996, the RFU National Playing Committee decided against sacking him on the proviso that the older members of his playing staff were replaced within the next twelve months.

Consequently, the victory over Ireland represented a last hurrah for Rory Underwood and Dean Richards, both of whom were awarded their first caps against the same opposition, Underwood in 1984 and Richards two years later. In thirteen seasons he won 85 caps and scored 49 tries, in addition to a Test-clinching touchdown for the British Isles versus New Zealand in 1993. Richards, the archetypal English forward and back-row lynchpin, made 54 international appearances, 48 wearing the red rose and six for the Lions.

Less than a year had passed since the IRB's historic proclamation, and already the professional revolution had galvanised rugby across the globe. The Super 12 competition was a monumental success: large crowds were treated to audacious, thrilling contests in which tries outweighed penalty goals. Much the same could be said of the inaugural Tri Nations tournament won by New Zealand. In twice beating Australia and South Africa, the All Blacks scored ten tries and amassed 119 points. Their exceptional performances would provide the benchmark by which all sides were judged.

Elsewhere, the advent of professionalism was more problematic. The RFU were in dispute with their club sides who, under the auspices of the newly formed English Professional Rugby Union Clubs, threatened to split from the governing body unless they received a greater share of sponsorship income and some say in the game's organisation. In an extraordinary endorsement of their team's position, England's players boycotted a national training session, and the conflict dragged on for several months until concessions were made, including the RFU's agreement to a twelve-club Division One.

In another power struggle, the RFU split from the Home Unions Committee to negotiate their own Five Nations television deal with BSkyB. The increased revenue was partly required to fund the growing financial demands of the domestic sides, and although the French have always done likewise the Celts took umbrage, accusing the RFU of greed and excluding England from the 1997 competition. Whether such an event would have been tenable without English participation remains uncertain, as the fractious parties were eventually reconciled by the RFU's agreement to pay a large chunk of their independently earned revenue to the other home unions.

In the midst of such chaos, Jack Rowell was somehow expected to finalise his squad for England's first match of the 1996–97 campaign, and also appoint a new captain. Of the prospective candidates Martin Johnson and Lawrence Dallaglio were thought the most likely to succeed Will Carling, with Phil de Glanville, Jason Leonard and Tim Rodber all in the frame. Three weeks before England's 23 November match with Italy, Rowell plumped for his former Bath centre Phil de Glanville. With Carling chosen to partner the captain there was no place in the team for Jeremy Guscott, one of seven changes to the side that had beaten Ireland in March. Five players – Stimpson (Newcastle), Adebayo (Bath), Gomarsall (Wasps), Shaw (Bristol) and Sheasby (Wasps) – and two more from the bench – Greening (Gloucester) and Hardwick (Coventry) – were making their first appearances, and Jason Leonard his 50th. Mike Catt was given a

third chance to establish himself at fly-half, and Tim Rodber was restored to the back row. On top of the myriad personnel changes, England's preparations had to incorporate several modifications to the game's laws. The erstwhile illegal practice of lifting in the line-out was now permitted, practically to guarantee possession on each team's own throw, and flankers were required to remain bound to the scrum until the ball had emerged. In another innovation, tactical substitutions, as opposed to injury replacements, were allowed for the first time.

Against Italy the revised legislation was not overly relevant. England won an astounding quantity of set-piece balls and the match, 54–21. At one stage they led by 35 points until the Italians punished a sloppy passage of play with three converted tries. Wasps pair Andy Gomarsall and Chris Sheasby scored debut tries, Gomarsall two, and considering the new faces the victory was promising.

Above Jason Leonard's one and only appearance as England captain, 14 December 1996. Argentina were beaten 20–18

history and left the world-renowned Jeremy Guscott to cool his heels on the sidelines. For England's next fixture, against Argentina on 14 December, Rowell tried to atone by selecting Guscott on the wing in place of his injured Bath clubmate Adedayo Adebayo. Ultimately the switch was unnecessary as de Glanville also picked up a late knock and Guscott moved inside to partner Will Carling for the final time. After his Jonah Lomu nightmare and a knee operation, Tony Underwood was considered sufficiently rehabilitated to step back into the fray, and the Northampton full-back Nick Beal replaced concussion victim Tim Stimpson.

Argentina had not beaten a side of any repute since their series victory over the Scots in June 1994. In the summer France had won a two-match rubber in Buenos Aires, and five months later South Africa had scored 90 points in the process of doing the same. Their record did not indicate they would greatly inconvenience England, but in an appalling game the home side were woeful. Mike Catt gave the sort of performance that could have ended a lesser player's career, and without a cogent fly-half England stumbled into a succession of blind alleys. Their play lacked shape or direction, and the Pumas were on the verge of a famous victory when acting skipper Jason Leonard scored an invaluable first international try six minutes from time. To his critics the 20–18 victory was barely pertinent, and the animated conjecture surrounding Rowell's future greatly increased.

He did little to placate it before England's 1997 championship curtain-raiser with Scotland, again replacing the esteemed Guscott with captain Phil de Glanville. Tim Stimpson and Paul Grayson also returned, for Nick Beal and Mike Catt respectively, and Saracens wing forward Richard Hill won his first cap on the open side. Chris Sheasby was omitted, and Tim Rodber moved to the middle of the back row. England had failed to cross the Scottish goal line since Tony Underwood's try in 1993, and the three intervening matches were won with eighteen penalties and a Rob Andrew drop goal. After a quarter of an hour New Zealand referee Paddy O'Brien ended the drought when he awarded England a questionable penalty try for, in his view and despite Scottish remonstrations, persistent transgression. Their riposte, a Ronnie Eriksson touchdown nine minutes later, closed the gap to three points, but Paul Grayson landed five penalty goals, and midway through the final quarter England led 22–3. Throughout the match they had played well intermittently, producing fleeting glimpses of an integrated game without ever reaching top gear. Until, that is, Martin Johnson created a try for Andy Gomarsall and the Scottish defences suddenly came crashing down. Will Carling immediately added another, his first in eleven appearances against Scotland, and Paul Grayson complemented his excellent place-kicking and 21 points by putting de Glanville away for the fourth. The 41–13 defeat was the heaviest the Scots had suffered against any of the Five Nation teams, and for the eighth successive occasion they had lost to England, a record between the two countries.

In Dublin, a fortnight later, the English were even more assured, and the best you could say about Ireland was that they

The following week the same inexperienced team met the New Zealand Barbarians. Peculiarly, the RFU did not see fit to award caps against essentially a full-strength Kiwi side, a decision rued by wing Jon Sleightholme and full-back Tim Stimpson, both of whom scored tries to take England six points ahead. Any chance of an improbable scalp disappeared on the hour when New Zealand benched their star fly-half Andrew Mehrtens; his replacement, the uncapped Carlos Spencer, scored thirteen points in a 34–9 Barbarians win.

In naming Phil de Glanville as captain, Jack Rowell had split the longest-serving centre three-quarters coupling in the game's were unlucky with injuries. Their two Erics, number eight Miller and fly-half Elwood, limped off either side of a Jon Sleightholme try, and at the interval the score was 11–6 in England's favour. Not an insurmountable deficit, but the Irish were tiring in the face of the forwards' onslaught, and when Andy Gomarsall scored his fourth international try in the 63rd minute the wheels fell off. In a final eight-minute salvo England recorded four more tries: two for Underwood, his first since the 1995 World Cup quarter-final, another for Sleightholme and one for Richard Hill. Substitute Austin Healy constructed Hill's score, and a second replacement, Jeremy Guscott, also made an immediate impact, creating mayhem in the slipshod Irish defence and contributing to both of Underwood's tries. The 46–6 victory was the largest in Five Nations annals, and England became the first team to score 40 points in consecutive championship matches.

The result was greeted with elation and relief in equal measure. Finally, Jack Rowell's talented players had delivered the type of sustained fifteen-man game perpetually discussed but seldom witnessed. Although there were still more than a few quibbles regarding the treatment of Guscott, given Will Carling's form and the record-breaking wins over Scotland and Ireland, it was difficult to fault Rowell for selecting the same team against France. Particularly after the first hour when England, in one of the finest passages of play since South Africa were overwhelmed in 1994, surged into a 20–6 lead. Lawrence Dallaglio charged over the line following a blistering 35-metre run, and Paul Grayson kicked four penalties and a drop goal. At times they were truly compelling, and even a carelessly conceded try in the fourth quarter – Christophe Lamaison's chip turned the defence and Tony Underwood's sluggish reaction allowed wing Laurent Leflamand to score in the corner – appeared to represent no more than a temporary setback. In the days of Brian Moore and Mick Skinner, England would have shrugged off the try as a solitary example of romantic French counter-attacking instinct. Lamentably, the current side, nine of which had never beaten the Tricolores, panicked. When it became imperative to relieve the growing pressure, several touch-kicks went astray and the game screamed out for one of the seasoned campaigners to kill the tempo. None were able to, and ten minutes from time Lamaison waltzed through the confused English ranks for a second French try. With the scores level there was only going to be one winner, and tormentor-in-chief Lamaison added a second penalty goal to his try, drop goal and two conversions to win the game 23–20.

It was the first time England had surrendered a fourteen-point lead in 126 years and 475 Test matches, and the inevitable post-match recriminations principally concentrated on their inability to defend an apparently unassailable position. With the ship floundering, Jack Rowell's dereliction in utilising his substitutes was also emphasised, and the first hour's brilliance was primarily ignored. Such were the fine margins by which sporting success or failure was now judged. To other, more discerning commentators the result did not detract from the encouraging aspects of the

Below Lawrence Dallagio surges fot the line to score a Five Nations try against France at Twickenham, March 1997. France, though, won the game 23–20

Thomas, Scott Gibbs and top try-scorer Ieuan Evans were among those missing, and six minutes into the match emergency full-back Neil Jenkins withdrew with a fractured arm. Even so, it took England 48 minutes and the half-time intervention of the mercurial Jeremy Guscott to impose their game. Guscott's poise conjured tries for Tim Stimpson and Richard Hill, and in between a Tony Underwood break left a mass of red shirts sprawling in his wake. Phil de Glanville completed the rout after a beguiling solo run from Catt. Leicester's prop Darren Garforth came on for a first cap, and, as in the corresponding fixture of 1996, Robert Howley scored a consolation try for Wales.

The 34–13 victory was England's largest at the Arms Park in what was the last international at the temple of Welsh rugby. Following the Swalec Cup final the ground was to be demolished and a new stadium erected to host the 1999 World Cup. The Arms Park had staged its first game on 12 April 1884, the home side beating Ireland by two tries and a drop goal to nil, and of the major Test match venues only Lansdowne Road was older. To the legion of Welsh disciples it was a spiritual home, and even to many neutrals its destruction was hard to comprehend.

In the Five Nations, England had finished runners-up to France, who beat Scotland 47–20 to win their first Grand Slam for a decade. The indifferent twenty minutes against the French were costly, but the players could take great solace from their fabulous performances and from the fact that they scored fifteen tries and more points – 141 – than any country in championship history (since surpassed on numerous occasions). They had also won a third successive Triple Crown, and when the British Lions party to South Africa was named, eighteen Englishmen were included. Lock Martin Johnson would captain the tourists, while the England helm Phil de Glanville, ignored by the Lions selectors, had the consolation of captaining a much-weakened squad to Argentina for a two-match series.

Before either side's departure, Tim Rodber – first-choice skipper Lawrence Dallaglio was still recovering from a virus – led an England team to Hong Kong to defend the World Cup sevens title won four years previously at Murrayfield. The then captain Andrew Harriman was now manager, Les Cusworth was again coach, and all but Dave Scully of the ten-man squad had been capped at senior level. With the tournament commencing less than a week after the meeting with Wales, there was little time to prepare adequately, and accordingly England did not do themselves justice. They compiled four routine victories over weak opposition – Canada (twice), Zimbabwe and the Cook Islands – before being eliminated by Western Samoa in the quarter-finals. In the final, sevens maestros Fiji, playing the version of the game closest to their hearts, beat South Africa 24–21. There were fears that with the English colony shortly to be restored to Chinese sovereignty the annual Hong Kong sevens contest could be threatened. The opposite was in fact the case. A new sponsor was found for the 1998 competition, and Fiji collected £75,000 by defeating the Samoans. Pointedly, none of the home unions entered teams.

Nine of the ten sevens party were involved in international duty that summer. Five headed to South Africa with the British Isles, and four – Adedayo Adebayo, Mike Catt, Chris Sheasby

performance, nor from the dramatic progress made by Rowell's players, the majority of whom merited, and were afforded, a chance to redeem themselves against Wales. Only scrum half Andy Gomarsall was dropped, for Austin Healy, though Paul Grayson and Lawrence Dallaglio also missed out. Mike Catt took over at fly-half, and Ben Clarke on the blindside. Rob Andrew was recalled to the squad after two years, predominantly as cover for Catt's kicking foot, and he and Will Carling fittingly made their final international appearances together. In coming on for the last few minutes, Andrew won his 71st England cap, one less than former captain Carling. Andrew scored a record 396 points (later surpassed by Wilkinson), and each made a colossal contribution to the national cause. Jonathan Davies was also making his farewell in a Welsh side ravaged by injuries. Arwel

and Jon Sleightholme – joined the 30-strong Argentina-bound England side. Sixteen of the squad were uncapped, and a further seven had played five or fewer matches.

Some observers though that given the limited resources available and the increasing potency of the emerging nations, there might come a time when the wisdom of undertaking such trips was called into question. Those in favour argued that the experience was essential for the development of young players. But whatever their own views, Jack Rowell and his coaching retinue had to fashion a competitive team in time for the opening Test on 30 May.

Of the fifteen that had narrowly defeated Argentina in December 1996, only Sleightholme and Catt remained, while the Pumas had twelve of the players who started that match. Six of the side were new to the top flight, and Nigel Redman returned after a three-year hiatus. Ben Clarke, out of favour until Lawrence Dallaglio cried off in Cardiff, retained his back-row berth, and scrum half Kyran Bracken was recalled. During a first half in which the lead was exchanged five times, Wasps centre Nick Greenstock and Saracens flanker Tony Diprose scored debut tries and England went into the break four points to the good. Hooker Phil Greening was forced to retire after 25 minutes with concussion, allowing Richard Cockerill to become the third of Leicester's front-row trinity – after Graham Rowntree and Darren Garforth – to be capped. In the second period wing Adebayo opened his international account with two tries, and Ben Clarke and Mike Catt added two more. Back in December Catt had given his worst display in an England shirt, but he responded against the same opposition with one of his best. He struck five of six conversions, two penalty goals and recorded a try of the highest order, catching his own chip beyond the Pumas' full-back, Jurado, and racing clear from 50 metres to touch down under the posts. For a makeshift outfit England had performed valiantly, and the 46–20 victory was one of the most memorable of Jack Rowell's stewardship.

The result had not gone unnoticed in South Africa, and when several of the British Isles team returned home with injuries Mike Catt and Nigel Redman answered the call. The pair had played under Rowell at Bath, and while the England manager would have been delighted with their Lions recognition their absence posed further selection headaches. Gloucester's Mark Mapletoft replaced Catt at fly-half, and Coventry lock Danny Grewcock was drafted in for Redman. Both were making their debuts, and the team that lined up for the final Test had a collective aggregate of 88 caps, 32 of them won by Ben Clarke; with Cockerill retained as hooker, the remaining pack members totalled seven appearances. Pitted against the mighty Argentine forwards England battled to remain in contention, and had just about held on until full-back Jim Mallinder and Adebayo made a hash of a dummy-scissors and Soler ran through for the opening try. His score sounded the English death knell, and in the second half the Pumas ran in three more tries. Substitute Alex King, Rowell's 21st new cap in eight matches, pulled one back, and in the final throes Grewcock completed the scoring in a 33–13 defeat. A basically worthwhile series was shared, and two more of England's players, Kyran Bracken and Tony Diprose, found themselves heading to South Africa for Lions duty.

Three-times England captain and tour manager Fran Cotton had played all four Tests in the unbeaten 1974 series, as had Scottish coach Ian McGeechan, now on his fifth Lions foray, three as coach. Compatriot Jim Telfer assisted McGeechan, and kicking guru Dave Alred, Rob Andrew's one-time informal mentor, was also included to work with, among others, Neil Jenkins. English lock Martin Johnson captained a squad containing a strong rugby league contingent. John Bentley had played union for England in 1988, and four years later league for Great Britain, and prodigal Welsh son Scott Gibbs, star of the 1993 Lions, returned to his roots after switching codes in 1994.

To foreign eyes British and Irish rugby was considered sterile and unenlightened, and the tourists were not given a prayer against the world champions. Perceptions started to change slightly when they began to dismantle South Africa's most feared provincial sides. Playing a creative game based on powerful mobile forwards supporting each other at every phase, the Lions won nine of ten regional games. So intense was the competition for places during these preliminary matches that the majority of the fifteen selected for the first Test in Cape Town had not

Below An Englishman abroad – a composed Jack Rowell during the Summer tour to Argentina

Above Lawrence Dallaglio scores a try for England as France's Phillipe Carbonneau attempts a tackle

previously played together. Scott Gibbs and Jeremy Guscott rekindled their 1993 centre three-quarters union, and Ieuan Evans and Alan Tait were named on opposing wings. With Robert Howley missing as one of six forced to return home through injury, the scrum half vacancy was filled by Matt Dawson. Neil Jenkins wore the number fifteen jersey, and fly-half Gregor Townsend completed a mouthwatering back division. Of the pack, England supplied a back row of Lawrence Dallaglio, Richard Hill and Tim Rodber, as well as lock Martin Johnson. Ireland provided his partner, Jeremy Davidson, hooker Keith Wood and tighthead Paul Wallace. Scotland's Tom Smith was given the loosehead berth in preference to Graham Rowntree.

The home side began the series in confident mood, taking the game to the visitors and scoring the first try after 21 minutes. Gary Teichmann created a second for half-time replacement Russell Bennett, but the Lions weathered the storm and on the hour Neil Jenkins kicked them to within one point with his fifth penalty. In the final quarter the visitors grew in stature and ambition, and seven minutes from time the Springboks' profligacy was punished. From the base of the scrum Matt Dawson

scampered away on the blindside, selling three bemused South Africans an outrageous dummy and strolling home unmolested. The shattered Boks were dead in the water, and minutes later, following a penetrating burst from Scott Gibbs, the quick hands of Dawson, Tim Rodber and Jenkins enabled Alan Tait to complete a stirring 25–16 victory. The one sour note was an injury to Ieuan Evans, which ended his tour and a run of seven consecutive Lions Tests. The Welsh wing was replaced by John Bentley for the next game in Durban.

South Africa started the second Test in identical manner to the first, only on this occasion they maintained their momentum to dominate almost the entire match. They outscored the Lions by three tries to nil and would have won but for a failure to capitalise on even a fraction of their enormous territorial advantage. Crucially, three different players missed all six of their kicks at goal, while the Lions' Neil Jenkins despatched five penalties from as many attempts. At the interval the tourists led

6–5 before enduring the worst possible start to the third quarter. Alan Tait's misplaced one-handed pass gifted Percy Montgomery a try, and fourteen minutes later Andre Joubert brushed aside a weak challenge from Bentley to increase their advantage. Trailing 15–9, the Lions redoubled their efforts and Jenkins kept his nerve to kick them level. Sensing victory, they surged forward. Gregor Townsend was stopped short of the South African line, Dawson recycled and Guscott with great aplomb dropped the winning goal. The Springboks were undone, and despite their furious assaults in a thrilling finale, the Lions stood firm. They were only the third touring side to win a series on South African soil, following their predecessors in 1974 and New Zealand in 1996.

For the final Test Celts Tait, Townsend and Wood, all casualties of a debilitating tour, were replaced by three Englishmen making their first Lions appearances: Tony Underwood, Mike Catt and Mark Regan. In the one tactical switch of the series Neil Back ousted Richard Hill, and on the day of the match Rob Wainwright deputised for flu victim Rodber. Attempting to avoid the indignity of a first home whitewash, the Springboks had more to play for than the Lions, who had already achieved all they set out to. Even so, their weary and emotionally drained players actually constructed some of their best moves of the rubber, but in opening the game they left daylight for the South Africans to exploit. Montgomery scored on the overlap, and scrum half Joost van der Westhuizen, after Guscott's departure with a broken arm, went on one of his distinctive mazy runs for the second. Not to be outdone, the Lions' number nine Dawson wriggled over, and with less than fifteen minutes remaining they trailed by the value of a converted try. On the day, that was probably about the only difference between the two sides, rather than the nineteen points the Boks eventually won by. Two late tries may have gone some way towards sparing their blushes, but they in no way tarnished the tourists' accomplishments.

In Argentina, Jack Rowell's reserves played just about well enough to vindicate the decision to organise concurrent England and British Isles tours. There was no such justification, though, in arranging an international against Australia within a week of a Lions Test. In less than nine months Mike Catt had completed a full English season, visited Hong Kong for the World Cup Sevens and played Test matches in Argentina, South Africa and Australia. This was being professional in financial terms only; it was simply impossible for players repeatedly to give of their best on that type of schedule. Twelve of the team that took the field against the Wallabies had spent the previous six weeks on one of the most arduous tours imaginable. No other country in the world would have allowed their national side to compete on such an unequal footing, and the Australians were no doubt rubbing their hands in glee when the sacrificial English lambs touched down from South Africa. They arrived just three days before kick-off, and were unsurprisingly slaughtered 25–6. It was the first match in which the two nations contested the newly conceived biannual Cook Trophy, and also the last game of the Jack Rowell regime.

During the summer months widespread substantiated rumours suggested that the RFU were seeking to replace Rowell as coach. His hitherto part-time post had been upgraded, and Graham Henry of Auckland and the successful Lions assistant Ian McGeechan were approached with a view to becoming England's first full-time professional coach. Captain of industry Rowell had never been able to devote himself slavishly to the cause, and the additional demands of the job were certainly a factor in his mid-August resignation. In three years Rowell had steered England to the Grand Slam, two championships, three Triple Crowns and the

Below England practise lineouts during training at Twickenham in 1997

World Cup semi-final; 21 out of 29 matches were won, including two victories in six fixtures against the top southern hemisphere sides. In the debit column they lost three times to France, home and away against South Africa and conclusively to New Zealand. Aided by some admittedly abstract team selections, the media often portrayed Rowell as a man who did not know his own mind. However, his persona belied a keen intellect and his superlative record at Bath was testimony to an almost unrivalled knowledge of the game. In his final season England had approached the high standards Rowell expected, and who knows whether his good intentions would have materialised given time. He certainly deserved better than the unseemly courting of his replacement while still in office.

As previous incumbents Geoff Cooke and Rowell could testify, the England coaching position was now as strenuous as its soccer equivalent. Since the 1991 World Cup the number of column inches devoted to rugby had increased tenfold, and Rowell's successor knew he would be operating in a goldfish bowl. Nevertheless, when asked, the recently appointed Bath coach Clive Woodward agreed to take up the poisoned chalice. His credentials were good, and he enjoyed the added advantage of having experienced international rugby as a player. The former Leicester centre was capped 21 times by England between 1980 and 1984, scoring four tries, and twice by the British Isles on the 1980 tour of South Africa.

Though the term 'baptism of fire' has been with us for centuries, it could easily have been penned for Woodward, who had barely a month to prepare a squad for the opening matches of the 1997–98 season with Australia, New Zealand, South Africa and New Zealand again. Against Australia he replaced current captain Phil de Glanville with the popular Wasps skipper Lawrence Dallaglio. De Glanville retained his place at centre – Jeremy Guscott's damaged arm ruled him out until Christmas – and Woodward introduced five new caps: full-back Matt Perry, wing David Rees, centre Will Greenwood, hooker Andy Long and prop Will Green. Mike Catt was selected at his club position of fly-half, a practice roundly condemned when instigated by Jack Rowell back in 1995. The new players bedded in quickly, and England played well in patches to draw a fitful match 15–15. Catt kicked five penalty goals, Australia scored two tries and both sides had chances to win. Adedayo Adebayo was checked inches short, and Steve Larkham took Catt out when the fly-half was favourite to gather his chip and score. The cynical professional foul was an unsavoury by-product of the contemporary game, and it was gratifying to see Catt exact retribution by brushing himself off and converting the match-saving penalty.

A week later England faced the formidable All Blacks. In August, New Zealand had completed their second clean sweep of the Tri-Nations competition and were unbeaten since losing a

Below England's Mike Catt celebrates scoring a try with Austin Healey and Neil Back in the Five Nations Championship against Ireland in 1998

'dead' match, of a victorious series, to the Springboks in 1996. For the first union international staged at Old Trafford Woodward made two changes to his front row: Richard Cockerill for hooker Long, and Darren Garforth for Green at tight-head. Psyched up by the incredible atmosphere generated by a full house in a compact stadium, Cockerill made a controversial impact by refusing to stand down to Norm Hewitt during the haka. He was later accused of not respecting a New Zealand tradition, but as every All Black knows this customary pre-match ritual is designed to intimidate opponents and definitely provides a tangible psychological edge. Cockerill's statement of intent had the desired effect. England defended gallantly against ceaseless pressure, and the 25–8 defeat contained more positives than the score might indicate.

Martin Johnson was cited for punching New Zealand captain Justin Marshall, and Clive Woodward suspended the Leicester lock for the impending Twickenham clash with world champions South Africa. The Springboks were in the middle of a European tour and Johnson was one of five changes made against a team that had beaten Italy and France twice. The Boks had won the second of these matches 52–10 at the Parc des Princes, scoring seven tries, four by their wing Pieter Rossouw to emulate Chester Williams' World Cup feat and the South African record. Undaunted, Woodward's men took an 11–0 lead with a couple of Mike Catt penalties and a try from Nick Greenstock. If England had managed to preserve their advantage until the interval, the outcome might have been different. Disastrously, fate decreed otherwise, and seconds before the whistle they suffered a triple blow. Prop Adrian Garvey bulldozed over for the first South African try, Mike Catt was stretchered off with a head injury sustained while attempting to defend the score and Henry Honiball converted with the last kick of the half. Instead of changing ends eleven points to the good, England led by an insufficient four, and in the second half the Springboks crafted three more tries. The final score of 29–11 was put into perspective the next weekend when the South Africans moved north and thumped Scotland 68–10.

If not for the huge scorelines, anyone taking a cursory glance at New Zealand's 1997 tour results could easily have been forgiven for momentarily confusing their sports. Ireland were beaten 63–15 at Lansdowne Road, where the Republic also play their football internationals, England 25–8 at Manchester United's 'theatre of dreams' and Wales 42–7 at Wembley Stadium. Another victory over England and the All Blacks would return to the Land of the Long White Cloud with a one hundred per cent record. Martin Johnson was restored to the second row after his slapped wrist, and Austin Healy, a replacement in the previous four outings, was given his first start under Woodward. Having missed out against South Africa, Phil de Glanville replaced Nick Greenstock at centre. Kyran Bracken did likewise for Matt Dawson at scrum half, and Paul Grayson, substitute for the prostrate Catt in the same game, remained at fly-half.

In the 1995 World Cup semi-final England had been annihilated by New Zealand's Jonah Lomu-inspired onslaught, and their second encounter of 1997 began identically, only this time the roles were reversed and it was the All Blacks who failed to withstand the English tempest. David Rees caught a steepling Andrew Mehrtens clearance and from his own half ran at the New Zealand back line, lobbing their defensive cover and collecting a favourable bounce to bravely ground the ball by the corner flag. It was a superb individual try, and within minutes England contrived an equally impressive team effort. Grayson and Healy combined to free Will Greenwood, and his brilliant swerving run presented Richard Hill with the easiest of scores. Seventh heaven for the ecstatic Twickenham faithful, and then, still in the first quarter, skipper Dallaglio capitalised on a New Zealand blunder to beat Lomu and Justin Marshall in a race to the posts. Grayson converted, after narrowly missing two attempts from the touchline, and England changed ends leading by fourteen points.

Three penalties from the dependable Mehrtens had kept the All Blacks in touch, and when he converted his own try at the start of the second half they ominously closed to within seven. Mehrtens added another penalty, and his two extra points, following a Walter Little touchdown, looked to have turned the match irreparably in the tourists' favour. England thought otherwise, and countered with all guns blazing. Three times they were held up on their opponents' goal line until eventually New Zealand buckled and conceded a penalty. With everyone else's nerve ends jangling, Paul Grayson, calmness personified, stepped up and drove his kick unerringly between the posts. An enthralling contest finished with honours even at 26–26.

Below Mike Catt can't shrug off Ireland's Denis Hickie but England went on to record a 35–17 victory in April 1998

In the midst of a transitional period England had competed creditably against the very best sides, and coach Woodward had rapidly prepared a strong foundation on which to launch his first Five Nations challenge in the new year. Six months before hosting the football World Cup final, the recently completed Stade de France was the magnificent setting for Woodward's opening sortie. He made three changes to the side held by the All Blacks, restoring the recuperated Catt at full-back, Guscott at centre and Mark Regan in the middle of the front row. Given the two teams' comparative displays against New Zealand, France were not considered likely to trouble unduly a confident and, in light of the result, perhaps complacent England. Dallaglio's men performed well below expectation, and after two French tries in the first twenty minutes were ultimately relieved to lose only 24–17. Clive Woodward's fifth match without a win was also England's seventh, their longest barren spell since 1972.

Predictably, Wales made every effort to extend the run at Twickenham, and after almost half an hour and two Allan Bateman tries the omens for a home victory looked anything but promising. However, a second international score for David Rees and a pushover try by Neil Back re-established the equilibrium, and for the rest of the match England, their game etched with class, proceeded to rip Wales asunder. Six tries followed, and Matt Dawson's, dropping his shoulder and running home a tap-penalty from 50 metres, was the best of a very good bunch. England's 60 points, in a 60–26 victory, were the most scored in a championship fixture and equalled the tally achieved against Japan in 1987 and Canada in 1994. On his 50th appearance, Jeremy Guscott extended his enviable record of never having lost a Five Nations game at Twickenham to thirteen matches.

A fifth successive win against Wales was followed, almost as handsomely, by a ninth over Scotland. The obdurate Scottish defence held out for longer than their Celtic cousins, but a penalty try broke their spirit and after 80 minutes England led 34–6. Although converted injury-time touchdowns from Tony Stanger and Shaun Longstaff reduced the arrears by fourteen points, England still won 34–20. Matt Dawson and Austin Healy both scored tries, and Paul Grayson claimed his own unique historical niche by becoming the first English player to record a try, a penalty goal, a conversion and a drop goal in a single championship game.

Having registered a further fifteen points against Ireland at Twickenham, Grayson came within a hair's breadth of breaking another Five Nations record: he completed the season with 66 points, one less than Jon Webb in 1992. England, though, did tread new ground. By beating the Irish 35–17 they won a fourth successive Triple Crown, a feat equalled only by Wales in 1979, and their 146 points, two more than the French accrued while completing a second Grand Slam in two years, were the most scored since the competition's hazy inception. Mike Catt, playing his first game on the wing, and Matt Perry were the beneficiaries of some sparkling midfield interchanges between the half-backs

Right Clive Woodward feels the heat as a drastically under-strength England have a tough time of it on the Summer 1998 tour to the southern hemisphere. Almost 200 points were conceded in just four tests

Will Greenwood and Jeremy Guscott, and the destructive forays of Neil Back created scores for Richard Cockerill and former captain Phil de Glanville. For the final two minutes England introduced the eighteen-year-old Newcastle back Jonny Wilkinson, their youngest international since the Harlequins fly-half Henri Laird made his debut against Wales in 1927.

In playing terms, new coach Clive Woodward enjoyed a fair season, but off the field England's ambitions were undermined by the disingenuous conflict that resurfaced between the clubs and the RFU. The discord concerning the game's structure and development raged unabated until the mutually acceptable Mayfair Agreement was unveiled in May 1998. The Premiership was to be increased to fourteen teams, and in return clubs agreed to undertake domestic fixtures on international weekends. While the deal produced a cessation in hostilities, a mass withdrawal of senior players had already wrecked England's summer tour of the southern hemisphere.

Teams were accused of refusing to release their assets, and while some were certainly more willing to do so than others until the Mayfair compromise, and a clarification of the relegation and European situation, so much uncertainty existed that most chairmen adopted a points-on-the-board policy. They declined to rest players and consequently several picked up serious injuries. Kyran Bracken, Mike Catt, Lawrence Dallaglio, Will Greenwood, Richard Hill, Martin Johnson, David Rees, Tim Rodber and Tony Underwood were all *hors de combat*. Paul Grayson was excused to attend the birth of his first child, and Jeremy Guscott, Jason Leonard and Phil de Glanville opted to rest after an exhausting season.

Attempting to play the best nations in world rugby with so many first-team players unavailable was tantamount to sporting suicide, and England duly suffered, in four matches, their three

heaviest defeats of all time, losing 76–0 to Australia, 64–22 and 40–10 to the All Blacks and finally 18–0 to South Africa. The humiliating reverse in Brisbane was the worst between senior member nations of the International Board, and four Australian supporters, completing press-ups for every point their team scored, were so tired by the end that they began performing sit-ups instead!

Some players did emerge with credit. Matt Dawson scored two good tries and led the side as well as could be expected, and hooker Richard Cockerill greatly improved his international prospects. The versatile full-back Matt Perry and Leicester wing Austin Healy also impressed, but as a whole the trip was an unmitigated disaster derided by all and sundry. The chairman of the Australian Union, Dick McGruther, rather appallingly described the tour party as 'the biggest English sell-out since Gallipoli', and the only slightly more restrained South African coach, Nick Mallett, insisted that given better playing conditions than a waterlogged Newlands pitch his side would have won by 50 points. It was cheering to see Clive Woodward remind Mallett that the teams would meet again in a few months, and that England would have a very different fifteen available.

With Lawrence Dallaglio recovering from a twisted knee, lock Martin Johnson was chosen to captain England for the World Cup qualifying matches against Holland and Italy at Huddersfield Town's McAlpine Stadium. In beating the Dutch 110–0 England made a mockery of the decision to increase the number of teams participating in the 1999 tournament from sixteen to twenty. Neil Back and Jeremy Guscott each scored four times, Back generously eschewing an England record-equalling fifth to provide NEC Harlequins wing Dan Luger with a debut try. Paul Grayson landed fifteen of sixteen conversions to tie Rob Andrew's record of 30 points in a game. Grayson and Luger were on the mark again a week later in a less than convincing 23–15 win against a deeply committed Italian team intent on inflicting the utmost discomfort. Luger and Will Greenwood both scored tries, but England had to look to the boot of Grayson for victory. The Northampton fly-half passed 250 career points with three penalty goals and two conversions.

Assured of World Cup qualification, as were the Italians by virtue of their 67–7 win over Holland, Clive Woodward began fine-tuning his side for the penultimate match of 1998 against Australia. In the pack Ben Clarke and the Leicester number eight Martin Corry made way for Lawrence Dallaglio and Richard Hill, while Tim Rodber was switched to the second row in his first start under Woodward. Another long-term absentee, Tony Underwood, returned to win his first cap since the 1997 defeat of Wales in Cardiff and Phil de Glanville replaced the injured Greenwood.

A stirring display by the unbowed forwards and Rodber's impressive conversion to lock were by and large the only positive features of an eminently forgettable contest. A propensity to drop the ball in promising situations allied to a lack of creativity in the final third dashed England's chances of beating an equally uninspired Australian side. Jeremy Guscott scored the game's solitary try, only for Mike Catt, a replacement for the injured

Grayson, to scuff the conversion that would have taken England four points clear. Instead, the Australian captain John Eales kicked his fourth penalty and Woodward's charges slumped to a 12–11 defeat.

Paul Grayson was still unavailable for the following week's meeting with South Africa, joining Matt Perry, Will Greenwood and Kyran Bracken on England's casualty list. Nick Beal deputised for full-back Perry, Catt continued at fly-half and Dan Luger supplanted Austin Healy on the left wing. Woodward named en bloc the pack beaten by Australia, seven of whom had appeared in the 26–26 draw with New Zealand a year earlier.

South Africa had won seventeen consecutive matches to equal the world record set by Brian Lochore's insuperable All Blacks side of the 1960s. Their triumphant procession included a clean

Right An armour-plated Lawrence Dallaglio gets down to the nitty gritty of training at Roehampton, November 1998

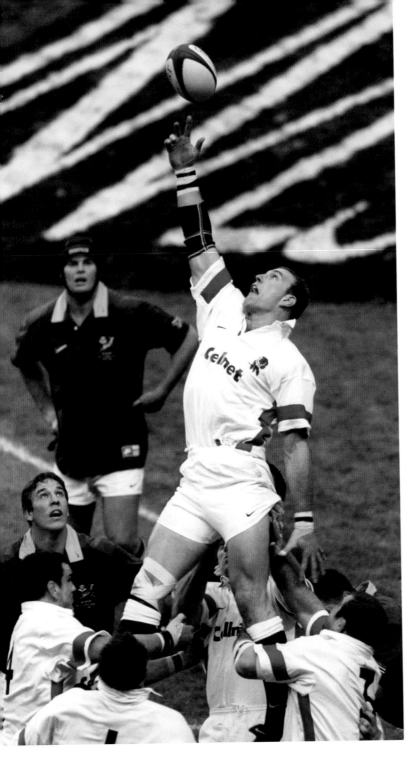

Left The influential Dallaglio leads his country to a remarkable 13–7 victory over the Springboks at Twickenham in December 1998, a result that prevented the South Africans from breaking the world record of five consecutive test wins

absence of Grayson, converted Guscott's 25th international try before driving England 13–7 ahead with two second-half penalties. As the minutes ticked away, the Springboks strove frantically to preserve their dreams of a record-breaking win. Their full-back Montgomery bungled a gimme in front of the posts, and Luger, making another enormous contribution in his third appearance, thwarted a South African counter-attack heading inexorably for the line. In an almost superhuman effort, particularly by the forwards, England clung on for one of the greatest-ever Twickenham victories.

Having beaten the world champions, England approached the last Five Nations championship in ebullient mood – Italy were to make a deserved entrance to the competition in 2000 – and with an immaculate sense of timing one of the oldest sporting showpieces reserved its greatest drama for its final act. On the opening weekend Scotland and France recorded wins, and a fortnight later England kick-started their campaign with a 24–21 victory over the Scots at Twickenham. In an otherwise unchanged team, the Newcastle fly-half Jonny Wilkinson was selected at centre and David Rees replaced Tony Underwood on the wing. Tries from Tim Rodber and Dan Luger established a fourteen-point cushion before some uncharacteristic defensive lapses allowed Scotland to make sizeable inroads. Nick Beal, alive to a typical dart from the scrum by Matt Dawson, restored England's advantage, but thereafter Mike Catt dropped the ball in Gregor Townsend's lap and the Scottish fly-half strolled away unopposed to level the try-count. Kenny Logan and Wilkinson converted all six scores, and ultimately only a penalty goal from Wilkinson divided the sides. Having crafted three tries against a team that had conceded just one in four pre-Christmas internationals, Scotland stole the post-match plaudits and England had to settle for the minor consolation of a tenth consecutive victory over the Celts.

After faint praise had all but damned England at Twickenham, press reaction to their hard-earned 27–15 win at Lansdowne Road was more even-handed. Paul Grayson and Kyran Bracken renewed their half-back collaboration, and Matt Perry returned for Nick Beal at full-back. Blindside Lawrence Dallaglio and number eight Richard Hill exchanged positions in the pack, and the previously well-regarded Irish eight waned before the English forwards' remorseless advance. Their first try, an exemplary contemporary move between forward and back divisions, took from conception to climax all of nineteen seconds to execute. Tim Rodber safely gathered line-out possession and he and Martin Johnson drove onwards, committing the Irish midfield. Bracken added width, and from his quick ball Wilkinson's miss-pass created space for Perry to step inside and score. A drop goal by Grayson, fourteen points from the phenomenally mature Wilkinson and a second championship try of the season for Rodber rounded off a satisfactory afternoon's work for Woodward's side.

In Paris, meanwhile, Wales were destroying French dreams of a third successive Grand Slam in a seven-try thriller at the Stade

sweep of the third Tri Nations competition and a crushing 96–13 victory over Wales, to surpass Australia's 76–0 win against England as the largest victory between senior International Board countries. Their tour of Britain and Ireland had already yielded Test match wins over three of the home unions, and coach Nick Mallett, the same man who had rubbished Woodward's reserves during their horrendous summer tour, brought his team to Twickenham in search of an eighteenth win and rugby immortality.

England, without a major southern hemisphere conquest in twelve matches, replied to an early Pieter Rossouw try and Percy Montgomery conversion with an intelligently worked score direct from the training ground. Dan Luger, rising smartly to out-leap Terblanche, made a stunning catch of Mike Catt's adroit crossfield kick and slipped a pass for Guscott to ghost home on the outside. Matt Dawson, handed the kicking chores in the de France. Six years after frustrating an England team seeking the same prize, their unflappable fly-half Neil Jenkins kicked Wales into a late one-point lead despite a hat-trick from French wing Emile Ntamack. An injury-time penalty looked to have handed France a possible reprieve, but Thomas Castaignede's kick drifted wide of the post and Wales claimed an improbable, though richly deserved, 34–33 victory.

The defeat shattered France, and the fifteen that took the field at Twickenham were a pale shadow of the side that had won the last two championships in tremendous style. Some brave tackling apart, their usual self-confidence was notable for its absence, and Castaignede, the scourge of England in 1996, flattered only to deceive. Jonny Wilkinson, coached at Newcastle by his country's previous dead-ball expert, Rob Andrew, despatched seven penalties in a 21–10 win, England's first against the French since 1995. An inability to convert their multiple opportunities prevented England from posting a more decisive victory. Mike Catt ignored a glaring two-man overlap, and Wilkinson, betrayed by a slight lack of pace, was held up agonisingly short of a first international try. Jeremy Guscott missed another good chance when Luger intelligently palmed back the same type of diagonal kick that had unlocked South Africa's back door.

But if England lacked penetration they were still creating openings, and had also honed an almost impregnable defence. For some months the former Great Britain and Widnes rugby league coach Phil Larder had been familiarising the side with the defensive principles employed in the thirteen-man game. By stretching a line across the pitch, with fast backs covering the flanks, opposing teams either have to switch inside, where they become easy prey for the forwards, or punt hopefully over the top. Even Franck Comba's injury-time consolation, when France were trailing 21–3, had more than an element of fluke about it, Philippe Carbonneau's speculative chip bouncing away from England's cover and directly into the path of the big centre.

Although playing to different agendas, one for pride and the other for an outside chance of winning the title, two weeks later France and Scotland served up one of the most extraordinary and engaging 40 minutes in the Five Nations' long and illustrious history. In basically the rugby equivalent of two boxers standing in the middle of the ring trading punches, both sides skipped the defensive formalities and instead ran at each other at every conceivable opportunity. Emile Ntamack's early try set the tone, and within 25 minutes Scotland had five to their name. From a neutral point of view it looked as if both countries were intent on playing touch-rugby, and at half-time Scotland led a match almost devoid of set-pieces 33–22. The feast of glorious offensive play – or woeful, shambolic defence, depending on your perspective – blew itself out in the second half, and a Kenny Logan penalty was the only addition to the score. Alan Tait finished the season with five tries, and Gregor Townsend scored in each game, only the fifth player so to do and the first since Philippe Sella in 1986. In all, Scotland amassed a record 120

Above right Tim Rodber gets his pass away before Cameron Murray can get to him

Right Teenage sensation Jonny Wilkinson slots home another penalty against the Scots

points, including sixteen tries, and if England were to lose the next day to Wales coach Jim Telfer, captain of their Grand Slam team in 1984, would receive Scotland's first championship crown for nine years.

On 11 April 1999, Wembley Stadium staged England's final Five Nations contest, technically a home game for Welsh opposition awaiting the completion of their new Millennium Stadium in Cardiff. In addition to the Grand Slam, England were chasing a fifth successive Triple Crown, but would do so without several first-choice players: Grayson, who missed the game against France, failed to recover in time to face Wales and was joined on the sidelines by Kyran Bracken, Jeremy Guscott and David Rees. In response, Clive Woodward awarded debuts to two Sale backs, centre Barrie Jon Mather and nineteen-year-old wing Steve Hanley. Mather, capped by Great Britain at rugby league, had already played at Wembley, in the Wigan team that beat Leeds in the 1994 Challenge Cup final. Loosehead prop Jason Leonard was making his 71st international appearance in a pack unchanged for six games.

In a near metaphysical transportation to the old Arms Park, Max Boyce and Tom Jones rallied a predominantly Welsh crowd in the rousing pre-match festivities, Jones singing 'Delilah' before joining the masses in one of the most passionate renditions of 'Cwm Rhondda' heard this side of the Severn. By kick-off England's revered national stadium was a seething, cacophonous ocean of red, and the atmosphere had long since attained fever pitch. The imperturbable countenance of captain Lawrence Dallaglio and his players' resolute demeanour suggested that, far from being intimidated, they would revel in the occasion.

After twenty minutes Dan Luger and Steve Hanley had temporarily lowered the decibel level with fine tries, and just before half-time Richard Hill added a third when Shane Howarth and Gareth Thomas collided trying to field Matt Dawson's chip-kick. England were in the box seat at 25–15, but through a combination of poor decision making and elementary mistakes they somehow contrived to snatch defeat from the jaws of victory. Twice the ball was fumbled in front of a sparsely defended Welsh line, Jonny Wilkinson missed a simple conversion, and a series of trivial infringements were penalised by the referee and punished by Neil Jenkins. Darren Garforth's injudicious swipe yards from play cost another three points, and all the time Jenkins kept Wales alive with a place-kicking master-class. The fly-half buried six penalties, and two minutes into the second half converted Howarth's well-worked try. With England still leading by six points, Dallaglio rejected an opportunity to put the result beyond doubt when he instructed Wilkinson to kick a penalty to touch rather than at goal. The move petered out, and in injury-time Wales exploited the captain's barely credible and ultimately catastrophic decision. Tim Rodber was harshly adjudged to have tackled dangerously, when he did nothing of the kind, and Jenkins thumped the

resulting penalty deep into English territory. From the line-out Scott Gibbs eluded the distracted Rodber and a third of the England team to add his name to the pantheon of immortal Welsh backs worshipped in the valleys. Jenkins was never going to miss the conversion, and though sufficient time remained for Mike Catt to sky a desperate drop goal attempt, Wales won 32–31.

The result was a tragedy for England who, despite unhelpful mutterings to the contrary from the New Zealand-born Welsh coach Graham Henry, far from being complacent worked tremendously hard to prepare for what they knew would be a severe test. In rugby, teams seldom learn a great deal in victory, and just as the bitter experience of defeat by Scotland in 1990 forged the most successful England team of all time, so the current side would be stronger for having lost at Wembley.

1999-2004

Taking on the world

EXPECTATIONS FOR ENGLAND'S PERFORMANCE IN 1999 WERE RELATIVELY HIGH AFTER THE DISAPPOINTMENT OF 1995, BUT IT TOOK LONGER THAN RUGBY FANS HAD HOPED BEFORE THEY WERE TO SEE THE WEBB ELLIS CUP CLASPED IN THE HANDS OF THE ENGLAND CAPTAIN.

AS thoughts turned away from England's failure to land the Grand Slam, having gone down to Wales at Wembley, and ahead, instead, to the forthcoming 1999 World Cup, captain Lawrence Dallaglio could not have imagined what was to hit him next. In May, the *News of the World* newspaper made drug abuse and drug dealing allegations against him and, eventually, after summit talks with Clive Woodward and RFU officials, it resulted in him stepping down as England skipper. Martin Johnson was the man chosen to take over the reins from Dallaglio, having initially been deemed Woodward's second choice as successor to Phil de Glanville in October 1997.

Johnson's first game after this appointment came one month later in June, ironically in Sydney's Stadium Australia where, four years later, he would lift the Rugby World Cup. England were defeated 22–15 in an international to mark 100 years of Australian international rugby. Doubts had been cast over the feasibility of England travelling Down Under for this centenary game, but a 35-man squad restored optimism ahead of the World Cup, despite slipping to defeat by four tries to two in front of an 81,006 crowd.

While an inquiry went on into the allegations made against Dallaglio, the burly forward was reunited with his international team-mates during summer training camps. (Later he was fined £15,000 and made to pay £10,000 costs after being found guilty of deliberately concealing the truth from the RFU committee set up for the investigation.) He returned to the England line-up in a 106–8 hammering of the United States at Twickenham six weeks prior to the start of the World Cup, yet did not cross the line for one of the sixteen tries England ran in. One week later, and happily freed from the scandal, Dallaglio was in unstoppable form as he inspired England to a 36–11 victory in their final warm-up game against Canada at Twickenham. Again he was not on the score-sheet, but he was inspirational and deservedly collected the man-of-the-match award.

Unfortunately, ahead of the World Cup, England lost Kyran Bracken to a long-term back injury, while wing David Rees

succumbed to a groin problem. The pair were replaced in a 30-man squad by Martyn Wood and Leon Lloyd.

At a sell-out 75,000-capacity Twickenham, where England played their games on home soil despite Wales being the official hosts of the World Cup, Woodward's men recorded a comfortable 67–7 victory over Italy, the country scheduled to join an extended Six Nations in 2000, in their tournament opener.

In the inevitable pool decider at Twickenham, England lost out to New Zealand once again. Having been destroyed by that one-man rugby machine Jonah Lomu at the semi-final stage in South Africa in 1995, the giant winger returned to taunt Woodward's men as he powered past four defenders and over the line for the second of three All Black tries. England lost 30–16. Despite this defeat, England hit back with a tasty 101–10 win over Tonga in the final pool game, a victory which included thirteen tries and secured a play-off showdown with Fiji for a place in the quarter-finals against South Africa. A 45–24 triumph over the South Pacific islanders was not as comfortable as the score suggested with Woodward's side drawn into a sometimes brutal battle, but it resulted in a last eight showdown with the Springboks, at the Stade de France, in Paris.

England had stumbled into the quarter-finals and it was no surprise when Clive Woodward's World Cup ambitions were knocked on the head with defeat in the French capital, courtesy of a sublime kicking performance from South African Jannie De Beer. The fly-half had not been considered a first-choice, but he kicked a world record five drop goals, scored five penalties and converted tries from Joost van der Westhuizen and Pieter Rossouw in a 34-points haul to which England could not respond. Grayson, preferred to the younger Jonny Wilkinson, was successful with six penalties before being replaced by the 20-year-old, who slotted over another penalty. The 44–21 defeat marked the end of the road for England, and for Jeremy Guscott, too, as he called time on a glittering international career. The quarter-final exit was England's worst World Cup showing since 1987 and, as is the critics' way, pressure grew on Woodward with calls from within the media for him to stand down, a year before his contract was due to expire. Fortunately, Woodward was unmoved by the speculation and flatly refused to call a day on the project he had begun, that of creating a side capable of beating anyone in the world, playing a free-flowing and expansive game.

Woodward's self-confidence and the RFU's decision to stand by their man was rewarded, in March 2000, when England claimed victory in the first Six Nations competition, following the addition of Italy, and narrowly missed out on the Grand Slam. Playing without injured skipper Johnson, who was ruled out for the mandatory 21 days after suffering concussion, Matt Dawson captained England to a 50–18 win over Ireland, a record score between the two nations, in the championship-opener in which new caps Ben Cohen, the nephew of England's World Cup-winning soccer player George Cohen, and Mike Tindall both celebrated their debuts with tries. Two weeks later, fielding an unchanged side, England took the scalp of World Cup finalists France, who had lost to Australia in Cardiff's Millennium Stadium, in an epic 15–9 win. Wilkinson was the hero with five successful penalty kicks to take his points total to more than 200 in just sixteen internationals. It was a victory in which the passion, power, pace and intensity that Woodward was striving for finally

came together. England had tournament victory in sight.

Liam Botham, the son of legendary England cricketer Ian, was one of ten new call-ups to a 36-man squad for the third Six Nations fixture but, once again, the same fifteen were named to face Wales at Twickenham. Revenge was duly gained over the Welsh with a dominant and emphatic 46–12 triumph, Wilkinson kicking 21 points as the back-row trio of Neil Back, Richard Hill and Lawrence Dallaglio all put their names on the score-sheet. Talk of a Grand Slam echoed around the West London stadium with trips to face underdogs Italy and reigning champions Scotland, who had failed to live up to expectations.

Basking in the victory over Wales, RFU Chief Executive Francis Baron declared the governing body ready to offer Clive Woodward a new three-year contract, which would take him through to the end of the 2003 World Cup in Australia. That was, after all, the trophy he so desperately wanted to lift. At the same time, the RFU were attempting to foil New Zealand's plans to appoint John Mitchell as coach, in the hope of holding onto Woodward's assistant.

With the political dialogue continuing in the background, England made their maiden Six Nations trip to Rome's Stadio Flaminio to play Italy. The previously unchanged line-up was finally altered, although the only change was brought about by the absence of Phil Vickery, forced onto the sidelines after suffering delayed concussion. Darren Garforth stepped into the breach. The outcome in the full international was never in doubt

Below Phil de Glanville heads for the tryline during the Rugby World Cup Pool B match between England and Italy played at Twickenham. The game finished in a 67–7 win for England

FOURTH WORLD CUP – 1999

Italy	New Zealand	Tonga	Fiji	South Africa
02.10.1999	09.10.1999	15.10.1999	20.10.1999	24.10.1999
Twickenham	Twickenham	Twickenham	Twickenham	Paris
Pool	Pool	Pool	Pool	Pool
Won 67–7	Lost 30–16	Won 101–10	Won 45–24	Lost 44–21
M B Perry	M B Perry	M B Perry	M B Perry	M B Perry
D Luger	A Healey	A Healey	N D Beal	N D Beal
W J H Greenwood	J C Guscott	W J H Greenwood	M Catt	P de Glanville
P de Glanville	P de Glanville	J C Guscott	W J Greenwood	W J Greenwood
A Healey	D Luger	D Luger	D Luger	D Luger
J P Wilkinson	J P Wilkinson	P Grayson	J P Wilkinson	P J Grayson
M J S Dawson	M J S Dawson	M J S Dawson	A Healey	M J S Dawson
J Leonard	J Leonard	G C Rowntree	J Leonard	J Leonard
R Cockerill	R Cockerill	P B T Greening	P B T Greening	P B T Greening
P J Vickery	P J Vickery	P J Vickery	D J Garforth	P J Vickery
M Johnson*	M Johnson*	M Johnson*	M Johnson*	M Johnson*
D Grewcock	D Grewcock	G Archer	G Archer	D Grewcock
R A Hill	R A Hill	J P R Worsley	J P R Worsley	R A Hill
N Back	N Back	R A Hill	N Back	N Back
L Dallaglio	L Dallaglio	L Dallaglio	L Dallaglio	L Dallaglio

Replacements	Replacements	Replacements	Replacements	Replacements
J C Guscott (12)	D J Garforth (3)	N D Beal (9)	G C Rowntree (1)	A Healey (14)
P B T Greening (2)	T A K Rodber (5)	D Grewcock (4)	P de Glanville (11)	J P Wilkinson (10)
D J Garforth (1)	P J Grayson (10)	M Catt (12)	M J S Dawson (9)	M Catt (12)
G C Rowntree (3)	P B T Greening (2)	R Cockerill (8)	R A Hill (6)	M J Corry (9)
N D Beal (15)	M J Corry (7)		T A K Rodber (5)	
M J Corry (5)			R Cockerill (2)	
			P J Grayson (10)	

Points Scorers	Points Scorers	Points Scorers	Points Scorers	Points Scorers
J Wilkinson – 32	J Wilkinson – 11	P J Grayson – 36	J Wilkinson – 23	P J Grayson – 18
M B Perry – 5	P de Glanville – 5	A Healey – 10	N D Beal – 5	J Wilkinson – 3
D Luger – 5		W Greenwood – 10	D Luger – 5	
P de Glanville – 5		J C Guscott – 10	P B T Greening – 5	
M Dawson – 5		D Luger – 10	N Back – 5	
R A Hill – 5		P B T Greening – 10	M J S Dawson –2	
N Back – 5		M Dawson – 5		
M J Corry – 5		R A Hill – 5		
		M Perry – 5		

from the moment the England backs eventually took charge, late in the first-half, despite Italy leading 7–6 after 28 minutes of play. The 59–12 victory included three tries from Austin Healey, two from Cohen and Dawson and a penalty try. It meant that victory in the Calcutta Cup showdown with Scotland, facing the wooden spoon after defeat to Italy, would give England the Grand Slam.

Johnson had played only two full senior matches in four months and was left out of a 25-man squad to travel to Murrayfield, which included the returning Vickery, Greenwood and hooker Mark Regan. But it was a case of déjà vu as the Grand Slam bid failed for the second year running, as Scotland spoiled the party by claiming an unlikely 19–13 win. Scotland fly-half Duncan Hodge scored all nineteen points and his try, six minutes from time, sealed England's fate. The championship was already won, but the Grand Slam had proved elusive. The trophy was lifted four days later at a bizarre ceremony at an eerily empty Twickenham. All that remained to be seen was whether Woodward could agree new terms with his deal due to expire in August, but within weeks of the Scotland defeat, he had agreed on a three-year deal and the signatures were eventually inked in place.

The completion of terms ensured he would lead England on their summer tour of South Africa. Johnson was welcomed back into the fold as captain, with Dawson ruled out of a 40-man touring party after suffering shoulder damage in domestic action,

joining Iain Balshaw, Andy Gomarsall, Vickery, Garath Archer, Grayson and Nick Beal on the sick list. Woodward opted to take eleven uncapped players, including Botham, for the two showdowns with South Africa in Pretoria and Bloemfontein, and also included Bracken, who had fought his way back from seven months out with a serious back injury. Bracken was given the number nine shirt for the opener in Pretoria and his Saracens club-mate Dan Luger was surprisingly chosen on the wing over Six Nations starlet Cohen. Julian White was handed a debut in the front row.

In April 2000, the IRB agreed to extend the trial of video referees used in the Super-12 to international matches. The video referee was to play a controversial role in England's visit to South Africa.

A heroic, though patchy, performance was not enough for victory as England were once again undone by the kicking of the Springboks, and the South African video referee declined a potential penalty try which would have given England victory. This time, it was the boot of Braam van Straaten, with six penalties, that proved the match-winner as the South Africans triumphed 18–13. Tim Stimpson, brought into the starting line-up after Wilkinson succumbed to a bug before kick-off, struck two penalties of his own and converted Luger's try, but it was not enough. In the second Test seven days later, it was Wilkinson's turn to take the plaudits on his return with a 27-point haul, comprising eight penalties and a drop goal, ensuring the series was drawn 1–1 as England won 27–22, in Bloemfontein, despite another controversial try awarded to the home team by the South African video referee. The two controversial decisions made by the South Africans led to calls for neutral video referees.

Ahead of three autumn internationals against Australia, Argentina and South Africa, Woodward named the uncapped Ben Johnston, Steve Borthwick and Alex Sanderson in a training squad. Of the trio, Borthwick was included on the bench to face world champions Australia at Twickenham, but Cohen, preferred to Healey on the wing, withdrew from the starting line-up following the death of his father Peter. The game was decided seven minutes into injury time when Luger stretched to reach a chip from Balshaw. After the video referee confirmed the try, Twickenham was awash with scenes of jubilation as the Wallabies were defeated 22–19. Wilkinson and Matt Burke had traded penalties before the Australian wing converted his own try, but England refused to accept defeat and

Luger produced the goods. But the joy of the success soon turned sour in one of the worst weeks in English rugby history.

Although it didn't come to placards and picket lines, Woodward's squad went on strike over a match/win fee split and refused to attend training ahead of the second scheduled test against Argentina. Four hours of talks with RFU representatives failed to conclude an agreement over new playing contracts, even though the initial negotiations had started some twelve months earlier. Woodward issued a threat to players that if they did not show for training the next day, he would never pick them for England again. An embarrassing wait followed before an agreement was eventually reached, leaving Woodward free to name his side to face the Pumas. He made five changes, handing a full debut to Iain Balshaw, recalling Cohen, preferring Dawson to Bracken at scrum half with White and Regan coming into the front row. Leonard was given the honour of leading England out at Twickenham to mark his 86th cap, surpassing Rory Underwood's record. In a 19–0 win in atrocious conditions at Twickenham, Wilkinson became the youngest-ever Test player to reach 300 international points with fourteen points on the day, while Cohen dedicated his try to his late father. Proving that the victory on the summer tour was no fluke, Greenwood also claimed a try and the man-of-the-match award in a 25–17 victory over South Africa as another 20 points went over from Wilkinson.

Below Austin Healey chips the ball over the defence during the Six Nations 2000 Championship match against Italy played at the Stadio Flaminio, in Rome, Italy. England won the match 59–12

Above Mike Tindall tries to break the tackle of Stirling Mortlock and Joe Roff of Australia during the International match between England and Australia at Twickenham

Ahead of the 2001 Six Nations, Johnson was banned for 35 days after being found guilty of foul play on three counts in domestic league action for Leicester. Controversially, the reduction of the mandatory sentence by seven days enabled his suspension to be lifted just one day prior to England's Six Nations opener against Wales, allowing him to lead England to a 44–15 win. Dorian West made his international bow at hooker in the absence of the injured Phil Greening but it was Greenwood who took centre stage with a hat-trick of tries, with Dawson (two) and Cohen also crossing the line. Jason Robinson, the former rugby league player who switched codes and joined Sale Sharks, was named as a substitute to face Italy, at Twickenham, with Healey replacing the injured Luger in the only change to the starting line-up. In fact, Robinson became the first man who moved from League to Union to be capped by England at both in a 30-minute appearance. He did not score one of the eleven tries, but his place was written in the history books.

The previous year's defeat at Murrayfield was happily wiped from collective English memories two weeks later when, at Twickenham, Woodward's men disposed of Scotland with a record 43–3 victory. It was yet another impressive team display, another unchanged line-up and another six tries. Once again, the Grand Slam was on offer for England, although doubts surrounded the completion of the Six Nations campaign following an outbreak of foot-and-mouth disease. Like various other sporting events England's trip to Dublin to face Ireland was cancelled, and the decision taken to complete the tournament later in the year. Before then, three changes were made by Woodward to the side to face France as Danny Grewcock and Vickery succumbed to injuries and were replaced by the uncapped Borthwick and White. Greening, out injured for the opening three games, came in for West at hooker. A second-half display to match the previous three Six Nations victories saw off the French 48–19 and another excellent kicking performance from Wilkinson, still only 21, put him in the record books as England's leading points scorer as he overtook Rob Andrew's 396 points.

Before England could attempt to secure the Grand Slam in Dublin in October, a summer tour of Canada and the United States allowed Woodward to assess some of the options available to him. The Lions tour was to see Jason Robinson come into his own and Martin Johnson become the first player to lead the Lions twice. It was the first time that the Lions lost to Australia and some players caused controversy with diaries of the tour.

With eighteen of his regulars on tour with the British Lions, Woodward called-up little-known fly-half Olly Barkley, Paul Sampson, Paul Sackey, Tom Voyce and Michael Stephenson to his party and handed the captaincy to scrum half Bracken. Against Canada in Markham it took two tries from Josh Lewsey to see off the determined hosts 22–10. An eight-try romp to a 59–20 victory a week later was England's tenth successive win and equalled the previous best set between 1982 and 1986. When the United States were defeated 48–19 in San Francisco in the final game of the tour a new record was set for a run of victories as Woodward's 'second string' enjoyed another eight-try demolition of the opposition.

Woodward opted to blend his returning British Lions with the eager youngsters who had been, so successful in North America,

in a 30-man squad to face Ireland in the Six Nations decider in October, with Dawson named as captain and Robinson handed his first start. But England could not complete the Grand Slam as Woodward's men failed to recover from an early Keith Wood try. Not even a late try for Healey could prevent a 20–14 defeat. England were crowned Six Nations champions but the eleven-match unbeaten run was ended.

New Zealand-born Henry Paul, another convert from Rugby League after signing for Gloucester, was called up for the three autumn tests with Australia, Romania and South Africa, with Northampton hooker Steve Thompson and Sale Sharks fly-half Charlie Hodgson also earning places in a 26-man squad. With a hand injury keeping Johnson out, Neil Back was handed the captaincy and he was a proud man after a 21–15 triumph against Australia. Yet again, England had Wilkinson's kicking to thank after being out-scored by two tries to none. Seven days later, in a much-changed side, England relished their biggest ever Test victory when they hammered Romania 134–0, debutant Hodgson scoring 44 points, Leonard winning his 93rd cap to become the most capped forward in Test history, and 20 tries being scored in total, including four from Jason Robinson. A third successive victory over South Africa the following week, by a record 29–9 margin between the two nations proved the growing authority of Woodward's side.

England's stranglehold on the Six Nations was brought to an end in 2002 with a defeat to France in the third game. Hooker Thompson was given his first cap and young scrum half Nick Duncombe played the entire second-half to complete a meteoric rise to international rugby as England beat Scotland 29–3 in the campaign-opener to lift the Calcutta Cup. Robinson scored two early tries, and Tindall and Cohen also added to the score with Wilkinson kicking seven points. Two weeks later, a 45–11 rout to gain revenge over Ireland propelled Woodward's men to the top of the world rankings. Four first-half tries from Wilkinson, Cohen, Greenwood and Worsley put the game beyond doubt, before Kay and Greenwood crossed the line late on.

This Six Nations campaign was hit, however, by the 20–15 defeat, in Paris, where the French secured a victory that would

earn them their first Six Nations title. Johnson led England, after appealing against a three-week suspension, imposed following a punch on Saracens' Robbie Russell in a domestic fixture for Leicester. This left him clear to play until the appeal hearing; but an excellent first-half performance by France, in which Gerald Merceron and Imanol Harinordoquy both scored tries, was the foundation for their success. Cohen and Robinson both got tries for England, but the boot of Merceron proved decisive with two conversions and two penalties. Although merely a consolation, a 50–10 win over Wales secured England's first Triple Crown since 1998. It was the biggest winning margin over the Welsh as five tries were scored, this time without Johnson, who had eventually been suspended despite his appeal, and the injured Robinson. The flying fullback was handed a recall for the final game in

Rome against Italy, but Johnson was left on the bench. In his absence Back led out England for his 50th cap, in a game made all but meaningless, as France had wrapped up the title 24 hours earlier. The Italians were disposed of 45–9 and six tries scored in a comfortable England victory.

With the 2002 Six Nations tournament navigated in respectable, but slightly disappointing, fashion, Woodward embarked on a demanding twelve months in which England were to emerge as favourites to win the 2003 World Cup and in which he would have to make tough decisions about his final line-up for the tournament. The first of England's challenges came on 22 June, just a week after Woodward had been awarded the OBE in the Queen's Birthday honours list, in the form of a typically physical Argentina in Buenos Aires.

Starting with five debutants in the line-up, England struggled, but eventually emerged as 26–18 winners. The performance of what was largely an England second-string underlined the strength and depth available. And, at last, progress on the pitch was supported by the signing of a vital agreement off it, between the RFU and club representatives, which would allow Woodward an extra 20 days with an élite squad of players in the year building up to the World Cup. The agreement gave both sides a basis on which to focus their efforts, with Woodward insisting that the deal could only benefit England's World Cup preparations. On a less positive note came news, at the start of October, of the ten-week suspension of Bristol prop Julian White. The suspension ruled White out of three vital matches against the best of the southern hemisphere at Twickenham and came close to ending his hopes of a place in the World Cup.

Above The undefeated England team after the game between England and USA at Balboa Park, San Francisco

The matches against New Zealand, Australia and South Africa on consecutive Sundays in early November were billed by the media as the first of a long series of tests to determine England's World Cup credentials. Woodward, typically bullish, was in no mood to play down the significance of the three games. The first, against the All Blacks, was a nerve-jangling classic in which England overcame another ground-trembling performance from Lomu and a stirring late New Zealand fight-back to claim a 31–28 win. A stirring rendition of 'Swing Low Sweet Chariot' during the All Blacks' traditional 'Haka' (guaranteed to raise a few hackles!) made it clear that the match had lost none of its

significance to home supporters. Despite conceding converted tries to Lomu and Tana Umaga, England held a 17–14 half-time lead, thanks to Wilkinson's kicking and a late Lewis Moody try, before a moment of brilliance from Wilkinson in the second half saw him touch down following a dummy for a drop goal, before catching his own chip-kick to score under the posts, which he duly converted. Lomu steam-rolled home his second try of the game, as New Zealand cut the deficit to 31–28 heading into the final minutes, but a series of last-gasp tackles denied the rampant All-Blacks. Ben Kay then stole a lineout on the England five-metre line to seal the victory.

The clash with Australia a week later, in which England claimed their third consecutive win over their typically outspoken Antipodean rivals, saw an outstanding early try from Cohen that set the scene for a first half in which England matched Australia tit for tat in terms of brains and front-line brawn, but tries either side of half-time from Elton Flatley and then another from Wendell Sailor turned a 16–6 lead into a 28–16 deficit. England fought back through the tried and tested boot of Wilkinson before Cohen, with just five minutes remaining, latched on to a pass from James Simpson-Daniel to go under the posts for a match-winning try that was predictably converted by Wilkinson.

The win sent Australia home from a gruelling tour somewhat humbled but no less reticent in forwarding theories and excuses for their defeat. After the exertions, both physically and mentally, of laying down a statement of World Cup intent, revenge was the dish of the day as England completed their November tests with a rampaging win over a disjointed South Africa. As England bulldozed their way to a 53–3 win that marked the heaviest defeat in South African Test history, it was hard to believe that, only three years previously, the Spingboks had put an early end to Woodward's hopes of World Cup success. The controversial sending-off of Springbok lock Jannes Labuschagne for a late tackle on Wilkinson, after 23 minutes, basically ended the game as a spectacle, but a victory in a sometimes brutal encounter completed the first-ever hat-trick of wins over the big three of the southern hemisphere by a northern hemisphere nation.

The three-match series had been England's chance to show their World Cup intent. South Africa left humiliated, while New Zealand and Australia lined up a plethora of excuses for their narrow defeats. Whatever! Three weeks in November 2002 had, quite literally, turned the rugby world upside down. The trio of wins rounded off twelve months in which England had scored a total of 868 points and conceded just 286 in reply. Fortress Twickenham had not seen an England defeat for eighteen games and the 'red rose' team were ranked as the best side in the world. But flattering statistics meant little if you subsequently fell flat on your face and the fact was England had not completed the Grand Slam since 1995. The bar had been raised again – anything other than a Grand Slam in 2003 would be seen as a failure.

Luckily, the balance between securing the expected five wins and giving potential World Cup squad members a chance to impress was made easier to strike by the 20-day élite player release scheme in the build up to the Six Nations. In addition the new, shorter seven-week time-span of the tournament would allow Woodward an unprecedented amount of time with his squad. The championship opener with France was to be England's only true test of nerve, one that was passed with flying colours. 'Le Crunch', as it was billed, turned into a war of attrition and 20 points from the boot of Wilkinson combined with superb ball retention by the pack and a try from Robinson helped England to win 25–17. Wilkinson's performance, in which he claimed his 600th point in international rugby, was made the more remarkable given the

Opposite left Joe Worsley of England wins the line out from Simon Taylor of Scotland during the Six Nations Championship match between Scotland and England at Murrayfield, Edinburgh

Right Ben Kay in action during the Investec Challenge Match between England and New Zealand at Twickenham, on 9 November 2002

Above Lawrence Dallaglio is tackled by Imanol Harinordoquy of France during the RBS Six Nations International match between England and France on 15 February 2003, held at Twickenham. England won the match 25–17

tragic news of the death of young England and NEC Harlequins scrum half Nick Duncombe while recovering from a hamstring injury, who had partnered Wilkinson in the Six Nations just a year previously. A late try from Damien Traille gave the scoreline some token of respectability for a French side who had, for the main, been outplayed.

Woodward's side almost threw away their hard work immediately when they were confronted next at the Millennium Stadium by a fiery Wales side that was aiming to make amends for an opening day defeat by Italy. England were lucky to go in at half-time level at 9–9 and started the second half with only fourteen men due to Phil Christophers' sin-binning seconds before the break. A half-time re-jig by Woodward appeared to do the trick as England withstood the pressure of the Welsh before Greenwood scored a try on the break. Having seen Wales dominate for an hour of the game, England added to their winning margin through a late Worsley try, but the manner of the 26–9 victory, and a late injury picked up by Wilkinson, frayed nerves and raised doubts over England's resolve away from home.

Wins and improved performances at Twickenham over Italy and Scotland, by scores of 40–5 and 40–9, kept the Grand Slam bid on course. But the Italy game proved costly when Wilkinson's

recurring shoulder injury saw him depart after an hour. Worse was to come when, shortly after replacing Wilkinson at fly-half, Charlie Hodgson picked up a knee injury. Unfortunately, the injury forced him out of contention for the World Cup. His absence resulted in Grayson playing against Scotland, making his first England appearance since the World Cup quarter-final defeat by South Africa in 1999.

The victories set up a Grand Slam decider between England and the unbeaten Irish at Lansdowne Road, England's fourth final-hurdle Grand Slam clash in five seasons. The Irish themselves were looking for a first Grand Slam since 1955 and were hoping to capitalise on the question marks over England's ability on their travels and tendency to choke with the Grand Slam in their sights. The manner of the 42–6 win ended any doubts about England's determination and ability. A Dallaglio try and opportunist kicking from Wilkinson saw England take a 13–6 lead at half-time despite Dawson and Hill requiring some medical repairs. After the break, Tindall powered through

Geordan Murphy on the Irish line before Grayson, on for the blood-binned Wilkinson, slotted over the conversion. Greenwood got England's third try, giving Woodward enough breathing space to experiment with Robinson at centre in place of Tindall. Greenwood and wing-replacement Luger both touched down in the closing stages.

In winning the Grand Slam, England had once again met the challenge set by their doubters and the demands made by Woodward. The nature of the victories over France at Twickenham and Ireland in Dublin in particular highlighted the growing dominance of the England pack, led by captain Johnson, and the increasing cohesion and imagination of a back line marshalled by Wilkinson. Significantly, Woodward would make only two changes from the line-up that defeated Ireland and the side that would eventually conquer Australia in the World Cup final some six months later.

Expectations were high after the Six Nations and, for the first time in many years, the prospect of travelling to play New Zealand in Wellington and Australia in Melbourne was now more eagerly anticipated than anxiously awaited. The mood was palpable that not only did England have the ability to claim their second-ever victory over the All Blacks on New Zealand soil but that a first-ever victory over Australia Down Under could be added a week later. Woodward, as usual quietly determined, insisted that although defeat would be a disappointment it would not be a setback.

After a 'reserve' side had defeated the New Zealand Maoris in a warm-up game, the battle proper began in Wellington on 14 June. And what a battle! England named an unchanged team from the Grand Slam decider win in Ireland, while New Zealand

also enjoyed the luxury of selecting their best fifteen. Wind and rain made for difficult conditions in the Westpac Stadium and saw a game dominated by forward play and a battle between the two fly-halves, Jonny Wilkinson and Carlos Spencer. The key period of the game came mid-way through the first half with England 9–6 ahead as Dallaglio and Back were sin-binned in quick succession for killing the ball. The ferocity of the English defence intensified despite being two men short and captain Johnson was magnificent as the tourists held on until their full compliment of players was restored. This was even more remarkable given the fact that with two men short in the scrum, they managed repeatedly to hold out on the five-metre line. A Wilkinson penalty and drop-goal then put England further ahead before a Rob Howlett try moved New Zealand back within two points. Carlos Spencer and Wilkinson both missed late penalties under intense pressure in the dying stages before the final whistle. It was their first win on New Zealand soil since 1973, but the nature of the victory inevitably did little to impress the ever critical Australian. England were labelled 'boring', overly dependent on Wilkinson and the monotonous power of the pack. Woodward and England, to their credit, turned the other cheek and awaited their chance to shine in Melbourne.

Seven days after beating New Zealand, England's critics were made to eat their words. Not only did they defeat Australia for the second time in six months, they comprehensively outplayed the

Below The England players celebrate winning the Grand Slam after the RBS Six Nations Championship match between Ireland and England held on 30 March 2003 at Lansdowne Road in Dublin, Ireland. England won the match 42–6

France	Wales	Italy	Scotland	Ireland
15.02.2003	22.02.2003	09.03.2003	22.03.2003	30.03.2003
Twickenham	Cardiff	Twickenham	Twickenham	Dublin
Won 25–17	Won 26–9	Won 40–5	Won 40–9	Won 42–6

France	Wales	Italy	Scotland	Ireland
J Robinson	J Robinson	J Lewsey	J Lewsey	J Lewsey
B C Cohen	B C Cohen	J Simpson-Daniel	J Robinson	J Robinson
W J H Greenwood	W J H Greenwood	W J H Greenwood	W J H Greenwood	W J H Greenwood
C Hodgson	C Hodgson	M J Tindall	M J Tindall	M J Tindall
D Luger	D Luger	D Luger	B Cohen	B Cohen
J P Wilkinson	J P Wilkinson	J P Wilkinson*	J P Wilkinson	J P Wilkinson
A Gomersall	K Bracken	M J S Dawson	M J S Dawson	M J S Dawson
J Leonard	G C Rowntree	G C Rowntree	G C Rowntree	G C Rowntree
S Thompson	S Thompson	S Thompson	S Thompson	S Thompson
J White	R Morris	R Morris	J Leonard	J Leonard
M Johnson*	M Johnson*	D J Grewcock	M Johnson*	M Johnson*
B J Kay	B J Kay	B J Kay	B Kay	B Kay
L W Moody	R A Hill	J P R Worsley	R A Hill	R A Hill
N Back	N Back	R A Hill	N Back	N Back
R A Hill	L Dallaglio	L Dallaglio	L Dallaglio	L Dallaglio

Replacements

France	Wales	Italy	Scotland	Ireland
G C Rowntree (1)	P Christophers (15)	A Sanderson (8) (7)	D Luger (12)	J P R Worsley (6t)
L Dallaglio (6)	J P R Worsley (7)	C Hodgon (10)	D Grewcock (5)	K Bracken (9t X 2)
M P Regan (17)	D Grewcock (5)	O Smith (21)	P Grayson (10)	T J Woodman (1)
D J Grewcock (5)	A Gomarsall (11)	S D Shaw (5)	T J Woodman (1)	D Grewcock (5t)
	J Simpson-Daniel (10)	M Worsley (3)	J P R Worsley (8)	P Grayson (10t)
		M P Regan (2)		D Luger (12)
		K Bracken (15)		

Points Scorers

France	Wales	Italy	Scotland	Ireland
J Wilkinson – 20	J Wilkinson – 16	J Lewsey – 10	J Wilkinson – 18	J Wilkinson – 15
J Robinson – 5	W Greenwood – 5	J Wilkinson – 8	J Robinson – 10	W Greenwood – 10
	J P R Worsley – 5	M Tindall – 5	B Cohen – 5	M Tindall – 5
		D Luger – 5	J Lewsey – 5	L Dallaglio – 5
		S Thompson – 5	P Grayson – 2	D Luger – 5
		J Simpson-Daniel 5		P Grayson – 2
		M Dawson – 2		

Wallabies in every area of the field. Both sides attacked from the outset, with tactical considerations left on the backburner. Dallaglio stole an early Australian lineout and phase after phase of English pressure finally ended with Greenwood breaking through Steve Kefu's tackle to touch down. If anything, England's impatience to add to their tally actually hindered their cause and one or two errors allowed Australia back into the game before a fluid move in the backs saw Tindall score, helping England to a 12–3 lead at the interval. Joe Roff narrowed the deficit to three with two penalties before Wilkinson responded in kind. Cohen then added a third try after breaking through the Australian defensive line from deep. As

the clock ran down, England's defence was finally breached by Wendell Sailor. The effort was not enough, however, and the men in white tasted a satisfying victory in Australia for the first time.

The RFU was certainly aware of the significance of England's record-breaking exploits and responded by handing Woodward a new four-year contract that would see him through to the 2007 World Cup. Shaking off England's usual Antipodean travel sickness had made it ten wins in a row against the 'big three' of Australia, New Zealand and South Africa. It also extended Woodward's record to 30 wins in 33 tests. Having famously asked to be judged on the 1999 World

Cup, the contract gave Woodward leeway to prove himself over three World Cups and nine years. Further good news came in July when a dispute between England's players and the Rugby World Cup organisers was resolved. England's players, led by captain Martin Johnson, had been unhappy at the conditions drawn up by RWC organisers concerning commercial issues and image rights. Many of the players due to take part in the World Cup had also been in dispute because of the absence of prize money from an event that had projected profits of £50 million. It seemed only fair that the RWC organisers should introduce a

Right Jonny Wilkinson (right) chases for possesion with Caleb Ralph during the game between the New Zealand All Blacks and England on 14 June 2003, at Westpac Stadium, Wellington, New Zealand

Below Steve Thompson in action during the Rugby World Cup Pool C match between England and Georgia at Subiaco Oval 12 October 2003 in Perth, Australia

compensation package, and England's players were satisfied and their participation assured.

The final preparations for the World Cup came in August and September. A warm-up game, in Wales, was followed by back-to-back fixtures against France. The Wales clash was as much a training exercise as a real test as England's fringe players romped to a 43–9 victory, erasing memories of their Six Nations struggle. The game was more significant for the return to action of the versatile Healey in an experimental side. Eleven changes were made as England travelled to the Stade Vélodrome, in Marseille, where a record run of fourteen victories finally came to an end with a 16–11 defeat. England's second-string were undone by the kicking of Frederic Michalak and a solitary Nicolas Brusque try, while Grayson was impressive on his return as fly-half. The tables were turned a week later at Twickenham when France fielded an experimental side of their own which was swept away by a strong England line-up, which ran in five tries in a 45–14 win on their final appearance on home soil before the World Cup.

On 7 September, Woodward named the final 30 who would get on the plane to Australia. Much of the group was predictable, but Catt was a surprise inclusion while Healey, Simpson-Daniel, Rowntree, Smith and the particularly unfortunate Simon Shaw failed to make the final cut. Injuries to Hodgson and Alex King opened the door for Catt, who had not played for England since picking up his 56th cap against South Africa, in November, 2001. In a young and vibrant back-line Catt, a throwback to the days of Guscott and Stuart Barnes, provided valuable experience.

Squad chosen, Woodward set about his final preparations for the World Cup. Simple as that sounds, all was not quite as it seemed as Woodward called in the experts to brief his team on 'espionage' threats during the forthcoming tournament. SPECTRE may not have posed a threat, but rumours suggested that the team's Pennyhill Park Hotel in Bagshot was swept for bugging devices in the summer. In addition, Woodward struck a deal with the World Cup organisers that each training session would only be made open for the first 20 minutes for fear of spies getting the inside track on tactics. The high-security policy was a far cry from the 1995 World Cup where, as Will Carling recalled, team psychologist Austin Swain was sent to spy on the Australians cunningly disguised as a back-packer (no wonder they didn't recognise him!). According to Carling 'he returned having seen the whole training session and actually drunk some of the management's beer'.

Spooks consulted and details finalised, England departed for Perth, in Western Australia, in the early hours of 1 October. The team arrived ten days in advance of their opening Pool C match with minnows Georgia. The second game of the group, with South Africa, had been billed as England's first, and only, true test in the group stages, with games against Samoa and Uruguay drawing the pool to a close. The South Africa game also carried huge importance due to the likelihood that the vanquished team would have to face New Zealand in the quarter-finals, as the All Blacks were hot favourites to dominate their group.

Right Lawrence Dallaglio powers forward during the Rugby World Cup Quarter-final match between England and Wales at Suncorp Stadium 9 November 2003 in Brisbane, Australia

After a largely untroubled training camp in Perth, England began their campaign with a crushing 84–6 victory over Georgia, running in twelve tries. While the win was easy enough in itself, news in the following days that all three scrum halves – Dawson, Bracken and Gomarsall – were injury doubts for the South Africa game prompted Bath's Martyn Wood to be summoned as cover. It turned out to be no more than a flying visit as fortunately Bracken's back injury was not serious enough to rule him out, and Gomarsall was fit enough for the bench. An injury to the inspirational Hill, however, forced him out until the semi-final and handed an opportunity to Moody. South Africa's preparations had been undermined by an unsettling on-going race row within the camp. A war of words had been raging with England over their brutal encounter a year previously. South African captain Corne Krige, somewhat ironically given his own chequered disciplinary past, labelled Martin Johnson as 'one of the dirtiest captains in world rugby' despite television evidence, after the Twickenham clash, showing clearly that Krige punched Robinson and Wilkinson, butted Dawson, shoulder-charged Tindall and stamped on Vickery. The England camp remained largely tight-lipped, although Johnson predicted a 'ferocious' encounter.

With everyone expecting another brutal game both teams appeared on their best behaviour, despite the importance of the match at the Subiaco Oval in Perth. Wilkinson struck an early penalty, but fierce tackling from South Africa helped Louis Koen kick South Africa level at half-time. England abandoned their head-on tactics and played a more expansive game. South Africa could not match or counter the creativity of England's back-line, fed by Bracken, as Woodward's side claimed nineteen unanswered

points in the second half through the unnervingly accurate boot of Wilkinson and a Greenwood try, which followed a charge down of Louis Koen's clearance kick by Lewis Moody. The 25–6 win marked the final exorcism of the memories of England's World Cup quarter-final defeat at the hands of South Africa, and the boot of Jannie de Beer, back in 1999.

With the major test of the pool passed with relative ease, it was anticipated that games against Samoa and Uruguay would be easy, allowing some of the fringe players in the squad the chance for a taste of the World Cup. But the 35–22 win over 'underdogs' Samoa proved to be a far sterner test than anticipated and for an hour in Melbourne it appeared that the biggest shock in World Cup history was on the cards. Samoan fly-half Earl Va'a kicked an early penalty and then converted a try from captain Semi Sitti to give the would-be party-poopers a 10–0 lead. England weren't aided by Wilkinson having an 'off day', even missing kicks infront of the posts. Having gone toe-to-toe with the powerful and cunning Samoan backs, England attempted to reassert their dominance in the second period by going through their forwards and persistent pressure in the scrum saw England awarded a penalty try to leave England 22–20 down heading into the final quarter. Late tries from Balshaw and Vickery sealed victory, but it was no gentle passage. Afterwards, it emerged that England had briefly played with sixteen men when Luger had run on to replace Tindall, who was still receiving treatment on the pitch. The Australian media howled for a harsh punishment, but the Rugby World Cup organisers saw sense and England received a £10,000 fine for their error of judgement. In addition, fitness coach Dave Reddin was suspended for two matches for ignoring the instructions of a match official. And it was all compounded by the news that Grewcock would miss the remainder of the tournament with a broken hand, so London Wasps' Simon Shaw was flown out as his replacement.

The Samoa encounter had been rather an embarrassment and a near catastrophe, so the final pool match against Uruguay came as welcome relief. The 111–13 result, in which Josh Lewsey ran in an English record-equalling five tries and back-up fly-half Grayson claimed 22 points, reflected a game of total dominance as Woodward mixed and matched ahead of the quarter-finals. The only blemish came when Worsley was sin-binned for a high tackle on Joaquin Pastore in the closing stages and dented England's popularity by clapping at the crowd.

Wales' fighting 53–37 defeat by the All Blacks in their final group game meant that England would take on Steve Hansen's side in the last eight. A semi-final with either France or Ireland awaited the victors. Wales were happy to be billed as the underdogs, but had shown in their defeat to New Zealand that they could pose a threat on the attack. Their tenacity and resolve in the face of a refreshed England pushed Woodward's side to its limits. Indeed, Wales outscored England by three tries to one as 23 points from Wilkinson once again lead England out of trouble in a 28–17 win. Welsh aggression saw them take a 10–3 lead into halftime. England's starting line-up boasted a total of 704 caps between them (Jason Leonard's 111th English appearance equalling Phillippe Sella's record for international caps), but Wales' less experienced team battled gamely with free-flowing attacking moves that perplexed the English defence. The game finally turned in England's favour with the introduction of Catt at centre, Tindall switching to the wing in place of the substituted Luger. The move was a masterstroke, taking the pressure off Wilkinson, as Catt took charge of tactical kicking in the centre of the field. As England found their feet, Robinson tore through the Welsh defence and allowed Greenwood to go over in the corner. The try was converted and England looked like a different team. Martyn Williams claimed a late try for Wales, but it was not enough. The game was a massive effort for Wales, but the reaction of the England players at the final whistle, however, reflected their disappointment at their own performance.

If moods were low after the Welsh game, however, they would have dipped even further upon viewing the performance of semi-final opponents France in a 43–21 demolition of Ireland. The French backs had, it appeared, returned to their mercurial best, with the back row of Serge Betsen, Olivier Magne and Imanol Harinordoquy tagged as the 'Three Musketeers' for their rampaging forays forward and biting tackles. England's performances in the tournament had been slightly uninspiring, whereas the French had swashbuckled their way to the last four. The battle for the title of the best of the northern hemisphere was on and, in many quarters, the French were the favourites to come out on top.

There was good news from inside the England camp ahead of the game when Hill was finally pronounced fit to return and

Above Jason Leonard recieves a commemorative number 112 jersey from Head Coach Clive Woodward after setting a new world record of 112 international apppearances for England, during the Rugby World Cup semi-final match between England and France at Telstra Stadium 16 November 2003 in Sydney, Australia

Woodward named his preferred 22-man squad for the match. Given the hype and the massive build-up to the clash, the game itself, while understandably tense, was reduced to a battle of attrition due to the appalling conditions at the Telstra Stadium in Sydney. High winds and torrential rain ended hopes of a battle of running rugby and prompted a struggle between the two packs as Michalak and Wilkinson went head-to-head in a kicking contest. Despite the reputation of the French back row, it was Hill, Back and Dallaglio who dominated proceedings as England took control. Betsen stole a lineout near the England line and crashed over against the run of play to score a try validated by the video referee, which Michalak converted, but it was his first and last score of the day as Wilkinson delivered a kicking masterclass. Christophe Dominici received a yellow card for a blatant trip on Robinson and Wilkinson added a second drop-goal and two penalties before halftime to put England in the ascendancy. France tried to inject some free-running play into the game and looked to have England rattled before Betson was yellow-carded for a late tackle on Wilkinson. The England fly-half dusted himself off before kicking the penalty squarely between the posts, putting England beyond the reaches of a converted try. Michalak's discontent was complete when, after he missed his fifth penalty kick of the game, French coach Bernarde Laport replaced him with Gerald Merceron. The battle of the fly-halves was won, comprehensively, by Wilkinson. He claimed all England's points in a 24–7 win. But much of the credit for the win had to go to England's back row and scrum half, who dominated at the breakdown of play, turning the screws on the French. In the midst of the battle, Jason Leonard came on for his 112th England cap and an undisputed place in the record books.

And, so, to the Rugby World Cup final... And the small matter of facing Australia, the hosts, in Sydney. The media circus that assembled and prepared the mood for the final was of an unprecedented level. England were accused in the Australian press of being boring, arrogant and overly dependent on the boot of Wilkinson. Woodward's experienced line-up was branded as a 'Dad's Army' and the likes of Back, Leonard, Hill and Johnson as 'Grumpy Old Men'. Previous losses to England were written off as flukes aided by Australian injury concerns and the whole of Australia had good reason to be confident. Rumours circulated that, despite the increased security, Australia had rumbled England's lineout calls. In contrast to England's stuttering progress, Australia's route to the final had included wins over an impressive Ireland and a mighty New Zealand in the semis. The 22–10 win over the All Blacks had been clinical and was roundly applauded. A team that could out-fight the hard-tackling All Blacks could surely not be out-fought by 'boring old' England? In the World Cup final? In front off the biggest worldwide television audience for a rugby union match? In Australia's own back yard? Never... The England camp kept their cool in face of extensive provocation. As always, they decided to do their talking on the pitch.

Rugby could not have asked for a more dramatic end to the best Rugby World Cup ever held. A crowd of 82,957 was packed into the Telstra Stadium, in Sydney, to witness Wilkinson kicking a winning drop-goal seconds before the end of extra-time. The kick was exactly the right answer to his critics and those of English rugby. The match itself was outstanding in terms of quality, strength

under pressure, determination and sheer bloody-mindedness. Nerve-wracking for spectators, the two sides matched each other blow for blow from the start. Lote Tuqiri towered above Robinson to catch a superb Stephen Larkham bomb for an early try. Stephen Larkham's conversion hit the post which proved costly for Australia. But England were not rattled and continued with their game-plan of back play based on the dominance of the forwards. Wilkinson kicked two penalties while Larkham was blood-binned, for the first of several visits, after coming off worse in an off-the-ball tackle on Cohen. Then, almost perfectly on cue, England scored a try of the highest quality. Robinson returned an Australian kick and from the ensuing ruck Dallaglio powered through the Australian defence and passed inside to Wilkinson, who fed the flying Robinson, who touched down in the corner. Crucially, Wilkinson missed the conversion, and Australia trailed 14–5 at half-time.

England's second half pushes had been a feature of their World Cup campaign, but it was Australia who hit back in the second period as constant pressure allowed a seemingly cool Elton Flatley to chip in with two penalties. With only a few seconds left, the England scrum was penalised by South African referee Andre Watson as Woodman stood up. This gifted Flatley

Above Telstra Stadium during the Rugby World Cup Final match between England and Australia
Opposite right Jonny Wilkinson kicks the winning drop goal for England's victory during the Rugby World Cup Final match, 22 November 2003 in Sydney, Australia

Left Martin Johnson of England recieves the William Webb Ellis Cup from Australian Prime Minister John Howard after England won the Rugby World Cup Final match between Australia and England
Below English coach Clive Woodward holds the Webb Ellis Cup during the celebrations after the final at the Olympic Park Stadium in Sydney, 22 November 2003. England beat Australia 17–20

a chance to level the scores and, with great coolness, he stepped up to make it 14–14 with the last kick of normal time and send the match into extra time. Both teams had had chances to win in normal time. Ben Kay dropped a pass with the try line at his mercy, Mat Rogers just denied Will Greenwood a try, Sterling Mortlock narrowly failed to score and Wilkinson missed several drop-goal attempts on his favoured left foot.

As nerves continued to jangle, Wilkinson kicked a penalty: 17–14. Flatley responded: 17–17. And then: the final scene of a drama of sustained excitement through every act. Three minutes remained and both sides were on the verge of total exhaustion when England gained possession. A drop-goal was always, it seemed, on – and the entire crowd, not to mention a television audience of millions that sat with hearts in mouths all round the world, was transfixed. Dawson broke through the Australian defence and set up a ruck on the 22-yard line. Everyone expected the ball to go to Wilkinson, but with Dawson at the bottom of the ruck captain Johnson wisely ran it, piling through the Australian defence to edge a yard closer to the try-line. Another ruck, a pause, and then Dawson spun the ball back to Wilkinson. For a moment it seemed the world had slowed in motion. He set himself in the manner seen a thousand times in training and club matches for Newcastle Falcons and then his drop-kick (this time from his 'unfavoured' right foot) sailed straight through the uprights. There was no time for an Australian comeback. England had won the World Cup, in front of the biggest worldwide television audience for a rugby union match, in Australia's back yard. 'Dad's Army' had done it. Captain Mainwaring would have been proud. 'Boring' Old

Georgia

12.10.2003
Subiaco Oval
Pool C
Won 84–6

J Lewsey
J Robinson
W Greenwood
M Tindall
B Cohen
J Wilkinson
M Dawson

T Woodman
S Thompson
P Vickery
M Johnson*
B Kay
R Hill
N Back
L Dallaglio

Replacements
M Regan (2)
J Leonard (1t & 3)
L Moody (6)
A Gomarsall (9)
P Grayson (10)
D Luger (13)

Points Scorers
J Wilkinson – 16
B Cohen – 10
W Greenwood – 10
P Grayson - 8
M Tindall – 5
M Dawson – 5
M Regan – 5
S Thompson – 5
N Back – 5
L Dallaglio – 5
J Robinson – 5
D Luger – 5

Samoa

26.10.2003
Telstra Dome
Pool C
Won 35–22

J Lewsey
J Robinson
W Greenwood
M Tindall
B Cohen
J Wilkinson
K Bracken

T Woodman
S Thompson
P Vickery
M Johnson*
B Kay
L Moody
N Back
L Dallaglio

Replacements
J P R Worsley (7t)
D Luger (12)
J Leonard (1)

Points Scorers
J Wilkinson – 20
W Greenwood – 5

Samoa

26.10.2003
Telstra Dome
Pool C
Won 35–22

J Robinson
I Balshaw
S Abbott
M Tindall
B Cohen
J Wilkinson
M Dawson

J Leonard
M Regan
J White
M Johnson*
B Kay
J Worsley
N Back
L Dallaglio

Replacements
S Thompson (2)
P Vickery (3)
L Moody (6)
M Catt (13)

Points Scorers
J Wilkinson – 15
N Back – 5
I Balshaw – 5
P Vickery – 5
Penalty try – 5

Uruguay

02.11.2003
Suncorp stadium
Pool C
111–13

J Lewsey
I Balshaw
S Abbott
M Catt
D Luger
P Grayson
A Gomarsall

J Leonard
D West
P Vickery*
M Corry
D Grewcock
J Worsley
L Moody
L Dallaglio

Replacements
J White (3)
M Johnson (4)
K Bracken (9)
W Greenwood (10)
J Robinson (14)

Points Scorers
J Lewsey – 25
P Grayson – 22
M Catt – 14
I Balshaw – 10
A Gomarsall – 10
J Robinson – 10
D Luger – 5
S Abbott – 5
W Greenwood – 5
L Moody – 5

Wales	France	Australia
09.11.2003	16.11.2003	22.11.2003
Suncorp stadium	Telstra Stadium	Telstra Stadium
Quarter-finals	Semi-finals	Final
Won 28–17	Won 24–7	Won 20–17
J Robinson	J Lewsey	J Lewsey
D Luger	J Robinson	J Robinson
W Greenwood	W Greenwood	W Greenwood
M Tindall	M Catt	M Tindall
B Cohen	B Cohen	B Cohen
J Wilkinson	J Wilkinson	J Wilkinson
M Dawson	M Dawson	M Dawson
J Leonard	T Woodman	T Woodman
S Thompson	S Thompson	S Thompson
P Vickery	P Vickery	P Vickery
M Johnson*	M Johnson*	M Johnson*
B Kay	B Kay	B Kay
L Moody	R Hill	R Hill
N Back	N Back	N Back
L Dallaglio	L Dallaglio	L Dallaglio

Replacements

Wales	France	Australia
T Woodman (1)	D West (1)	J Leonard (3)
K Bracken	J Leonard (3B & 1)	L Moody (6)
M Catt (14)	L Moody (6)	M Catt (12)
S Abbott (13)	K Bracken (9B & 9)	I Balshaw (15)
	M Tindall (12)	

Points Scorers

Wales	France	Australia
J Wilkinson – 23	J Wilkinson – 24	J Wilkinson – 15
W Greenwood – 5		J Robinson – 5

England were the world champions.

The celebrations that marked the victory were unprecedented in the history of English rugby union. In Australia, England's players proudly received their medals (at double quick speed thanks to the hosts' prime minister) and Johnson let out an almighty roar as he lifted the Webb Ellis Cup. Players paraded around the pitch and family members found their way onto the turf to join in the fun. The media scrum that met the victory indicated that the manner of England's win had at least gone some way to captivate Australian and worldwide audiences as much as the viewing public back at home. In England, the celebrations were even more pronounced. Every newspaper led with pictures of England's victory and the moment Wilkinson kicked the winning drop-goal, with many of the tabloids taking the opportunity to hit back at the remorseless abuse that that the Australian press had aimed at the England squad. Politicians and celebrities clamoured to send their congratulations to Woodward's squad as victory saw the entire squad acclaimed as heroes. Captain Johnson and Wilkinson, for a while at least, had emerged as the biggest celebrities in England. Johnson was hailed as England's 'captain colossus', while 'golden-boot' Wilkinson was lifted onto the type of pedestal usually reserved for pop-stars and David Beckham. Wilkinson's winning drop kick was repeated endlessly on television, with pundits claiming the moment would join Geoff Hurst's fourth goal for the England football team in the 1966 World Cup final as one of the most readily recognised

sporting moments in the history of English sport.

Pressure from the public saw the squad come together at the start of December to parade the World Cup trophy around the crammed streets of London before taking tea with the Queen and visiting Number Ten Downing Street for a party with the Prime Minister. The players, back-room staff and officials in and around the England squad savoured the moment – but there was still better to come. Speculation had suggested Woodward, Wilkinson, Johnson and some of England's more experienced players would have their efforts recognised with awards in the Queen's New Year's honours list. In fact, every member of the squad was recognised. Clive Woodward received a knighthood, Johnson the CBE and Wilkinson was made an OBE with the rest of the squad made MBEs. Never had the English nation responded so positively and in such numbers to an English rugby squad. Their efforts had sparked an unprecedented interest in rugby that would see attendances at domestic league fixtures swell massively. The entire squad were stars. But, inevitably, it would all have to come to an end sooner or later.

The start of the New Year saw attentions turn away from the victory in Australia and towards the start of the 2004 Six Nations. Speculation was rife over which, of England's squad, would retire before the competition and how Woodward would change his line-up after the success. Taking the decision to end a glorious career on a World Cup high, the first retirement came with Martin Johnson announcing he was to step down

Above The England team celebrate victory over Australia

from international rugby with immediate effect in mid-January. Within days Woodward named Dallaglio as his successor as captain. Neil Back then followed in Jason Leonard's footsteps and announced he would retire at the end of the Six Nations. Kyran Bracken stepped down with immediate effect. As well as spelling the end of a number of glittering England careers, the massive effort of the World Cup win had also taken its toll physically and Wilkinson revealed he would miss the whole of the Six Nations and the subsequent summer tour with a shoulder injury aggravated in the final in Sydney. Tindall similarly feared he would miss all five games.

Refusing to let the World Cup win cloud his determination to claim another Grand Slam, Sir Clive Woodward named a side to start in Italy that, apart from some small but significant changes, was recognisable as the successful side from Down Under. Gone were Johnson and Wilkinson, and in came Grewcock and Grayson. Woodward controversially omitted Back, insisting he would not allow the Six Nations to turn into a retirement party, and brought in Worsley. Luger was left out to give him time to settle in France after moving to Perpignan. Perhaps the biggest headache for Woodward was Tindall's absence. His injury saw Robinson move to outside centre, Lewsey pushed to the wing and Balshaw handed the full-back slot. The only truly unforced tactical changes from Woodward came with the dropping of Catt and the replacement of Dawson with Gomarsall who finally, it appeared, would get his chance to shine in an England jersey. Whatever the chosen side, England were expected to romp to victory and they did so by a score of 50–9. This was to be the last appearance for Jason Leonard as he totalled 114 England and five Lion caps. The Calcutta Cup followed, England fielding a similar line-up to that which had strolled past Italy, but the nature of the 35–13 win over Scotland at Twickenham gave the first indications that England could be suffering from a 'World Cup hangover' as they frequently looked leaderless in a largely drab affair.

The stage looked set for the World Cup bubble to burst and Ireland provided the necessary pin at Twickenham on 6 March. England's lineout, minus Johnson and the injured Grewcock, struggled and new captain Dallaglio had a performance to forget as England's usually formidable back row was outplayed. England's back line, re-jigged without Wilkinson and Tindall, looked unable to pass or catch the ball with any confidence. Ireland dominated for vast periods of the game and a Matt Dawson try could not hide England's deficiencies, although the home side finally came to life in the dying stages. The effort, though admirable, came too late and England's 22-match unbeaten run at Twickenham was ended. It had to happen sooner or later. Everyone was aware that England were beatable, but the tag of World Champions and the remarkable run of success had given England a veneer of invincibility that was incorrectly attributed, especially with so many changes coming after the World Cup.

A narrow 31–21 victory over Wales, in which Olly Barkley returned to fly-half with Grayson injured, put England back in contention for the Six Nations championship and set up a game with France that would decide the tournament's eventual winners.

The match at the Stade de France was the chance for the French to gain revenge for their semi-final defeat and an opportunity for England's reformed team to prove that a post-World Cup collapse was not imminent. In truth, France's 24–21 win saw both scenarios come true. France looked brighter, keener and more creative and scrum half Dimitri Yachvili was outstanding as France took a strong 24–6 lead. It looked as though England were on their way to a humiliating defeat, but the introduction of Mike Catt from the substitutes' bench turned the game in England's favour – as it had in times of trouble for England in the World Cup. Cohen and Lewsey touched down and Barkley's kicking got England to within three points in a frantic finale. But England could not get the score they needed and France were able to celebrate revenge with a fine win that their first-half performance richly deserved. As France lifted the Six Nations trophy, England's players remained by the side of the pitch to applaud their conquerors in a memorable display of sportsmanship.

The 2004 Six Nations had marked the end of England's total dominance of the world game but it had also, in its dying stages, illustrated that even an England side struggling to find its direction could still push France all the way.

Disappointment of defeat put aside, Woodward joined his team in applauding France from the sidelines safe in the knowledge that, once again, he had four years ahead of him to build a team good enough to retain the Webb Ellis Cup in France.

Above The crowd in Trafalgar Square wave flags as the team bus arrives
Below The England Rugby World Cup team victory parade on 8 December 2003 in London. Up to half a million supporters flocked to central London for the procession

Player profiles

STUART ABBOTT

Full Name Stuart Richard Abbott
Born 03.06.1978 – Cape Town, South Africa
Clubs London Wasps
Position Centre
Debut 23.08.2003 – Wales
Last Match 09.11.2003 – Wales
England Appearances 5 (won 5, drew 0, lost 0)
Points 10 – 2 tries
International Championship 0
Triple Crown 0
World Cup 2003 (winner)

Stuart Abbott became the eighth South African-born player to play for England when he made his full international debut against Wales in the Millenium Stadium in August 2003, where he scored the try that helped him become a surprise selection for the tournament in Australia. He only made fleeting appearances in the World Cup, but did score a try as a substitute against Uruguay. He came to the attention of the England set-up with a series of outstanding performances for London Wasps in their Zurich Premiership winning side and many see him as a threat to both Mike Tindall and Will Greenwood in the centre of the field. Educated in South Africa, he also made an appearance for South Africa's Under-23 side before joining Wasps in 2001. He was awarded the MBE in 2003.

ROB ANDREW

Full Name Christopher Robert Andrew
Born 18.02.1963 – Richmond, Yorkshire
Clubs Cambridge University, Nottingham, Wasps, Toulouse, Newcastle
Position Fly-half
Debut 05.01.1985 – Romania
Last Match 15.03.1997 – Wales
England Appearances 71 (won 50, drew 2, lost 19)
Points 396 – 2 tries, 21 drop goals, 86 penalty goals, 33 conversions
British Lions Appearances 5 (won 3, drew 0, lost 2)
Points 11 – 2 drop goals, 1 penalty goal, 1 conversion
Grand Slam 1991, 1992, 1995
International Championship: 1991, 1992, 1995
Triple Crown 1991, 1992, 1995, 1997
World Cup 1987 (quarter-final), 1991 (runner-up), 1995 (semi-final; 4th)
Cambridge Blue 1982, 1983, 1984
England Captain 2,1989–95 (won 2, drew 0, lost 0)

England's most capped fly-half and all-time leading scorer. Despite eighteen points on debut against Romania in 1985, Rob Andrew was initially too inconsistent to be considered a specialist place-kicker. Only spasmodically entrusted with the kicking duties he scored 151 points in his first 55 internationals, compared to 245 in the next fifteen. Permanently handed the role in 1994, following the retirement of full-back Jon Webb, with the assistance of kicking guru David Alred, Andrew completely remodelled his technique and went on to break almost every English scoring record. On seven occasions he registered more than twenty points in a game, and nine times accrued all of his country's points in a match. Against South Africa in 1994 Andrew became the first Englishman to accomplish every possible method of scoring in a single fixture when he notched a try, a drop goal, five penalties and two

conversions in the 32–15 First Test victory. His total of 27 points, a national record, was further improved in the 60–19 win over Canada in December 1994. The Wasps fly-half landed twelve out of twelve goal attempts and his tally of 30 points remained unequalled until Paul Grayson converted all but one of England's sixteen tries in the 110–0 annihilation of Holland in 1998. Frequently criticised for his supposedly negative tactics and often compared unfavourably with Bath's Stuart Barnes, Andrew always responded in the best possible fashion, and his finest moment was undoubtedly the dramatic late drop goal that beat Australia in the 1995 World Cup quarter-final. He was the class-mate of another latter-day English hero, Rory Underwood – the pair were in the same cricket team at Barnard Castle School. In addition to his three rugby Blues at Cambridge, Andrew played in two Varsity cricket matches. A middle order left-hand batsman, he compiled a first-class century against Nottinghamshire in 1984 and took twelve career wickets with his gentle off break bowling. In 1995 he was appointed director of rugby at Newcastle, leading them to the Allied Dunbar Premiership title in 1998, and after an absence of two years he made his farewell international appearance as a replacement against Wales at Cardiff Arms Park. The golden boy of English rugby, Andrew was passed over as captain by manager Geoff Cooke, but deputised for Will Carling on two occasions and also had the honour of representing the Lions in both Australia and New Zealand.

NEIL BACK

Born 16.01.1969 – Coventry, West Midlands
Clubs Leicester Tigers
Position Flanker
Debut 05.02.1994 – Scotland
Last Match 22.11.2003 – Australia
England Appearances 66
Points 83 – 16 tries, 1 drop goal
British Lions Appearances 4 (won 3, drew 0, lost 1)
Points 5 – 1 try
Grand Slam 2003
International Championship 2001, 2003
Triple Crown 1998, 2002, 2003
World Cup 1995 (semi-final; 4th), 1999 (quarter-final), 2003 (winner)

Alongside Lawrence Dallaglio and Richard Hill, Neil Back was one of the back row trio, nicknamed the 'grumpy old men' by the Australian media, who helped England lift the World Cup. He made an intermittent start to his international career, hampered by a six-month ban for pushing over referee Steve Lander in the 1996 English Cup final, but it was blamed on his small 5ft 10in stature. He made it into the 1995 World Cup squad because of his ferocious tackling and unrivalled fitness and his performances ensured he was ever present on the Lions tour in 1997, the 1999 World Cup and the 2001 Lions tour. He came on strongly before the 2003 World Cup and was consistently outstanding during the tournament, playing in six of the seven World Cup matches and scoring two tries. A Leicester stalwart, after joining from

Nottingham in 1990, he holds the club's try-scoring record and helped them to consecutive European titles in 2001 and 2002. Awarded the MBE in 2003, he retired from international rugby at the end of the 2004 RBS 6 Nations championship.

IAIN BALSHAW

Full Name Iain Robert Balshaw
Born 14.04.1979, Blackburn, Lancashire
Clubs Bath
Position Full-back
Debut 05.02.2000 – Ireland
Last Match 06.03.2004 – Ireland
England Appearances 22
Points 55 – 11 tries
British Lions Appearances 3 (won 2, drew 0, lost 1)
International Championship 2001
Triple Crown 2002
World Cup 2003 (winner)

One of England's most exciting talents in the late 1990s, Iain Balshaw's performances for Bath helped him gain an international debut as a replacement against Ireland in 2000. His starting debut came against Wales a year later and his potential was recognised when the Lions called on him for their tour of Australia, selecting him for all three intense test matches. Despite his undoubted pace, strong tackling and attacking flair Balshaw was still only 24 and he suffered a dip in form and confidence during the tour and followed it with just nine games in eleven months for Bath, hampered by a shoulder injury. After surgery, Balshaw returned to his best in the 2002–03 season and made his international comeback – after an 18-month absence – in the World Cup warm-up match with France. The battle between Jason Robinson and John Lewsey relegated Balshaw to a role as able replacement, but he scored a vital try against Samoa and featured in the dying seconds of the final. He was awarded the MBE in 2003.

MARTIN BAYFIELD

Full Name Martin Christopher Bayfield
Born 21.12.1966 – Bedford, Bedfordshire
Clubs Northampton, Bedford
Position Lock
Debut 20.07.1991 – Fiji
Last Match 03.02.1996 – Wales
England Appearances 31 (won 22, drew 0, lost 9)
British Lions Appearances 3 (won 1, drew 0, lost 2)
Grand Slam 1992, 1995
International Championship 1992, 1995, 1996
Triple Crown 1992, 1995, 1996
World Cup 1995 (semi-final; 4th)

An England B representative, Martin Bayfield first appeared for the national side on the 1991 tour of Fiji and Australia, playing

in both Test matches as a replacement for the injured lock Wade Dooley. Overlooked for the subsequent World Cup, he became a regular member of the side following Paul Ackford's post-tournament retirement. He started all three Tests on the 1993 Lions tour of New Zealand, but suffered a neck and spine problem which forced him to miss England's 15–9 defeat of the All Blacks and briefly threatened his career. In 1996 he took a prolonged leave from the police force to concentrate on his rugby career, only to be permanently discarded by manager Jack Rowell. England's outstanding performer in the 1995 World Cup, Bayfield partnered Martin Johnson eighteen times in the second row and played in all eight of the 1992 and 1995 Grand Slam matches.

BILL BEAUMONT

Full Name William Blackledge Beaumont
Born 09.03.1952 – Preston, Lancashire
Clubs Fylde
Position Lock
Debut 18.01.1975 – Ireland
Last Match 16.01.1982 – Scotland
England Appearances 34 (won 14, drew 3, lost 17)
British Lions Appearances 7 (won 2, drew 0, lost 5)
Grand Slam 1980
International Championship 1980
Triple Crown 1980
England Captain 21, 1978–82 (won 11, drew 2, lost 8)

One of the most influential figures in English rugby and captain of the 1980 Grand Slam side, Bill Beaumont led his country on 21 occasions. With the Gosforth lock Roger Uttley incapacitated by a back problem, he was awarded a first cap opposite the Irish legend Willie John McBride at Lansdowne Road in 1975. Dropped as a result of Uttley's recovery and not the 12–9 defeat, Beaumont returned for that summer's tour of Australia and went on to contest 33 consecutive internationals, a record for the position eventually surpassed by Wade Dooley. Courageous and self-effacing, he was tragically forced to retire at just 29 years of age after receiving one blow to the head too many in the 1982 County Championship final between Lancashire and the North Midlands. Called up as a replacement for the Lions 1977 tour of New Zealand, he appeared in the last three Tests and captained the team in all four matches of the 1980 Springboks series. He also led the North of England to an improbable 21–9 victory over the All Blacks in 1979 and won the County Championship

three times with Lancashire. The recipient of an OBE in 1982, once retired Beaumont turned effortlessly to a career in broadcasting, appearing as a pundit for both the BBC and Sky Sports, as well as as a captain on the popular celebrity quiz A Question of Sport. He later joined the RFU management board.

JOHN BIRKETT

Full Name John Guy Giberne Birkett
Born 27.12.1884 – Richmond, Surrey
Clubs Harlequins, Brighton
Position Centre
Debut 17.03.1906 – Scotland
Last Match 08.04.1912 – France
England Appearances 21 (won 12, drew 2, lost 7)
Points 34 – 10 tries, 1 drop goal
International Championship 1910, 1912
England Captain 5, 1908–11 (won 2, drew 0, lost 3)

With ten tries to his name in 21 appearances, John Birkett retired as England's most capped player and top try-scorer, records later surpassed by the wing Cyril Lowe. He scored for the first time in the 1907 massacre of France, a match celebrated for the five tries registered by Daniel Lambert to equal the world record established by Scotland's George Lindsay against Wales in 1887. Prolific in his own right, Birkett twice scored two tries in a game, against Wales in 1908 and Scotland in 1910, and signed off with a tenth touchdown in the 18–8 victory over France on Easter Monday, 1912. He hailed from an impressive sporting lineage: his father, Reginald Birkett, represented England four times at rugby and once at soccer, and his uncle, Louis Birkett, won rugby caps against Scotland in 1875 and 1877. A captain with the Royal Field Artillery, Birkett served with distinction in the First World War and was mentioned in despatches in 1918.

KYRAN BRACKEN

Full Name Kyran Paul Patrick Bracken
Born 22.11.1971 – Dublin, Ireland
Clubs Bristol, Saracens
Position Scrum half
Debut 27.11.1993 – New Zealand
Last Match 16.11.2003 – France
England Appearances 51
Points 15, 3 tries
Grand Slam 1995, 2003
International Championship 1995, 2001, 2003
Triple Crown 1995, 1998, 2002, 2003
World Cup 1995 (semi-final; 4th), 2003 (winner)

The England career of Kyran Bracken was marked by a series of highs and lows and ended with the World Cup victory in Australia. He made his mark with Bristol and gained England under-21 and 'A' honours before making his debut against New Zealand in 1993, when he was stamped on by New Zealand flanker Jamie Joseph. He lost his place to Dewi Morris and sat out the South Africa tour of 1994 to complete his law exams but, after passing those, he put himself back in contention under Jack Rowell and played in all four games of the 1995 Five Nations. He sat on the bench after Morris regained his place for the 1995 World Cup but replaced his retiring rival at Saracens only to find Matt Dawson emerging as new competition at scrum half. He consequently saw only on-off action, despite winning the Tetley's Bitter Cup in 1998, and a back injury ruled him out of the 1999 World Cup. He missed the Lions tour of 2001 and, after captaining England in the tour of North America and starting both games in the back-to-back wins over Australia and New Zealand in the tour in 2003, he lost his place to Dawson for the world cup finals and retired from international rugby at the end of the tournament, having also been awarded the MBE in 2003.

JEFF BUTTERFIELD

Full Name Jeffrey Butterfield
Born 09.08.1929 – Heckmondwike, West Yorkshire
Clubs Northampton
Position Centre
Debut 28.02.1953 – France
Last Match 21.03.1959 – Scotland
England Appearances 28 (won 16, drew 5, lost 7)
Points 15 – 5 tries

British Lions Appearances 4 (won 2, drew 0, lost 2)
Points 12 – 3 tries, 1 drop goal
Grand Slam 1957
International Championship 1953, 1954, 1957, 1958
Triple Crown 1954, 1957
England Captain 4, 1959 (won 1, drew 2, lost 1)

Called into the side for the last two games of the 1952–53 season, Jeff Butterfield scored a try in each as England claimed their first outright championship title since 1937. Ever-present until a thigh injury prematurely ended his career on the 1959 Lions tour of Australia and New Zealand, the stylish three-quarter represented his country on 28 occasions, a record for a centre later broken by Paul Dodge. He played in all four of the 1957 Grand Slam fixtures and captained England throughout 1959. Due to the vagaries of team selection he partnered Phil Davies, another exceptional centre, only nine times, although the pair did combine to great effect for the British Isles against the Springboks in 1955. Butterfield registered tries in the first three Tests, but South Africa levelled the series when Davies was inexplicably dropped for the final match.

JOHN CARLETON

Full Name John Carleton
Born 24.11.1955 – Orrell, Lancashire
Clubs Orrell
Position Wing
Debut 24.11.1979 – New Zealand
Last Match 03.11.1984 – Australia
England Appearances 26 (won 12, drew 3, lost 11)
Points 28 – 7 tries
British Lions Appearances 6 (won 1, drew 0, lost 5)
Grand Slam 1980
International Championship 1980
Triple Crown 1980

Having won a first cap in the lacklustre 1979 defeat against the All Blacks, John Carleton played 25 consecutive matches for his country until business commitments forced him to miss the 1984 tour of South Africa. He wore the England jersey on just one more occasion, that autumn's 19–3 reverse against Australia at Twickenham. A one-time schoolmaster, the Orrell wing played three Tests on the 1980 British Isles tour of South Africa, and the same number in New Zealand three years later. His hat-trick of tries in the 1980 Grand Slam victory over Scotland was the first by an Englishman since Herbert Jacob against France in 1924.

WILL CARLING

Full Name William David Charles Carling
Born 12.12.1965 – Bradford-on-Avon, Wiltshire
Clubs Durham University, Harlequins
Position Centre
Debut 16.01.1988 – France
Last Match 15.03.1997 – Wales

England Appearances 72 (won 53, drew 1, lost 18)
Points 54 – 12 tries
British Lions Appearances 1 (won 0, drew 0, lost 1)
Grand Slam 1991, 1992, 1995
International Championship 1991, 1992, 1995, 1996
Triple Crown 1991, 1992, 1995, 1996, 1997
World Cup 1991 (runner-up), 1995 (semi-final; 4th)
England Captain 59, 1988–96 (won 44, drew 1, lost 14)

Brought into the side by manager Geoff Cooke at the age of 22, and handed the leadership within ten months, Will Carling exacted more influence over the England team than any previous incumbent. In a seven-year tenure, he captained his country on 59 occasions and three Grand Slam-winning teams. In addition he holds the national record for most appearances at centre and for having played the most consecutive internationals. A run of 44 successive matches was brought to an abrupt end in the 1995 World Cup, when an ankle injury prevented his participation in the meeting with Italy. Although a powerful and destructive centre, who scored twelve England tries, in some quarters there lingered the perception that Carling's own game was often stifled by the responsibilities of captaincy. Certainly no other leader was more involved in team strategy and selection. If, due to the weight of expectation, he was not always able to express himself as a player, as a captain he transformed the England team from a laughing stock into one of the most competitive outfits in world rugby. Only comfortable when immersed in the national set-up, he was forced to withdraw from the 1989 Lions tour of Australia due to shin splints, and was dropped in New Zealand four years later after the First Test. He was awarded the OBE in 1992 and on retiring developed his business career and has also worked as a TV pundit.

MIKE CATT

Full Name Michael John Catt
Born 17.09.1971 – Port Elizabeth, South Africa
Club Bath
Positions Full-back, fly-half, wing, centre, scrum half
Debut 19.03.1994 – Wales
Last Match 27.03.04 – France
England Appearances 63 (won 46, drew 1, lost 16)
Points 142 – 7 tries, 3 drop goals, 22 penalty goals, 16 conversions
British Lions Appearances 1 (won 0, drew 0, lost 1)
Grand Slam 1995, 2003
International Championship 1995, 1996, 2000, 2001, 2003
Triple Crown 1995, 1996, 1997, 1998, 2003
World Cup 1995 (semi-final; 4th), 1999 (quarter-final), 2003 (winner)

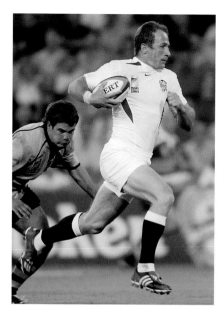

Just as the respective merits of Rob Andrew and Stuart Barnes once polarised the nation, the choice between Mike Catt and Paul Grayson for the England fly-half position attracted a similar heated debate in the late 1990s before Jonny Wilkinson made the position his own. Catt gained his reputation for being able to turn a game with a single flash of brilliance, although consistency always hindered his opportunities for England. Born in Port Elizabeth, South Africa, to an English mother, he began his international career with ten straight wins, including the four 1995 Grand Slam victories, but was brought down to earth in the semi-finals of the World Cup the same year when he was trampled on by Jonah Lomu. Appearing in the 1999 World Cup and the 2001 Lions Tour, injury forced him out of the 2002 Six Nations and he did not feature in the Grand Slam squad of 2003. But as his international career seemed doomed, his experience helped him into the 2003 World Cup squad and he proved integral. As a tactical choice to relieve the pressure from Wilkinson, his introduction against Samoa changed the game in England's favour and he went on to feature in the games against Wales, France and Australia in the final.

BEN CLARKE

Full Name Benjamin Bevan Clarke
Born 15.04.1968 – Bishop's Stortford, Hertfordshire
Clubs Bath, Richmond, Saracens
Positions Number eight, flanker
Debut 14.11.1992 – South Africa
Last Match 26.06.99 – Australia
England Appearances 40 (won 26, drew 0, lost 14)
Points 15 – 3 tries
British Lions Appearances 3 (won 1, drew 0, lost 2)
Grand Slam 1995
International Championship 1995, 1996
Triple Crown 1995, 1996, 1997
World Cup 1995 (semi-final; 4th)

An accomplished number eight or flanker, Ben Clarke commenced his international career with seventeen victories in twenty games. Selected for the Lions 1993 tour of New Zealand after just five England appearances, he was outstanding in all three Tests and within two years had won a Grand Slam and played in a World Cup semi-final. Less successful when Clive Woodward replaced Jack Rowell as coach, he missed eight successive matches, but was one of only a handful of senior players to undertake the 1998 southern hemisphere tour. A substitute in the record 76–0 defeat by Australia, Clarke stood head and shoulders above the majority of his team-mates in the remaining two Tests against the All Blacks and the one-off encounter with South Africa. Surprisingly again out of favour following the autumnal World Cup qualifiers with Holland and Italy, he was not required for the remainder of the 1998–99 season. A big-money signing by Richmond, he helped them to the Second Division title in 1997, having missed the end of Bath's 1995–96 double-winning campaign through injury. He returned to Bath in 1999 as captain, leaving 2001 to go to Worcester for a brief spell as a player/coach.

BEN COHEN

Full Name Ben Christopher Cohen
Born 14.09.1978, Northampton, Northamptonshire
Clubs Northampton Saints
Position Wing
Debut 05.02.2000 – Ireland
Last Match 27.03.2004 – France
England Appearances 40
Points 145 – 29 tries
Grand Slam 2003
International Championship 2001, 2003
Triple Crown 2002, 2003
World Cup 2003 (winner)

Not many families can boast a World Cup winner in their ranks – let alone two – but Ben Cohen followed in the footsteps of his uncle George, winner of the football World Cup in 1966, with his exploits in Australia in 2003. At 16 stones, Cohen proved a formidable opponent on the wing in both attack and defence and burst onto the international scene with two tries against Ireland in 2000. He joined Austin Healey and Brian O'Driscoll as the tournament's highest scorers the same season. A product of Northampton's academy, Cohen was drafted into the Lions squad in 2001 and demonstrated his blistering turn of pace in the 2002–03 season, scoring a try against the All Blacks and then two against Australia at Twickenham. He established himself in Clive Woodward's plans for the World Cup by scoring again when England defeated Australia in 2003 to complete the southern hemisphere tour unbeaten. He featured in all but one of England's games in the World Cup finals, scoring two tries in the process. He was awarded the MBE in 2003.

MARTIN CORRY

Full Name Martin Corry
Born 12.10.1972, Birmingham, Midlands
Clubs Leicester Tigers
Position Flanker/Number eight

Debut 31.05.1997 – Argentina
Last Match 02.11.2003 – Uruguay
England Appearances 29
Points 10 – 2 tries
British Lions Appearances 4 (won 3, drew 0, lost 1)
Points 5 – 1 try
International Championship 2001
Triple Crown 2002
World Cup 1999 (quarter-final), 2003 (winner)

Rising through the ranks of English rugby, Martin Corry first represented England at under-18 level in 1992 and went on to represent England Universities in 1995. Later that same year he made the England A tour to Australia and Fiji but with Richard Hill, Lewis Moody, Lawrence Dallaglio, Neil Back and Joe Worsley, competition for back row positions was tough. He threw his name into the hat when he made his debut in 1997, moving from Bristol to Leicester in the same year and playing a major part in their hat-trick of Premiership titles from 1999 and the 2001 Heineken Cup win. He has played a part in every Five/Six Nations tournament since 1999 but his only appearance in the World Cup came against Uruguay. He was awarded the MBE in 2003.

FRAN COTTON

Full Name Francis Edward Cotton
Born 03.01.1948 – Wigan, Lancashire
Clubs Loughborough College, Coventry, Sale
Position Prop
Debut 20.03.1971 – Scotland
Last Match 17.01.1981 – Wales
England Appearances 31 (won 13, drew 0, lost 18)
Points 4 – 1 try
British Lions Appearances 7 (won 4, drew 1, lost 2)
Grand Slam 1980
International Championship 1973, 1980
Triple Crown 1980
England Captain 3, 1975 (won 0, drew 0, lost 3)

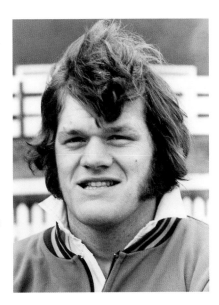

The son of a rugby league international, Fran Cotton won his first cap against Scotland during the 1971 centenary season; despite suffering a debilitating run of injuries, he retired in 1981 having made more appearances than any other English prop. Built like a carthorse, with a heart of roughly the same size, Cotton was of genuine world class on either side of the scrum. Equally secure at one or three, he occupied the loose-head berth for England's 1980 Grand Slam campaign and played at tighthead in all four Tests of the Lions' famed 1974 series victory against the Springboks.

A reserve for their 1971 jaunt, he represented the British Isles in New Zealand six years later, and in 1980 embarked on a second tour of South Africa. A certainty for the Test team, chest pains and a presumed heart attack, later diagnosed as a less serious condition, curtailed his trip, and although he recovered sufficiently to play for England against Wales in 1981, recurring problems after a hamstring injury precipitated his retirement.

RONNIE COVE-SMITH

Full Name Dr Ronald Cove-Smith
Born 26.11.1899 – Edmonton, London
Clubs Cambridge University, King's College Hospital, Old Merchant Taylors
Positions Lock, prop
Debut 19.03.1921 – Scotland
Last Match 09.02.1929 – Ireland
England Appearances 29 (won 22, drew 2, lost 5)
Points 3 – 1 try
British Lions Appearances 4 (won 0, drew 1, lost 3)
Grand Slam 1921, 1923, 1924, 1928
International Championship 1921,1923,1924,1928
Triple Crown 1921, 1923, 1924, 1928
Cambridge Blue 1919, 1920, 1921
England Captain 7, 1928–29 (won 6, drew 0, lost 1)

During a decade in which England completed four Grand Slams, Ronnie Cove-Smith was the only player to participate in each. He was captain of the side for their final title in 1928, having previously led the British Isles to South Africa in 1924. Unbeaten in thirteen matches since debut, his record was ended in 1925 by Cliff Porter's 'Invincibles'. The All Blacks won 17-11 at Twickenham, despite a one and only international try by Cove-Smith. An officer in the Grenadier Guards, after World War One he studied medicine at Cambridge University and played alongside Wavell Wakefield in the 1921 Varsity match, the first staged at Twickenham. In all he won three Blues, and also represented Cambridge at swimming and water polo.

LAWRENCE DALLAGLIO

Full Name Lawrence Bruno Nero Dallaglio
Born 10.08.1972 – Shepherd's Bush, London
Clubs London Wasps
Positions Flanker, number eight
Debut 18.11.1995 – South Africa
Last Match 27.03.04 – France
England Appearances 70 (won 53, drew 2, lost 15)
Points 70 – 14 tries
British Lions Appearances 3 (won 2, drew 0, lost 1)
Grand Slam 2003
International Championship 1996, 2000, 2001, 2003
Triple Crown 1996, 1997, 1998, 2002, 2003
England Captain 19, 1997–04 (won 10, drew 2, lost 7)

An inspirational leader and world-class forward, Lawrence Dallaglio made his first 23 international appearances as a flanker before switching to the number eight berth against Ireland in March 1999. A 1997 Lion and Clive Woodward's preferred choice as captain, he was first hampered by injury and then, after an off-pitch scandal in the build-up to the 1999 World Cup, he was forced to resign. Returning to the Lions fold in 2001, he was then dropped to the bench by Woodward in late 2002 and early 2003, but his positive reaction to adversity saw him fight back for a starting place in the successful tour to the southern hemisphere and he went on to start all seven of England's games in the World Cup finals. Named England captain for the second time in January 2004 after Martin Johnson's retirement from international rugby, he was awarded the MBE in 2003.

DAVE DAVIES

Full Name William John Abbott Davies
Born 21.06.1890 – Pembroke, Wales
Clubs United Services, Royal Navy, Combined Services
Position Fly-half
Debut 04.01.1913 – South Africa
Last Match 02.04.1923 – France
England Appearances 22 (won 20, drew 1, lost 2)
Points 24 – 4 tries, 3 drop goals
Grand Slam 1913, 1914,1921, 1923
International Championship 1913, 1914, 1920, 1921, 1923
Triple Crown 1913, 1914, 1921, 1923
England Captain 11, 1921–23 (won 10, drew 1, lost 0)

After playing in the losing side in his first international, Dave Davies made a further 21 appearances without tasting defeat. A mercurial talent, he remained England's most capped fly-half until the rise of Rob Andrew, and established a record halfback partnership with Cyril Kershaw. Originally united for the Grand Fleet versus the Rest of the Navy in 1919, the pair combined on fourteen occasions, resulting in thirteen victories and one draw. One of the earliest tactical kickers, Davies was equally proficient at dropping goals, nursing the touchlines or completing short pressure-relieving punts over the top. He served in World War One aboard HMS *Iron Duke* and HMS *Queen Elizabeth*, and in 1919 received an OBE for his naval duty. He captained his country on eleven unbeaten occasions and guided England to Grand Slams in 1921 and 1923.

MATT DAWSON

Full Name Matthew James Sutherland Dawson
Born 31.10.1972 – Birkenhead, Merseyside.
Clubs Northampton Saints
Position Scrum Half
Debut 16.12.1995 – Western Samoa
Last Match 27.03.2004 – France
England Appearances 62
Points 96 – 14 tries, 3 penalty goals, 6 conversions
British Lions Appearances 5 (won 3, drew 0, lost 2)
Points 10 – 2 tries
Grand Slam 2003
International Championship 1996, 2001, 2003
Triple Crown 1996, 1998, 2002, 2003
World Cup 1999 (quarter-final), 2003 (winner)
England Captain 1998–2001 (won 4, drew 0, lost 5)

Matt Dawson celebrated his 50th cap for England on the day that England won the Grand Slam in Ireland in 2003. A mainstay of the England team for eight years following his debut in 1995, Dawson gained recognition as one of the finest scrum halves of the modern game, an outstanding exponent of the tap-and-go penalty and a persistent nuisance to the opposition at the scrum. Brought up in High Wycombe, where he played alongside future England team-mate Nick Beal, Dawson went on to join Northampton, where his progress saw him usurp Kyran Bracken as England's first choice behind the pack. A part of the Lions' tours of South Africa and Australia, in 1997 and 2001, Dawson stood in as captain in the absence of Martin Johnson to guide England to the Six Nations title in 2001. Dawson was pivotal to England's World Cup success, supplying the pass that saw Jonny Wilkinson kick the winning drop goal in the final against Australia.

PHIL DE GLANVILLE

Full Name Philip Ranulph de Glanville
Born 01.10.1968 – Loughborough, Leicestershire
Clubs Bath
Position Centre

Debut 14.11.1992 – South Africa
Last Match 24.10.99 – South Africa
England Appearances 38 (won 24, drew 2, lost 12)
Points 40 – 8 tries
International Championship 1996
Triple Crown 1996, 1997, 1998
World Cup 1995 (semi-final; 4th), 1999 (quarter-final)
Oxford Blue 1990
England Captain 8, 1996–97 (won 5, drew 0, lost 3)

Phil de Glanville's first-team opportunities were few and far between until a serious injury to Jeremy Guscott provided an extended opening in 1994. He made his debut from the bench against South Africa in 1992, and a year later was given a first start in the 15–9 victory over New Zealand – a particularly sweet occasion for the Bath centre, who had recently sustained a horrific eye wound as a result of some characteristically mindless All Blacks rucking in their regional encounter with the South West Division. He was Jack Rowell's choice to replace Will Carling as captain and led England in eight internationals before being relieved of his captaincy duties by Rowell's successor as coach, Clive Woodward. He made eight appearances under the new regime, three as substitute, but withdrew from the 1998 southern hemisphere tour and missed the 1999 Five Nations with an injury. After winning numerous honours with Bath, and captaining them to the League and Cup double in 1996, he retired in 2001.

PAUL DODGE

Full Name Paul William Dodge
Born 26.05.1958 – Leicester
Clubs Leicester
Position Centre
Debut 04.02.1978 – Wales
Last Match 08.06.1985 – New Zealand
England Appearances 32 (won 14, drew 5, lost 13)
Points 15 – 1 try, 3 penalty goals, 1 conversion
British Lions Appearances 2 (won 1, drew 0, lost 1)
Grand Slam 1980
International Championship 1980
Triple Crown 1980
England Captain 7, 1985 (won 2, drew 1, lost 4)

Although his 32 appearances exceeded Jeff Butterfield's record for an English centre, Paul Dodge would have represented his country on many more occasions if not for the broken leg he sustained in 1983. Forced to sit out the 1984 Five Nations

Championship and the ensuing tour of South Africa, he returned against Romania a year later when he was also named as England's 100th captain. His seven-game tenure was not overly successful, and ended in a record 42–15 defeat at the hands of the All Blacks in Wellington. Dodge scored only one try in his international career, albeit a match winner against Ireland at Lansdowne Road, but did kick three penalty goals and also converted Nick Jeavons' try in the 15–11 victory over Australia in 1982. Between 1978 and 1989 he was a member of the Leicester team that reached six John Player/ Pilkington Cup finals, winning three in succession from 1979 to 1981 and losing the remainder. In 1980 he was summoned to South Africa as a replacement on the Lions tour, arriving in time to join the team for the last two Tests, a 12–10 defeat in Port Elizabeth and a 17–3 victory in Pretoria.

WADE DOOLEY

Full Name Wade Anthony Dooley
Born 02.10.1957 – Warrington, Cheshire
Clubs Preston Grasshoppers, Fylde
Position Lock
Debut 05.01.1985 – Romania
Last Match 20.03.1993 – Ireland
England Appearances 55 (won 33, drew 2, lost 20)
Points 12 – 3 tries
British Lions Appearances 2 (won 2, drew 0, lost 0)
Grand Slam 1991, 1992
International Championship 1991, 1992
Triple Crown 1991, 1992
World Cup 1987 (quarter-final), 1991 (runner-up)

Standing 6ft 8in tall and weighing almost eighteen stone, for nine seasons man mountain Wade Dooley was the backbone of his country's pack. Exceptional in the lineout and relentless in the scrum, from debut to retirement he played in 55 of England's 63 Test matches and barely took a backward step in each. Like his father, Dooley originally gravitated towards rugby league,

switching codes as an eighteen-year-old police cadet and joining Preston Grasshoppers, whom he represented for almost a decade before eventually receiving international recognition in 1985. England's most capped lock, he marked his 50th appearance by scoring the final try in the 1992 Grand Slam win over Wales. Although by no means a dirty player, he was less intimidated than most in the hostile Celtic strongholds, and was

briefly suspended in 1987 for throwing the haymaker that broke Phil Davies's cheekbone in the thick of the notorious battle of Cardiff Arms Park. He contested the two Lions victories against Australia in 1989, but in an unparalleled display of bureaucratic insensitivity, was disgracefully denied permission to rejoin their 1993 tour of New Zealand after returning to England to attend his father's funeral.

DAVID DUCKHAM

Full Name David John Duckham
Born 28.06.1946 – Coventry, West Midlands
Clubs Coventry
Positions Centre, wing
Debut 08.02.1969 – Ireland
Last Match 21.02.1976 – Scotland
England Appearances 36 (won 11, drew 2, lost 23)
Points 36 – 10 tries
British Lions Appearances 3 (won 1, drew 1, lost 1)
International Championship 1973

An enormously talented attacking wing or centre, David Duckham had the misfortune to play in an era when English rugby was at its lowest ebb. His seven-year career coincided with the championship whitewashes of 1972 and 1976, four wooden spoons and ten consecutive defeats between March 1971 and February 1973. His achievement, therefore, in retiring as England's second-highest try-scorer to Cyril Lowe was all the more remarkable, and one suspects that if born either twenty years earlier or later, Duckham would certainly have been recognised in the same class as Jeff Butterfield and Jeremy Guscott. He claimed three tries in his first three appearances, including a debut score against Ireland and a brace in the 1969 Calcutta Cup victory at Twickenham. For the British Isles Duckham starred in the last three Tests of the victorious 1971 New Zealand series and holds the Lions' record for most tries in a provincial match, scoring six times against West Coast-Buller. He captained Coventry to successive John Player Cup final wins over Bristol in 1973 and London Scottish a year later.

ERIC EVANS

Full Name Eric Evans
Born 01.02.1921 – Droylsden, Manchester
Clubs Sale
Positions Hooker, prop
Debut 03.01.1948 – Australia
Last Match 15.03.1958 – Scotland
England Appearances 30 (won 17, drew 3, lost 10)
Points 15 – 5 tries
Grand Slam 1957
International Championship 1953, 1954, 1957, 1958
Triple Crown 1954, 1957
England Captain 13, 1956–58 (won 9, drew 2, lost 2)

After winning his first cap as a loose-head prop in 1948, Eric Evans made just one more appearance in the next three years before establishing himself in 1951 as England's premier hooker. He missed the entire 1955 Five Nations season, but, having already captained Lancashire, returned a year later to skipper England in his last thirteen internationals, equalling the captaincy record established by Wavell Wakefield and Nim Hall. He ended his career with an unbeaten nine-match run, during which he led England to the Grand Slam in 1957, a second outright championship title in 1958 and, in the same season, a monumental victory over the touring Australians. A student at the outbreak of World War Two, Evans served as a sergeant in the Border Regiment and was elected a national selector in 1963. His record of 29 appearances in the number two shirt was eventually bettered by John Pullin.

ANDY GOMARSALL

Full Name Andrew Charles Thomas Gomarsall
Born 24.07.1974
Clubs Wasps, Bedford, Bath, Gloucester
Position Scrum half
Debut 23.11.1996 – Italy
Last Match 21.02.2004 – Scotland
England Appearances 17
Points 34 – 6 tries, 2 conversions
Grand Slam 2003
International Championship 2003
Triple Crown 2003
World Cup 2003 (winner)

Despite making sporadic appearances following his debut in 1996, Andy Gomarsall's England career looked over until he was drafted in against Argentina in 2002 after 27 months in the international wilderness. Gomarsall made his debut aged 22 after captaining the England schools under-18 team to their first Grand Slam in 11 years in 1992. He always faced stiff competition for England recognition with Matt Dawson and Kyran Bracken establishing themselves ahead of him but was part of Wasps' Powergen Cup success in 1999 before moving to Bedford and eventually finding his way to Gloucester, where he won the Powergen Cup in 2003. That helped him force his way back into the England set-up and after an excellent performance in the World Cup warm-up game he travelled to the World Cup as England's third choice scrum half, playing an important role as back-up. With both Dawson and Bracken struggling with injuries,

he started the game against Uruguay and scored two tries in the tournament. He was awarded the MBE in 2003.

PAUL GRAYSON

Full Name Paul James Grayson
Born 30.05.1971, Chorley, Lancashire
Clubs Northampton Saints
Position Fly Half
Debut 16.12.1995 – Western Samoa
Last Match 06.03.2004 – Ireland
England Appearances 32
Points 400 - 2 tries, 6 drop goals, 72 penalty goals, 78 conversions
International Championship 1996
Triple Crown 1996, 1997, 1998
World Cup 1999 (quarter-final), 2003 (winner)

When Jonny Wilkinson made the number ten shirt virtually his own, Northampton stalwart Paul Grayson was left to be patient and learn to wait for his chance for England. Having made his debut in 1995, Grayson emerged as England's first choice fly-half between 1996 and 1999, but struggled to maintain his position after the 1999 World Cup, despite kicking six penalties as England fell to South Africa. He broke the 1,000 points mark for Northampton and is England's second highest points scorer of all time behind Wilkinson. Grayson re-emerged as the preferred second choice to Wilkinson in the build up to the 2003 World Cup, playing a part in the 2003 Grand Slam and scoring 11 points as England's 14-match unbeaten run was ended by France in Marseilles. A Lion in 1997, Grayson came on for a deserved but brief appearance in the World Cup final. He retired from international rugby in May 2004.

WILL GREENWOOD

Full Name Will John Heaton Greenwood
Born 20.10.1972 – Blackburn, Lancashire
Clubs Leicester, NEC Harlequins
Position Centre
Debut 15.11.1997 – New Zealand
Last Match 27.03.2004 – France
England Appearances 52
Points 150 – 30 tries
Grand Slam 2003
International Championship 2001, 2003
Triple Crown 1998, 2002, 2003
World Cup 1999 (quarter-final), 2003 (winner)

Will Greenwood, the son of former England captain and national coach Richard Greenwood, was one of the unsung heroes of England's World Cup-winning side, a colossus alongside centre partner Mike Tindall and England's joint-highest try-scorer of the tournament. Excelling in both defence and attack, Greenwood scored vital tries in the narrow wins over South Africa and Wales and was involved in all but one of England's tries during the tournament, scoring five himself. His one-game absence came as he returned home on compassionate leave to be by the side of his pregnant wife. Thrown in at the deep end with a debut against New Zealand in 1997, Will Greenwood repeatedly showed his ability and commitment. His partnership with Tindall, in combination with Wilkinson, saw England's defence emerge as possibly the strongest in the world. Greenwood toured with the British Lions in 1997 before making his England debut and also toured in 2001. He is an RFU Cup winner with Leicester and went on to play for Harlequins. He was awarded the MBE in 2003.

DANNY GREWCOCK

Full Name Daniel Jonathon Grewcock
Born 07.11.1972 – Coventry, West Midlands
Clubs Bath, Saracens
Position Lock
Debut 07.06.1997 – Argentina
Last Match 27.03.2004 – France
England Appearances 47
Points 10 – 2 tries
British Lions Appearances 3 (won 1, drew 0, lost 1)
Grand Slam 2003
International Championship 2001, 2003
Triple Crown 1998, 2002, 2003
World Cup 1999 (quarter-final), 2003 (winner)

An accomplished lineout jumper, Coventry-born lock Danny Grewcock made his name with Saracens before moving to Bath, whom he went on to captain. Grewcock made his debut in 1997 where he scored the solitary try of his England career to date. Affectionately nicknamed 'Robolock', Grewcock holds the dubious distinction of being only the second ever England rugby player to be sent off in a Test match when he was dismissed against the All Blacks on England's tour of New Zealand in 1998 for excessive use of the boot. A much-underrated part of England's resurgence after the 1999 World Cup, Grewcock was named in the Lions tour of Australia in 2001 where he played in all three tests against the Wallabies. Fighting off the challenge of Ben Kay, he soon emerged as Clive Woodward's preferred companion alongside Martin Johnson. His World Cup campaign was cruelly cut short by a broken hand picked up against Uruguay, but he remained with the squad to bear witness to the eventual victory.

JEREMY GUSCOTT

Full Name Jeremy Clayton Guscott
Born 07.07.1965 – Bath, Avon
Clubs Bath
Position Centre
Debut 13.05.1989 – Romania
Last Match 15.10.1999 – Tonga
England Appearances 65 (won 47, drew 0, lost 12)

Points 113 – 24 tries, 2 drop goals
British Lions Appearances 8 (won 5, drew 0, lost 3)
Points 7 – 1 try, I drop goal
Grand Slam 1991, 1992, 1995
International Championship 1991, 1992, 1995, 1996
Triple Crown 1991, 1992, 1995, 1996, 1997, 1998
World Cup 1991 (runner-up), 1995 (semi-final; 4th), 1999 (quarter-final)

England's second-highest try-scorer with 24, Jeremy Guscott began his international career with a hat-trick in the 58–3 victory over Romania, and went one better with four against Holland in 1998. He scored his country's only try in the infamous defeat by Scotland in 1990 and also their one touchdown in the considerably more satisfying 1998 win versus a South African side seeking an eighteenth consecutive victory. An attacking centre, able to deceive unwitting defences with a barely perceptible change of pace, Guscott played sixteen championship matches at Twickenham, each of which England won. In combination with Will Carling, he holds the world record for the most international appearances by a centre three-quarter alliance: the pair played the last of their 45 matches against Argentina in 1996. After missing the entire 1993–94 season with a pelvic injury, he featured only intermittently in England's 1996–97 campaign, when manager Jack Rowell rather belatedly discovered he could no longer accommodate both Guscott and Carling, having selected another centre, Phil de Glanville, as captain. He scored a decisive try on debut during the 1989 Lions tour of Australia, and the drop goal that won the Second Test and the series against South Africa in 1997. In 1998 Guscott helped Bath to a first European Cup triumph, and England to a sixth Triple Crown in eight seasons. He retired in 2001 and now commentates for the BBC.

DUSTY HARE

Full Name William Henry Hare
Born 29.11.1952 – Newark, Nottinghamshire
Clubs Nottingham, Leicester
Position Full-back
Debut 16.03.1974 – Wales
Last Match 09.06.1984 – South Africa
England Appearances 25 (won 11, drew 2, lost 12)
Points 240 – 2 tries, 1 drop goal, 67 penalty goals, 14 conversions

Grand Slam 1980
International Championship 1980
Triple Crown 1980

Despite beginning his international career in England's first victory over Wales for eleven years, Dusty Hare made just two more appearances in the next five seasons. He finally established himself during the 1979–80 Grand Slam campaign by despatching an injury-time penalty goal to beat Wales 9–8 in the penultimate championship fixture. A composed and highly skilled place-kicker, Hare retired as England's leading scorer and most capped full-back, records later surpassed by Jon Webb. He twice registered nineteen points in a match, against Wales in 1981 and France twelve months later, and his 1984 Five Nations tally of 44 points remained a national best until Simon Hodgkinson scored 60 in 1991. A British Lion in New Zealand, Hare failed to command a Test place and, notwithstanding his world record 7,337 senior points, was still dropped on several occasions by England. Awarded an MBE in 1989, he won three John Player Cup finals with Leicester and also represented Nottinghamshire County Cricket Club in ten first-class games. A right-hand, middle order batsman, he accrued 171 runs in eighteen innings.

RICHARD HILL

Full Name Richard Anthony Hill
Born 23.05.1973, Dormansland, Surrey
Club Saracens
Position Flanker
Debut 01.02.1997 – Scotland
Last Match 27.03.2004 – France
England Appearances 68
Points 55 – 11 tries
British Lions Appearances 4 (won 3, drew 0, lost 1)
Grand Slam 2003
International Championship 2003 2001
Triple Crown 1997, 1998, 2002, 2003
World Cup 1999 (quarter-final), 2003 (winner)

Richard Hill's reputation as England's 'Mr Dependable' was so important that it was feared his injury problems at the start of the 2003 World Cup could undermine England's chances. Despite being limited to three games in the tournament, Hill was outstanding against France and Australia in the semi-final and final. Indeed, Hill's absence in the games against South Africa, Samoa and Wales was blamed in some quarters for England's struggles. A regular in the England side since his debut in 1997, Hill scored 11 tries for England whilst proving equally proficient in defence as part of the 'Holy Trinity' with Neil Back and Martin Johnson. Able to play anywhere in the back row, Hill donned the number 6, 7 and 8 shirts during the 2003 Six Nations. Having represented England at every level from schools upwards, Hill's showing in the 1997 Five Nations saw him selected for the Lions tour the same year and he returned to Lions duty in 2001. Hilda, as he is known, gained a reputation as a fierce competitor, a softly spoken giant and a consummate professional. He was awarded an MBE in 2003.

RICHARD HILL

Full Name Richard John Hill
Born 04.05.1961 – Birmingham, West Midlands
Club Bath
Position Scrum half
Debut 02.06.1984 – South Africa
Last Match 02.11.1991 – Australia
England Appearances 29 (won 16, drew 0, lost 13)
Points 8 – 2 tries
Grand Slam 1991
International Championship 1991
Triple Crown 1991
World Cup 1987 (quarter-final), 1991 (runner-up)
England Captain: 3, 1987 (won 0, drew 0, lost 3)

Handed the England captaincy after just five internationals, all but two as a replacement, Richard Hill was dismissed three matches later when his torrent of anti-Welsh invective was deemed to have provoked the unsavoury brawl at Cardiff Arms Park in 1987. While the Welsh authorities chose to ignore their players' role in the incident, Hill's outburst was to prove costly. In addition to losing the captaincy, he was suspended for that season's Calcutta Cup and made only one more appearance in the next two and a half years. Recalled on the strength of innumerable convincing performances for Bath, he won a further twenty caps in succession to transcend Steve Smith's record number of games by an English scrum half. Along with the Harlequins lock Paul Ackford, he last represented his country in the 1991 World Cup final defeat and was denied an opportunity to pull on a Lions jersey when their 1986 tour to South Africa was cancelled on political grounds. At club level a loyal servant to Bath, in a glittering eleven-year career Hill won eight John Player/Pilkigton Cup finals and six League Championships.

RON JACOBS

Full Name Charles Ronald Jacobs
Born 28.10.1928 – Whittlesey, Cambridgeshire
Club Northampton
Position Prop
Debut 21.01.1956 – Wales
Last Match 21.03.1964 – Scotland
England Appearances 29 (won 14, drew 5, lost 10)
Grand Slam 1957
International Championship 1957, 1958, 1960
Triple Crown 1957, 1960
England Captain 2, 1964 (won 1, drew 0, lost 1)

From his debut against Wales in 1956, Ron Jacobs played in thirteen consecutive internationals and eventually retired as his country's most capped prop, a record not overtaken until Fran Cotton made his 30th appearance in the 1980 Grand Slam victory over Scotland at Murrayfield. In 1957 he was an ever-present member of the previous England team to win all four championship fixtures and was named captain in 1964. Sadly, after an initial 6–3 win over France, his career ended in a disappointing 15–6 defeat against Scotland, their first success in fourteen matches against England. Later a national selector, Jacobs also represented the East Midlands and the Barbarians.

DICKIE JEEPS

Full Name Richard Eric Gautrey Jeeps
Born 25.11.1931 – Willingham, Cambridgeshire
Clubs Northampton
Position Scrum half
Debut 21.01.1956 – Wales
Last Match 17.03.1962 – Scotland
England Appearances 24 (won 13, drew 6, lost 5)
British Lions Appearances 13 (won 4, drew 1, lost 8)
Grand Slam 1957
International Championship 1957, 1958, 1960
Triple Crown 1957, 1960
England Captain 13, 1960–62 (won 5, drew 4, lost 4)

The fourth player to captain England thirteen times, Dickie Jeeps made the same number of appearances for the British Isles. Missing just one Test in eight years, he toured South Africa in 1955 when still uncapped by his country, Australia and New Zealand in 1959 and South Africa again three years later. Only the legendary Irish lock Willie John McBride has represented the Lions on more occasions, winning seventeen caps on five tours between 1962 and 1974. A resilient scrum half with great vision under pressure, Jeeps featured in nine unbeaten matches during which England won a Grand Slam and another Five Nations title. He assumed the captaincy when Jeff Butterfield's one season in charge ended without a try and immediately led his side to a third championship in four seasons. An England selector for six years, he was appointed RFU President in 1976, but his attempts to introduce much-needed change to the national set-up did not meet with universal approval and he moved on to become chairman of the Sports Council in 1978.

MARTIN JOHNSON

Full Name Martin Osborne Johnson
Born 09.03.1970 – Solihull, West Midlands
Clubs Wigston, Leicester Tigers
Position Lock
Debut 16.01.1993 – France
Last Match 22.11.2003 – Australia
England Appearances 84 (won 67, drew 2, lost 15)
Points 10 – 2 tries

British Lions Appearances 8 (won 4, drew 0, lost 4)
Grand Slam 1995, 2003
International Championship 1995, 1996
Triple Crown 1995, 1996, 1997, 1998, 2002, 2003
World Cup 1995 (semi-final; 4th), 1999 (quarter-final), 2003 (winner)
England Captain 39, 1998–2003 (won 34, drew 0, lost 5)

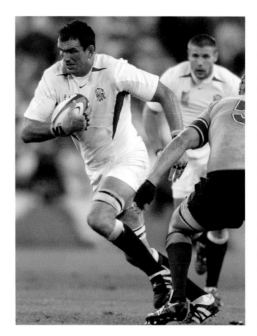

Arguably England's greatest captain, Martin Johnson became the first ever captain of a northern hemisphere team to lift the World Cup when he guided England to triumph in Australia. Initially ignored for the captain's armband in favour of Phil de Glanville, he was named as skipper following the resignation of Lawrence Dallaglio in 1999 after proving his leadership in the 1997 Lions tour in South Africa. By the time he became England captain he was a veteran of six years of international rugby and, despite the disappointment of the World Cup of 1999 and the Lions tour in 2001, the Grand Slam success in 2003 built his confidence up for the World Cup. He started six of the seven World Cup games as captain and featured in the win over Uruguay, although he was supposed to be resting. An outstanding technician in the lineout, fearsome in the scrum and in open play, Johnson's burst through the Australian defence set the scene for Jonny Wilkinson's World Cup winning drop-goal in the final. He retired in January 2004 before the start of the Six Nations. He was awarded the CBE in 2003.

BEN KAY

Full Name Benedict James Kay
Born 14.12.1975 – Liverpool, Merseyside
Clubs Leicester, Waterloo
Position Lock
Debut 02.06.2001 – Canada
Last Match 27.03.2004 – France
England Appearances 33
Points 10 – 2 tries
Grand Slam 2003
International Championship 2003
Triple Crown 2002, 2003
World Cup 2003 (winner)

Ben Kay confirmed his status as a key component in England's World Cup success by playing in all but one of England's games, including the final in Sydney. Having made the switch from Waterloo to Leicester in 1999, Kay broke onto the international scene during the landmark tour of North America in 2001 with many of England's regulars on Lions duty. Kay subsequently played in every game of the 2002 and 2003 Six Nations tournaments, although he faced serious competition from Danny Grewcock for the right to join Martin Johnson in the England second row for the World Cup. After Grewcock's tournament was cut short by injury, Kay emerged as a massive influence alongside Johnson, excelling in the semi-final victory over France. Although academic considering the final result, Kay will forever be remembered for fumbling the ball with the try line beckoning during the final after popping up on the wing. He was awarded the MBE in 2003.

JASON LEONARD

Full Name Jason Leonard
Born 14.08.1968 – Barking, London
Clubs Barking, Saracens, Harlequins
Position Prop
Debut 28.07.1990 – Argentina
Last Match 15.02.2004 – Italy
England Appearances 114 (won 86, drew 2, lost 24)
Points 5 – 1 try
British Lions Appearances 5 (won 3, drew 0, lost 2)
Grand Slam 1991, 1992, 1995, 2003
International Championship 1991,1992,1995,1996, 2000, 2001, 2003
Triple Crown 1991, 1992, 1995, 1996, 1997, 1998, 2002, 2003
World Cup 1991 (runner-up), 1995 (semi-final; 4th), 1999 (quarter-final), 2003 (winner)
England Captain 2, 1996–2003 (won 2, drew 0, lost 0)

A World Cup winner and world record holder for the most international caps, Leonard's legend speaks for itself. He made his England debut 13 years before he lifted the Webb Ellis trophy when he became an immediate hit in a brutal encounter with Argentina. He appeared in 40 consecutive tests for England

at the start of his career and missed only one game in his first five years of international play. With a playing record at club and international level that speaks for itself, he is rightly considered one of the finest front rows ever, with reliability, power, determination and competitiveness. A veteran Lion and one of few squad members who played in the amateur days, he was picked for his fourth World Cup in

2003 and, regularly used as a replacement during the finals, was one of the experienced heads that provided vital cohesion in the England squad under intense pressure in Australia. Awarded the OBE in 2003, he retired from international rugby at the end of the 2004 RBS 6 Nations championship.

JOSH LEWSEY

Full Name Owen Joshua Lewsey
Born 30.11.1976, Bromley, Kent
Clubs Bristol, Wasps
Position Full-back, wing
Debut 20.06.1998 – New Zealand
Last Match 27.03.2004 – France
England Appearances 23
Points 80 – 16 tries
Grand Slam 2003
International Championship 2003
Triple Crown 2003
World Cup 2003 (winner)

Josh Lewsey overcame significant pre-tournament fears over his fitness to play a part in England's World Cup victory. Lewsey's try-scoring potency was demonstrated by a record five-try haul against Uruguay, but his proficiency also allowed Jason Robinson to work his magic on the wing. The five tries in a World Cup game bettered the three scored by Mike Harrison against Japan in 1987. First capped aged 21 on England's 'tour of hell' to Australia in 1998, Lewsey was part of England's North American tour in 2001, but really returned to England contention in 2002 when scoring twice in the Six Nations win over Italy. He went on to enjoy Grand Slam success with England in 2003 and, also in 2003, wrote himself into England folklore with an outstanding tackle on Australia's Mat Rogers in the closing stages of England's 25–14 win in the southern hemisphere. Lewsey was awarded the MBE in 2003.

CYRIL LOWE

Full Name Cyril Nelson Lowe
Born 07.10.1891 – Holbeach, Lincolnshire
Clubs Cambridge University, Old Alleynians, Richmond, Blackheath
Position Wing
Debut 04.01.1913 – South Africa
Last Match 02.04.1923 – France
England Appearances 25 (won 21, drew 1, lost 3)
Points 58 – 18 tries, 1 drop goal
Grand Slam 1913, 1914, 1921, 1923
International Championship 1913, 1914, 1920, 1921, 1923
Triple Crown 1913, 1914, 1921, 1923
Cambridge Blue 1911, 1912, 1913

Rather overshadowed in 1913 by the exploits of Vince Coates and Cherry Pillman, Cyril Lowe came into his own the following year when he completed hat-tricks against Scotland and France and a brace against Ireland. Although equalled by Scotland's Ian Smith in 1925, his total of eight tries in a single championship term has never been bettered. Between 1913 and 1923 he made 25 consecutive appearances, a record for his country later surpassed by Wavell Wakefield, and played in all sixteen matches of England's first four Grand Slams. In his time a try-scorer nonpareil, Lowe's national record of eighteen touchdowns stood for almost 67 years. During World War One Lowe served with the Royal Flying Corps as an ace fighter pilot, rising to the rank of Group Captain. A recipient of both the Distinguished Flying Cross and Military Cross, he is thought to have downed as many as 31 enemy aircraft and was officially credited with nine kills. A dashing post-war figure, Lowe inspired P.G. Wodehouse's poem 'The Great Day', and many believe he was also the inspiration behind Biggles, the fictional air ace in W E Johns' ripping yarns. At the height of his career Lowe lost six years to the war, and exactly how many tries he would have scored without this interruption remains one of the great sporting imponderables.

DAN LUGER

Full Name Daniel Darko Luger
Born 11.01.1975 – Chiswick, Middlesex
Clubs Harlequins, Saracens, Perpignan
Position Wing
Debut 14.11.1998 – Netherlands
Last Match 09.11.2003 – Wales
England Appearances 38
Points 120 – 24 tries
Grand Slam 2003
International Championship 2001, 2003
Triple Crown 2002, 2003
World Cup 1999 (quarter-final) 2003 (winner)

The son of a Croatian father and Czech mother, Dan Luger holds a remarkable scoring record; only three players have scored more tries for England. Starting his club career with Harlequins, Luger join Saracens, briefly returned to Harlequins and then moved to play for Perpignan in France. Tries in his first two international games set Luger on his way to dominating the left-wing berth, but he has subsequently struggled with a long line of injury concerns. A neck injury ruled Luger out of the 2001 Six Nations, but he

returned in time for the Lions tour of 2001. He scored a hat-trick in the opening game of the tour, but was subsequently ruled out with a broken jaw. An outstanding talent, Luger's injury jinx stopped him from breaking through to as an England regular but, when he finally returned to full fitness, Luger capped England's Grand Slam win of 2003 with the final try in a decisive match with Ireland. Jason Robinson's switch to the

wing, with Josh Lewsey at full-back, meant Luger was limited to just two starting appearances in the World Cup. He was awarded the MBE in 2003.

LEWIS MOODY

Full Name Lewis Walton Moody
Born 12.06.1978 – Ascot, Berkshire
Clubs Leicester
Position Flanker
Debut 02.06.2001 – Canada
Last Match 22.11.2003 – Australia
England Appearances 24
Points 30 – 6 tries
Grand Slam 2003
International Championship 2003
Triple Crown 2003, 2002
World Cup 2003 (winner)

Lewis Moody figured in all seven of England's games in the 2003 World Cup capping a meteoric rise of a player who only made his first appearance for England two-and-a-half years previously. An England schoolboy international, he became the youngest player to feature for Leicester in a league game in 1996 aged 18 and went on to represent England at under-21 level before touring with the full England squad in 1998. He finally proved his international ability during the 2001 tour to North America and began to challenge for a place in England's back line when he was called into the squad for the decisive Six Nations game with Ireland, despite the likes of Neil Back and Richard Hill returning from Lions duty. Improving physical conditioning and impressive form in the build up to the World Cup, including a try in the pre-tournament win over Wales, secured Moody's place in Clive Woodward's squad. He was awarded the MBE in 2003.

BRIAN MOORE

Full Name Brian Christopher Moore
Born 11.01. 1962 – Birmingham, West Midlands
Clubs Nottingham, Harlequins, Richmond
Position Hooker
Debut 04.04.1987 – Scotland
Last Match 22.06.1995 – France
England Appearances 64 (won 45, drew 1, lost 18)
Points 4 – 1 try
British Lions Appearances 5 (won 3, drew 0, lost 2)
Grand Slam 1991, 1992, 1995
International Championship 1991, 1992, 1995
Triple Crown 1991, 1992, 1995
World Cup 1987 (quarter-final), 1991 (runner-up), 1995 (semi-final; 4th)

Notoriously labelled 'Pit Bull' by Wade Dooley, those who believe Brian Moore's game was all bristling aggression and physical confrontation do a great disservice to the most technically

proficient English hooker of all time. Constantly having to contend with the popular theory that hookers should be built like props, through his superior skills Moore sustained an eight-year international career and eventually retired as England's most capped forward. From debut against Scotland in 1987 he missed just four of his country's next 68 fixtures and was ever-present in the three Grand Slam campaigns between 1991 and 1995. He represented the British Lions on five occasions, three times during the 1989 tour of Australia and twice in New Zealand four years later. An outspoken anti-establishment figure, Moore campaigned to end the double standards that saw an increasingly commercial sport inherit millions, while players struggled to maintain professional and family commitments.

DEWI MORRIS

Full Name Colin Dewi Morris
Born 09.02.1964 – Crickhowell, Wales
Clubs Liverpool, St Helens, Orrell
Position Scrum half
Debut 05.11.1988 – Australia
Last Match 22.06.1995 – France
England Appearances 26 (won 19, drew 1, lost 6)
Points 21 – 5 tries
British Lions Appearances 3 (won 1, drew 0, lost 2)
Grand Slam 1992, 1995
International Championship 1992, 1995
Triple Crown 1992, 1995
World Cup 1995 (semi-final; 4th)

Dewi Morris enjoyed a meteoric rise to international recognition, scoring a try on debut against Australia in 1988 and winning five England caps in his first full season of senior rugby. However, after losing to Wales with the Five Nations Championship at stake, his descent was just as rapid. Usurped by Richard Hill, Morris waited almost four years for another chance and spent the entire 1991 World Cup sitting on the bench as an unused replacement. When he did finally return, he did so in some style, registering tries in the first three matches of England's 1992 Grand Slam. After making ten consecutive appearances, flu prevented him from playing against the 1993 inbound All Blacks, and his number nine jersey was handed to a young Kyran Bracken. Both excellent scrum halves, the pair alternated until Bracken was given the nod for the 1995 championship and his more experienced compatriot was restricted to a cameo role as a temporary substitute in the Grand Slam decider with Scotland. Vowing to return, Morris was one of England's major stars of the 1995 World Cup. He retired following the third-place play-off defeat against France, having partnered fly-half Rob Andrew on 22 occasions to equal the half-back record Andrew had formerly established with Richard Hill. Born in Wales, but utterly committed to England, Morris also featured in all three Tests on the 1993 Lions tour of New Zealand.

TONY NEARY

Full Name Anthony Neary
Born 25.11.1949 – Manchester
Club Broughton Park
Position Flanker
Debut 16.01.1971 – Wales
Last Match 15.03.1980 – Scotland
England Appearances 43 (won 15, drew 3, lost 25)
Points 19 – 5 tries
British Lions Appearances 1 (won 0, drew 0, lost 1)
Grand Slam 1980
International Championship 1973, 1980
Triple Crown 1980
England Captain 7, 1975–76 (won 2, drew 0, lost 5)

After ten seasons of unwavering commitment to predominantly lost causes, Tony Neary fittingly concluded his career with four consecutive victories in England's first Grand Slam for 23 years. In his farewell performance, a dazzling 30–18 triumph at Murrayfield, the penetrating open side eclipsed John Pullin's national record of 42 international appearances. A flanker with considerable pace and exceptional handling skills, he scored five tries, three of them in successive matches, including a memorable winner against the All Blacks in 1973. Although perceived by many to be the best number seven of his generation, Neary's obvious talents were never fully recognised by the British Lions management. During tours to South Africa and New Zealand he played in only one Test, and business responsibilities prevented his involvement in the 1980 series against the Springboks. His brief reign as England captain commenced with a one-point defeat of Scotland at Twickenham, but sadly ended in the ignominious Five Nations whitewash of 1976.

GARY PEARCE

Full Name Gary Stephen Pearce
Born 02.03.1956 – Dinton, Buckinghamshire
Clubs Northampton
Position Prop
Debut 03.02.1979 – Scotland
Last Match 11.10.1991 – United States
England Appearances 36 (won 12, drew 5, lost 19)
World Cup 1987 (quarter-final), 1991 (runner-up)

Ever present in the 1979 Five Nations Championship, Gary Pearce was jettisoned after an horrendous 27–3 savaging by Wales in Cardiff and did not play again until a depleted England squad toured Argentina in 1981. Impressive in a tight but ultimately successful series, he established himself as a regular member of the side for the next five years, winning a 32nd cap in the opening match of the 1987 World Cup, to overtake Fran Cotton's record number of appearances by an English prop. After losing his place to Jeff Probyn in the aftermath of a disappointing tournament, he briefly reappeared during the 1988 tour of Australia and Fiji, playing in the Test victory in Suva, before making his international farewell three years later against the United States. A former skipper of England B, he captained the Northampton team beaten in extra-time by Harlequins in the 1991 Pilkington Cup final.

RONNIE POULTON

Full Name Ronald William Poulton (later Poulton-Palmer)
Born 12.09.1889 – Oxford
Clubs Oxford University, Harlequins, Liverpool
Positions Wing, centre
Debut 30.01.1909 – France
Last Match 13.04.1914 – France
England Appearances 17 (won 14, drew 0, lost 3)
Points 28 – 8 tries, 1 drop goal
Grand Slam 1913, 1914
International Championship 1910,1912,1913,1914
Triple Crown 1913, 1914
Oxford Blue 1909, 1910, 1911
England Captain 4, 1914 (won 4, drew 0, lost 0)

Educated at Rugby School, Ronnie Poulton represented Oxford in three Varsity matches, scoring five tries in the 1909 game and a combined total of 24 points. Also a triple hockey Blue, he captained England in the 1914 championship and his four touchdowns that season against France remain a record for a Five Nations fixture. A sublimely gifted individual, equally adept in the centre or on the wing, Poulton ended his international career with eight consecutive victories as England completed back-to-back Grand Slams. Sadly, the candle that burns twice as brightly burns half as long, and he was only 25 when killed by a sniper in a muddy trench on the Western Front. A lieutenant in the Royal Berkshire Regiment, he died Poulton-Palmer after changing his name in order to satisfy the requirements of his uncle's will.

JEFF PROBYN

Full Name Jeffrey Alan Probyn
Born 27.04.1956 – London
Clubs Wasps, Askeans, Bedford, Barking
Position Prop
Debut 16.01.1988 – France
Last Match 20.03.1993 – Ireland
England Appearances 37 (won 25, drew 1, lost 11)
Points 12 – 3 tries
Grand Slam 1991, 1992
International Championship 1991, 1992
Triple Crown 1991, 1992
World Cup 1991 (runner-up)

Selected for England's 1987 World Cup squad at 31 years of age, Jeff Probyn took no part in the inaugural competition and instead experienced a further six-month delay before making a long overdue debut against France in 1988. Having quickly established himself as the best tight-head in Britain, he appeared in 37 of England's next 44 internationals, a record for a prop since passed by Jason Leonard. A Barbarian, Probyn was twice overlooked by the Lions, but did tour South Africa with a World XV in 1989 and was also a member of the Wasps side that won the Courage League Championship a year later. Along with Stuart Barnes, Wade Dooley Mike Teague, Peter Winterbottom and Jon Webb, he proudly wore the England shirt for the last time in a disappointing 17–3 defeat at the hands of Ireland at Lansdowne Road in 1993.

JOHN PULLIN

Full Name John Vivian Pullin
Born 01.11.1941 – Australia
Clubs Bristol, Saracens
Position Hooker
Debut 15.01.1966 – Wales
Last Match 20.03.1976 – France
England Appearances 42 (won 13, drew 4, lost 25)
Points 3 – 1 try
British Lions Appearances 7 (won 2, drew 2, lost 3)
International Championship 1973
England Captain 13, 1972–75 (won 6, drew 1, lost 6)

Having endured a frustrating two-year exile following a debut defeat by Wales, the dependable hooker John Pullin returned to international duty against the same opposition in 1968. On this occasion, however, the contest was drawn, and Pullin went on to play 36 consecutive matches, ultimately establishing a record number of appearances unsurpassed until Tony Neary won his 43rd cap against Scotland in 1980. Remarkably, considering his country's then lamentable reputation, Pullin was the first player to captain England to victories over rugby's three superpowers: Australia, South Africa and New Zealand. Since then Will Carling and Martin Johnson have repeated the feat, but Pullin was the first to do so at Twickenham. With seven caps for the British Isles, Pullin had already experienced the satisfaction of beating the All Blacks at home. He appeared in all four Tests on the triumphant 1971 Lions tour, after playing three times during a fruitless series against South Africa in 1968. Like two other stalwarts of the national team, Rosslyn Park number eight Andy Ripley and Coventry three-quarter

David Duckham, his distinguished career ended in the 1976 Five Nations whitewash, England's second such humiliation in five years.

MARK REGAN

Full Name Mark Regan
Born 28.01.1972 – Bristol
Clubs Bristol, Bath, Leeds Tykes
Position Hooker
Debut 18.11.1995 – South Africa
Last Match 06.03.2004 – Ireland
England Appearances 30
Points 15 – 3 tries
Grand Slam 2003
International Championship 1996, 2001, 2003
Triple Crown 1996, 1997, 2003
World Cup 2003 (winner)

Mark Regan wrote his own small piece of international history during the opening game of the World Cup when he became the first Leeds Tykes player to score a try for England. After making his England debut in 1995, having come through the ranks at Bristol, he moved to Bath and toured South Africa with the Lions in 1997 before joining Leeds in 2002. Despite early promise, two years in the international wilderness saw him miss the 1999 World Cup before returning to play against South Africa in June 2000. Sporadic international appearances followed, but his switch to Leeds revitalised his England career and, singled out for his tireless work ethic, he featured in England's build up to the World Cup. He found his role in the tournament limited by Steve Thompson but he did start in one game against Samoa. He was awarded the MBE in 2003.

DEAN RICHARDS

Full Name Dean Richards
Born 11.07.1963 – Nuneaton, Warwickshire
Clubs Leicester, Hinckley
Position Number eight
Debut 01.03.1986 – Ireland
Last Match 16.03.1996 – Ireland
England Appearances 48 (won 35, drew 1, lost 12)
Points 24 – 6 tries
British Lions Appearances 6 (won 3, drew 0, lost 3)
Grand Slam 1991, 1992, 1995
International Championship 1991,1992,1995,1996
Triple Crown 1991, 1992, 1995, 1996
World Cup 1987 (quarter-final), 1991 (runner-up), 1995 (semi-final; 4th)

A colossus in the English pack for a decade and the current holder of the world record for most appearances by a number eight, Dean Richards announced his arrival on the international scene by scoring two tries on debut in the 25–20 victory over Ireland in 1986. An enormously powerful individual, superb at close quarters, his career suffered several disruptions, partially as a result of a recurring dislocated shoulder but also due to a lack of faith shown by certain coaches. Viewed as a dinosaur in some less perceptive quarters, deemed unable to contribute to an expansive game on hard, fast surfaces, Richards was not always a regular choice in the England side. Replaced by Mick Skinner in the 1991 World Cup quarter-final, he missed the final against Australia and was overlooked by Jack Rowell for the entire 1993 Five Nations. That season's Lions management were more prudent, and Richards was selected for all three Tests in New Zealand, to add to the three caps obtained in Australia four years earlier. A regular member of the 1995 side that completed the Grand Slam and reached the World Cup semi-final, Dean Richards was considered too old for the 1996 championship and was again discarded. On this occasion his exile lasted precisely two games before Rowell, cap in hand, recalled the big man to rescue a disappointing English season. As was so often the case, he duly obliged and bossed the team to victories over Scotland and Ireland. It was certainly no coincidence that Richards contested sixteen consecutive wins between 1991 and 1995, and once established in the national set-up was on the losing side only four times in his final 29 internationals. Although he never captained his country, he led Leicester to the 1995 Courage League Championship and coached them to four successive Premiership titles and back-to-back wins of the Heineken European Cup in 2001 and 2002.

JASON ROBINSON

Full Name Jason Robinson
Born 30.07.1974 – Leeds, North Yorkshire
Clubs Bath, Sale
Position Full back/wing
Debut 17.02.2001 – Italy
Last Match 27.03.2004 – France
England Appearances 33
Points 95 – 19 tries
British Lions Appearances 3 (won 2, drew 0, lost 1)
Points 10 – 2 tries
Grand Slam 2003
International Championship 2001, 2003
Triple Crown 2002, 2003
World Cup 2003 (winner)

After mesmerising defences in Rugby League, having scored 184 tries in 302 games, Jason Robinson switched codes again to Union in November 2000 when he moved to Sale after a brief spell with Bath in the mid 1990s. Not surprisingly, given his record, Robinson's switch was eagerly awaited by English union fans and his impact was swift. He was handed his first England cap against Italy in February 2001 and immediately chosen for the 2001 Lions tour to Australia, where he played in all three tests and scored two tries. Robinson's forays forward from full back and his power and pace on the wing helped England top the world rankings and his importance to England's World Cup triumph can be illustrated by the fact that he played in all seven of the games during the tournament and scored England's try in the final when he latched on to Jonny Wilkinson's pass to touch down in the corner. He was awarded the MBE in 2003.

TIM RODBER

Full Name Timothy Andrew Keith Rodber
Born 02.07.1969 – Richmond, Yorkshire
Clubs Army, Northampton
Positions Flanker, number eight, lock
Debut 18.01.1992 – Scotland
Last Match 11.04.1999 – Wales
England Appearances 44 (won 33, drew 0, lost 11)
Points 25 – 5 tries
British Lions Appearances 2 (won 2, drew 0, lost 0)
Grand Slam 1992, 1995
International Championship 1992, 1995, 1996
Triple Crown 1992, 1995, 1996, 1997
World Cup 1995 (semi-final; 4th), 1999 (quarter-final)

A versatile and athletic forward, Tim Rodber won the majority of his first 32 England caps at blind-side until future captain Lawrence Dallaglio was preferred in the position and Jack Rowell switched the Green Howards army officer to number eight. Despite becoming only the second Englishman to be dismissed in England colours, for retaliation against an unacceptably combative Eastern Province outfit, his commanding performances were a major factor in the 1995 Grand Slam as well as England's progression to fourth place in that year's World Cup. More a victim of Rowell's increasingly erratic selection policy than any actual loss of form, he was in and out of the team in 1996, but returned twelve months later to contest every Five Nations match and stake a successful claim for a place on the Lions tour to

South Africa.
A member of the side that established an unassailable series lead by dramatically winning the first two Tests, he was forced to withdraw from the third with flu. Having sustained a string of niggling injuries, including damaged knee ligaments, Rodber played no international rugby during the 1997–98 season, missing Clive Woodward's first twelve fixtures as coach, before rejoining the fray as a

replacement in the 1998 World Cup qualifying victories over Holland and Italy. A revelation when asked to partner Martin Johnson in the second row, he excelled in the position throughout the Five Nations, scoring successive tries against Scotland and Ireland.

BUDGE ROGERS

Full Name Derek Prior Rogers
Born 20.06.1935 – Bedford, Bedfordshire
Clubs Bedford
Position Flanker
Debut 11.02.1961 – Ireland
Last Match 12.04.1969 – Wales
England Appearances 34 (won 10, drew 6, lost 18)
Points 9 – 3 tries
British Lions Appearances 2 (won 0, drew 0, lost 2)
International Championship 1963
England Captain 7, 1966–69 (won 2, drew 1, lost 4)

A rampaging open-side flanker, Budge Rogers scored a try on debut against Ireland in 1961 and retired eight years later as England's record cap holder. A member of the 1963 Five Nations Championship-winning side, he captained his country on seven occasions and twice represented the Lions during the 1962 tour of South Africa. He played for the Barbarians against New Zealand in 1964, and in the same season registered his last two international tries in defeats by Ireland and Scotland. A loyal servant to Bedford throughout his career, Rogers also competed in the County Championship for the East Midlands and was awarded an OBE for his services to the game. A judicious chairman of the national selectors, he presided over the England team that won the 1980 Grand Slam.

JOHN SCOTT

Full Name John Phillip Scott
Born 28.09.1954 – Exeter, Devon
Clubs Rosslyn Park, Cardiff
Positions Number eight, lock
Debut 21.01.1978 – France
Last Match 09.06.1984 – South Africa
England Appearances 34 (won 14, drew 3, lost 17)
Points 4 – 1 try
Grand Slam 1980
International Championship 1980
Triple Crown 1980
England Captain 4, 1983-84 (won 0, drew 0, lost 4)

The only English forward to score a try in the 1980 Grand Slam season, John Scott played 34 times for his country, once as a replacement, three times in the second row and on 30 occasions at number eight, the latter a record for the position broken by Dean Richards in 1992. The first man to lead Cardiff in four consecutive seasons, his fleeting stint as a national captain was considerably less auspicious. All four of his games were ignobly lost, and in the process England conceded 115 points. The last two defeats during the 1984 tour of South Africa marked the end of his international career. Severely mauled by the press, Scott's shoddy treatment did not prevent him from memorably describing a fledgling Rob Andrew as the worst player ever to have represented England. Surprisingly ignored by the Lions in 1980, he did have the consolation of helping Cardiff to win five of the six Welsh Rugby Union Challenge Cup finals they contested between 1981 and 1987.

MICKY SKINNER

Full Name Michael Gordon Skinner
Born 26.11.1958 – Newcastle-upon-Tyne, Tyne and Wear
Clubs Harlequins, Blackheath
Position Flanker
Debut 16.01.1988 – France
Last Match 07.03.1992 – Wales
England Appearances 21 (won 16, drew 0, lost 5)
Points 12 – 3 tries
Grand Slam 1992
International Championship 1992
Triple Crown 1992
World Cup 1991 (runner-up)

Summoned as a replacement to Australia for the 1987 World Cup, Micky Skinner was not required to play in the competition and eventually made his England debut, along with Will Carling and Jeff Probyn, at the Parc des Princes in 1988. A hard-hitting flanker, he assumed both the blind-side and open-side positions, before losing his place to Mike Teague. Recalled for the last pool match of the 1991 World Cup, Skinner remained in the side, at Dean Richard's expense, for the quarter-final in Paris, where his crunching tackle on Marc Cecillon psychologically destroyed the French. The only English forward to score a try in the tournament, he was retained for the 1991–92 season and scored again in his last international, the Grand Slam-clinching victory over Wales at Twickenham. A member of the Harlequins team that won the John Player/Pilkington Cup in 1988 and 1991, he also played for Kent in their 1985 County Championship final defeat against Warwickshire. He earned the sobriquet 'Mick the Munch', more for his insatiable appetite than his equally voracious tackling.

MIKE SLEMEN

Full Name Michael Anthony Charles Slemen
Born 11.05.1951 – Liverpool
Clubs Liverpool
Position Wing
Debut 06.03.1976 – Ireland
Last Match 04.02.1984 – Scotland
England Appearances 31 (won 15, drew 2, lost 14)
Points 32 – 8 tries
British Lions Appearances 1 (won 0, drew 0, lost 1)
Grand Slam 1980
International Championship 1980
Triple Crown 1980

At one time England's most capped wing, Mike Slemen scored eight international tries, including four against Scotland and two in the 1980 Grand Slam season. Dropped following the 1984 defeat at Murrayfield, he was replaced by Rory Underwood, the same player who ultimately exceeded his record total of 31 international appearances. Despite having to return home after the First Test, Slemen was the British Isles' leading try scorer on the 1980 tour of South Africa. One of his touchdowns, versus a South African Invitation XV, rivalled for pure brilliance the perennially screened Barbarians score against the All Blacks in 1973. His diagonal run completed a move involving three separate rucks, 33 passes and just about the entire team. As perceptive a judge as Bill Beaumont rated the Liverpool schoolmaster one of the best wings to wear a Lions shirt, and in the mid 1990s his talents were put to good use when he was invited to coach England's back division.

STEVE SMITH

Full Name Stephen James Smith
Born 22.07.1951 – Stockport, Lancashire
Club Sale
Position Scrum half
Debut 10.02.1973 – Ireland
Last Match 05.03.1983 – Scotland
England Appearances 28 (won 13, drew 4, lost 11)
Points 8 – 2 tries
Grand Slam 1980
International Championship 1973, 1980
Triple Crown 1980
England Captain 5, 1982–83 (won 2, drew 1, lost 2)

Even at a time when England's selectors were renowned for their eccentricities, the treatment of Steve Smith beggared belief. One of the proudest and most gifted scrum halves to represent his country, Smith was discarded four times and played in only nine of 33 internationals between February 1973 and March 1979. When eventually permitted a prolonged run of nineteen consecutive matches, he helped England to the 1980 Grand Slam and earned the captaincy for five championship games. Unfortunately, his career ended as badly as it had begun. Stripped of the leadership and dropped against Scotland in 1983, Smith graciously agreed to step back into the breach when his replacement Nigel Melville was injured. England lost 22–12, and though Melville was still incapacitated for the forthcoming fixture with Ireland, Smith's loyalty was rewarded by being permanently jettisoned. England's most capped scrum half until Richard Hill contested the 1991 World Cup final, he scored tries against Ireland and Scotland in 1980 and was twice called upon by the Lions without playing a Test.

PETER SQUIRES

Full Name Peter John Squires
Born 04.08.1951 – Ripon, Yorkshire
Clubs Harrogate, Headingley
Position Wing
Debut 24.02.1973 – France
Last Match 17.03.1979 – Wales
England Appearances 29 (won 12, drew 2, lost 15)
Points 24 – 6 tries
British Lions Appearances 1 (won 0, drew 0, lost 1)
International Championship 1973

A Yorkshire county cricketer, Peter Squires was one of five players to incur the selectors' permanent displeasure in the wake of an excruciating 27–3 defeat at the Arms Park in 1979. He represented England 29 times, a record for a wing surpassed in 1984 by fellow teacher Mike Slemen, and scored six tries, including three in his first six internationals. After appearing in the last two games of the 1972–73 season, when every nation won their home fixtures and the championship was shared five ways, Squires notched the second of England's three tries in their first victory on the All Blacks' home turf. His next trip to the Antipodes, a two-match series against Australia in 1975, was far less agreeable. Although he scored a try in each of the Test defeats, a sorry tour was marred by the selectors' foolhardy decision to send a squad of rookies, and also by Australian attempts to win both contests with the type of thuggery normally reserved for a bare-knuckle brawl. Thirteen years would pass before an England team returned to Australia, but Squires did revisit New Zealand with the 1977 Lions, playing in the opening Test of a four-match rubber won 3–1 by the All Blacks.

MIKE TEAGUE

Full Name Michael Clive Teague
Born 08.10.1950 – Gloucester, Gloucestershire
Clubs Gloucester, Moseley
Positions Flanker, number eight
Debut 02.02.1985 – France
Last Match 20.03.1993 – Ireland
England Appearances 27 (won 16, drew 2, lost 9)
Points 12 – 3 tries
British Lions Appearances 3 (won 3, drew 0, lost 0)
Grand Slam 1991

International Championship 1991
Triple Crown 1991
World Cup 1991 (runner-up)

After winning a first cap as a replacement for John Hall against France in 1985, Mike Teague featured in both Test match defeats on that summer's tour of New Zealand and was then discarded for the best part of four years. Recalled for the 12–12 draw with Scotland in 1989, he became a regular member of the England side and played in the 1991 Grand Slam and World Cup final. A versatile forward, who occupied every position in the back row, he was unavailable, through a combination of exhaustion and injury, for the 1992 Five Nations Championship, but returned to complete his international career in the 1992–93 season. One of the few players to maintain a 100 per cent record for the British Isles, he appeared in the two victories over Australia in 1989 and came on as a temporary replacement in the Second Test against New Zealand in 1993, the Lions' only win of the series. Having missed the opening Test in Australia, Teague's form in the next two was outstanding, and he justifiably received the accolade of Player of the Series. On the domestic front he represented Gloucester in two Cup finals. In 1982 they shared the John Player Cup with Moseley, and eight years later were beaten 48–6 by Bath in the Pilkington Cup, the most one-sided Twickenham showpiece in the history of England's premier knock-out competition.

STEVE THOMPSON

Full Name Steve Thompson
Born 15.07.1978 – Hemel Hemstead, Hertfordshire
Clubs Northampton Saints
Position Hooker
Debut 02.02.2002 – Scotland
Last Match 27.03.2004 – France
England Appearances 29
Points 10 – 2 tries
Grand Slam 2003
International Championship 2003
Triple Crown 2003 2002
World Cup 2003 (winner)

One of the most mobile hookers in the history of England rugby, Steve Thompson took the fast track to World Cup glory after usurping Phil Greening in the centre of the front row. Thompson fought off the challenge of Argentine Federico Mendez to become first-choice in 2000 as the Saints claimed victory in the European Cup. Having already appeared for the England under-21 side Thompson travelled on England's tour of North America in 2001 and made his debut against Scotland in 2002. He impressed with his handling skills and throwing at the lineout and retained his place, missing only two of England's 17 tests in 2003 and scoring his second try for his country in the opening game of the World Cup with Georgia. Thompson proposed to his fiancé in Sydney just hours after lifting the Webb Ellis Trophy. He was awarded the MBE in 2003.

MIKE TINDALL

Full Name Michael James Tindall
Born 18.10.1978 – Wakefield, West Yorkshire
Clubs Bath Rugby
Position Centre
Debut 05.02.2000 – Ireland
Last Match 27.03.2004 – France
England Appearances 35
Points 45 – 9 tries
Grand Slam 2003
International Championship 2001, 2003
Triple Crown 2002, 2003
World Cup 2003 (winner)

In an international game that increasingly demands power and inventiveness from its backs, Mike Tindall shot onto the world scene in February 2000 and soon became one of the most powerful runners and tacklers in the England side. Tindall, a product of Bath's Academy, was called up to replace Jeremy Guscott in the 1999 World Cup squad, when aged just 21, having represented the England under-21 side, before gaining his first full cap against Ireland. Tindall scored a try in the win over Australia, Down Under in 2003, and put in an outstanding defensive performance as England won on Australian soil for the first time. He received criticism for his unconventional style at the tail end of 2002, but his outstanding form in 2003 alongside Jonny Wilkinson made him a certainty for the World Cup squad. Tindall played in six of the seven games. A giant for the England team, when under pressure, Tindall has gained wide recognition as one of Clive Woodward's most respected lieutenants. He was awarded the MBE in 2003.

SAM TUCKER

Full Name John Samuel Tucker
Born 01.06.1895 – Bristol, Avon
Clubs Bristol
Position Hooker
Debut 21.01.1922 – Wales
Last Match 17.01.1931 – Wales
England Appearances 27 (won 14, drew 4, lost 9)
Points 6 – 2 tries
Grand Slam 1928
International Championship 1928, 1930
Triple Crown 1928
England Captain 3, 1930–31 (won 1, drew 2, lost 0)

Discarded after just one appearance in 1922, a 28–6 thrashing by Wales, Sam Tucker was recalled to the national side against the All Blacks three years later. He played in 26 of England's next 27 internationals and was honoured with the captaincy for his last three matches. A try scorer in the 1926 championship defeat at the hands of Scotland, he added a second in 1928 against New South Wales, England's first victory over Australian opposition. Not originally selected for the 1930 fixture at the Arms Park, Tucker

was flown from Bristol to Cardiff on the morning of the match after Bob Sparks injured himself in a motorcycle accident. A tough, uncompromising hooker, he served with the Royal Engineers in the Great War and was wounded at the Battle of the Somme.

RORY UNDERWOOD

Full Name Rory Underwood
Born 19.06.1963 – Middlesbrough, Cleveland
Clubs RAF, Leicester, Bedford
Position Wing
Debut 18.02.1984 – Ireland
Last Match 16.03.1996 – Ireland
England Appearances 85 (won 55, drew 2, lost 28)
Points 210 – 49 tries
British Lions Appearances 6 (won 3, drew 0, lost 3)
Points 5 – 1 try
Grand Slam 1991, 1992, 1995
International Championship 1991, 1992, 1995, 1996
Triple Crown 1991, 1992, 1995, 1996
World Cup 1987 (quarter-final), 1991 (runner-up), 1995 (semi-final; 4th)

Cast from the Cyril Lowe mould of RAF fighter pilot and dashing wing, Rory Underwood still holds the record for most England tries from his thirteen-year career. His country's most capped player and record try scorer, between February 1984 and March 1996 the Leicester three-quarter missed just nine of 94 fixtures, six of them when RAF commitments took precedence over two-match tours to South Africa, New Zealand and Argentina. Including his blistering run to the corner for the Lions against the All Blacks in 1993, Underwood scored 50 international tries, the second-highest total in world rugby behind the 64 crafted by the Australian David Campese. His five touchdowns against Fiji in 1989 equalled the world record originally established by George Lindsay in 1887. He scored eleven times in fifteen World Cup contests – a far cry from the early days, when he cut a disconsolate figure, playing in an indifferent team with neither the vision nor inclination to make use of Twickenham's wide expanse. Although by no means the finished article – his lack of concentration cost England vital tries – when presented with even the slightest opening Underwood's searing pace was lethal, and his ability to beat defences over the final few metres was almost unsurpassed. Capable of feinting inside or out at high speed, he left back lines around the world grasping at shadows, and once clear was rarely caught. Away from England, with whom he won three Grand Slams, Underwood helped Leicester to League

Championship honours in 1988 and 1995, the Pilkington Cup in 1993 and the 1997 European Cup final. When Rory briefly retired in 1992, he had the unique distinction of being replaced by his brother Tony, who went on to win 27 England caps and scored thirteen tries. After finishing his rugby career, Rory went into management consultancy.

PHIL VICKERY

Full Name Philip John Vickery
Born 04.03.1976 – Barnstaple, Devon
Clubs Gloucester
Position Prop
Debut 21.01.1998 – Wales
Last Match 27.03.2004 – France
England Appearances 43
Points 5 – 1 try
British Lions Appearances 3 (won 2, drew 0, lost 1)
International Championship 2001
Triple Crown 1998. 2002
World Cup 1999 (quarter final), 2003 (winner)

Typifying his indomitable comeback style, Phil Vickery returned from a back injury, which forced him to miss the whole of the Six Nations tournament in 2003, to play in all seven of England's games in the World Cup, captaining his country for the first time against Uruguay. His rise to international level was fast – he was handed his international debut after only 34 games for Gloucester and just 81 days after his first England A cap – but his career has been blighted by injury and previously he only just recovered from neck problems in time to play in the 1999 World Cup. He made three appearances for the Lions in 2001 and captained a young England side to victory in Buenos Aires in 2002. Proud of his Cornwall roots, Vickery's honest determination and resolve helped him established a place alongside Gloucester team-mate Trevor Woodman in England's victorious World Cup side. He was awarded the MBE in 2003.

TOM VOYCE

Full Name Anthony Thomas Voyce
Born 18.05.1897
Clubs Gloucester, Cheltenham, Richmond, Blackheath, The Army
Positions Flanker, lock
Debut 14.02.1920 – Ireland
Last Match 20.03.1926 – Scotland
England Appearances 27 (won 19, drew 3, lost 5)
Points 15 – 5 tries
British Lions Appearances 2 (won 0, drew 1, lost 1)
Points 6 – 1 try, 1 penalty goal
Grand Slam 1921, 1923, 1924
International Championship 1920,1921,1923,1924
Triple Crown 1921, 1923, 1924

An integral member of England's influential pack, from his debut in a 14–11 victory over Ireland Tom Voyce appeared in 27 consecutive internationals. He contributed to three Grand Slams and only once finished on the losing side in his first eighteen matches. Following in the footsteps of Cherry Pillman, one of the first flankers genuinely effective in the loose, Voyce responded to Wavell Wakefield's tactical ingenuity by scoring tries against all of England's Five Nations opposition. He notched two against Scotland, and his only non-championship score came during the 1924 Lions trip to South Africa. On a tour blighted by injury, Voyce was required to assume wing and full-back responsibilities and even landed a penalty goal in the absence of a regular place-kicker. As a young officer he sustained an eye wound in the Great War, but served again during the century's second global conflict as a major in the Royal Army Service Corps. Gloucester's representative on the RFU for 39 years, he was elected president of rugby's oldest governing body in 1960 and awarded an OBE in 1962.

WAVELL WAKEFIELD

Full Name William Wavell Wakefield
Born 10.03.1898 – Beckenham, London
Clubs Cambridge University, Harlequins, RAF, Leicester
Positions Flanker, number eight, lock
Debut 17.01.1920 – Wales
Last Match 02.04.1927 – France
England Appearances 31 (won 20, drew 3, lost 8)
Points 18 – 6 tries
Grand Slam 1921, 1923, 1924
International Championship 1920, 1921, 1923, 1924
Triple Crown 1921, 1923, 1924
Cambridge Blue 1921, 1922
England Captain 13, 1924–26 (won 7, drew 2, lost 4)

An innovative and inspirational leader, Wavell Wakefield captained England on thirteen occasions and his national record of 31 appearances stood for 42 years. He served with the Royal Flying Corps during World War One, and after making his international debut against Wales in 1920, won the first of two Cambridge Blues the following year. England's 50th captain and a member of three Grand Slam teams, he played 29 games in succession and scored six championship tries, including two against both France and Scotland. Similarly deft at lock or in the back row, Wakefield was a man of tremendous vision whose unconventional use of his pack at set pieces and in the loose radically redefined the role of the previously immobile forward. An all-round sportsman, he was the RAF 440 yards champion in 1920 and played cricket for the MCC. Upon retirement he embarked on an equally illustrious career in administration. A pilot in the Second World War, he was knighted in 1944 and elected RFU president six years later. He also served on the International Rugby Board, and later became the first Baron Wakefield of Kendal.

JONATHAN WEBB

Full Name Jonathan Mark Webb
Born 24.08.1963 – Ealing, London
Clubs Bristol, Bath
Position Full-back
Debut 23.05.1987 – Australia
Last Match 20.03.1993 – Ireland
England Appearances 33 (won 20, drew 1, lost 12)
Points 296 – 4 tries, 66 penalty goals, 41 conversions
Grand Slam 1992
International Championship 1992
Triple Crown 1992
World Cup 1987 (quarter-final), 1991 (runner-up)

Between them Jon Webb and his one-time rival Simon Hodgkinson rewrote every major English scoring record. Webb made his debut in the first match of the 1987 World Cup when he replaced the concussed Marcus Rose after barely five minutes of the defeat by hosts Australia. He remained in the side for all but one of the next sixteen fixtures before being dropped for Hodgkinson in the aftermath of the Cardiff Arms Park reverse that cost England the 1989 Five Nations title. An exceptional goal kicker, the Nottingham full-back scored 203 points in fourteen appearances and in the process established two significant national records, each later broken by Webb. Against Argentina in November 1990 he landed three penalty goals and seven conversions to better by one Daniel Lambert's tally of 22 points in an England international and during the same season he registered 60 points, a Championship best, in a first Grand Slam for eleven years. Back in favour for the 1991 World Cup, Webb topped both records within twelve months. His 24 points against Italy featured a maiden senior try and the 67 scored in a second consecutive Grand Slam has yet to be equalled in a Five/Six Nations campaign. Although Hogkinson was the more reliable kicker, Webb's attacking instincts and vision gave him the edge at the highest level and consequently he enjoyed the more substantial career. He was he first full-back to score two tries in an international, and he was also his country's leading scorer, exceeding Dusty Hare's total of 240 points in the 1992 victory over Wales at Twickenham. A surgeon by profession, he retired in 1993 to concentrate on his medical duties.

DORIAN WEST

Full Name Dorian Edward West
Born 05.10.1967 – Wrexham, Wales
Clubs British Police, Welsh Exiles, Midlands, Leicester Tigers
Position Hooker
Debut 07.02.1998 – France
Last Match 16.11.2003 – France
England Appearances 21

Points 15, 3 tries
International Championship 2001
Triple Crown 1998, 2002
World Cup 2003 (winner)

England's first choice at hooker ahead of the World Cup after the warm-up matches against Wales and twice against France, Dorian West, known as 'Nobby', was handed the captaincy for the clash with Les Bleus in Marseille. Despite this, he had to play second fiddle to Steve Thompson in the finals and was limited to a start against Uruguay and an appearance as substitute against France. He started his first game for England against Wales in 2001, two years after earning his first cap from the bench against France in Paris, and he excelled in the tour of North America. His humble roots included playing for the British Police, Welsh Exiles and the Midlands, and he first played for Leicester in 1988. He was awarded the MBE in 2003.

PETER WHEELER

Full Name Peter John Wheeler
Born 26.11.1948 – South Norwood, London
Clubs Leicester, Old Borckleyans
Position Hooker
Debut 01.02.1975 – France
Last Match 17.03.1984 –Wales
England Appearances 41 (won 17, drew 2, lost 22)
British Lions Appearances 7 (won 2, drew 0, lost 5)
Grand Slam 1980
International Championship 1980
Triple Crown 1980
England Captain 5,1983–84 (won 2, drew 0, lost 3)

A world-class and ultra competitive hooker, Peter Wheeler was the mainstay of England's front row for ten seasons. He represented his country on 41 occasions, just two short of the record established by Tony Neary, and in 1980 participated in a first championship Grand Slam for 23 years. A member of the Lions tour party to New Zealand in 1977 and to South Africa in 1980, Wheeler won seven consecutive caps on the two trips and was extremely unfortunate when not selected for a second crack at the All Blacks in 1983. Although captain of Leicester in three successive John Player Cup final victories, his forthright opinions regarding the game's administration delayed his appointment as England skipper until November 1983. A week short of his 35th birthday, Wheeler seized his opportunity, inspiring a first defeat of the All Blacks since 1975. Four matches later he effectively ended his own international career by asking not to be considered for the 1984 tour of South Africa.

JULIAN WHITE

Full Name Julian White
Born 14.05.1973 – Plymouth, Devon
Clubs Saracens, Bristol, Leicester Tigers
Position Prop

Debut 17.06.2000 – South Africa
Last Match 27.03.2004 – France
England Appearances 21
Points 0
International Championship 2001
Triple Crown 2002
World Cup 2003 (winner)

From rural roots in deepest Devon, Julian White emerged to make his debut in the 2000 tour to South Africa having made his Premiership debut in 1999 for Saracens. Prior to that, his mixed history included spells with Bridgend and for Hawkes Bay and Canterbury Crusaders in New Zealand. In battle with Phil Vickery for a regular place in the England side, he formed a powerful relationship with Graham Rowntree and Dorian West in the England front row in 2002 before all three were usurped in time for the World Cup. He made the World Cup squad, despite being suspended for ten weeks for butting Rowntree during a club game in an incident that set back his hopes of emerging as first choice for England. Even so, he started the game against Samoa and came on as a replacement against Uruguay during the finals. He was awarded the MBE in 2003.

JONNY WILKINSON

Full Name Jonathan Peter Wilkinson
Born 25.05.1979 – Frimley, Surrey.
Clubs Newcastle
Position Fly-half
Debut 04.04.1998 – Ireland
Last Match 22.11.2003 – Australia
England Appearances 52
Points 817 – 5 tries, 21 drop goals, 161 penalty goals, 123 conversions
British Lions Appearances 3
Points 41 – 1 try, 7 penalty goals, 5 conversions
Grand Slam 2003
International Championship 2001, 2003
Triple Crown 1998, 2002, 2003
World Cup 1999 (quarter-final), 2003 (winner)

The finest fly half of the modern game, Jonny Wilkinson wrote his name into the sporting history books by kicking a drop goal, just seconds from the end of extra-time, in a dramatic final, that won England the World Cup in 2003. A prodigious points scorer for Newcastle and England, Wilkinson made his international debut aged eighteen, becoming the youngest England debutant for 71 years and went on to feature in the 1999 World Cup campaign. A remarkable total of 817 points from 52 test appearances helped Wilkinson on his way to becoming England's highest ever points scorer at the tender age of 24. Eight points against Dublin in 2001 also made Wilkinson the record points scorer in a Championship season with a total of 89, which included another record through his 35-point haul against Italy. The first choice fly-half for the Lions tour to Australia in 2001, Wilkinson scored 18 points in three matches and demonstrated a

remarkable fierceness and power in the tackle. He won the Tetley's Bitter Cup in the same season. Renowned for his rigorous and lengthy fitness and training regimes, Wilkinson earned himself a place as one of the best-known faces in World Rugby. Awarded the OBE in 2003, his inherent modesty has kept his media profile to a minimum despite his being labelled a rugby legend with the potential to carry on re-writing the record books in years to come.

PETER WINTERBOTTOM

Full Name Peter James Winterbottom
Born 31.05.1960 – Horsforth, Leeds
Clubs Headingley Harlequins
Position Flanker
Debut 02.01.1982 – Australia
Last Match 20.03.1993 – Ireland
England Appearances 58 (won 31, drew 2, lost 25)
Points 13 – 3 tries
British Lions Appearances 7 (won 1, drew 0, lost 6)
Grand Slam 1991, 1992
International Championship 1991, 1992
Triple Crown 1991, 1992
World Cup 1987 (quarter-final), 1991 (runner-up)

One of the most accomplished flanker England has ever produced, Peter Winterbottom made his debut in the 15–11 Twickenham victory over Australia in 1982. During the next twelve seasons he represented his country on 58 occasions and was a Test match ever-present on the 1983 and 1993 British Lions tours of New Zealand. Dubbed the 'Straw Man' due to his striking blond locks, Winterbottom was anything but. Brian Moore, no shrinking violet in the physical stakes, described him as the hardest man he ever met, and many an international opponent could testify to his massive commitment to the England cause. Technically adept, quick to the breakdown and forever recycling second-phase possession, as his handling skills developed so Winterbottom matured into the consummate openside. Towards the end of a career for years blighted by England's spectacular underachievement, he at last began to reap the rewards befitting his tireless service. In addition to a World Cup final appearance against Australia in 1991, he played in two Grand Slam teams and, at club level, captained Harlequins to three successive Pilkington Cup finals, the first of which, versus Northampton in 1991, was won 25–13.

TREVOR WOODMAN

Full Name Trevor James Woodman
Born 04.08.1976 – Plymouth, Devon
Clubs Gloucester, Bath
Position Prop
Debut 21.08.1999 – United States
Last Match 27.03.2004 – France
England Appearances 20
Points 0
Grand Slam 2003
International Championship 2001, 2003
Triple Crown 2003
World Cup 2003 (winner)

A relative newcomer to the England throng, Trevor Woodman made an immediate impact on the international scene with a commanding and physical performance against the All Blacks on his starting debut in 2002. He had been forced to wait three years for a full game, despite coming on as a replacement for England in 1999 and holding down a place in Gloucester's mighty front row. Injuries had previously hindered his chances of making an international breakthrough and a neck injury following the New Zealand game ruled him out of the remaining autumn internationals. His luck eventually turned in 2003 when he made a return to the England squad in the Six Nations and remained injury free and able to take his place in the World Cup squad. Keeping out the massively experienced Jason Leonard, Woodman started four of the seven World Cup matches including the crunch group game with South Africa, the semi-final and final. He was awarded the MBE in 2003.

CLIVE WOODWARD

Full Name Sir Clive Ronald Woodward
Born 06.01.1956
Clubs Leicester, Loughborough College, Manley
Position Centre
Debut 19.01.1980 – Ireland
Last Match 17.03.1984 – Wales
England Appearances 21 (won 12, drew 2, lost 7)
Points 16 – 4 tries
British Lions Appearances 2 (won 0, drew 0, lost 2)
Grand Slam 1980
International Championship 1980
Triple Crown 1980

Although now chiefly known for his leading England to victory in the 2003 World Cup as head coach, Clive Woodward was actually a skilful and elusive centre, scoring four tries for his country, including two against Argentina in a 19–19 draw in Buenos Aires, the first full international between the two countries. Despite twice suffering a broken leg, Woodward racked up 21 England appearances, starting with his debut as a replacement for Tony Bond in the first Grand Slam match of 1980, and was also selected for two British Lions tours. He played in two Tests

during the 1980 tour to South Africa but didn't play a Test on the 1983 trip to New Zealand. After a spell playing for Manley in Australia, Woodward made a smooth transition to coaching. While coach at Bath, he was appointed to replace Jack Rowell in the England job in 1997. His first international was a 15–15 draw with Australia at Twickenham in November of that year. The following summer's tour to the southern hemisphere was a severe test of his coaching abilities as Woodward's greatly depleted team suffered three record defeats. His side bounced back, though, to beat the all-conquering South Africans in December and then come within a whisker of a Grand Slam the following Spring. A disappointing performance in the 1999 World Cup spurred the squad on to better things and Woodward's perseverance led to a Grand Slam in 2003 followed by a highly successful tour of the southern hemisphere in the summer and then a return visit to Australia where England beat Australia in a tense final to lift the Webb Ellis trophy. He was knighted in 2003 for his services to rugby.

JOE WORSLEY

Full Name Joe Paul Richard Worsley
Born 14.06.1977 – Redbridge, Hampshire
Clubs Welwyn Garden City, London Wasps
Position Flanker
Debut 15.10.1999 – Tonga
Last Match 27.03.2004 – France
England Appearances 34
Points 10 – 8 tries
Grand Slam 2003
International Championship 2001, 2003
Triple Crown 2002, 2003
World Cup 1999 (quarter-final), 2003 (winner)

Coming out of the considerable shadow of Lawrence Dallaglio on the international stage and at club level with Wasps, Joe Worsley emerged as an important back-up to the established back row of Neil Back, Richard Hill and Dallaglio for England's World Cup triumph. Despite the outstanding level of competition for a place in England's back row, Worsley made 30 appearances for England up to and including the World Cup – although nearly half came from the substitutes' bench or in the absence of Dallaglio. Brought up in Digswell, in Hertfordshire, Worsley played for Welwyn Garden City before moving onto Wasps, aged sixteen. Learning his trade from Dallaglio, he became the youngest player capped at England Under-21 level and, unusually, Worsley became an England international for the first time during the 1999 World Cup. Worsley's unselfish play, fierce tackling and personable character made him a favourite in the England squad. He was awarded the MBE in 2003.

ENGLAND
RUGBY

Statistics

INTERNATIONAL RESULTS 1871–2004

1 – 1	27.03.1871	Scotland	Edinburgh	Single Test	Lost 1T–1G 1T
2 – 2	05.02.1872	Scotland	The Oval	Single Test	Won 1G 1DG 2T–1DG
3 – 3	03.03.1873	Scotland	Glasgow	Single Test	Drew 0–0
4 – 4	23.02.1874	Scotland	The Oval	Single Test	Won 1DG–1T
5 – 1	15.02.1875	Ireland	The Oval	Single Test	Won 1G 1DG 1T–0
6 – 5	08.03.1875	Scotland	Edinburgh	Single Test	Drew 0–0
7 – 2	13.12.1875	Ireland	Rathmines	Single Test	Won 1G 1T–0
8 – 6	06.03.1876	Scotland	The Oval	Single Test	Won 1G 1T–0
9 – 3	05.02.1877	Ireland	The Oval	Single Test	Won 2G 2T–0
10 – 7	05.03.1877	Scotland	Edinburgh	Single Test	Lost 0–1 DG
11 – 8	04.03.1878	Scotland	The Oval	Single Test	Drew 0–0
12 – 4	11.03.1878	Ireland	Dublin	Single Test	Won 2G 1T–0
13 – 9	10.03.1879	Scotland	Edinburgh	Single Test	Drew 1G–1DG
14 – 5	24.03.1879	Ireland	The Oval	Single Test	Won 2G 1DG 2T–0
15 – 6	30.01.1880	Ireland	Dublin	Single Test	Won 1G 1T–1T
16 – 10	28.02.1880	Scotland	Manchester	Single Test	Won 2G 3T–1G
17 – 7	05.02.1881	Ireland	Manchester	Single Test	Won 2G 2T–0
18 – 1	19.02.1881	Wales	Blackheath	Single Test	Won 7G 1DG 6T–0
19 – 11	19.03.1881	Scotland	Edinburgh	Single Test	Drew 1DG 1T–1G 1T
20 – 8	06.02.1882	Ireland	Dublin	Single Test	Drew 2T–2T
21 – 12	04.03.1882	Scotland	Manchester	Single Test	Lost 0–2T
22 – 2	16.12.1882	Wales	Swansea	Four Nations	Won 2G 4T–0
23 – 9	05.02.1883	Ireland	Manchester	Four Nations	Won 1G 3T–1T
24 – 13	03.03.1883	Scotland	Edinburgh	Four Nations	Won 2T–1T
25 – 3	05.01.1884	Wales	Leeds	Four Nations	Won 1G 2T–1G
26 – 10	04.02.1884	Ireland	Dublin	Four Nations	Won 1G–0
27 – 14	01.03.1884	Scotland	Blackheath	Four Nations	Won 1G–1T
28 – 4	03.01.1885	Wales	Swansea	Four Nations	Won 1G 4T–1G 1T
29 – 11	07.02.1885	Ireland	Manchester	Four Nations	Won 2T–1T
30 – 5	02.01.1886	Wales	Blackheath	Four Nations	Won 1GM 2T–1G
31 – 12	06.02.1886	Ireland	Dublin	Four Nations	Won 1T–0
32 – 15	13.03.1886	Scotland	Edinburgh	Four Nations	Drew 0–0
33 – 6	08.01.1887	Wales	Llanelli	FourNations	Drew 0–0
34 – 13	05.02.1887	Ireland	Dublin	Four Nations	Lost 0–2G
35 – 16	05.03.1887	Scotland	Manchester	Four Nations	Drew 1T–1T
36 – 1	16.02.1889	NZ Natives	Blackheath	Single Test	Won 1G–4T
37 – 7	15.02.1890	Wales	Dewsbury	Four Nations	Lost 0–1T
38 – 17	01.03.1890	Scotland	Edinburgh	Four Nations	Won 1G 1T–0
39 – 14	15.03.1890	Ireland	Blackheath	Four Nations	Won 3T–0
40 – 8	03.01.1891	Wales	Newport	Four Nations	Won 7–3
41 – 15	07.02.1891	Ireland	Dublin	Four Nations	Won 9–0
42 – 18	07.03.1891	Scotland	Richmond	Four Nations	Lost 3–9
43 – 9	02.01.1892	Wales	Blackheath	Four Nations	Won 17–0
44 – 16	06.02.1892	Ireland	Manchester	Four Nations	Won 7–0
45 – 19	05.03.1892	Scotland	Edinburgh	Four Nations	Won 5–0
46 – 10	07.01.1893	Wales	Cardiff	Four Nations	Lost 11–12
47 – 17	04.02.1893	Ireland	Dublin	Four Nations	Won 4–0
48 – 20	04.03.1893	Scotland	Leeds	Four Nations	Lost 0–8
49 – 11	06.01.1894	Wales	Birkenhead	Four Nations	Won 24–3
50 – 18	03.02.1894	Ireland	Blackheath	Four Nations	Lost 5–7
51 – 21	17.03.1894	Scotland	Edinburgh	Four Nations	Lost 0–6
52 – 12	05.01.1895	Wales	Swansea	Four Nations	Won 14–6
53 – 19	02.02.1895	Ireland	Dublin	Four Nations	Won 6–3
54 – 22	09.03.1895	Scotland	Richmond	Four Nations	Lost 3–6
55 – 13	04.01.1896	Wales	Blackheath	Four Nations	Won 25–0
56 – 20	01.02.1896	Ireland	Leeds	Four Nations	Lost 4–10

57 – 23	14.03.1896	Scotland	Glasgow	Four Nations	Lost 0–11
58 – 14	09.01.1897	Wales	Newport	Four Nations	Lost 0–11
59 – 21	06.02.1897	Ireland	Dublin	Four Nations	Lost 9–13
60 – 24	13.03.1897	Scotland	Manchester	Four Nations	Won 12–3
61 – 22	05.02.1898	Ireland	Richmond	Four Nations	Lost 6–9
62 – 25	12.03.1898	Scotland	Edinburgh	Four Nations	Drew 3–3
63 – 15	02.04.1898	Wales	Blackheath	Four Nations	Won 14–7
64 – 16	07.01.1899	Wales	Swansea	Four Nations	Lost 3–26
65 – 23	04.02.1899	Ireland	Dublin	Four Nations	Lost 0–6
66 – 26	11.03.1899	Scotland	Blackheath	Four Nations	Lost 0–5
67 – 17	06.01.1900	Wales	Gloucester	Four Nations	Lost 3–13
68 – 24	03.02.1900	Ireland	Richmond	Four Nations	Won 15–4
69 – 27	10.03.1900	Scotland	Edinburgh	Four Nations	Drew 0–0
70 – 18	05.01.1901	Wales	Cardiff	Four Nations	Lost 0–13
71 – 25	09.02.1901	Ireland	Dublin	Four Nations	Lost 6–10
72 – 28	09.03.1901	Scotland	Blackheath	Four Nations	Lost 3–18
73 – 19	11.01.1902	Wales	Blackheath	Four Nations	Lost 8–9
74 – 26	08.02.1902	Ireland	Leicester	Four Nations	Won 6–3
75 – 29	15.03.1902	Scotland	Edinburgh	Four Nations	Won 6–3
76 – 20	10.01.1903	Wales	Swansea	Four Nations	Lost 5–21
77 – 27	14.02.1903	Ireland	Dublin	Four Nations	Lost 0–6
78 – 30	21.03.1903	Scotland	Richmond	Four Nations	Lost 6–10
79 – 21	09.01.1904	Wales	Leicester	Four Nations	Drew 14–14
80 – 28	13.02.1904	Ireland	Blackheath	Four Nations	Won 19–0
81 – 31	19.03.1904	Scotland	Edinburgh	Four Nations	Lost 3–6
82 – 22	14.01.1905	Wales	Cardiff	Four Nations	Lost 0–25
83 – 29	11.02.1905	Ireland	Cork	Four Nations	Lost 3–17
84 – 32	18.03.1905	Scotland	Richmond	Four Nations	Lost 0–8
85 – 1	02.12.1905	New Zealand	Crystal Palace	Single Test	Lost 0–15
86 – 23	13.01.1906	Wales	Richmond	Four Nations	Lost 3–16
87 – 30	10.02.1906	Ireland	Leicester	Four Nations	Lost 6–16
88 – 33	17.03.1906	Scotland	Edinburgh	Four Nations	Won 9–3
89 – 1	22.03.1906	France	Paris	Single Test	Won 35–8
90 – 1	08.12.1906	South Africa	Crystal Palace	Single Test	Drew 3–3
91 – 2	05.01.1907	France	Richmond	Single Test	Won 41–13
92 – 24	12.01.1907	Wales	Swansea	Four Nations	Lost 0–22
93 – 31	09.02.1907	Ireland	Dublin	Four Nations	Lost 9–17
94 – 34	16.03.1907	Scotland	Blackheath	Four Nations	Lost 3–8
95 – 3	01.01.1908	France	Paris	Single Test	Won 19–0
96 – 25	18.01.1908	Wales	Bristol	Four Nations	Lost 18–28
97 – 32	08.02.1908	Ireland	Richmond	Four Nations	Won 13–3
98 – 35	21.03.1908	Scotland	Edinburgh	Four Nations	Lost 10–16
99 – 1	09.01.1909	Australia	Blackheath	Single Test	Lost 3–9
100 – 26	16.01.1909	Wales	Cardiff	Four Nations	Lost 0–8
101 – 4	30.01.1909	France	Leicester	Single Test	Won 22–0
102 – 33	13.02.1909	Ireland	Dublin	Four Nations	Won 11–5
103 – 36	20.03.1909	Scotland	Richmond	Four Nations	Lost 8–18
104 – 27	15.01.1910	Wales	Twickenham	Five Nations	Won 11–6
105 – 34	12.02.1910	Ireland	Twickenham	Five Nations	Drew 0–0
106 – 5	03.03.1910	France	Paris	Five Nations	Won 11–3
107 – 37	19.03.1910	Scotland	Edinburgh	Five Nations	Won 14–5
108 – 28	21.01.1911	Wales	Swansea	Five Nations	Lost 11–15
109 – 6	28.01.1911	France	Twickenham	Five Nations	Won 37–0
110 – 35	11.02.1911	Ireland	Dublin	Five Nations	Lost 0–3
111 – 38	18.03.1911	Scotland	Twickenham	Five Nations	Won 13–8
112 – 29	20.01.1912	Wales	Twickenham	Five Nations	Won 8–0
113 – 39	16.03.1912	Scotland	Edinburgh	Five Nations	Lost 3–8
115 – 7	08.04.1912	France	Paris	Five Nations	Won 18–8
116 – 2	04.01.1913	South Africa	Twickenham	Single Test	Lost 3–9
117 – 30	18.01.1913	Wales	Cardiff	Five Nations	Won 12–0
118 – 8	25.01.1913	France	Twickenham	Five Nations	Won 20–0
119 – 37	08.02.1913	Ireland	Dublin	Five Nations	Won 15–4
120 – 40	15.03.1913	Scotland	Twickenham	Five Nations	Won 3–0
121 – 31	17.01.1914	Wales	Twickenham	Five Nations	Won 10–9
122 – 38	14.02.1914	Ireland	Twickenham	Five Nations	Won 17–12
123 – 41	21.03.1914	Scotland	Edinburgh	Five Nations	Won 16–15
124 – 9	13.04.1914	France	Paris	Five Nations	Won 39–13
125 – 32	17.01.1920	Wales	Swansea	Five Nations	Lost 5–19
126 – 10	31.01.1920	France	Twickenham	Five Nations	Won 8–3
127 – 39	14.02.1920	Ireland	Dublin	Five Nations	Won 14–11
128 – 42	20.03.1920	Scotland	Twickenham	Five Nations	Won 13–4
129 – 33	15.01.1921	Wales	Twickenham	Five Nations	Won 18–3
130 – 40	12.02.1921	Ireland	Twickenham	Five Nations	Won 15–0
131 – 43	19.03.1921	Scotland	Edinburgh	Five Nations	Won 18–0
132 – 11	28.03.1921	France	Paris	Five Nations	Won 10–6

133 – 34	21.01.1922	Wales	Cardiff	Five Nations	Lost 6–28
134 – 41	11.02.1922	Ireland	Dublin	Five Nations	Won 12–3
135 – 12	25.02.1922	France	Twickenham	Five Nations	Drew 11–11
136 – 44	18.03.1922	Scotland	Twickenham	Five Nations	Won 11––5
137 – 35	20.01.1923	Wales	Twickenham	Five Nations	Won 7–3
138 – 42	10.02.1923	Ireland	Leicester	Five Nations	Won 23–5
139 – 45	17.03.1923	Scotland	Edinburgh	Five Nations	Won 8–6
140 – 13	02.04.1923	France	Paris	Five Nations	Won 12–3
141 – 36	19.01.1924	Wales	Swansea	Five Nations	Won 17–9
142 – 43	09.02.1924	Ireland	Belfast	Five Nations	Won 14–3
143 – 14	23.02.1924	France	Twickenham	Five Nations	Won 19–7
144 – 46	15.03.1924	Scotland	Twickenham	Five Nations	Won 19–0
145 – 2	03.01.1925	New Zealand	Twickenham	Single Test	Lost 11–17
146 – 37	17.01.1925	Wales	Twickenham	Five Nations	Won 12–6
147 – 44	14.02.1925	Ireland	Twickenham	Five Nations	Drew 6–6
148 – 47	21.03.1925	Scotland	Edinburgh	Five Nations	Lost 11–14
149 – 15	13.04.1925	France	Paris	Five Nations	Won 13–11
150 – 38	16.01.1926	Wales	Cardiff	Five Nations	Drew 3–3
151 – 45	13.02.1926	Ireland	Dublin	Five Nations	Lost 15–19
152 – 16	27.02.1926	France	Twickenham	Five Nations	Won 11–0
153 – 48	20.03.1926	Scotland	Twickenham	Five Nations	Lost 9–17
154 – 39	15.01.1927	Wales	Twickenham	Five Nations	Won 11–9
155 – 46	12.02.1927	Ireland	Twickenham	Five Nations	Won 8–6
156 – 49	19.03.1927	Scotland	Edinburgh	Five Nations	Lost 13–21
157 – 17	02.04.1927	France	Paris	Five Nations	Lost 0–3
158 – 2	07.01.1928	Australia	Twickenham	Single Test	Won 18–11
159 – 40	21.01.1928	Wales	Swansea	Five Nations	Won 10–8
160 – 47	11.02.1928	Ireland	Dublin	Five Nations	Won 7–6
161 – 18	25.02.1928	France	Twickenham	Five Nations	Won 18–8
162 – 50	17.03.1928	Scotland	Twickenham	Five Nations	Won 6–0
163 – 41	19.01.1929	Wales	Twickenham	Five Nations	Won 8–3
164 – 48	09.02.1929	Ireland	Twickenham	Five Nations	Lost 5–6
165 – 51	16.03.1929	Scotland	Edinburgh	Five Nations	Lost 6–12
166 – 19	01.04.1929	France	Paris	Five Nations	Won 16–6
167 – 42	18.01.1930	Wales	Cardiff	Five Nations	Won 11–3
168 – 49	08.02.1930	Ireland	Dublin	Five Nations	Lost 3–4
169 – 20	22.02.1930	France	Twickenham	Five Nations	Won 11–5
170 – 52	15.03.1930	Scotland	Twickenham	Five Nations	Drew 0–0
171 – 43	17.01.1931	Wales	Twickenham	Five Nations	Drew 11–11
172 – 50	14.02.1931	Ireland	Twickenham	Five Nations	Lost 5–6
173 – 53	21.03.1931	Scotland	Edinburgh	Five Nations	Lost 19–28
174 – 21	06.04.1931	France	Paris	Five Nations	Lost 13–14
175 – 3	02.01.1932	South Africa	Twickenham	Single Test	Lost 0–7
176 – 44	16.01.1932	Wales	Swansea	Four Nations	Lost 5–12
177 – 51	13.02.1932	Ireland	Dublin	Four Nations	Won 11–8
178 – 54	19.03.1932	Scotland	Twickenham	Four Nations	Won 16–3
179 – 45	21.01.1933	Wales	Twickenham	Four Nations	Lost 3–7
180 – 52	11.02.1933	Ireland	Twickenham	Four Nations	Won 17–6
181 – 55	18.03.1933	Scotland	Edinburgh	Four Nations	Lost 0–3
182 – 46	20.01.1934	Wales	Cardiff	Four Nations	Won 9–0
183 – 53	10.02.1934	Ireland	Dublin	Four Nations	Won 13–3
184 – 56	17.03.1934	Scotland	Twickenham	Four Nations	Won 6–3
185 – 47	19.01.1935	Wales	Twickenham	Four Nations	Drew 3–3
186 – 54	09.02.1935	Ireland	Twickenham	Four Nations	Won 14–3
187 – 57	16.03.1935	Scotland	Edinburgh	Four Nations	Lost 7–10
188 – 3	04.01.1936	New Zealand	Twickenham	Single Test	Won 13–0
189 – 48	18.01.1936	Wales	Swansea	Four Nations	Drew 0–0
190 – 55	08.02.1936	Ireland	Dublin	Four Nations	Lost 3–6
191 – 58	21.03.1936	Scotland	Twickenham	Four Nations	Won 9–8
192 – 49	16.01.1937	Wales	Twickenham	Four Nations	Won 4–3
193 – 56	13.02.1937	Ireland	Twickenham	Four Nations	Won 9–8
194 – 59	20.03.1937	Scotland	Edinburgh	Four Nations	Won 6–3
195 – 50	15.01.1938	Wales	Cardiff	Four Nations	Lost 8–14
196 – 57	12.02.1938	Ireland	Dublin	Four Nations	Won 36–14
197 – 60	19.03.1938	Scotland	Twickenham	Four Nations	Lost 16–21
198 – 51	21.01.1939	Wales	Twickenham	Four Nations	Won 3–0
199 – 58	11.02.1939	Ireland	Twickenham	Four Nations	Lost 0–5
200 – 61	18.03.1939	Scotland	Edinburgh	Four Nations	Won 9–6
201 – 52	18.01.1947	Wales	Cardiff	Five Nations	Won 9–6
202 – 59	08.02.1947	Ireland	Dublin	Five Nations	Lost 0–22
203 – 62	15.03.1947	Scotland	Twickenham	Five Nations	Won 24–5
204 – 22	19.04.1947	France	Twickenham	Five Nations	Won 6–3
205 – 3	03.01.1948	Australia	Twickenham	Single Test	Lost 0–11
206 – 53	17.01.1948	Wales	Twickenham	Five Nations	Drew 3–3
207 – 60	14.02.1948	Ireland	Twickenham	Five Nations	Lost 10–11

208 – 63	20.03.1948	Scotland	Edinburgh	Five Nations	Lost 3–6
209 – 23	29.03.1948	France	Paris	Five Nations	Lost 0–15
210 – 54	15.01.1949	Wales	Cardiff	Five Nations	Lost 3–9
211 – 61	12.02.1949	Ireland	Dublin	Five Nations	Lost 5–14
212 – 24	26.02.1949	France	Twickenham	Five Nations	Won 8–3
213 – 64	19.03.1949	Scotland	Twickenham	Five Nations	Won 19–3
214 – 55	21.01.1950	Wales	Twickenham	Five Nations	Lost 5–11
215 – 62	11.02.1950	Ireland	Twickenham	Five Nations	Won 3–0
216 – 25	25.02.1950	France	Paris	Five Nations	Lost 3–6
217 – 65	18.03.1950	Scotland	Edinburgh	Five Nations	Lost 11–13
218 – 56	20.01.1951	Wales	Swansea	Five Nations	Lost 5–23
219 – 63	10.02.1951	Ireland	Dublin	Five Nations	Lost 0–3
220 – 26	24.02.1951	France	Twickenham	Five Nations	Lost 3–11
221 – 66	17.03.1951	Scotland	Twickenham	Five Nations	Won 5–3
222 – 4	05.01.1952	South Africa	Twickenham	Single Test	Lost 3–8
223 – 57	19.01.1952	Wales	Twickenham	Five Nations	Lost 6–8
224 – 67	15.03.1952	Scotland	Edinburgh	Five Nations	Won 19–3
225 – 64	29.03.1952	Ireland	Twickenham	Five Nations	Won 3–0
226 – 27	05.04.1952	France	Paris	Five Nations	Won 6–3
227 – 58	17.01.1953	Wales	Cardiff	Five Nations	Won 8–3
228 – 65	14.02.1953	Ireland	Dublin	Five Nations	Drew 9–9
229 – 28	28.02.1953	France	Twickenham	Five Nations	Won 11–0
230 – 68	21.03.1953	Scotland	Twickenham	Five Nations	Won 26–8
231 – 59	16.01.1954	Wales	Twickenham	Five Nations	Won 9–6
232 – 4	30.01.1954	New Zealand	Twickenham	Single Test	Lost 0–5
233 – 66	13.02.1954	Ireland	Twickenham	Five Nations	Won 14–3
234 – 69	20.03.1954	Scotland	Edinburgh	Five Nations	Won 13–3
235 – 29	10.04.1954	France	Paris	Five Nations	Lost 3–11
236 – 60	22.01.1955	Wales	Cardiff	Five Nations	Lost 0–3
237 – 67	12.02.1955	Ireland	Dublin	Five Nations	Drew 6–6
238 – 30	26.02.1955	France	Twickenham	Five Nations	Lost 9–16
239 – 70	19.03.1955	Scotland	Twickenham	Five Nations	Won 9–6
240 – 61	21.01.1956	Wales	Twickenham	Five Nations	Lost 3–8
241 – 68	11.02.1956	Ireland	Twickenham	Five Nations	Won 20–0
242 – 71	17.03.1956	Scotland	Edinburgh	Five Nations	Won 11–6
243 – 31	14.04.1956	France	Paris	Five Nations	Lost 9–14
244 – 62	19.01.1957	Wales	Cardiff	Five Nations	Won 3–0
245 – 69	09.02.1957	Ireland	Dublin	Five Nations	Won 6–0
246 – 32	23.02.1957	France	Twickenham	Five Nations	Won 9–5
247 – 72	16.03.1957	Scotland	Twickenham	Five Nations	Won 16–3
248 – 63	18.01.1958	Wales	Twickenham	Five Nations	Drew 3–3
249 – 4	01.02.1958	Australia	Twickenham	Single Test	Won 9–6
250 – 70	08.02.1958	Ireland	Twickenham	Five Nations	Won 6–0
251 – 33	01.03.1958	France	Paris	Five Nations	Won 14–0
252 – 73	15.03.1958	Scotland	Edinburgh	Five Nations	Drew 3–3
253 – 64	17.01.1959	Wales	Cardiff	Five Nations	Lost 0–5
254 – 71	14.02.1959	Ireland	Dublin	Five Nations	Won 3–0
255 – 34	28.02.1959	France	Twickenham	Five Nations	Drew 3–3
256 – 74	21.03.1959	Scotland	Twickenham	Five Nations	Drew 3–3
257 – 65	16.01.1960	Wales	Twickenham	Five Nations	Won 14–6
258 – 72	13.02.1960	Ireland	Twickenham	Five Nations	Won 8–5
259 – 35	27.02.1960	France	Paris	Five Nations	Drew 3–3
260 – 75	19.03.1960	Scotland	Edinburgh	Five Nations	Won 21–12
261 – 5	07.01.1961	South Africa	Twickenham	Single Test	Lost 0–5
262 – 66	21.01.1961	Wales	Cardiff	Five Nations	Lost 3–6
263 – 73	11.02.1961	Ireland	Dublin	Five Nations	Lost 8–11
264 – 36	25.02.1961	France	Twickenham	Five Nations	Drew 5–5
265 – 76	18.03.1961	Scotland	Twickenham	Five Nations	Won 6–0
266 – 67	20.01.1962	Wales	Twickenham	Five Nations	Drew 0–0
267 – 74	10.02.1962	Ireland	Twickenham	Five Nations	Won 16–0
268 – 37	24.02.1962	France	Paris	Five Nations	Lost 0–13
269 – 77	17.03.1962	Scotland	Edinburgh	Five Nations	Drew 3–3
270 – 68	19.01.1963	Wales	Cardiff	Five Nations	Won 13–6
271 – 75	09.02.1963	Ireland	Dublin	Five Nations	Drew 0–0
272 – 38	23.02.1963	France	Twickenham	Five Nations	Won 6–5
273 – 78	16.03.1963	Scotland	Twickenham	Five Nations	Won 10–8
274 – 5	25.05.1963	New Zealand	Auckland	First Test	Lost 11–21
275 – 6	01.06.1963	New Zealand	Christchurch	Second Test	Lost 6–9
276 – 5	04.06.1963	Australia	Sydney	Single Test	Lost 9–18
277 – 7	04.01.1964	New Zealand	Twickenham	Single Test	Lost 0–14
278 – 69	18.01.1964	Wales	Twickenham	Five Nations	Drew 6–6
279 – 76	08.02.1964	Ireland	Twickenham	Five Nations	Lost 5–18
280 – 39	22.02.1964	France	Paris	Five Nations	Won 6–3
281 – 79	21.03.1964	Scotland	Edinburgh	Five Nations	Lost 6–15
282 – 70	16.01.1965	Wales	Cardiff	Five Nations	Lost 3–14

283 – 77	13.02.1965	Ireland	Dublin	Five Nations	Lost 0–5
284 – 40	27.02.1965	France	Twickenham	Five Nations	Won 9–6
285 – 80	20.03.1965	Scotland	Twickenham	Five Nations	Drew 3–3
286 – 71	15.01.1966	Wales	Twickenham	Five Nations	Lost 6–11
287 – 78	12.02.1966	Ireland	Twickenham	Five Nations	Drew 6–6
288 – 41	26.02.1966	France	Paris	Five Nations	Lost 0–13
289 – 81	19.03.1966	Scotland	Edinburgh	Five Nations	Lost 3–6
290 – 6	07.01.1967	Australia	Twickenham	Single Test	Lost 11–23
291 – 79	11.02.1967	Ireland	Dublin	Five Nations	Won 8–3
292 – 42	25.02.1967	France	Twickenham	Five Nations	Lost 12–16
293 – 82	18.03.1967	Scotland	Twickenham	Five Nations	Won 27–14
294 – 72	15.04.1967	Wales	Cardiff	FiveNations	Lost 21–34
295 – 8	04.11.1967	New Zealand	Twickenham	Single Test	Lost 11–23
296 – 73	20.01.1968	Wales	Twickenham	Five Nations	Drew 11–11
297 – 80	10.02.1968	Ireland	Twickenham	Five Nations	Drew 9–9
298 – 43	24.02.1968	France	Paris	Five Nations	Lost 9–14
299 – 83	16.03.1968	Scotland	Edinburgh	Five Nations	Won 8–6
300 – 81	08.02.1969	Ireland	Dublin	Five Nations	Lost 15–17
301 – 44	22.02.1969	France	Twickenham	Five Nations	Won 22–8
302 – 84	15.03.1969	Scotland	Twickenham	Five Nations	Won 8–3
303 – 74	12.04.1969	Wales	Cardiff	Five Nations	Lost 9–30
304 – 6	20.12.1969	South Africa	Twickenham	Single Test	Won 11–8
305 – 82	14.02.1970	Ireland	Twickenham	Five Nations	Won 9–3
306 – 75	28.02.1970	Wales	Twickenham	Five Nations	Lost 13–17
307 – 85	21.03.1970	Scotland	Edinburgh	Five Nations	Lost 5–14
308 – 45	18.04.1970	France	Paris	Five Nations	Lost 13–35
309 – 76	16.01.1971	Wales	Cardiff	Five Nations	Lost 6–22
310 – 83	13.02.1971	Ireland	Dublin	Five Nations	Won 9–6
311 – 46	27.02.1971	France	Twickenham	Five Nations	Drew 14–14
312 – 86	20.03.1971	Scotland	Twickenham	Five Nations	Lost 15–16
313 – 87	27.03.1971	Scotland	Edinburgh	Single Test	Lost 6–26
314 – 1	17.04.1971	RFU President's XV	Twickenham	Single Test	Lost 11–28
315 – 77	15.01.1972	Wales	Twickenham	Five Nations	Lost 3–12
316 – 84	12.02.1972	Ireland	Twickenham	Five Nations	Lost 12–16
317 – 47	26.02.1972	France	Paris	Five Nations	Lost 12–37
318 – 88	18.03.1972	Scotland	Edinburgh	Five Nations	Lost 9–23
319 – 7	03.06.1972	South Africa	Johannesburg	Single Test	Won 18–9
320 – 9	06.01.1973	New Zealand	Twickenham	Single Test	Lost 0–9
321 – 78	20.01.1973	Wales	Cardiff	Five Nations	Lost 9–25
322 – 85	10.02.1973	Ireland	Dublin	Five Nations	Lost 9–18
323 – 48	24.02.1973	France	Twickenham	Five Nations	Won 14–6
324 – 89	17.03.1973	Scotland	Twickenham	Five Nations	Won 20–13
325 – 10	15.09.1973	New Zealand	Auckland	Single Test	Won 16–10
326 – 7	17.11.1973	Australia	Twickenham	Single Test	Won 20–3
327 – 90	02.02.1974	Scotland	Edinburgh	Five Nations	Lost 14–16
328 – 86	16.02.1974	Ireland	Twickenham	Five Nations	Lost 21–26
329 – 49	02.03.1974	France	Paris	Five Nations	Drew 12–12
330 – 79	16.03.1974	Wales	Twickenham	Five Nations	Won 16–12
331 – 87	18.01.1975	Ireland	Dublin	Five Nations	Lost 9–12
332 – 50	01.02.1975	France	Twickenham	Five Nations	Lost 20–27
333 – 80	15.02.1975	Wales	Cardiff	Five Nations	Lost 4–20
334 – 91	15.03.1975	Scotland	Twickenham	Five Nations	Won 7–6
335 – 8	24.05.1975	Australia	Sydney	First Test	Lost 9–16
336 – 9	31.05.1975	Australia	Brisbane	Second Test	Lost 21–30
337 – 10	03.01.1976	Australia	Twickenham	Single Test	Won 23–6
338 – 81	17.01.1976	Wales	Twickenham	Five Nations	Lost 9–21
339 – 92	21.02.1976	Scotland	Edinburgh	Five Nations	Lost 12–22
340 – 88	06.03.1976	Ireland	Twickenham	Five Nations	Lost 12–13
341 – 51	20.03.1976	France	Paris	Five Nations	Lost 9–30
342 – 93	15.01.1977	Scotland	Twickenham	Five Nations	Won 26–6
343 – 89	05.02.1977	Ireland	Dublin	FiveNations	Won 4–0
344 – 52	19.02.1977	France	Twickenham	Five Nations	Lost 3–4
345 – 82	05.03.1977	Wales	Cardiff	Five Nations	Lost 9–14
346 – 53	21.01.1978	France	Paris	Five Nations	Lost 6–15
347 – 83	04.02.1978	Wales	Twickenham	Five Nations	Lost 6–9
348 – 94	04.03.1978	Scotland	Edinburgh	Five Nations	Won 15–0
349 – 90	18.03.1978	Ireland	Twickenham	Five Nations	Won 15–9
350 – 11	25.11.1978	New Zealand	Twickenham	Single Test	Lost 6–16
351 – 95	03.02.1979	Scotland	Twickenham	Five Nations	Drew 7–7
352 – 91	17.02.1979	Ireland	Dublin	Five Nations	Lost 7–12
353 – 54	03.03.1979	France	Twickenham	Five Nations	Won 7–6
354 – 84	17.03.1979	Wales	Cardiff	Five Nations	Lost 3–27
355 – 12	24.11.1979	New Zealand	Twickenham	Single Test	Lost 9–10
356 – 92	19.01.1980	Ireland	Twickenham	Five Nations	Won 24–9
357 – 55	02.02.1980	France	Paris	Five Nations	Won 17–13

358 – 85	16.02.1980	Wales	Twickenham	Five Nations	Won 9–8
359 – 96	15.03.1980	Scotland	Edinburgh	Five Nations	Won 30–18
360 – 86	17.01.1981	Wales	Cardiff	Five Nations	Lost 19–21
361 – 97	21.02.1981	Scotland	Twickenham	Five Nations	Won 23–17
362 – 93	07.03.1981	Ireland	Dublin	Five Nations	Won 10–6
363 – 56	21.03.1981	France	Twickenham	Five Nations	Lost 12–16
364 – 1	30.05.1981	Argentina	Buenos Aires	First Test	Drew 19–19
365 – 2	06.06.1981	Argentina	Buenos Aires	Second Test	Won 12–6
366 – 11	02.01.1982	Australia	Twickenham	Single Test	Won 15–11
367 – 98	16.01.1982	Scotland	Edinburgh	Five Nations	Drew 9–9
368 – 94	06.02.1982	Ireland	Twickenham	Five Nations	Lost 15–16
369 – 57	20.02.1982	France	Paris	Five Nations	Won 27–15
370 – 87	06.03.1982	Wales	Twickenham	Five Nations	Won 17–7
371 – 58	15.01.1983	France	Twickenham	Five Nations	Lost 15–19
372 – 88	05.02.1983	Wales	Cardiff	Five Nations	Drew 13–13
373 – 99	05.03.1983	Scotland	Twickenham	Five Nations	Lost 12–22
374 – 95	19.03.1983	Ireland	Dublin	Five Nations	Lost 15–25
375 – 13	19.11.1983	New Zealand	Twickenham	Single Test	Won 15–9
376 –100	04.02.1984	Scotland	Edinburgh	Five Nations	Lost 6–18
377 – 96	18.02.1984	Ireland	Twickenham	Five Nations	Won 12–9
378 – 59	03.03.1984	France	Paris	Five Nations	Lost 18–32
379 – 89	17.03.1984	Wales	Twickenham	Five Nations	Lost 15–24
380 – 8	02.06.1984	South Africa	Port Elizabeth	First Test	Lost 15–33
381 – 9	09.06.1984	South Africa	Johannesburg	Second Test	Lost 9–35
382 – 12	03.11.1984	Australia	Twickenham	Single Test	Lost 3–19
383 – 1	05.01.1985	Romania	Twickenham	Single Test	Won 22–15
384 – 60	02.02.1985	France	Twickenham	Five Nations	Drew 9–9
385 – 101	16.03.1985	Scotland	Twickenham	Five Nations	Won 10–7
386 – 97	30.03.1985	Ireland	Dublin	Five Nations	Lost 10–13
387 – 90	20.04.1985	Wales	Cardiff	Five Nations	Lost 15–24
388 – 14	01.06.1985	New Zealand	Christchurch	First Test	Lost 13–18
389 – 15	08.06.1985	New Zealand	Wellington	Second Test	Lost 15–42
390 – 91	18.01.1986	Wales	Twickenham	Five Nations	Won 21–18
391 – 102	15.02.1986	Scotland	Edinburgh	Five Nations	Lost 6-33
392 – 98	01.03.1986	Ireland	Twickenham	Five Nations	Won 25–20
393 – 61	15.03.1986	France	Paris	Five Nations	Lost 10–29
394 – 99	07.02.1987	Ireland	Dublin	Five Nations	Lost 0–17
395 – 62	21.02.1987	France	Twickenham	Five Nations	Lost 15–19
396 – 92	07.03.1987	Wales	Cardiff	Five Nations	Lost 12–19
397 – 103	04.04.1987	Scotland	Twickenham	Five Nations	Won 21–12
398 – 13	23.05.1987	Australia	Sydney	World Cup	Lost 6–19
399 – 1	30.05.1987	Japan	Sydney	World Cup	Won 60–7
400 – 1	03.06.1987	United States	Sydney	World Cup	Won 34–6
401 – 93	08.06.1987	Wales	Brisbane	World Cup	Lost 3–16
402 – 63	16.01.1988	France	Paris	Five Nations	Lost 9–10
403 – 94	06.02.1988	Wales	Twickenham	Five Nations	Lost 3–11
404 – 104	05.03.1988	Scotland	Edinburgh	Five Nations	Won 9–6
405 – 100	19.03.1988	Ireland	Twickenham	Five Nations	Won 35–3
406 – 101	23.04.1988	Ireland	Dublin	Single Test	Won 21–10
407 – 14	29.05.1988	Australia	Brisbane	First Test	Lost 16–22
408 – 15	12.06.1988	Australia	Sydney	Second Test	Lost 8–28
409 – 1	17.06.1988	Fiji	Suva	Single Test	Won 25–12
410 – 16	05.11.1988	Australia	Twickenham	Single Test	Won 28–19
411 – 105	04.02.1989	Scotland	Twickenham	Five Nations	Drew 12–12
412 – 102	18.02.1989	Ireland	Dublin	Five Nations	Won 16–3
413 – 64	04.03.1989	France	Twickenham	Five Nations	Won 11–0
414 – 95	18.03.1989	Wales	Cardiff	Five Nations	Lost 9–12
415 – 2	13.05.1989	Romania	Bucharest	Single Test	Won 58–3
416 – 2	04.11.1989	Fiji	Twickenham	Single Test	Won 58–23
417 – 103	20.01.1990	Ireland	Twickenham	Five Nations	Won 23–0
418 – 65	03.02.1990	France	Paris	Five Nations	Won 26–7
419 – 96	17.02.1990	Wales	Twickenham	Five Nations	Won 34–6
420 – 106	17.03.1990	Scotland	Edinburgh	Five Nations	Lost 7–13
421 – 3	28.07.1990	Argentina	Buenos Aires	First Test	Won 25–12
422 – 4	04.08.1990	Argentina	Buenos Aires	Second Test	Lost 13–15
423 – 5	03.11.1990	Argentina	Twickenham	Single Test	Won 51–0
424 – 97	19.01.1991	Wales	Cardiff	Five Nations	Won 25–6
425 – 107	16.02.1991	Scotland	Twickenham	Five Nations	Won 21–12
426 – 104	02.03.1991	Ireland	Dublin	Five Nations	Won 16–7
427 – 66	16.03.1991	France	Twickenham	Five Nations	Won 21–19
428 – 3	20.07.1991	Fiji	Suva	Single Test	Won 28–12
429 – 17	27.07.1991	Australia	Sydney	Single Test	Lost 15–40
430 – 16	03.10.1991	New Zealand	Twickenham	World Cup	Lost 12–18
431 – 1	08.10.1991	Italy	Twickenham	World Cup	Won 36–6
432 – 2	11.10.1991	United States	Twickenham	World Cup	Won 37–9

433 – 67	19.10.1991	France	Paris	World Cup	Won 19–10
434 – 108	26.10.1991	Scotland	Edinburgh	World Cup	Won 9–6
435 – 18	02.11.1991	Australia	Twickenham	World Cup	Lost 6–12
436 – 109	18.01.1992	Scotland	Edinburgh	Five Nations	Won 25–7
437 – 105	01.02.1992	Ireland	Twickenham	Five Nations	Won 38–9
438 – 68	15.02.1992	France	Paris	Five Nations	Won 31–13
439 – 98	07.03.1992	Wales	Twickenham	Five Nations	Won 24–0
440 – 1	17.10.1992	Canada	Wembley	Single Test	Won 26–13
441 – 10	14.11.1992	South Africa	Twickenham	Single Test	Won 33–16
442 – 69	16.01.1993	France	Twickenham	Five Nations	Won 16–15
443 – 99	06.02.1993	Wales	Cardiff	Five Nations	Lost 9–10
444 – 110	06.03.1993	Scotland	Twickenham	Five Nations	Won 26–12
445 – 106	20.03.1993	Ireland	Dublin	Five Nations	Lost 3–17
446 – 17	27.11.1993	New Zealand	Twickenham	Single Test	Won 15–9
447 – 111	05.02.1994	Scotland	Edinburgh	Five Nations	Won 15–14
448 – 107	19.02.1994	Ireland	Twickenham	Five Nations	Lost 12–13
449 – 70	05.03.1994	France	Paris	Five Nations	Won 18–14
450 – 100	19.03.1994	Wales	Twickenham	Five Nations	Won 15–8
451 – 11	04.06.1994	South Africa	Pretoria	First Test	Won 32–15
452 – 12	11.06.1994	South Africa	Cape Town	Second Test	Lost 9–27
453 – 3	12.11.1994	Romania	Twickenham	Single Test	Won 54–3
454 – 2	10.12.1994	Canada	Twickenham	Single Test	Won 60–19
455 – 108	21.01.1995	Ireland	Dublin	Five Nations	Won 20–8
456 – 71	04.02.1995	France	Twickenham	Five Nations	Won 31–10
457 – 101	18.02.1995	Wales	Cardiff	Five Nations	Won 23–9
458 – 112	18.03.1995	Scotland	Twickenham	Five Nations	Won 24–12
459 – 6	27.05.1995	Argentina	Durban	World Cup	Won 24–18
460 – 2	31.05.1995	Italy	Durban	World Cup	Won 27–20
461 – 1	04.06.1995	Western Samoa	Durban	World Cup	Won 44–22
462 – 19	11.06.1995	Australia	Cape Town	World Cup	Won 25–22
463 – 18	18.06.1995	New Zealand	Cape Town	World Cup	Lost 29–45
464 – 72	22.06.1995	France	Pretoria	World Cup	Lost 9–19
465 – 13	18.11.1995	South Africa	Twickenham	Single Test	Lost 14–24
466 – 2	16.12.1995	Western Samoa	Twickenham	Single Test	Won 27–9
467 – 73	20.01.1996	France	Paris	Five Nations	Lost 12–15
468 – 102	03.02.1996	Wales	Twickenham	Five Nations	Won 21–15
469 – 113	02.03.1996	Scotland	Edinburgh	Five Nations	Won 18–9
470 – 109	16.03.1996	Ireland	Twickenham	Five Nations	Won 28–15
471 – 3	23.11.1996	Italy	Twickenham	Single Test	Won 54–21
472 – 7	14.12.1996	Argentina	Twickenham	Single Test	Won 20–18
473 – 114	01.02.1997	Scotland	Twickenham	Five Nations	Won 41–13
474 – 110	15.02.1997	Ireland	Dublin	Five Nations	Won 46–6
475 – 74	01.03.1997	France	Twickenham	Five Nations	Lost 20–23
476 – 103	15.03.1997	Wales	Cardiff	Five Nations	Won 34–13
477 – 8	30.05.1997	Argentina	Buenos Aires	First Test	Won 46–20
478 – 9	06.06.1997	Argentina	Buenos Aires	Second Test	Lost 13–33
479 – 20	12.07.1997	Australia	Sydney	Single Test	Lost 6–25
480 – 21	15.11.1997	Australia	Twickenham	Single Test	Drew 15–15
481 – 19	22.11.1997	New Zealand	Manchester	First Test	Lost 8–25
482 – 14	29.11.1997	South Africa	Twickenham	Single Test	Lost 11–29
483 – 20	06.12.1997	New Zealand	Twickenham	Second Test	Drew 26–26
484 – 75	07.02.1998	France	Paris	Five Nations	Lost 17–24
485 – 104	21.02.1998	Wales	Twickenham	Five Nations	Won 60–26
486 – 15	22.03.1998	Scotland	Edinburgh	Five Nations	Won 34–20
487 – 111	04.04.1998	Ireland	Twickenham	Five Nations	Won 35–17
488 – 22	06.06.1998	Australia	Brisbane	Single Test	Lost 0–76
489 – 21	20.06.1998	New Zealand	Dunedin	First Test	Lost 22–64
490 – 22	27.06.1998	New Zealand	Auckland	Second Test	Lost 10–40
491 – 15	04.07.1998	South Africa	Cape Town	Single Test	Lost 0–18
492 – 1	14.11.1998	Holland	Huddersfield	WC Qualifier	Won 110–0
493 – 4	22.11.1998	Italy	Huddersfield	WC Qualifier	Won 23–15
494 – 23	28.11.1998	Australia	Twickenham	Single Test	Lost 11–12
495 – 16	05.12.1998	South Africa	Twickenham	Single Test	Won 13–7
496 – 116	20.02.1999	Scotland	Twickenham	Five Nations	Won 24–21
497 – 112	06.03.1999	Ireland	Dublin	Five Nations	Won 27–15
498 – 76	20.03.1999	France	Twickenham	Five Nations	Won 21–10
499 – 105	11.04.1999	Wales	Wembley	Five Nations	Lost 31–32
500 – 24	26.06.1999	Australia	Sydney	Single Test	Lost 15–22
501 – 3	21.09.1999	USA	Twickenham	Single Test	Won 106–8
502 – 5	02.10.1999	Italy	Twickenham	Single Test	Won 67–7
503 – 23	09.10.1999	New Zealand	Twickenham	Single Test	Lost 16–30
504 – 1	15.10.1999	Tonga	Twickenham	World Cup	Won 101–10
505 – 4	20.10.1999	Fiji	Twickenham	World Cup	Won 45–24
506 – 17	24.10.1999	South Africa	Paris	World Cup	Lost 21–44
507 – 3	28.08.1999	Canada	Twickenham	Single Test	Won 36–11

508 – 113	05.02.2000	Ireland	Twickenham	Six Nations	Won 50–18
509 – 77	19.02.2000	France	Paris	Six Nations	Won 15–9
510 – 106	04.03.2000	Wales	Twickenham	Six Nations	Won 46–12
511 – 6	18.03.2000	Italy	Rome	Six Nations	Won 59–12
512 – 117	02.04.2000	Scotland	Edinburgh	Six Nations	Lost 13–19
513 – 18	17.06.2000	South Africa	Pretoria	First Test	Lost 13–18
514 – 19	24.06.2000	South Africa	Bloemfontein	Second Test	Won 27–22
515 – 25	18.11.2000	Australia	Twickenham	Single Test	Won 22–19
516 – 10	25.11.2000	Argentina	Twickenham	Single Test	Won 19–0
517 – 20	02.12.2000	South Africa	Twickenham	Single Test	Won 25–17
518 – 107	03.02.2001	Wales	Cardiff	Six Nations	Won 44–15
519 – 7	17.02.2001	Italy	Twickenham	Six Nations	Won 80–23
520 – 118	03.03.2001	Scotland	Twickenham	Six Nations	Won 43–3
521 – 78	07.04.2001	France	Twickenham	Six Nations	Won 48–19
522 – 4	02.06.2001	Canada	Markham	First Test	Won 22–10
523 – 5	09.06.2001	Canada	Burnaby	Second Test	Won 59–20
524 – 4	16.06.2001	USA	San Francisco	Single Test	Won 48–19
525 – 114	20.10.2001	Ireland	Dublin	Single Test	Lost 14–20
526 – 26	10.11.2001	Australia	Twickenham	Single Test	Won 21–15
527 – 4	17.11.2001	Romania	Twickenham	Single Test	Won 134–0
528 – 21	24.11.2001	South Africa	Twickenham	Single Test	Won 29–9
529 – 119	02.02.2002	Scotland	Edinburgh	Six Nations	Won 29–3
530 – 115	16.02.2002	Ireland	Twickenham	Six Nations	Won 45–11
531 – 79	02.03.2002	France	Paris	Six Nations	Lost 15–20
532 – 108	23.03.2002	Wales	Twickenham	Six Nations	Won 50–10
533 – 8	06.04.2002	Italy	Rome	Six Nations	Won 45–9
534 – 11	22.06.2002	Argentina	Buenos Aires	Single Test	Won 26–18
535 – 27	16.11.2002	Australia	Twickenham	Single Test	Won 32–31
536 – 24	09.11.2002	New Zealand	Twickenham	Single Test	Won 31–28
537 – 22	23.11.2002	South Africa	Twickenham	Single Test	Won 53–3
538 – 80	15.02.2003	France	Twickenham	Six Nations	Won 25–17
539 – 109	22.02.2003	Wales	Cardiff	Six Nations	Won 26–9
540 – 9	09.03.2003	Italy	Twickenham	Six Nations	Won 40–5
541 – 120	22.03.2003	Scotland	Twickenham	Six Nations	Won 40–9
542 – 116	30.03.2003	Ireland	Dublin	Six Nations	Won 42–6
543 – 25	14.06.2003	New Zealand	Wellington	Single Test	Won 15–13
544 – 28	21.06.2003	Australia	Melbourne	Single Test	Won 25–14
545 – 110	23.08.2003	Wales	Cardiff	Single Test	Won 43–9
546 – 81	30.08.2003	France	Marseilles	First Test	Lost 16–17
547 – 82	06.09.2003	France	Twickenham	Second Test	Won 45–14
548 – 23	18.10.2003	South Africa	Perth	World Cup	Won 25–6
549 – 1	12.10.2003	Georgia	Perth	World Cup	Won 84–6
550 – 3	26.10.2003	Samoa	Melbourne	World Cup	Won 35–22
551 – 1	02.11.2003	Uruguay	Brisbane	World Cup	Won 111–13
552 – 111	09.11.2003	Wales	Brisbane	World Cup	Won 28–17
553 – 83	16.11.2003	France	Sydney	World Cup	Won 24–7
554 – 29	22.11.2003	Australia	Sydney	World Cup	Won 20–17
555 – 10	15.02.2004	Italy	Rome	Six Nations	Won 50–9
556 – 121	21.02.2004	Scotland	Edinburgh	Six Nations	Won 35–13
557 – 117	06.03.2004	Ireland	Twickenham	Six Nations	Lost 13–19
558 – 112	20.03.2004	Wales	Twickenham	Six Nations	Won 31–21
559 – 84	27.03.2004	France	Paris	Six Nations	Lost 21–24

OPPOSITION	MAT	WON	DREW	LOST	PTS FOR	PTS AG
Argentina	11	6	1	2	223	141
Australia	29	12	1	16	412	571
Canada	5	5	0	0	203	73
Fiji	4	3	0	0	156	71
France	84	46	8	30	1243	952
Georgia	1	1	0	0	84	6
Holland	1	1	0	0	110	0
Ireland	117	69	8	40	1277	845
Italy	10	10	0	0	481	127
Japan	1	1	0	0	60	7
New Zealand	25	6	1	18	310	516
New Zealand Natives	1	1	0	0	7	0
RFU President's XV	1	0	0	1	11	28
Romania	4	4	0	0	268	21
Samoa	3	3	0	0	106	53
Scotland	121	63	19	39	1260	965
South Africa	23	10	1	12	367	372
Tonga	1	1	0	0	101	10

United States	2	2	0	0	71	15
Uruguay	1	1	0	0	11	13
Wales	112	51	12	49	1273	1193
Total	**559**	**301**	**51**	**207**	**8226**	**6024**

ENGLAND v. ARGENTINA 1981–2002

1	30.05.1981	Buenos Aires	First Test	Drew 19–19
2	06.06.1981	Buenos Aires	Second Test	Won 12–6
3	28.07.1990	Buenos Aires	First Test	Won 25–12
4	04.08.1990	Buenos Aires	Second Test	Lost 13–15
5	03.11.1990	Twickenham	Single Test	Won 51–0
6	27.05.1995	Durban	World Cup	Won 24–18
7	14.12.1996	Twickenham	Single Test	Won 20–18
8	30.05.1997	Buenos Aires	First Test	Won 46–20
9	06.06.1997	Buenos Aires	Second Test	Lost 13–33
10	25.11.2000	Twickenham	Single Test	Won 19–0
11	22.06.2002	Buenos Aires	Single Test	Won 26–18

VENUE	MAT	WON	DREW	LOST	PTS FOR	PTS AG
Home	3	3	0	0	901	18
Away	7	4	1	2	154	123
Neutral	1	1	0	0	24	18
Total	11	8	1	2	268	159

ENGLAND v. AUSTRALIA 1909–2004 (1928 v. New South Wales)

1	09.01.1909	Blackheath	Single Test	Lost 3–9
2	07.01.1928	Twickenham	Single Test	Won 18–11
3	03.01.1948	Twickenham	ingle Test	Lost 0–11
4	01.02.1958	Twickenham	Single Test	Won 9–6
5	04.06.1963	Sydney	Single Test	Lost 9–18
6	07.01.1967	Twickenham	Single Test	Lost 11–23
7	17.11.1973	Twickenham	Single Test	Won 20–3
8	24.05.1975	Sydney	First Test	Lost 9–16
9	31.05.1975	Brisbane	Second Test	Lost 21–30
10	03.01.1976	Twickenham	Single Test	Won 23–6
11	02.01.1982	Twickenham	Single Test	Won 15–11
12	03.11.1984	Twickenham	Single Test	Lost 3–19
13	23.05.1987	Sydney	World Cup	Lost 6–19
14	29.05.1988	Brisbane	First Test	Lost 16–22
15	12.06.1988	Sydney	Second Test	Lost 8–28
16	05.11.1988	Twickenham	Single Test	Won 28–19
17	27.07.1991	Sydney	Single Test	Lost 15–40
18	02.11.1991	Twickenham	World Cup	Lost 6–12
19	11.06.1995	Cape Town	World Cup	Won 25–22
20	12.07.1997	Sydney	Single Test	Lost 6–25
21	15.11.1997	Twickenham	Single Test	Drew 15–15
22	06.06.1998	Brisbane	Single Test	Lost 0–76
23	28.11.1998	Twickenham	Single Test	Lost 11–12
24	26.06.1999	Sydney	Single Test	Lost 15–22
25	18.11.2000	Twickenham	Single Test	Won 22–19
26	10.11.2001	Twickenham	Single Test	Won 21–15
27	16.11.2002	Twickenham	Single Test	Won 32–31
28	21.06.2003	Melbourne	Single Test	Won 25–14
29	22.11.2003	Sydney	World Cup	Won 20–17

VENUE	MAT	WON	DREW	LOST	PTS FOR	PTS AG
Home	16	9	1	6	237	222
Away	12	2	0	10	150	327
Neutral	1	1	0	0	25	22
Total	29	12	1	16	412	571

ENGLAND v. CANADA 1992–94

1	17.10.1992	Wembley	Single Test	Won 26–13
2	10.12.1994	Twickenham	Single Test	Won 60–19
3	28.08.1999	Twickenham	Single Test	Won 36–11
4	02.06.2001	Markham	First Test	Won 22–10
5	09.06.2001	Burnaby	Second Test	Won 59–20

VENUE	MAT	WON	DREW	LOST	PTS FOR	PTS AG
Home	3	2	0	0	122	43
Away	2	2	0	0	81	30
Total	5	5	0	0	203	73

ENGLAND v. FIJI 1988–99

1	17.06.1988	Suva	Single Test	Won 25–12
2	04.11.1989	Twickenham	Single Test	Won 58–23
3	20.07.1991	Suva	Single Test	Won 28–12
4	20.10.1999	Twickenham	World Cup	Won 45–24

VENUE	MAT	WON	DREW	LOST	PTS FOR	PTS AG
Home	2	2	0	0	103	47
Away	2	2	0	0	53	24
Total	4	4	0	0	156	71

ENGLAND v. FRANCE 1906–2004

1	22.03.1906	Paris	Single Test	Won 35–8
2	05.01.1907	Richmond	Single Test	Won 41–13
3	01.01.1908	Paris	Single Test	Won 19–0
4	30.01.1909	Leicester	Single Test	Won 22–0
5	03.03.1910	Paris	Five Nations	Won 11–3
6	28.01.1911	Twickenham	Five Nations	Won 37–0
7	08.04.1912	Paris	Five Nations	Won 18–8
8	25.01.1913	Twickenham	Five Nations	Won 20–0
9	13.04.1914	Paris	Five Nations	Won 39–13
10	31.01.1920	Twickenham	Five Nations	Won 8–3
11	28.03.1921	Paris	Five Nations	Won 10–6
12	25.02.1922	Twickenham	Five Nations	Drew 11–11
13	02.04.1923	Paris	Five Nations	Won 12–3
14	23.02.1924	Twickenham	Five Nations	Won 19–7
15	13.04.1925	Paris	Five Nations	Won 13–11
16	27.02.1926	Twickenham	Five Nations	Won 11–0
17	02.04.1927	Paris	Five Nations	Lost 0–3
18	25.02.1928	Twickenham	Five Nations	Won 18–8
19	01.04.1929	Paris	Five Nations	Won 16–6
20	22.02.1930	Twickenham	Five Nations	Won 11–5
21	06.04.1931	Paris	Five Nations	Lost 13–14
22	19.04.1947	Twickenham	Five Nations	Won 6–3
23	29.03.1948	Paris	Five Nations	Lost 0–15
24	26.02.1949	Twickenham	Five Nations	Won 8–3
25	25.02.1950	Paris	Five Nations	Lost 3–6
26	24.02.1951	Twickenham	Five Nations	Lost 3–11
27	05.04.1952	Paris	Five Nations	Won 6–3
28	28.02.1953	Twickenham	Five Nations	Won 11–0
29	10.04.1954	Paris	Five Nations	Lost 3–11
30	26.02.1955	Twickenham	Five Nations	Lost 9–16
31	14.04.1956	Paris	Five Nations	Lost 9–14
32	23.02.1957	Twickenham	Five Nations	Won 9–5
33	01.03.1958	Paris	Five Nations	Won 14–0
34	28.02.1959	Twickenham	Five Nations	Drew 3–3
35	27.02.1960	Paris	Five Nations	Drew 3–3
36	25.02.1961	Twickenham	Five Nations	Drew 5–5
37	24.02.1962	Paris	Five Nations	Lost 0–13
38	23.02.1963	Twickenham	Five Nations	Won 6–5
39	22.02.1964	Paris	Five Nations	Won 6–3
40	27.02.1965	Twickenham	Five Nations	Won 9–6
41	26.02.1966	Paris	Five Nations	Lost 0–13
42	25.02.1967	Twickenham	Five Nations	Lost 12–16
43	24.02.1968	Paris	Five Nations	Lost 9–14
44	22.02.1969	Twickenham	Five Nations	Won 22–8
45	18.04.1970	Paris	Five Nations	Lost 13–35
46	27.02.1971	Twickenham	Five Nations	Drew 14–14
47	26.02.1972	Paris	Five Nations	Lost 12–37
48	24.02.1973	Twickenham	Five Nations	Won 14–6
49	02.03.1974	Paris	Five Nations	Drew 12–12
50	01.02.1975	Twickenhamn	Five Nations	Lost 20–27
51	20.03.1976	Paris	Five Nations	Lost 9–30

52	19.02.1977	Twickenham	Five Nations	Lost 3–4
53	21.01.1978	Paris	Five Nations	Lost 6–15
54	03.03.1979	Twickenham	Five Nations	Won 7–6
55	02.02.1980	Paris	Five Nations	Won 17–13
56	21.03.1981	Twickenham	Five Nations	Lost 12–16
57	20.02.1982	Paris	Five Nations	Won 27–15
58	15.01.1983	Twickenham	Five Nations	Lost 15–19
59	03.03.1984	Paris	Five Nations	Lost 18–32
60	02.02.1985	Twickenham	Five Nations	Drew 9–9
61	15.03.1986	Paris	Five Nations	Lost 10–29
62	21.02.1987	Twickenham	Five Nations	Lost 15–19
63	16.01.1988	Paris	Five Nations	Lost 9–10
64	04.03.1989	Twickenham	Five Nations	Won 11–0
65	03.02.1990	Paris	Five Nations	Won 26–7
66	16.03.1991	Twickenham	Five Nations	Won 21–19
67	19.10.1991	Paris	World Cup	Won 19–10
68	15.02.1992	Paris	Five Nations	Won 31–13
69	16.01.1993	Twickenham	Five Nations	Won 16–15
70	05.03.1994	Paris	Five Nations	Won 18–14
71	04.02.1995	Twickenham	Five Nations	Won 31–10
72	22.06.1995	Pretoria	World Cup	Lost 9–19
73	20.01.1996	Paris	Five Nations	Lost 12–15
74	01.03.1997	Twickenham	Five Nations	Lost 20–23
75	07.02.1998	Paris	Five Nations	Lost 17–24
76	20.03.1999	Twickenham	Five Nations	Won 21–10
77	19.02.2000	Paris	Six Nations	Won 15–9
78	07.04.2001	Twickenham	Six Nations	Won 48–19
79	02.03.2002	Paris	Six Nations	Lost 15–20
80	15.02.2003	Twickenham	Six Nations	Won 25–17
81	30.08.2003	Marseilles	Single Test	Lost 16–17
82	06.09.2003	Twickenham	Single Test	Won 45–14
83	16.11.2003	Sydney	World Cup	Won 24–7
84	27.03.2004	Paris		Lost 21–24

VENUE	MAT	WON	DREW	LOST	PTS FOR	PTS AG
Home	40	26	5	9	648	375
Away	42	19	2	21	562	551
Neutral	2	1	0	1	33	26
Total	84	46	7	31	1243	952

ENGLAND v. GEORGIA 2003

| 1 | 12.10.2003 | Perth | World Cup | Won 84–6 |

VENUE	MAT	WON	DREW	LOST	PTS FOR	PTS AG
Home	1	1	0	0	84	6
Total	1	1	0	0	84	6

ENGLAND v. HOLLAND 1998

| 1 | 14.11.1998 | Huddersfield | WC Qualifier | Won 110–0 |

VENUE	MAT	WON	DREW	LOST	PTS FOR	PTS AG
Home	1	1	0	0	110	0
Total	1	1	0	0	110	0

ENGLAND v. IRELAND 1875–2004

1	15.02.1875	The Oval	Single Test	Won 1G 1DG 1T–0
2	13.12.1875	Rathmines	Single Test	Won 1G 1T–0
3	05.02.1877	The Oval	Single Test	Won 2G 2T–0
4	11.03.1878	Dublin	Single Test	Won 2G 1T–0
5	24.03.1879	The Oval	Single Test	Won 2G 1DG 2T–0
6	30.01.1880	Dublin	Single Test	Won 1G 1T–1T
7	05.02.1881	Manchester	Single Test	Won 2C 2T–0
8	06.02.1882	Dublin	Single Test	Drew 2T–2T
9	05.02.1883	Manchester	Four Nations	Won 1G 3T–1T

10	04.02.1884	Dublin	Four Nations	Won 1G–0
11	07.02.1885	Manchester	Four Nations	Won 2T–1T
12	06.02.1886	Dublin	Four Nations	Won 1T–0
13	05.02.1887	Dublin	Four Nations	Lost 0–2C
14	15.03.1890	Blackheath	Four Nations	Won 3T–0
15	07.02.1891	Dublin	Four Nations	Won 9–0
16	06.02.1892	Manchester	Four Nations	Won 7–0
17	04.02.1893	Dublin	Four Nations	Won 4–0
18	03.02.1894	Blackheath	Four Nations	Lost 5–7
19	02.02.1895	Dublin	Four Nations	Won 6–3
20	01.02.1896	Leeds	Four Nations	Lost 4–10
21	06.02.1897	Dublin	Four Nations	Lost 9–13
22	05.02.1898	Richmond	Four Nations	Lost 6–9
23	04.02.1899	Dublin	Four Nations	Lost 0–6
24	03.02.1900	Richmond	Four Nations	Won 15–4
25	09.02.1901	Dublin	Four Nations	Lost 6–10
26	08.02.1902	Leicester	Four Nations	Won 6–3
27	14.02.1903	Dublin	Four Nations	Lost 0–6
28	13.02.1904	Blackheath	Four Nations	Won 19–0
29	11.02.1905	Cork	Four Nations	Lost 3–17
30	10.02.1906	Leicester	Four Nations	Lost 6–16
31	09.02.1907	Dublin	Four Nations	Lost 9–17
32	08.02.1908	Richmond	Four Nations	Won 13–3
33	13.02.1909	Dublin	Four Nations	Won 11–5
34	12.02.1910	Twickenham	Five Nations	Drew 0–0
35	11.02.1911	Dublin	Five Nations	Lost 0–3
36	10.02.1912	Twickenham	Five Nations	Won 15–0
37	08.02.1913	Dublin	Five Nations	Won 15–4
38	14.02.1914	Twickenham	Five Nations	Won 17–12
39	14.02.1920	Dublin	Five Nations	Won 14–11
40	12.02.1921	Twickenham	Five Nations	Won 15–0
41	11.02.1922	Dublin	Five Nations	Won 12–3
42	10.02.1923	Leicester	Five Nations	Won 23–5
43	09.02.1924	Belfast	Five Nations	Won 14–3
44	14.02.1925	Twickenham	Five Nations	Drew 6–6
45	13.02.1926	Dublin	Five Nations	Lost 15–19
46	12.02.1927	Twickenham	Five Nations	Won 8–6
47	11.02.1928	Dublin	Five Nations	Won 7–6
48	09.02.1929	Twickenham	Five Nations	Lost 5–6
49	08.02.1930	Dublin	Five Nations	Lost 3–4
50	14.02.1931	Twickenham	Five Nations	Lost 5–6
51	13.02.1932	Dublin	Four Nations	Won 11–8
52	11.02.1933	Twickenham	Four Nations	Won 17–6
53	10.02.1934	Dublin	Four Nations	Won 13–3
54	09.02.1935	Twickenham	Four Nations	Won 14–3
55	08.02.1936	Dublin	Four Nations	Lost 3–6
56	13.02.1937	Twickenham	Four Nations	Won 9–8
57	12.02.1938	Dublin	Four Nations	Won 36–14
58	11.02.1939	Twickenham	Four Nations	Lost 0–5
59	08.02.1947	Dublin	Five Nations	Lost 0–22
60	14.02.1948	Twickenham	Five Nations	Lost 10–11
61	12.02.1949	Dublin	Five Nations	Lost 5–14
62	11.02.1950	Twickenham	Five Nations	Won 3–0
63	10.02.1951	Dublin	Five Nations	Lost 0–3
64	29.03.1952	Twickenham	Five Nations	Won 3–0
65	14.02.1953	Dublin	Five Nations	Drew 9–9
66	13.02.1954	Twickenham	Five Nations	Won 14–3
67	12.02.1955	Dublin	Five Nations	Drew 6–6
68	11.02.1956	Twickenham	Five Nations	Won 20–0
69	09.02.1957	Dublin	Five Nations	Won 6–0
70	08.02.1958	Twickenham	Five Nations	Won 6–0
71	14.02.1959	Dublin	Five Nations	Won 3–0
72	13.02.1960	Twickenham	Five Nations	Won 8–5
73	11.02.1961	Dublin	Five Nations	Lost 8–11
74	10.02.1962	Twickenham	Five Nations	Won 16–0
75	09.02.1963	Dublin	Five Nations	Drew 0–0
76	08.02.1964	Twickenham	Five Nations	Lost 5–18
77	13.02.1965	Dublin	Five Nations	Lost 0–5
78	12.02.1966	Twickenham	Five Nations	Drew 6–6
79	11.02.1967	Dublin	Five Nations	Won 8–3
80	10.02.1968	Twickenham	Five Nations	Drew 9–9
81	08.02.1969	Dublin	Five Nations	Lost 15–17
82	14.02.1970	Twickenham	Five Nations	Won 9–3
83	13.02.1971	Dublin	Five Nations	Won 9–6
84	12.02.1972	Twickenham	Five Nations	Lost 12–16
85	10.02.1973	Dublin	Five Nations	Lost 9–18

86	16.02.1974	Twickenham	Five Nations	Lost 21–26
87	18.01.1975	Dublin	Five Nations	Lost 9–12
88	06.03.1976	Twickenham	Five Nations	Lost 12–13
89	05.02.1977	Dublin	Five Nations	Won 4–0
90	18.03.1978	Twickenham	Five Nations	Won 15–9
91	17.02.1979	Dublin	Five Nations	Lost 7–12
92	19.01.1980	Twickenham	Five Nations	Won 24–9
93	07.03.1981	Dublin	Five Nations	Won 10–6
94	06.02.1982	Twickenham	Five Nations	Lost 15–16
95	19.03.1983	Dublin	Five Nations	Lost 15–25
96	18.02.1984	Twickenham	Five Nations	Won 12–9
97	30.03.1985	Dublin	Five Nations	Lost 10–13
98	01.03.1986	Twickenham	Five Nations	Won 25–20
99	07.02.1987	Dublin	Five Nations	Lost 0–17
100	19.03.1988	Twickenham	Five Nations	Won 35–3
101	23.04.1988	Dublin	Single Test	Won 21–10
102	18.02.1989	Dublin	Five Nations	Won 16–3
103	20.01.1990	Twickenham	Five Nations	Won 23–0
104	02.03.1991	Dublin	Five Nations	Won 16–7
105	01.02.1992	Twickenham	Five Nations	Won 38–9
106	20.03.1993	Dublin	Five Nations	Lost 3–17
107	19.02.1994	Twickenham	Five Nations	Lost 12–13
108	21.01.1995	Dublin	Five Nations	Won 20–8
109	16.03.1996	Twickenham	Five Nations	Won 28–15
110	15.02.1997	Dublin	Five Nations	Won 46–6
111	04.04.1998	Twickenham	Five Nations	Won 35–17
112	06.03.1999	Dublin	Five Nations	Won 27–15
113	05.02.2000	Twickenham	Six Nations	Won 50–18
114	20.10.2001	Dublin	Single Test	Lost 14–20
115	16.02.2002	Twickenham	Six Nations	Won 45–11
116	30.03.2003	Dublin	Six Nations	Won 42–6
117	06.03.2004	Twickenham	Six nations	Lost 13–19

VENUE	MAT	WON	DREW	LOST	PTS FOR	PTS AG
Home	58	39	4	15	739	393
Away	59	30	4	25	538	452
Total	117	69	8	40	1277	845

ENGLAND v. ITALY 1991–2004

1	08.10.1991	Twickenham	World Cup	Won 36–6
2	31.05.1995	Durban	World Cup	Won 27–20
3	23.11.1996	Twickenham	Single Test	Won 54–21
4	22.11.1998	Huddersfield	WC Qualifier	Won 23–15
5	02.10.1999	Twickenham	Single Test	Won 67–7
6	18.03.2000	Rome	Six Nations	Won 59–12
7	17.02.2001	Twickenham	Six Nations	Won 80–23
8	06.04.2002	Rome	Six Nations	Won 45–9
9	09.03.2003	Twickenham	Six Nations	Won 40–5
10	15.02.2004	Rome	Six Nations	Won 50–9

VENUE	MAT	WON	DREW	LOST	PTS FOR	PTS AG
Home	6	6	0	0	300	77
Neutral	1	1	0	0	27	20
Away	3	3	0	0	154	30
Total	10	10	0	0	481	127

ENGLAND v. JAPAN 1987

1	30.05.1987	Sydney	World Cup	Won 60–7

VENUE	MAT	WON	DREW	LOST	PTS FOR	PTS AG
Neutral	1	1	0	0	60	7
Total	1	1	0	0	60	7

ENGLAND v. NEW ZEALAND 1905–2003

1	02.12.1905	Crystal Palace	Single Test	Lost 0–15
2	03.01.1925	Twickenham	Single Test	Lost 11–17
3	04.01.1936	Twickenham	Single Test	Won 13–0
4	30.01.1954	Twickenham	Single Test	Lost 0–5
5	25.05.1963	Auckland	First Test	Lost 11–21
6	01.06.1963	Christchurch	Second Test	Lost 6–9
7	04.01.1964	Twickenham	Single Test	Lost 0–14
8	04.11.1967	Twickenham	Single Test	Lost 11–23
9	06.01.1973	Twickenham	Single Test	Lost 0–9
10	15.09.1973	Auckland	Single Test	Won 16–10
11	25.11.1978	Twickenham	Single Test	Lost 6–16
12	24.11.1979	Twickenham	Single Test	Lost 9–10
13	19.11.1983	Twickenham	Single Test	Won 15–9
14	01.06.1985	Christchurch	First Test	Lost 13–18
15	08.06.1985	Wellington	Second Test	Lost 15–42
16	03.10.1991	Twickenham	World Cup	Lost 12–18
17	27.11.1993	Twickenham	Single Test	Won 15–9
18	18.06.1995	Cape Town	World Cup	Lost 29–45
19	22.11.1997	Manchester	First Test	Lost 8–25
20	06.12.1997	Twickenham	Second Test	Drew 26–26
21	20.06.1998	Dunedin	First Test	Lost 22–64
22	27.06.1998	Auckland	Second Test	Lost 10–40
23	09.10.1999	Twickenham	Single Test	Lost 16–30
24	09.11.2002	Twickenham	Single Test	Won 31–28
25	14.06.2003	Wellington	Single Test	Won 15–13

VENUE	MAT	WON	DREW	LOST	PTS FOR	PTS AG
Home	16	4	1	11	173	254
Away	8	2	0	6	108	217
Neutral	1	0	0	1	29	45
Total	25	6	1	18	310	516

ENGLAND v. NEW ZEALAND NATIVES 1889

1	16.02.1889	Blackheath	Single Test	Won 1G 4T–0 (7–0)

VENUE	MAT	WON	DREW	LOST	PTS FOR	PTS AG
Home	1	1	0	0	7	0
Total	1	1	0	0	7	0

ENGLAND v. RFU PRESIDENT'S XV 1971

1	17.04.1971	Twickenham	Single Test	Lost 11–28

VENUE	MAT	WON	DREW	LOST	PTS FOR	PTS AG
Home	1	0	0	1	11	28
Total	1	0	0	1	11	28

ENGLAND v. ROMANIA 1985–2001

1	05.01.1985	Twickenham	Single Test	Won 22–15
2	13.05.1989	Bucharest	Single Test	Won 58–3
3	12.11.1994	Twickenham	Single Test	Won 54–3
4	17.11.2001	Twickenham	Single Test	Won 134–0

VENUE	MAT	WON	DREW	LOST	PTS FOR	PTS AG
Home	3	3	0	0	210	18
Away	1	1	0	0	58	3
Total	4	4	0	0	268	21

1	27.03.1871	Edinburgh	Single Test	Lost 1T–1G 1T
2	05.02.1872	The Oval	Single Test	Won 1G 1DG 2T–1DG
3	03.03.1873	Glasgow	Single Test	Drew 0–0
4	23.02.1874	The Oval	Single Test	Won 1DG–1T
5	08.03.1875	Edinburgh	Single Test	Drew 0–0
6	06.03.1876	The Oval	Single Test	Won 1G 1T–0
7	05.03.1877	Edinburgh	Single Test	Lost 0–1DG
8	04.03.1878	The Oval	Single Test	Drew 0–0
9	10.03.1879	Edinburgh	Single Test	Drew 1G–1DG
10	28.02.1880	Manchester	Single Test	Won 2G 3T–1G
11	19.03.1881	Edinburgh	Single Test	Drew 1DG 1T–1G 1T
12	04.03.1882	Manchester	Single Test	Lost 0–2T
13	03.03.1883	Edinburgh	Four Nations	Won 2T–1T
14	01.03.1884	Blackheath	Four Nations	Won 1G–1T
15	13.03.1886	Edinburgh	Four Nations	Drew 0–0
16	05.03.1887	Manchester	Four Nations	Drew 1T–1T
17	01.03.1890	Edinburgh	Four Nations	Won 1G–1T–0
18	07.03.1891	Richmond	Four Nations	lost 3–9
19	05.03.1892	Edinburgh	Four Nations	Won 5–0
20	04.03.1893	Leeds	Four Nations	Lost 0–8
21	17.03.1894	Edinburgh	Four Nations	Lost 0–6
22	09.03.1895	Richmond	Four Nations	Lost 3–6
23	14.03.1896	Glasgow	Four Nations	Lost 0–11
24	13.03.1897	Manchester	Four Nations	Won 12–3
25	12.03.1898	Edinburgh	Four Nations	Drew 3–3
26	11.03.1899	Blackheath	Four Nations	Lost 0–5
27	10.03.1900	Edinburgh	Four Nations	Drew 0–0
28	09.03.1901	Blackheath	Four Nations	Lost 3–18
29	15.03.1902	Edinburgh	Four Nations	Won 6–3
30	21.03.1903	Richmond	Four Nations	Lost 6–10
31	19.03.1904	Edinburgh	Four Nations	Lost 3–6
32	18.03.1905	Richmond	Four Nations	Lost 0–8
33	17.03.1906	Edinburgh	Four Nations	Won 9–3
34	16.03.1907	Blackheath	Four Nations	Lost 3–8
35	21.03.1908	Edinburgh	Four Nations	Lost 10–16
36	20.03.1909	Richmond	Four Nations	Lost 8–18
37	19.03.1910	Edinburgh	Five Nations	Won 14–5
38	18.03.1911	Twickenham	Five Nations	Won 13–8
39	16.03.1912	Edinburgh	Five Nations	Lost 3–8
40	15.03.1913	Twickenham	Five Nations	Won 3–0
41	21.03.1914	Edinburgh	Five Nations	Won 16–15
42	20.03.1920	Twickenham	Five Nations	Won 13–4
43	19.03.1921	Edinburgh	Five Nations	Won 18–0
44	18.03.1922	Twickenham	Five Nations	Won 11–5
45	17.03.1923	Edinburgh	Five Nations	Won 8–6
46	15.03.1924	Twickenham	Five Nations	Won 19–0
47	21.03.1925	Edinburgh	Five Nations	Lost 11–14
48	20.03.1926	Twickenham	Five Nations	Lost 9–17
49	19.03.1927	Edinburgh	Five Nations	Lost 13–21
50	17.03.1928	Twickenham	Five Nations	Won 6–0
51	16.03.1929	Edinburgh	Five Nations	Lost 6–12
52	15.03.1930	Twickenham	Five Nations	Drew 0–0
53	21.03.1931	Edinburgh	Five Nations	Lost 19–28
54	19.03.1932	Twickenham	Four Nations	Won 16–3
55	18.03.1933	Edinburgh	Four Nations	Lost 0–3
56	17.03.1934	Twickenham	Four Nations	Won 6–3
57	16.03.1935	Edinburgh	Four Nations	Lost 7–10
58	21.03.1936	Twickenham	Four Nations	Won 9–8
59	20.03.1937	Edinburgh	Four Nations	Won 6–3
60	19.03.1938	Twickenham	Four Nations	Lost 16–21
61	18.03.1939	Edinburgh	Four Nations	Won 9–6
62	15.03.1947	Twickenham	Five Nations	Won 24–5
63	20.03.1948	Edinburgh	Five Nations	Lost 3–6
64	19.03.1949	Twickenham	Five Nations	Won 19–3
65	18.03.1950	Edinburgh	Five Nations	Lost 11–13
66	17.03.1951	Twickenham	Five Nations	Won 5–3
67	15.03.1952	Edinburgh	Five Nations	Won 19–3
68	21.03.1953	Twickenham	Five Nations	Won 26–8
69	20.03.1954	Edinburgh	Five Nations	Won 13–3
70	19.03.1955	Twickenham	Five Nations	Won 9–6
71	17.03.1956	Edinburgh	Five Nations	Won 11–6

72	16.03.1957	Twickenham	Five Nations	Won 16–3
73	15.03.1958	Edinburgh	Five Nations	Drew 3–3
74	21.03.1959	Twickenham	Five Nations	Drew 3–3
75	19.03.1960	Edinburgh	Five Nations	Won 21–12
76	18.03.1961	Twickenham	Five Nations	Won 6–0
77	17.03.1962	Edinburgh	Five Nations	Drew 3–3
78	16.03.1963	Twickenham	Five Nations	Won 10–8
79	21.03.1964	Edinburgh	Five Nations	Lost 6–15
80	20.03.1965	Twickenham	Five Nations	Drew 3–3
81	19.03.1966	Edinburgh	Five Nations	Lost 3–6
82	18.03.1967	Twickenham	Five Nations	Won 27–14
83	16.03.1968	Edinburgh	Five Nations	Won 8–6
84	15.03.1969	Twickenham	Five Nations	Won 8–3
85	21.03.1970	Edinburgh	Five Nations	Lost 5–14
86	20.03.1971	Twickenham	Five Nations	Lost 15–16
87	27.03.1971	Edinburgh	Single Test	Lost 6–26
88	18.03.1972	Edinburgh	Five Nations	Lost 9–23
89	17.03.1973	Twickenham	Five Nations	Won 20–13
90	02.02.1974	Edinburgh	Five Nations	Lost 14–16
91	15.03.1975	Twickenham	Five Nations	Won 7–6
92	21.02.1976	Edinburgh	Five Nations	Lost 12–22
93	15.01.1977	Twickenham	Five Nations	Won 26–6
94	04.03.1978	Edinburgh	Five Nations	Won 15–0
95	03.02.1979	Twickenham	Five Nations	Drew 7–7
96	15.03.1980	Edinburgh	Five Nations	Won 30–18
97	21.02.1981	Twickenham	Five Nations	Won 23–17
98	16.01.1982	Edinburgh	Five Nations	Drew 9–9
99	05.03.1983	Twickenham	Five Nations	Lost 12–22
100	04.02.1984	Edinburgh	Five Nations	Lost 6–18
101	16.03.1985	Twickenham	Five Nations	Won 10–7
102	15.02.1986	Edinburgh	Five Nations	Lost 6–33
103	04.04.1987	Twickenham	Five Nations	Won 21–12
104	05.03.1988	Edinburgh	Five Nations	Won 9–6
105	04.02.1989	Twickenham	Five Nations	Drew 12–12
106	17.03.1990	Edinburgh	Five Nations	Lost 7–13
107	16.02.1991	Twickenham	Five Nations	Won 21–12
108	26.10.1991	Edinburgh	World Cup	Won 9–6
109	18.01.1992	Edinburgh	Five Nations	Won 25–7
110	06.03.1993	Twickenham	Five Nations	Won 26–12
111	05.02.1994	Edinburgh	Five Nations	Won 15–14
112	18.03.1995	Twickenham	Five Nations	Won 24–12
113	02.03.1996	Edinburgh	Five Nations	Won 18–9
114	01.02.1997	Twickenham	Five Nations	Won 41–13
115	22.03.1998	Edinburgh	Five Nations	Won 34–20
116	20.02.1999	Twickenham	Five Nations	Won 24–21
117	02.04.2000	Edinburgh	Six Nations	Lost 13–14
118	03.03.2001	Twickenham	Six Nations	Won 43–3
119	02.02.2002	Edinburgh	Six Nations	Won 29–3
120	22.03.2003	Twickenham	Six Nations	Won 40–9
121	21.02.2004	Edinburgh	Six Nations	Won 35–13

VENUE	MAT	WON	DREW	LOST	PTS FOR	PTS AG
Home	59	38	7	14	687	421
Away	62	26	10	26	523	544
Total	121	64	17	40	1260	965

ENGLAND v. SOUTH AFRICA 1906–2003

1	08.12.1906	Crystal Palace	Single Test	Drew 3–3
2	04.01.1913	Twickenham	Single Test	Lost 3–9
3	02.01.1932	Twickenham	Single Test	Lost 0–7
4	05.01.1952	Twickenham	Single Test	Lost 3–8
5	07.01.1961	Twickenham	Single Test	Lost 0–5
6	20.12.1969	Twickenham	Single Test	Won 11–8
7	03.06.1972	Johannesburg	Single Test	Won 18–9
8	02.06.1984	Port Elizabeth	First Test	Lost 15–33
9	09.06.1984	Johannesburg	Second Test	Lost 9–35
10	14.11.1992	Twickenham	Single Test	Won 33–16
11	04.06.1994	Pretoria	First Test	Won 32–15
12	11.06.1994	Cape Town	Second Test	Lost 9–27
13	18-11.1995	Twickenham	Single Test	Lost 14–24
14	29.11.1997	Twickenham	Single Test	Lost 11–29
15	04.07.1998	Cape Town	Single Test	Lost 0–18

16	05.12.1998	Twickenham	Single Test	Won 13–7
17	24.10.1999	Paris	World Cup	Lost 21–44
18	17.06.2000	Pretoria	First Test	Lost 13–18
19	24.06.2000	Bloemfontein	Second Test	Won 27–22
20	02.12.2000	Twickenham	Single Test	Won 25–17
21	24.11.2001	Twickenham	Single Test	Won 29–9
22	23.11.2002	Twickenham	Single Test	Won 53–3
23	18.10.2003	Perth	World Cup	Won 25–6

VENUE	MAT	WON	DREW	LOST	PTS FOR	PTS AG
Home	13	6	1	6	198	145
Neutral	2	3	0	1	46	50
Away	8	2	0	5	123	177
Total	23	10	1	12	367	372

ENGLAND v. TONGA 1998

1	15.10.1999	Twiockenham	World Cup	Won 101–10

VENUE	MAT	WON	DREW	LOST	PTS FOR	PTS AG
Home	1	1	0	0	101	10
Total	1	1	0	0	101	10

ENGLAND v. UNITED STATES 1987–2001

1	03.06.1987	Sydney	World Cup	Won 34–6
2	11.10.1991	Twickenham	World Cup	Won 37–9
3	21.09.1999	Twickenham	Single Test	Won 106–8
4	16.06.2001	San Franscisco	Single Test	Won 48–19

VENUE	MAT	WON	DREW	LOST	PTS FOR	PTS AG
Home	2	2	0	0	143	17
Neutral	1	1	0	0	34	6
Away	1	1	0	0	48	19
Total	4	4	0	0	225	42

ENGLAND v. URUGUAY 1998

1	02.11.2003	Brisbane	World Cup	Won 111–13

VENUE	MAT	WON	DREW	LOST	PTS FOR	PTS AG
Home	1	1	0	0	111	13
Total	1	1	0	0	111	13

ENGLAND v. WALES 1881–2004

1	19.02.1881	Blackheath	Single Test	Won 7G 1DG 6T–7
2	16.12.1882	Swansea	Four Nations	Won 2G 4T–0
3	05.01.1884	Leeds	Four Nations	Won 1G 2T–1G
4	03.01.1885	Swansea	Four Nations	Won 1G 4T–1G 1T
5	02.01.1886	Blackheath	Four Nations	Won 1GM 2T–1G
6	08.01.1887	Llanelli	Four Nations	Drew 0–0
7	15.02.1890	Dewsbury	Four Nations	Lost 0–1T
8	03.01.1891	Newport	Four Nations	Won 7–3
9	02.01.1892	Blackheath	Four Nations	Won 17–0
10	07.01.1893	Cardiff	Four Nations	Lost 11–12
11	06.01.1894	Birkenhead	Four Nations	Won 24–3
12	05.01.1895	Swansea	Four Nations	Won 14–6
13	04.01.1896	Blackheath	Four Nations	Won 25–0
14	09.01.1897	Newport	Four Nations	Lost 0–11
15	02.04.1898	Blackheath	Four Nations	Won 14–7
16	07.01.1899	Swansea	Four Nations	Lost 3–26
17	06.01.1900	Gloucester	Four Nations	Lost 3–13
18	05.01.1901	Cardiff	Four Nations	Lost 0–13

19	11.01.1902	Blackheath	Four Nations	Lost 8–9
20	10.01.1903	Swansea	Four Nations	Lost 5–21
21	09.01.1904	Leicester	Four Nations	Drew 14–14
22	14.01.1905	Cardiff	Four Nations	Lost 0–25
23	13.01.1906	Richmond	Four Nations	Lost 3–16
24	12.01.1907	Swansea	Four Nations	Lost 0–22
25	18.01.1908	Bristol	Four Nations	Lost 18–28
26	16.01.1909	Cardiff	Four Nations	Lost 0–8
27	15.01.1910	Twickenham	Five Nations	Won 11–6
28	21.01.1911	Swansea	Five Nations	Lost 11–15
29	20.01.1912	Twickenham	Five Nations	Won 8–0
30	18.01.1913	Cardiff	Five Nations	Won 12–0
31	17.01.1914	Twickenham	Five Nations	Won 10–9
32	17.01.1920	Swansea	Five Nations	Lost 5–19
33	15.01.1921	Twickenham	Five Nations	Won 18–3
34	21.01.1922	Cardiff	Five Nations	Lost 6–28
35	20.01.1923	Twickenham	Five Nations	Won 7–3
36	19.01.1924	Swansea	Five Nations	Won 17–9
37	17.01.1925	Twickenham	Five Nations	Won 12–6
38	16.01.1926	Cardiff	Five Nations	Drew 3–3
39	15.01.1927	Twickenham	Five Nations	Won 11–9
40	21.01.1928	Swansea	Five Nations	Won 10–8
41	19.01.1929	Twickenham	Five Nations	Won 8–3
42	18.01.1930	Cardiff	Five Nations	Won 11–3
43	17.01.1931	Twickenham	Five Nations	Drew 11–11
44	16.01.1932	Swansea	Four Nations	Lost 5–12
45	21.01.1933	Twickenham	Four Nations	Lost 3–7
46	20.01.1934	Cardiff	Four Nations	Won 9–0
47	19.01.1935	Twickenham	Four Nations	Drew 3–3
48	18.01.1936	Swansea	Four Nations	Drew 0–0
49	16.01.1937	Twickenham	Four Nations	Won 4–3
50	15.01.1938	Cardiff	Four Nations	Lost 8–14
51	21.01.1939	Twickenham	Four Nations	Won 3–0
52	18.01.1947	Cardiff	Five Nations	Won 9–6
53	17.01.1948	Twickenham	Five Nations	Drew 3–3
54	15.01.1949	Cardiff	Five Nations	Lost 3–9
55	21.01.1950	Twickenham	Five Nations	Lost 5–11
56	20.01.1951	Swansea	Five Nations	Lost 5–23
57	19.01.1952	Twickenham	Five Nations	Lost 6–8
58	17.01.1953	Cardiff	Five Nations	Won 8–3
59	16.01.1954	Twickenham	Five Nations	Won 9–6
60	22.01.1955	Cardiff	Five Nations	Lost 0–3
61	21.01.1956	Twickenham	Five Nations	Lost 3–8
62	19.01.1957	Cardiff	Five Nations	Won 3–0
63	18.01.1958	Twickenham	Five Nations	Drew 3–3
64	17.01.1959	Cardiff	Five Nations	Lost 0–5
65	16.01.1960	Twickenham	Five Nations	Won 14–6
66	21.01.1961	Cardiff	Five Nations	Lost 3–6
67	20.01.1962	Twickenham	Five Nations	Drew 0–0
68	19.01.1963	Cardiff	Five Nations	Won 13–6
69	18.01.1964	Twickenham	Five Nations	Drew 6–6
70	16.01.1965	Cardiff	Five Nations	Lost 3–14
71	15.01.1966	Twickenham	Five Nations	Lost 6–11
72	15.04.1967	Cardiff	Five Nations	Lost 21–34
73	20.01.1968	Twickenham	Five Nations	Drew 11–11
74	12.04.1969	Cardiff	Five Nations	Lost 9–30
75	28.02.1970	Twickenham	Five Nations	Lost 13–17
76	16.01.1971	Cardiff	Five Nations	Lost 6–22
77	15.01.1972	Twickenham	Five Nations	Lost 3–12
78	20.01.1973	Cardiff	Five Nations	Lost 9–25
79	16.03.1974	Twickenham	Five Nations	Won 16–12
80	15.02.1975	Cardiff	Five Nations	Lost 4–20
81	17.01.1976	Twickenham	Five Nations	Lost 9–21
82	05.03.1977	Cardiff	Five Nations	Lost 9–14
83	04.02.1978	Twickenham	Five Nations	Lost 6–9
84	17.03.1979	Cardiff	Five Nations	Lost 3–27
85	16.02.1980	Twickenham	Five Nations	Won 9–8
86	17.01.1981	Cardiff	Five Nations	Lost 19–21
87	06.03.1982	Twickenham	Five Nations	Won 17–7
88	05.02.1983	Cardiff	Five Nations	Drew 13–13
89	17.03.1984	Twickenham	Five Nations	Lost 15–24
90	20.04.1985	Cardiff	Five Nations	Lost 15–24
91	18.01.1986	Twickenham	Five Nations	Won 21–18
92	07.03.1987	Cardiff	Five Nations	Lost 12–19
93	08.06.1987	Brisbane	World Cup	Lost 3–16

94	06.02.1988	Twickenham	Five Nations	Lost 3–11	
95	18.03.1989	Cardiff	Five Nations	Lost 9–12	
96	17.02.1990	Twickenham	Five Nations	Won 34–6	
97	19.01.1991	Cardiff	Five Nations	Won 25–6	
98	07.03.1992	Twickenham	Five Nations	Won 24–0	
99	16.02.1993	Cardiff	Five Nations	Lost 9–10	
100	19.03.1994	Twickenhamn	Five Nations	Won 15–8	
101	18.02.1995	Cardiff	Five Nations	Won 23–9	
102	03.02.1996	Twickenham	Five Nations	Won 21–15	
103	15.03.1997	Cardiff	Five Nations	Won 34–13	
104	21.02.1998	Twickenham	Five Nations	Won 60–26	
105	11.04.1999	Wembley	Five Nations	Lost 31–32	
106	04.03.2000	Twickenham	Six nations	Won 46–12	
107	03.02.2001	Cardiff	Six Nations	Won 44–15	
108	23.03.2002	Twickenham	Six Nations	Won 50–10	
109	22.02.2003	Cardiff	Six Nations	Won 26–9	
110	23.08.2003	Cardiff	Single Test	Won 43–9	
111	09.11.2003	Brisbane	World Cup	Won 28–17	
112	20.03.2004	Twickenham	Six Nations	Won 31–21	

VENUE	MAT	WON	DREW	LOST	PTS FOR	PTS AG
Home	55	31	8	16	694	463
Away	55	19	4	32	548	697
Neutral	2	1	0	1	31	33
Total	112	51	12	49	1261	1193

ENGLAND v. SAMOA 1995–2003

1	04.06.1995	Durban	World Cup	Won 44–22	
2	16.12.1995	Twickenham	Single Test	Won 27–9	
3	26.10.2003	Melbourne	World Cup	Won 35–22	

VENUE	MAT	WON	DREW	LOST	PTS FOR	PTS AG
Home	1	1	0	0	27	9
Neutral	2	2	0	0	79	44
Total	3	3	0	0	106	53

HIGHEST SCORES

Result	Opposition	Date	Venue	Result	Opposition	Date	Venue
134–0	Romania	17.11.2001	Twickenham	50–10	Wales	23.03.2002	Twickenham
111–13	Uruguay	02.11.2003	Brisbane	50–18	Ireland	05.02.2000	Twickenham
110–0	Holland	14.11.1998	Huddersfield	48–19	France	07.04.2001	Twickenham
106–8	USA	21.08.1999	Twickenham	48–19	USA	16.06.2001	San Francisco
101–10	Tonga	15.10.1999	Twickenham	46–6	Ireland	15.02.1997	Dublin
84–6	Georgia	12.10.2003	Perth	46–12	Wales	04.03.2000	Twickenham
80–23	Italy	17.02.2001	Twickenham	46–20	Argentina	30.05.1997	Buenos Aires
67–7	Italy	02.10.1999	Twickenham	45–9	Italy	07.04.2002	Rome
60–7	Japan	30.05.1987	Sydney	45–11	Ireland	16.02.2002	Twickenham
60–19	Canada	10.12.1994	Twickenham	45–14	France	06.09.2003	Twickenham
60–26	Wales	21.02.1998	Twickenham	45–24	Fiji	20.10.1999	Twickenham
59–12	Italy	18.03.2000	Rome	44–15	Wales	03.02.2001	Cardiff
59–20	Canada	09.06.2001	Burnaby	44–22	Western Samoa	04.06.1995	Durban
58–23	Fiji	04.11.1989	Twickenham	43–3	Scotland	03.03.2001	Twickenham
58–3	Romania	13.05.1989	Bucharest	43–9	Wales	23.09.2003	Cardiff
54–3	Romania	12.11.1994	Twickenham	42–6	Ireland	30.03.2003	Dublin
54–21	Italy	23.11.1996	Twickenham	41–13	France	05.01.1907	Richmond
53–3	South Africa	23.11.2002	Twickenham	41–13	Scotland	01.02.1997	Twickenham
51–0	Argentina	03.11.1990	Twickenham	40–9	Scotland	22.03.2003	London
50–9	Italy	15.02.2004	Rome	40–5	Italy	09.03.2003	Twickenham

HIGHEST SCORES CONCEDED

Result	Opposition	Date	Venue	Result	Opposition	Date	Venue
76–0	Australia	06.06.1998	Brisbane	40–15	Australia	27.07.1991	Sydney
64–22	New Zealand	20.06.1998	Dunedin	40–10	New Zealand	27.06.1998	Auckland
45–29	New Zealand	18.06.1995	Cape Town	37–12	France	26.02.1972	Paris
42–15	New Zealand	08.06.1985	Wellington	35–13	France	18.04.1970	Paris
35–9	South Africa	09.06.1984	Johannesburg	34–21	Wales	15.04.1967	Cardiff

33–15	South Africa	02.06.1984	Port Elizabeth
33–6	Scotland	15.02.1986	Edinburgh
33–13	Argentina	06.06.1997	Buenos Aires
32–18	France	03.03.1984	Paris
32–31	Wales	11.04.1999	Wembley
32–31	Australia	16.11.2002	Twickenham
30–9	Wales	12.04.1969	Cardiff
30–21	Australia	31.05.1975	Brisbane
30–9	France	20.03.1976	Paris
21–44	South Africa	24.10.1999	Paris
30–16	New Zealand	09.10.1999	Twickenham

RECORD VICTORIES

Margin	Result	Opposition	Date	Venue
134	134–0	Romania	17.11.2001	Twickenham
110	110–0	Holland	14.11.1998	Huddersfield
98	111–13	Uruguay	02.11.2003	Brisbane
91	101–10	Tonga	13.10.1999	Twickenham
78	84–6	Georgia	12.10.2003	Perth
57	80–23	Italy	17.02.2001	Twickenham
55	58–3	Romania	13.05.1989	Bucharest
53	60–7	Japan	30.05.1987	Sydney
51	51–0	Argentina	03.11.1990	Twickenham
51	54–3	Romania	12.11.1994	Twickenham
50	53–3	South Africa	23.11.2002	Twickenham
47	59–12	Italy	18.03.2000	Rome
41	60–19	Canada	10.12.1994	Twickenham
41	50–9	Italy	15.02.2004	Rome
40	46–6	Ireland	15.02.1997	Dublin
40	43–3	Scotland	03.03.2001	Twickenham
40	50–10	Wales	23.03.2002	Twickenham
39	59–20	Canada	09.06.2001	Burnaby
37	37–0	France	28.01.1911	Twickenham
36	45–9	Italy	07.04.2002	Rome
36	42–6	Ireland	30.03.2003	Dublin
35	58–23	Fiji	04.11.1989	Twickenham
35	40–5	Italy	09.03.2003	Twickenham
34	60–26	Wales	21.02.1998	Twickenham
34	46–12	Wales	04.03.2000	Twickenham
34	45–11	Ireland	16.02.2002	Twickenham
34	43–9	Wales	23.08.2003	Cardiff
33	54–21	Italy	23.11.1996	Twickenham
32	35–3	Ireland	19.03.1988	Twickenham
32	50–18	Ireland	05.02.2000	Twickenham
31	40–9	Scotland	22.03.2003	Twickenham
31	45–14	France	06.09.2003	Twickenham
30	36–6	Italy	08.10.1991	Twickenham

RECORD DEFEATS

Margin	Result	Opposition	Date	Venue
76	76–0	Australia	06.06.1998	Brisbane
42	64–22	New Zealand	20.06.1998	Dunedin
30	40–10	New Zealand	27.06.1998	Auckland
27	42–15	New Zealand	08.06.1985	Wellington
27	33–6	Scotland	15.02.1986	Edinburgh
26	35–9	South Africa	09.06.1984	Johannesburg
25	25–0	Wales	14.01.1905	Cardiff
25	37–12	France	26.02.1972	Paris
25	40–15	Australia	27.07.1991	Sydney
24	27–3	Wales	17.03.1979	Cardiff
23	26–3	Wales	07.01.1899	Swansea
23	44–21	South Africa	24.10.1999	Paris
22	22–0	Wales	12.01.1907	Swansea
22	28–6	Wales	21.01.1922	Cardiff
22	22–0	Ireland	08.02.1947	Dublin
22	35–13	France	18.04.1970	Paris
21	30–9	Wales	12.04.1969	Cardiff
21	30–9	France	20.03.1976	Paris
20	33–13	Argentina	06.06.1997	Buenos Aires
20	26–6	Scotland	27.03.1971	Edinburgh
20	28–8	Australia	12.06.1988	Sydney

MOST CONSECUTIVE VICTORIES

Fourteen 2002–2003

1	23.03.2002	Wales	Twickenham	50–10
2	07.04.2002	Italy	Rome	45–9
3	22.06.2002	Argentina	Buenos Aires	26–18
4	09.11.2002	New Zealand	Twickenham	31–28
5	16.11.2002	Australia	Twickenham	32–31
6	23.11.2002	South Africa	Twickenham	53–3
7	15.02.2003	France	Twickenham	25–17
8	22.02.2003	Wales	Cardiff	26–9
9	09.03.2003	Italy	Twickenham	40–5
10	22.03.2203	Scotland	Twickenham	40–9
11	30.03.2003	Ireland	Dublin	40–26
12	14.06.2003	New Zealand	Wellington	15–13
13	21.06.2003	Australia	Melbourne	25–14
14	23.08.2003	Wales	Cardiff	43–9

Eleven 2000–2001

1	24.06.2000	South Africa	Bloemfontein	27–22
2	18.11.2000	Australia	Twickenham	22–19
3	25.11.2000	Argentina	Twickenham	19–0
4	02.12.2000	South Africa	Twickenham	25–17
5	03.02.2001	Wales	Cardiff	44–15
6	17.02.2001	Italy	Twickenham	80–23
7	03.03.2001	Scotland	Twickenham	43–3
8	07.04.2001	France	Twickenham	48–19
9	02.06.2001	Canada	Markham	22–10
10	09.06.2001	Canada	Burnaby	59–20
11	16.06.2001	USA	San Francisco	48–19

Ten 1882–86

1	16.12.1882	Wales	Swansea	2G 4T–0
2	05.02.1883	Ireland	Manchester	1G 3T–1T
3	03.03.1883	Scotland	Edinburgh	2T–1T
4	05.01.1884	Wales	Leeds	1G 2T–1G
5	04.02.1884	Ireland	Dublin	1G–0
6	01.03.1884	Scotland	Blackheath	1G–1T
7	03.01.1885	Wales	Swansea	1G 4T–1G 1T
8	07.02.1885	Ireland	Manchester	2T–1T
9	02.01.1886	Wales	Blackheath	1GM 2T–1G
10	06.02.1886	Ireland	Dublin	1T–0

Ten 1994–95

1	12.11.1994	Romania	Twickenham	54–3
2	10.12.1994	Canada	Twickenham	60–19
3	21.01.1995	Ireland	Dublin	20–8
4	04.02.1995	France	Twickenham	31–10
5	18.02.1995	Wales	Cardiff	23–9
6	18.03.1995	Scotland	Twickenham	24–12
7	27.05.1995	Argentina	Durban	24–18
8	31.05.1995	Italy	Durban	27–20
9	04.06.1995	Western Samoa	Durban	44–22
10	11.06.1995	Australia	Cape Town	25–22

Nine 1922–24

1	18.03.1922	Scotland	Twickenham	11–5
2	20.01.1923	Wales	Twickenham	7–3
3	10.02.1923	Ireland	Leicester	23–5
4	17.03.1923	Scotland	Edinburgh	8–6
5	02.04.1923	France	Paris	12–3
6	19.01.1924	Wales	Swansea	17–9
7	09.02.1924	Ireland	Belfast	14–3
8	23.02.1924	France	Twickenham	19–7
9	15.03.1924	Scotland	Twickenham	19–0

Eight 1913–14

1	18.01.1913	Wales	Cardiff	12–0
2	25.01.1913	France	Twickenham	20–0
3	08.02.1913	Ireland	Dublin	15–4
4	15.03.1913	Scotland	Twickenham	3–0
5	17.01.1914	Wales	Twickenham	10–9
6	14.02.1914	Ireland	Twickenham	17–12
7	21.03.1914	Scotland	Edinburgh	16–15
8	13.04.1914	France	Paris	39–13

MOST CONSECUTIVE DEFEATS

Seven 1904–06

1	19.03.1904	Scotland	Edinburgh	3–6
2	14.01.1905	Wales	Cardiff	0–25
3	11.02.1905	Ireland	Cork	3–17
4	18.03.1905	Scotland	Richmond	0–8
5	02.12.1905	New Zealand	Crystal Palace	0–15
6	13.01.1906	Wales	Richmond	3–16
7	10.02.1906	Ireland	Leicester	6–16

Seven 1971–72

1	20.03.1971	Scotland	Twickenham	15–16
2	27.03.1971	Scotland	Edinburgh	6–26
3	17.04.1971	RFU President's XV	Twickenham	11–28
4	15.01.1972	Wales	Twickenham	3–12
5	12.02.1972	Ireland	Twickenham	12–16
6	26.02.1972	France	Paris	12–37
7	18.03.1972	Scotland	Edinburgh	9–23

MOST MATCHES WITHOUT DEFEAT

Fourteen 2002–2003

1	23.03.2002	Wales	Twickenham	Won 50–10
2	07.04.2002	Italy	Rome	Won 45–9
3	22.06.2002	Argentina	Buenos Aires	Won 26–18
4	09.11.2002	New Zealand	Twickenham	Won 31–28
5	16.11.2002	Australia	Twickenham	Won 32–31
6	23.11.2002	South Africa	Twickenham	Won 53–3
7	15.02.2003	France	Twickenham	Won 25–17
8	22.02.2003	Wales	Cardiff	Won 26–9
9	09.03.2003	Italy	Twickenham	Won 40–5
10	22.03.2203	Scotland	Twickenham	Won 40–9
11	30.03.2003	Ireland	Dublin	Won 40–26
12	14.06.2003	New Zealand	Wellington	Won 15–13
13	21.06.2003	Australia	Melbourne	Won 25–14
14	23.08.2003	Wales	Cardiff	Won 43–9

Twelve 1882–87

1	16.12.1882	Wales	Swansea	Won 2G 4T–0
2	05.02.1883	Ireland	Manchester	Won 1G 3T–1T
3	03.03.1883	Scotland	Edinburgh	Won 2T–1T
4	05.01.1884	Wales	Leeds	Won 1G 2T–1G
5	04.02.1884	Ireland	Dublin	Won 1G–0
6	01.03.1884	Scotland	Blackheath	Won 1G–7T
7	03.01.1885	Wales	Swansea	Won 1G 4T–1G 1T
8	07.02.1885	Ireland	Manchester	Won 2T–1T
9	02.01.1886	Wales	Blackheath	Won 1GM 2T–1G
10	06.02.1886	Ireland	Dublin	Won 1T–0
11	13.03.1886	Scotland	Edinburgh	Drew 0–0
12	08.01.1887	Wales	Llanelli	Drew 0–0

Eleven 1922–24

1	11.02.1922	Ireland	Dublin	Won 12–3
2	25.02.1922	France	Twickenham	Drew 11–11
3	18.03.1922	Scotland	Twickenham	Won 11–5
4	20.01.1923	Wales	Twickenham	Won 7–3
5	10.02.1923	Ireland	Leicester	Won 23–5
6	17.03.1923	Scotland	Edinburgh	Won 8–6
7	02.04.1923	France	Paris	Won 12–3
8	19.01.1924	Wales	Swansea	Won 17–9
9	09.02.1924	Ireland	Belfast	Won 14–3
10	23.02.1924	France	Twickenham	Won 19–7
11	15.03.1924	Scotland	Twickenham	Won 19–0

Eleven 2000–2001

1	24.06.2000	South Africa	Bloemfontein	Won 27–22
2	18.11.2000	Australia	Twickenham	Won 22–19
3	25.11.2000	Argentina	Twickenham	Won 19–0
4	02.12.2000	South Africa	Twickenham	Won 25–17
5	03.02.2001	Wales	Cardiff	Won 44–15
6	17.02.2001	Italy	Twickenham	Won 80–23
7	03.03.2001	Scotland	Twickenham	Won 43–3
8	07.04.2001	France	Twickenham	Won 48–19

9	02.06.2001	Canada	Markham	Won 22–10
10	09.06.2001	Canada	Burnaby	Won 59–20
11	16.06.2001	USA	San Francisco	Won 48–19

Ten 1878–82

1	04.03.1878	Scotland	The Oval	Drew 0–0
2	11.03.1878	Ireland	Dublin	Won 2G 1T–0
3	10.03.1879	Scotland	Edinburgh	Drew 1G–1DG
4	24.03.1879	Ireland	The Oval	Won 2G 1DG 2T–0
5	30.01.1880	Ireland	Dublin	Won 1G 1T–1T
6	28.02.1880	Scotland	Manchester	Won 2G 3T–1G
7	05.02.1881	Ireland	Manchester	Won 2G 2T–0
8	19.02.1881	Wales	Blackheath	Won 7G 1DG 6T–0
9	19.03.1881	Scotland	Edinburgh	Drew 1DG 1T–1G 1T
10	06.02.1882	Ireland	Dublin	Drew 2T–2T

Ten 1994–95

1	12.11.1994	Romania	Twickenham	Won 54–3
2	10.12.1994	Canada	Twickenham	Won 60–19
3	21.01.1995	Ireland	Dublin	Won 20–8
4	04.02.1995	France	Twickenham	Won 31–10
5	18.02.1995	Wales	Cardiff	Won 23–9
6	18.03.1995	Scotland	Twickenham	Won 24–12
7	27.05.1995	Argentina	Durban	Won 24–18
8	31.05.1995	Italy	Durban	Won 27–20
9	04.06.1995	Western Samoa	Durban	Won 44–22
10	11.06.1995	Australia	Cape Town	Won 25–22

MOST MATCHES WITHOUT A VICTORY

Eight 1971–72

1	27.02.1971	France	Twickenham	Drew 14–14
2	20.03.1971	Scotland	Twickenham	Lost 15–16
3	27.03.1971	Scotland	Edinburgh	Lost 6–26
4	17.04.1971	RFU President's XV	Twickenham	Lost 11–28
5	15.01.1972	Wales	Twickenham	Lost 3–12
6	12.02.1972	Ireland	Twickenham	Lost 12–16
7	26.02.1972	France	Paris	Lost 12–37
8	18.03.1972	Scotland	Edinburgh	Lost 9–23

Seven 1904–06

1	19.03.1904	Scotland	Edinburgh	Lost 3–6
2	14.01.1905	Wales	Cardiff	Lost 0–25
3	11.02.1905	Ireland	Cork	Lost 3–17
4	18.03.1905	Scotland	Richmond	Lost 0–8
5	02.12.1905	New Zealand	Crystal Palace	Lost 0–15
6	13.01.1906	Wales	Richmond	Lost 3–16
7	10.02.1906	Ireland	Leicester	Lost 6–16

Seven 1930–32

1	15.03.1930	Scotland	Twickenham	Drew 0–0
2	17.01.1931	Wales	Twickenham	Drew 11–11
3	14.02.1931	Ireland	Twickenham	Lost 5–6
4	21.03.1931	Scotland	Edinburgh	Lost 19–28
5	06.04.1931	France	Paris	Lost 13–14
6	02.01.1932	South Africa	Twickenham	Lost 0–7
7	16.01.1932	Wales	Swansea	Lost 5–12

Seven 1948–49

1	03.01.1948	Australia	Twickenham	Lost 0–11
2	17.01.1948	Wales	Twickenham	Drew 3–3
3	14.02.1948	Ireland	Twickenham	Lost 10–11
4	20.03.1948	Scotland	Edinburgh	Lost 3–6
5	29.03.1948	France	Paris	Lost 0–15
6	15.01.1949	Wales	Cardiff	Lost 3–9
7	12.02.1949	Ireland	Dublin	Lost 5–14

Seven 1997–98

1	06.06.1997	Argentina	Buenos Aires	Lost 13–33
2	12.07.1997	Australia	Sydney	Lost 6–25
3	15.11.1997	Australia	Twickenham	Drew 15–15
4	22.11.1997	New Zealand	Manchester	Lost 8–25
5	29.11.1997	South Africa	Twickenham	Lost 11–29
6	06.12.1997	New Zealand	Twickenham	Drew 26–26
7	07.02.1998	France	Paris	Lost 17–24

INTERNATIONAL CHAMPIONSHIP 1893–2004

Year	Winners	Triple Crown	Grand Slam	Year	Winners	Triple Crown	Grand Slam
1883	England	England		1950	Wales	Wales	Wales
1884	England	England		1951	Ireland		
1885	Incomplete			1952	Wales	Wales	Wales
1886	England & Scotland			1953	England		
1887	Scotland			1954	England, France & Wales	England	
1888	Incomplete			1955	France & Wales		
1889	Incomplete			1956	Wales		
1890	England & Scotland			1957	England	England	England
1891	Scotland	Scotland		1958	England		
1892	England	England		1959	France		
1893	Wales	Wales		1960	England & France	England	
1894	Ireland	Ireland		1961	France		
1895	Scotland	Scotland		1962	France		
1896	Ireland			1963	England		
1897	Incomplete			1964	Scotland & Wales		
1898	Incomplete			1965	Wales	Wales	
1899	Ireland	Ireland		1966	Wales		
1900	Wales	Wales		1967	France		
1901	Scotland	Scotland		1968	France		France
1902	Wales	Wales		1969	Wales	Wales	
1903	Scotland	Scotland		1970	France & Wales		
1904	Scotland			1971	Wales	Wales	Wales
1905	Wales	Wales		1972	Incomplete		
1906	Ireland & Wales			1983	Quintuple tie		
1907	Scotland	Scotland		1974	Ireland		
1908	Wales	Wales	Wales	1975	Wales		
1909	Wales	Wales	Wales	1976	Wales	Wales	Wales
1910	England			1977	France	Wales	France
1911	Wales	Wales	Wales	1978	Wales	Wales	Wales
1912	England & Ireland			1979	Wales	Wales	
1913	England	England	England	1980	England	England	England
1914	England	England	England	1981	France		France
1920	England, Scotland & Wales			1982	Ireland	Ireland	
1921	England	England	England	1983	France & Ireland		
1922	Wales			1984	Scotland	Scotland	Scotland
1923	England	England	England	1985	Ireland	Ireland	
1924	England	England	England	1986	France & Scotland		
1925	Scotland	Scotland	Scotland	1987	France		France
1926	Ireland & Scotland			1988	France & Wales	Wales	
1927	Ireland & Scotland			1989	France		
1928	England	England	England	1990	Scotland	Scotland	Scotland
1929	Scotland			1991	England	England	England
1930	England			1992	England	England	England
1931	Wales			1993	France		
1932	England, Ireland & Wales			1994	Wales		
1933	Scotland	Scotland		1995	England	England	England
1934	England	England		1996	England	England	
1935	Ireland			1997	France	England	France
1936	Wales			1998	France	England	France
1937	England	England		1999	Scotland		
1938	Scotland	Scotland		2000	England		
1939	England, Ireland & Wales			2001	England		
1947	England & Wales			2002	France	England	France
1948	Ireland	Ireland	Ireland	2003	England	England	England
1949	Ireland	Ireland		2004	France	Ireland	France

INTERNATIONAL CHAMPIONSHIP RECORD

Year	Pos	P	W	D	L	Points	Tries	Pts	Scot	Ire	Wal	Fra
1883	1st	3	3	0	0	–	12–2	6	Won	Won	Won	–
1884	1st	3	3	0	0	–	5–2	6	Won	Won	Won	–
1885	–	2	2	0	0	–	7–3	4	–	Won	Won	–
1886	1st=	3	2	1	0	–	3–1	5	Drew	Won	Won	–
1887	3rd=	3	0	2	1	–	1–3	2	Drew	Lost	Drew	–
1888	–	–	–	–	–	–	–	–	–	–	–	–
1889	–	–	–	–	–	–	–	–	–	–	–	–
1890	1st=	3	2	0	1	–	5–1	4	Won	Won	Lost	–
1891	2nd	3	2	0	1	19–12	9–3	4	Lost	Won	Won	–
1892	1st	3	3	0	0	29–0	7–0	6	Won	Won	Won	–
1893	3rd=	3	1	0	2	15–20	6–3	2	Lost	Won	Lost	–
1894	2nd=	3	1	0	2	29–16	5–4	2	Lost	Lost	Won	–
1895	2nd	3	2	0	1	23–15	6–4	4	Lost	Won	Won	–

Year	Pos	P	W	D	L	For–Ag		Pts				
1896	3rd=	3	1	0	2	29–21	7–5	2	Lost	Lost	Won	–
1897	–	3	1	0	2	21–27	3–7	2	Won	Lost	Lost	–
1898	–	3	1	1	1	23–19	6–4	3	Drew	Lost	Won	–
1899	4th	3	0	0	3	3–37	1–8	0	Lost	Lost	Lost	–
1900	2nd	3	1	1	1	18–17	4–2	3	Drew	Won	Lost	–
1901	4th	3	0	0	3	9–41	2–9	0	Lost	Lost	Lost	–
1902	2nd	3	2	0	1	20–15	6–4	4	Won	Won	Lost	–
1903	4th	3	0	0	3	11–37	3–8	0	Lost	Lost	Lost	–
1904	2nd=	3	1	1	1	36–20	9–4	3	Lost	Won	Drew	–
1905	4th	3	0	0	3	3–50	1–14	0	Lost	Lost	Lost	–
1906	3rd=	3	1	0	2	18–35	6–9	2	Won	Lost	Lost	–
1907	4th	3	0	0	3	12–47	3–12	0	Lost	Lost	Lost	–
1908	2nd=	3	1	0	2	41–47	9–7	2	Lost	Won	Lost	–
1909	3rd	3	1	0	2	19–31	5–7	2	Lost	Won	Lost	–
1910	1st	4	3	1	0	36–14	9–4	7	Won	Drew	Wo	Won
1911	3rd	4	2	0	2	61–26	13–7	4	Won	Lost	Lost	Won
1912	1st=	4	3	0	1	44–16	12–4	6	Lost	Won	Won	Won
1913	1st	4	4	0	0	50–4	13–0	8	Won	Won	Won	Won
1914	1st	4	4	0	0	82–49	20–9	8	Won	Won	Won	Won
1920	1st=	4	3	0	1	40–37	9–5	6	Won	Won	Lost	Won
1921	1st	4	4	0	0	61–9	13–1	8	Won	Won	Won	Won
1922	2nd	4	2	1	1	40–47	10–13	5	Won	Won	Lost	Drew
1923	1st	4	4	0	0	50–17	10–4	8	Won	Won	Won	Won
1924	1st	4	4	0	0	69–19	17–5	8	Won	Won	Won	Won
1925	2nd=	4	2	1	1	42–37	9–9	5	Lost	Drew	Won	Won
1926	4th	4	1	1	2	38–39	10–8	3	Lost	Lost	Drew	Won
1927	3rd	4	2	0	2	32–39	5–9	4	Lost	Won	Won	Lost
1927	1st	4	4	0	0	41–22	9–6	8	Won	Won	Won	Won
1929	4th	4	2	0	2	35–27	9–9	4	Lost	Lost	Won	Won
1930	1st	4	2	1	1	25–12	6–2	5	Drew	Lost	Won	Won
1931	5th	4	0	1	3	38–59	9–11	1	Lost	Lost	Drew	Lost
1932	1st=	3	2	0	1	32–23	6–3	4	Won	Won	Lost	–
1933	2nd=	3	1	0	2	20–16	6–3	2	Lost	Won	Lost	–
1934	1st	3	3	0	0	28–6	8–2	6	Won	Won	Won	–
1935	2nd=	3	1	1	1	24–16	2–4	3	Lost	Won	Drew	–
1936	3rd=	3	1	1	1	12–14	4–3	3	Won	Lost	Drew	–
1937	1st	3	3	0	0	19–14	4–3	6	Won	Won	Won	–
1938	3rd	3	1	0	2	60–49	10–11	2	Lost	Won	Lost	–
1939	1st=	3	2	0	1	12–11	1–3	4	Won	Lost	Won	–
1947	1st=	4	3	0	1	39–36	7–8	6	Won	Lost	Won	Won
1948	5th	4	0	1	3	16–35	2–9	1	Lost	Lost	Drew	Lost
1949	2nd=	4	2	0	2	35–29	7–5	2	Won	Lost	Lost	Won
1950	5th	4	1	0	3	22–30	5–7	2	Lost	Won	Lost	Lost
1951	4th=	4	1	0	3	13–40	3–8	2	Won	Lost	Lost	Lost
1952	2nd	4	3	0	1	34–14	7–4	6	Won	Won	Lost	Won
1953	1st	4	3	1	0	54–20	11–3	7	Won	Drew	Won	Won
1954	1st=	4	3	0	1	39–23	10–4	6	Won	Won	Won	Lost
1955	4th	4	1	1	2	24–31	5–4	3	Won	Drew	Lost	Lost
1956	2nd=	4	2	0	2	43–28	5–5	4	Won	Won	Lost	Lost
1957	1st	4	4	0	0	34–8	7–1	8	Won	Won	Won	Won
1958	1st	4	2	2	0	26–6	5–0	6	Drew	Won	Drew	Won
1959	2nd=	4	1	2	1	9–11	0–1	4	Drew	Won	Lost	Drew
1960	1st=	4	3	1	0	46–26	7–2	7	Won	Won	Won	Drew
1961	4th	4	1	1	2	22–22	5–4	3	Won	Lost	Lost	Drew
1962	3rd=	4	1	2	1	19–16	3–3	4	Drew	Won	Drew	Lost
1963	1st	4	3	1	0	29–19	4–3	7	Won	Drew	Won	Won
1964	3rd=	4	1	1	2	23–42	5–10	3	Lost	Lost	Drew	Won
1965	4th	4	1	1	2	15–28	2–5	3	Drew	Lost	Lost	Won
1966	5th	4	0	1	3	15–36	2–6	1	Lost	Drew	Lost	Lost
1967	2nd=	4	2	0	2	68–67	8–9	4	Won	Won	Lost	Lost
1968	3rd	4	1	2	1	37–40	3–3	4	Won	Drew	Drew	Lost
1969	3rd	4	2	0	2	54–58	6–8	4	Won	Lost	Lost	Won
1970	4th=	4	1	0	3	40–69	7–11	2	Lost	Won	Lost	Lost
1971	3rd=	4	1	1	2	44–58	5–9	3	Lost	Won	Lost	Drew
1972	5th	4	0	0	4	36–88	2–11	0	Lost	Lost	Lost	Lost
1973	1st=	4	2	0	2	52–62	7–8	4	Won	Lost	Lost	Won
1974	5th	4	1	1	2	63–66	6–8	3	Lost	Lost	Won	Drew
1975	5th	4	1	0	3	40–65	5–9	2	Won	Lost	Lost	Lost
1976	5th	4	0	0	4	42–86	2–15	0	Lost	Lost	Lost	Lost
1977	3rd	4	2	0	2	42–24	5–3	4	Won	Won	Lost	Lost
1978	3rd	4	2	0	2	42–33	4–2	4	Won	Won	Lost	Lost
1979	4th	4	1	1	2	24–52	3–8	3	Drew	Lost	Lost	Won
1980	1st	4	4	0	0	80–48	10–6	8	Won	Won	Won	Won
1981	2nd=	4	2	0	2	64–60	6–6	4	Won	Won	Lost	Lost
1982	2nd=	4	2	1	1	68–47	5–4	5	Drew	Lost	Won	Won
1983	5th	4	0	1	3	55–79	1–8	1	Lost	Lost	Drew	Lost

Year	Pos	P	W	D	L	F–A						
1984	4th	4	1	0	3	51–83	2–8	2	Lost	Won	Lost	Lost
1985	4th	4	1	1	2	44–53	3–4	3	Won	Lost	Lost	Drew
1986	3rd=	4	2	0	2	62–100	5–11	4	Lost	Won	Won	Lost
1987	4th=	4	1	0	3	48–67	2–7	2	Won	Lost	Lost	Lost
1988	3rd=	4	2	0	2	56–30	6–3	4	Won	Won	Lost	Lost
1989	2nd=	4	2	1	1	48–27	4–2	5	Drew	Won	Lost	Won
1990	2nd	4	3	0	1	90–26	12–3	6	Lost	Won	Won	Won
1991	1st	4	4	0	0	83–44	5–4	8	Won	Won	Won	Won
1992	1st	4	4	0	0	118–29	15–4	8	Won	Won	Won	Won
1993	3rd	4	2	0	2	54–54	4–4	4	Won	Lost	Lost	Won
1994	2nd	4	3	0	1	60–49	2–4	6	Won	Lost	Won	Won
1995	1st	4	4	0	0	98–39	9–2	8	Won	Won	Won	Won
1996	1st	4	3	0	1	79–54	3–2	6	Won	Won	Won	Lost
1997	2nd	4	3	0	1	141–55	15–4	6	Won	Won	Won	Lost
1998	2nd	4	3	0	1	146–87	17–10	6	Won	Won	Won	Lost
1999	2nd	4	3	0	1	103–78	8–6	6	Won	Won	Lost	Won
2000	1st	5	4	0	1	183–10	12–3	8	Lost	Won	Won	Won Won
2001	1st	5	4	0	1	224–80	29–6	8	Won	Lost	Won	Won Won
2002	2nd	5	4	0	1	184–53	23–4	8	Won	Won	Won	Lost Won
2003	1st	5	5	0	0	173–46	18–4	10	Won	Won	Won	Won Won
2004	3rd	5	3	0	2	150–86	17–6	6	Won	Lost	Won	Lost Won
	403	212	38	153	4972–3781	753–585	462					

INTERNATIONAL APPEARANCES 1871–2004

Player	Caps	First International	Last International	
C D Aarvold	16	07.01.1928 – Australia	21.01.1933 – Wales	
S Abbott*	5	23.08.2003 – Wales		
P J Acktord	22	05.11.1988 – Australia	02.11.1991 – Australia	*still playing
A A Adams	1	03.03.1910 – France		
F R Adams	7	15.02.1875 – Ireland	24.03.1879 – Ireland	
A A Adebayo	6	23.11.1996 – Italy	22.03.1998 – Scotland	
G J Adey	2	06.03.1976 – Ireland	20.03.1976 – France	
S J Adkins	7	11.02.1950 – Ireland	21.03.1953 – Scotland	
A E Agar	7	05.01.1952 – South Africa	14.02.1953 – Ireland	
A Alcock	1	08.12.1906 – South Africa		
F H R Alderson	6	03.01.1891 – Wales	07.01.1893 – Wales	
H Alexander	7	03.02.1900 – Ireland	08.02.1902 – Ireland	
W Alexander	1	02.04.1927 – France		
D F Allison	7	21.01.1956 – Wales	15.03.1958 – Scotland	
A Allport	5	02.01.1892 – Wales	17.03.1894 – Scotland	
S Anderson	1	04.02.1899 – Ireland		
W F Anderson	1	06.01.1973 – New Zealand		
C Anderton	2	16.02.1889 – NZ Natives		
C R Andrew	71	05.01.1985 – Romania	15.03.1997 – Wales	
G Appleford	1	22.06.2002 – Argentina	22.06.2002 – Argentina	
G S Archer*	21	02.03.1996 – Scotland	02.04.2000 – Scotland	
H Archer	3	16.01.1909 – Wales	13.02.1909 – Ireland	
R Armstrong	1	17.01.1925 – Wales		
T G Arthur	2	15.01.1966 – Wales	12.02.1966 – Ireland	
R C Ashby	3	12.02.1966 – Ireland	07.01.1967 – Australia	
A Ashcroft	16	21.01.1956 – Wales	21.03.1959 – Scotland	
A H Ashcroft	1	09.01.1909 – Australia		
W Ashford	4	09.01.1897 – Wales	02.04.1898 – Wales	
A Ashworth	1	06.02.1892 – Ireland		
J G Askew	3	18.01.1930 – Wales	22.02.1930 – France	
A R Aslett	6	16.01.1926 – Wales	01.04.1929 – France	
E W Assinder	2	09.01.1909 – Australia	16.01.1909 – Wales	
R L Aston	2	01.03.1890 – Scotland	15.03.1890 – Ireland	
J R Auty	1	16.03.1935 – Scotland		
N A Back*	66	05.02.1994 – Scotland	22.11.2003 – Australia	
M D Bailey	7	02.06.1984 – South Africa	17.03.1990 – Scotland	
S Bainbridge	18	20.02.1982 – France	03.06.1987 – United States	
D G S Baker	4	22.01.1955 – Wales	19.03.1955 – Scotland	
E M Baker	7	05.01.1895 – Wales	09.01.1897 – Wales	
H C Baker	1	08.01.1887 – Wales		
I R Balshaw	22	05.02.2000 – Ireland	06.03.2004 – Ireland	
J F Bance	1	20.03.1954 – Scotland		
O Barkley	5	16.06.2001 – USA	27.03.2004 – France	

B Barley	7	18.02.1984 – Ireland	17.06.1988 – Fiji
S Barnes	10	03.11.1984 – Australia	20.03.1993 – Ireland
R J Barr	3	02.01.1932 – South Africa	13.02.1932 – Ireland
E I M Barrett	1	21.03.1903 – Scotland	
T J M Barrington	2	17.01.1931 – Wales	14.02.1931 – Ireland
L E Barrington-Ward	4	15.01.1910 – Wales	19.03.1910 – Scotland
J H Barron	3	14.03.1896 – Scotland	06.02.1897 – Ireland
J T Bartlett	1	20.01.1951 – Wales	
R M Bartlett	7	19.01.1957 – Wales	15.03.1958 – Scotland
J Barton	4	11.02.1967 – Ireland	26.02.1972 – France
T B Batchelor	1	05.01.1907 – France	
S M Bates	1	13.05.1989 – Romania	
A H Bateson	4	18.01.1930 – Wales	15.03.1930 – Scotland
H D Bateson	1	24.03.1879 – Ireland	
T Batson	3	05.02.1872 – Scotland	15.02.1875 – Ireland
J M Batten	1	23.02.1874 – Scotland	
J L Baume	1	18.03.1950 – Scotland	
J J N Baxendell*	2	27.06.1998 – New Zealand	04.07.1998 – South Africa
J Baxter	3	06.01.1900 – Wales	10.03.1900 – Scotland
M C Bayfield	31	20.07.1991 – Fiji	03.02.1996 – Wales
R C Bazley	10	29.03.1952 – Ireland	19.03.1955 – Scotland
N D Beal*	15	14.12.1996 – Argentina	24.10.1999 – South Africa
W B Beaumont	34	18.01.1975 – Ireland	16.01.1982 – Scotland
H Bedford	3	16.02.1889 – NZ Natives	15.03.1890 – Ireland
L L Bedford	2	17.01.1931 – Wales	14.02.1931 – Ireland
I D S Beer	2	26.02.1955 – France	19.03.1955 – Scotland
M C Beese	3	15.01.1972 – Wales	26.02.1972 – France
T D Beim*	2	20.06.1998 – New Zealand	27.06.1998 – New Zealand
F J Bell	1	06.01.1900 – Wales	
H Bell	1	04.02.1884 – Ireland	
J L Bell	1	11.03.1878 – Ireland	
P J Bell	4	20.01.1968 – Wales	16.03.1968 – Scotland
R W Bell	3	06.01.1900 – Wales	10.03.1900 – Scotland
G J Bendon	4	17.01.1959 – Wales	21.03.1959 – Scotland
N O Bennett	7	18.01.1947 – Wales	20.03.1948 – Scotland
W N Bennett	7	15.03.1975 – Scotland	17.03.1979 – Wales
B B Bennetts	2	09.01.1909 – Australia	16.01.1909 – Wales
J Bentley	4	23.04.1988 – Ireland	29.11.1997 – South Africa
J E Bentley	2	27.03.1871 – Scotland	05.02.1872 – Scotland
S Benton*	1	06.06.1998 – Australia	
M J Berridge	2	15.01.1949 – Wales	12.02.1949 – Ireland
H Berry	4	15.01.1910 – Wales	19.03.1910 – Scotland
J Berry	3	03.01.1891 – Wales	07.03.1891 – Scotland
J T W Berry	3	21.01.1939 – Wales	18.03.1939 – Scotland
E Beswick	2	06.02.1882 – Ireland	04.03.1882 – Scotland
J M Biggs	2	04.03.1878 – Scotland	24.03.1879 – Ireland
J G G Birkett	21	17.03.1906 – Scotland	08.04.1912 – France
L Birkett	3	08.03.1875 – Scotland	05.03.1877 – Scotland
R H Birkett	4	27.03.1871 – Scotland	05.02.1877 – Ireland
C C Bishop	1	02.04.1927 – France	
B H Black	10	18.01.1930 – Wales	21.01.1933 – Wales
J H Blacklock	2	05.02.1898 – Ireland	04.02.1899 – Ireland
P J Blakeway	19	19.01.1980 – Ireland	30.03.1985 – Ireland
A F Blakiston	17	20.03.1920 – Scotland	13.04.1925 – France
T Blatherwick	1	11.03.1878 – Ireland	
J A Body	2	05.02.1872 – Scotland	03.03.1873 – Scotland
C A Bolton	1	30.01.1909 – France	
R Bolton	5	21.01.1933 – Wales	12.02.1938 – Ireland
W N Bolton	11	06.02.1882 – Ireland	05.03.1887 – Scotland
M S Bonaventura	1	17.01.1931 – Wales	
A M Bond	6	25.11.1978 – New Zealand	06.02.1982 – Ireland
E Bonham-Carter	1	07.03.1891 – Scotland	
F Bonsor	7	02.01.1886 – Wales	16.02.1889 – NZ Natives
B Boobbyer	9	21.01.1950 – Wales	05.04.1952 – France
L A Booth	7	21.01.1933 – Wales	16.03.1935 – Scotland
S Borthwick	10	07.04.2001 – France	27.05.2004 – France
I J Botting	2	21.01.1950 – Wales	11.02.1950 – Ireland
H J Boughton	3	19.01.1935 – Wales	16.03.1935 – Scotland
C W Boyle	1	03.03.1873 – Scotland	
S B Boyle	3	05.02.1983 – Wales	19.03.1983 – Ireland
F Boylen	4	01.01.1908 – France	21.03.1908 – Scotland
K P P Bracken*	51	27.11.1993 – New Zealand	16.11.2003 – France
M S Bradby	2	11.02.1922 – Ireland	25.02.1922 – France
R Bradley	1	10.01.1903 – Wales	
H Bradshaw	7	05.03.1892 – Scotland	17.03.1894 – Scotland
S E Brain	13	09.06.1984 – South Africa	15.03.1986 – France

J Braithwaite	1	02.12.1905 – New Zealand	
B Braithwaite-Exley	1	15.01.1949 – Wales	
A T Brettargh	8	06.01.1900 – Wales	18.03.1905 – Scotland
J Brewer	1	13.12.1875 – Ireland	
A Briggs	3	02.01.1892 – Wales	05.03.1892 – Scotland
A Brinn	3	15.01.1972 – Wales	18.03.1972 – Scotland
T Broadley	6	07.01.1893 – Wales	14.03.1896 – Scotland
W E Bromet	12	03.01.1891 – Wales	01.02.1896 – Ireland
P W P Brook	3	15.03.1930 – Scotland	21.03.1936 – Scotland
T J Brooke	2	24.02.1968 – France	16.03.1968 – Scotland
F G Brooks	1	08.12.1906 – South Africa	
M J Brooks	1	23.02.1874 – Scotland	
T J Brophy	8	08.02.1964 – Ireland	26.02.1966 – France
J W Brough	2	03.01.1925 – New Zealand	17.01.1925 – Wales
H Brougham	4	20.01.1912 – Wales	08.04.1912 – France
A A Brown	1	19.03.1938 – Scotland	
L G Brown	18	21.01.1911 – Wales	21.01.1922 – Wales
S Brown*	2	06.06.1998 – Australia	04.07.1998 – South Africa
T W Brown	9	17.03.1928 – Scotland	18.03.1933 – Scotland
J Brunton	3	17.01.1914 – Wales	21.03.1914 – Scotland
E B Brutton	1	13.03.1886 – Scotland	
C C Bryden	2	13.12.1875 – Ireland	05.03.1877 – Scotland
H A Bryden	1	23.02.1874 – Scotland	
R A Buckingham	1	02.04.1927 – France	
A L Bucknall	10	20.12.1969 – South Africa	27.03.1971 – Scotland
J R D Buckton	3	05.11.1988 – Australia	04.08.1990 – Argentina
A Budd	5	11.03.1878 – Ireland	19.03.1881 – Scotland
R T D Budworth	3	15.02.1890 – Wales	07.03.1891 – Scotland
A G Bull	1	17.01.1914 – Wales	
E Bullough	3	02.01.1892 – Wales	05.03.1892 – Scotland
M P Bulpitt	1	21.03.1970 – Scotland	
A J Bulteei	1	13.12.1875 – Ireland	
W L Bunting	9	06.02.1897 – Ireland	09.03.1901 – Scotland
D W Burland	8	17.01.1931 – Wales	18.03.1933 – Scotland
B H Burns	1	27.03.1871 – Scotland	
G W Burton	6	10.03.1879 – Scotland	19.03.1881 – Scotland
H C Burton	1	16.01.1926 – Wales	
M A Burton	17	15.01.1972 – Wales	04.02.1978 – Wales
J A Bush	5	05.02.1872 – Scotland	06.03.1876 – Scotland
C J S Butcher	3	02.06.1984 – South Africa	03.11.1984 – Australia
W V Butcher	7	21.03.1903 – Scotland	18.03.1905 – Scotland
A G Butler	2	16.01.1937 – Wales	13.02.1937 – Ireland
P E Butler	2	24.05.1975 – Australia	20.03.1976 – France
J Butterfield	28	28.02.1953 – France	21.03.1959 – Scotland
F A Byrne	1	09.01.1897 – Wales	
J F Byrne	13	06.01.1894 – Wales	04.02.1899 – Ireland
J J Cain	1	21.01.1950 – Wales	
J E B Callard	5	27.11.1993 – New Zealand	18.11.1995 – South Africa
D A Campbell	2	16.01.1937 – Wales	13.02.1937 – Ireland
P L Candler	10	19.01.1935 – Wales	19.03.1938 – Scotland
L B Cannell	19	29.03.1948 – France	09.02.1957 – Ireland
D W N Caplan	2	04.03.1978 – Scotland	18.03.1978 – Ireland
R M Cardus	2	03.03.1979 – France	17.03.1979 – Wales
G M Carey	5	05.01.1895 – Wales	01.02.1896 – Ireland
J Carleton	26	24.11.1979 – New Zealand	03.11.1984 – Australia
W D C Carling	72	16.01.1988 – France	15.03.1997 – Wales
A D Carpenter	1	02.01.1932 – South Africa	
R S L Carr	3	21.01.1939 – Wales	18.03.1939 – Scotland
V H Carrwright	14	10.01.1903 – Wales	08.12.1906 – South Africa
H C Catcheside	8	19.01.1924 – Wales	19.03.1927 – Scotland
M J Catt*	63	19.03.1994 – Wales	27.03.2004 – France
R H B Cattell	7	05.01.1895 – Wales	06.01.1900 – Wales
J W Cave	1	16.02.1889 – NZ Natives	
W T C Cave	1	14.01.1905 – Wales	
R Challis	3	09.02.1957 – Ireland	16.03.1957 – Scotland
E L Chambers	3	01.01.1908 – France	12.02.1910 – Ireland
B S Chantrill	4	19.01.1924 – Wales	15.03.1924 – Scotland
C E Chapman	1	05.01.1884 – Wales	
D E Chapman*	1	06.06.1998 – Australia	
F E Chapman	7	15.01.1910 – Wales	14.02.1914 – Ireland
W I Cheesman	4	04.01.1913 – South Africa	08.02.1913 – Ireland
E C Cheston	5	03.03.1873 – Scotland	06.03.1876 – Scotland
G J Chilcott	14	03.11.1984 – Australia	13.05.1989 – Romania
P Christophers	3	22.06.2002 – Argentina	22.02.2003 – Wales
P Christopherson	2	03.01.1891 – Wales	07.03.1891 – Scotland
C W H Clark	1	13.12.1875 – Ireland	

A J Clarke	6	19.01.1935 – Wales	08.02.1936 – Ireland
B B Clarke*	40	14.11.1992 – South Africa	26.06.1999 – Australia
S J S Clarke	13	19.01.1963 – Wales	20.03.1965 – Scotland
J H Clayton	1	27.03.1871 – Scotland	
J W Clements	3	14.02.1959 – Ireland	21.03.1959 – Scotland
C R Cleveland	2	08.01.1887 – Wales	05.03.1887 – Scotland
W G Clibborn	7	02.01.1886 – Wales	05.03.1887 – Scotland
F J Clough	4	01.03.1986 – Ireland	03.06.1987 – United States
C H Coates	3	28.02.1880 – Scotland	04.03.1882 – Scotland
V H M Coates	5	04.01.1913 – South Africa	15.03.1913 – Scotland
W Cobby	1	06.01.1900 – Wales	
A Cockerharn	1	06.01.1900 – Wales	
R Cockerill*	27	30.05.1997 – Argentina	20.10.1999 – South Africa
A Codling	1	22.06.2002 – Argentina	22.06.2002 – Argentina
B C Cohen	40	05.02.2000 – Ireland	27.05.2004 – France
M J Colclough	25	04.03.1978 – Scotland	15.03.1986 – France
E Coley	2	01.04.1929 – France	16.01.1932 – Wales
P J Collins	3	15.03.1952 – Scotland	05.04.1952 – France
W E Collins	5	23.02.1874 – Scotland	06.03.1876 – Scotland
S G U Considine	1	13.04.1925 – France	
G S Conway	18	31.01.1920 – France	15.01.1927 – Wales
J G Cook	1	20.03.1937 – Scotland	
P W Cook	2	13.02.1965 – Ireland	27.02.1965 – France
D A Cooke	4	17.01.1976 – Wales	20.03.1976 – France
D H Cooke	12	17.01.1981 – Wales	08.06.1985 – New Zealand
P Cooke	2	21.01.1939 – Wales	11.02.1939 – Ireland
T Coop	1	05.03.1892 – Scotland	
J G Cooper	2	09.01.1909 – Australia	16.01.1909 – Wales
M J Cooper	11	24.02.1973 – France	05.03.1977 – Wales
S F Coopper	7	06.01.1900 – Wales	12.01.1907 – Wales
L J Corbett	16	28.03.1921 – France	02.04.1927 – France
B J Corless	10	03.01.1976 – Australia	18.03.1978 – Ireland
M J Corry*	29	30.05.1997 – Argentina	02.11.2003 – Uruguay
F E Cotton	31	20.03.1971 – Scotland	17.01.1981 – Wales
M J Coulman	9	07.01.1967 – Australia	16.03.1968 – Scotland
T J Coulson	3	15.01.1927 – Wales	21.01.1928 – Wales
E D Court	1	03.01.1885 – Wales	
H Coverdale	4	03.03.1910 – France	17.01.1920 – Wales
R Cove-Smith	29	19.03.1921 – Scotland	09.02.1929 – Ireland
R J Cowling	8	15.01.1977 – Scotland	17.02.1979 – Ireland
A R Cowrnan	5	20.03.1971 – Scotland	10.02.1973 – Ireland
N S Cox	1	09.03.1901 – Scotland	
P Cramner	16	20.01.1934 – Wales	19.03.1938 – Scotland
R N Creed	1	17.04.1971 – RFU President's XV	
A G Cridlan	3	19.01.1935 – Wales	16.03.1935 – Scotland
C A Crompton	1	27.03.1871 – Scotland	
C W Crosse	2	23.02.1874 –– Scotland	15.02.1875 – Ireland
B S Cumberlege	8	17.01.1920 – Wales	21.01.1922 – Wales
D C Cumming	2	21.03.1925 – Scotland	13.04.1925 – France
F L Cunliffe	1	23.02.1874 – Scotland	
F I Currey	1	05.02.1872 – Scotland	
J D Currie	25	21.01.1956 – Wales	24.02.1962 – France
D A Cusani	1	07.02.1987 – Ireland	
L Cusworth	12	24.11.1979 – New Zealand	06.02.1988 – Wales
F B G D'Aguilar	1	05.02.1872 – Scotland	
L B N Dallaglio*	70	18.11.1995 – South Africa	27.03.2004 – France
T J Dalton	1	15.03.1969 – Scotland	
T Danby	1	15.01.1949 – Wales	
J Daniell	7	07.01.1899 – Wales	19.03.1904 – Scotland
A J L Darby	1	04.02.1899 – Ireland	
A Davenport	1	27.03.1871 – Scotland	
J Davey	2	21.03.1908 – Scotland	16.01.1909 – Wales
R F Davey	1	17.01.1931 – Wales	
James Davidson	5	13.03.1897 – Scotland	11.03.1899 – Scotland
Joseph Davidson	2	07.01.1899 – Wales	11.03.1899 – Scotland
G H Davles	21	21.02.1981 – Scotland	15.03.1986 – France
P H Davies	1	12.02.1927 – Ireland	
V G Davies	2	21.01.1922 – Wales	03.01.1925 – New Zealand
W J A Davies	22	04.01.1913 – South Africa	02.04.1923 – France
W P C Davies	11	21.03.1953 – Scotland	18.01.1958 – Wales
A M Davis	16	19.01.1963 – Wales	21.03.1970 – Scotland
R G R Dawe	5	07.02.1987 – Ireland	04.06.1995 – Western Samoa
E F Dawson	1	11.03.1878 – Ireland	
M J S Dawson*	62	16.12.1995 – Western Samoa	27.03.2004 – France
H L V Day	4	17.01.1920 – Wales	20.03.1926 – Scotland
G J Dean	1	14.02.1931 – Ireland	

J M Dee	2	17.03.1962 – Scotland	25.05.1963 – New Zealand
Sir T G Devitt	4	13.02.1926 – Ireland	21.01.1928 – Wales
J H Dewhurst	5	08.01.1887 – Wales	15.02.1890 – Wales
P R De Glanville*	38	14.11.1992 – South Africa	24.10.1999 – South Africa
R F C De Winton	1	07.01.1893 – Wales	
R Dibble	19	17.03.1906 – Scotland	16.03.1912 – Scotland
J Dicks	8	20.01.1934 – Wales	13.02.1937 – Ireland
E W Dillon	4	09.01.1904 – Wales	14.01.1905 – Wales
A J Dingle	3	08.02.1913 – Ireland	13.04.1914 – France
A J Diprose*	10	30.05.1997 – Argentina	04.07.1998 – South Africa
P J Dixon	22	17.04.1971 – RFU President's XV	25.11.1978 – New Zealand
G E B Dobbs	2	13.01.1906 – Wales	10.02.1906 – Ireland
S A Doble	3	03.06.1972 – South Africa	20.01.1973 – Wales
D D Dobson	6	11.01.1902 – Wales	21.03.1903 – Scotland
T H Dobson	1	09.03.1895 – Scotland	
P W Dodge	32	04.02.1978 – Wales	08.06.1985 – New Zealand
M P Donnelly	1	08.02.1947 – Ireland	
W A Dooley	55	05.01.1985 – Romania	20.03.1993 – Ireland
B A Dovey	2	19.01.1963 – Wales	09.02.1963 – Ireland
P J Down	1	09.01.1909 – Australia	
A O Dowson	1	11.03.1899 – Scotland	
N J Drake-Lee	8	19.01.1963 – Wales	16.01.1965 – Wales
H Duckett	2	04.02.1893 – Ireland	04.03.1893 – Scotland
D J Duckham	36	08.02.1969 – Ireland	21.02.1976 – Scotland
H W Dudgeon	7	13.03.1897 – Scotland	11.03.1899 – Scotland
J M Dugdale	1	27.03.1871 – Scotland	
A F Dun	1	17.03.1984 – Wales	
R F H Duncan	3	11.02.1922 – Ireland	18.03.1922 – Scotland
N Duncombe	2	02.02.2002 – Scotland	16.02.2002 – Ireland
P E Dunkley	6	14.02.1931 – Ireland	21.03.1936 – Scotland
J Duthie	1	10.01.1903 – Wales	
J W Dyson	4	01.03.1890 – Scotland	04.03.1893 – Scotland
H Eagles	1	n/a 1888 Cap	1888 Cap
P J Ebdon	2	09.01.1897 – Wales	06.02.1897 – Ireland
J H Eddison	4	20.01.1912 – Wales	08.04.1912 – France
C S Edgar	1	09.03.1901 – Scotland	
R Edwards	11	15.01.1921 – Wales	03.01.1925 – New Zealand
D W Egerton	7	23.04.1988 – Ireland	04.08.1990 – Argentina
C H Elliot	1	02.01.1886 – Wales	
E W Elliot	4	05.01.1901 – Wales	09.01.1904 – Wales
W Elliot	7	13.02.1932 – Ireland	10.02.1934 – Ireland
A E Elliott	1	17.03.1894 – Scotland	
J Ellis	1	18.03.1939 – Scotland	
S S Ellis	1	30.01.1880 – Ireland	
C Emmott	1	02.01.1892 – Wales	
H J Enthoven	1	11.03.1878 – Ireland	
N S D Estcourt	1	19.03.1955 – Scotland	
B J Evans	2	12.06.1988 – Australia	17.06.1988 – Fiji
E Evans	30	03.01.1948 – Australia	15.03.1958 – Scotland
G W Evans	9	18.03.1972 – Scotland	16.03.1974 – Wales
N L Evans	5	16.01.1932 – Wales	11.02.1933 – Ireland
A M Evanson	4	16.12.1882 – Wales	01.03.1884 – Scotland
W A D Evanson	5	08.03.1875 – Scotland	24.03.1879 – Ireland
F Evershed	10	16.02.1889 – NZ Natives	04.03.1893 – Scotland
W C T Eyres	1	12.02.1927 – Ireland	
A R St L Fagan	2	05.02.1887 – Ireland	
K E Fairbrother	12	08.02.1969 – Ireland	27.02.1971 – France
C K T Faithfull	3	09.02.1924 – Ireland	20.03.1926 – Scotland
H Fallas	1	04.02.1884 – Ireland	
J H C Fegan	3	05.01.1895 – Wales	09.03.1895 – Scotland
C W L Fernandes	3	05.02.1881 – Ireland	19.03.1881 – Scotland
J H Fidler	4	30.05.1981 – Argentina	09.06.1984 – South Africa
R J Fidler*	2	27.06.1998 – New Zealand	04.07.1998 – South Africa
E Field	2	07.01.1893 – Wales	04.02.1893 – Ireland
K J Fielding	10	08.02.1969 – Ireland	18.03.1972 – Scotland
R T Finch	1	28.02.1880 – Scotland	
J F Finlan	13	11.02.1967 – Ireland	06.01.1973 – New Zealand
H W Finlinson	3	05.01.1895 – Wales	09.03.1895 – Scotland
S Finney	2	05.02.1872 – Scotland	03.03.1873 – Scotland
F Firth	3	06.01.1894 – Wales	17.03.1894 – Scotland
D Flatman	8	17.06.2000 – South Africa	22.06.2002 – Argentina
N C Fletcher	4	05.01.1901 – Wales	21.03.1903 – Scotland
T Fletcher	1	09.01.1897 – Wales	
W R B Fletcher	2	03.03.1873 – Scotland	08.03.1875 – Scotland
E F Fookes	10	04.01.1896 – Wales	11.03.1899 – Scotland
P J Ford	4	18.01.1964 – Wales	21.03.1964 – Scotland

J W Forrest	10	18.01.1930 – Wales	17.03.1934 – Scotland
R Forrest	6	07.01.1899 – Wales	21.03.1903 – Scotland
R T Foulds	2	19.01.1929 – Wales	09.02.1929 – Ireland
F D Fowler	2	04.03.1878 – Scotland	10.03.1879 – Scotland
H Fowler	3	04.03.1878 – Scotland	19.03.1881 – Scotland
R H Fowler	1	05.02.1877 – Ireland	
F H Fox	2	15.02.1890 – Wales	01.03.1890 – Scotland
T E S Francis	4	16.01.1926 – Wales	20.03.1926 – Scotland
G P Frankcom	4	16.01.1965 – Wales	20.03.1965 – Scotland
E C Fraser	1	15.02.1875 – Ireland	
G Fraser	5	11.01.1902 – Wales	14.02.1903 – Ireland
H D Freakes	3	15.01.1938 – Wales	11.02.1939 – Ireland
H Freeman	3	05.02.1872 – Scotland	23.02.1874 – Scotland
R J French	4	21.01.1961 – Wales	18.03.1961 – Scotland
H A Fry	3	20.01.1934 – Wales	17.03.1934 – Scotland
T W Fry	3	30.01.1880 – Ireland	19.02.1881 – Wales
H G Fuller	6	06.02.1882 – Ireland	05.01.1884 – Wales
B C Gadney	14	13.02.1932 – Ireland	15.01.1938 – Wales
H T Gamlin	15	07.01.1899 – Wales	19.03.1904 – Scotland
E R Gardner	10	15.01.1921 – Wales	02.04.1923 – France
H P Gardner	1	11.03.1878 – Ireland	
D J Garforth*	25	15.03.1997 – Wales	18.3.2000 – Italy
H W T Garnett	1	05.03.1877 – Scotland	
M N Gavins	1	21.01.1961 – Wales	
D J Gay	4	20.01.1968 – Wales	16.03.1968 – Scotland
D R Gent	5	02.12.1905 – New Zealand	12.02.1910 – Ireland
J S M Genth	2	23.02.1874 – Scotland	08.03.1875 – Scotland
J T George	3	15.03.1947 – Scotland	12.02.1949 – Ireland
R A Gerrard	14	02.01.1932 – South Africa	21.03.1936 – Scotland
G A Gibbs	2	19.04.1947 – France	14.02.1948 – Ireland
J C Gibbs	7	03.01.1925 – New Zealand	02.04.1927 – France
N Gibbs	2	20.03.1954 – Scotland	10.04.1954 – France
L F Giblin	3	04.01.1896 – Wales	13.03.1897 – Scotland
A S Gibson	1	27.03.1871 – Scotland	
C O P Gibson	1	05.01.1901 – Wales	
G R Gibson	2	07.01.1899 – Wales	09.03.1901 – Scotland
T A Gibson	2	14.01.1905 – Wales	18.03.1905 – Scotland
F G Gilbert	2	20.01.1923 – Wales	10.02.1923 – Ireland
R Gilbert	3	18.01.1908 – Wales	21.03.1908 – Scotland
J L Giles	6	19.01.1935 – Wales	19.03.1938 – Scotland
W J Gittings	1	04.11.1967 – New Zealand	
P B Glover	3	07.01.1967 – Australia	17.04.1971 – RFU President's XV
R E Godfray	1	02.12.1905 – New Zealand	
H O Godwin	11	28.02.1959 – France	04.11.1967 – New Zealand
A C T Gomarsall	17	23.11.1996 – Italy	21.02.2004 – Scotland
G W Gordon-Smith	3	06.01.1900 – Wales	10.03.1900 – Scotland
A L H Gotley	6	03.03.1910 – France	18.03.1911 – Scotland
D Graham	1	05.01.1901 – Wales	
H J Graham	4	15.02.1875 – Ireland	06.03.1876 – Scotland
J D G Graham	1	13.12.1875 – Ireland	
A Gray	3	18.01.1947 – Wales	15.03.1947 – Scotland
P J Grayson*	32	16.12.1995 – Western Samoa	06.03.2004 – Ireland
J Green	8	11.02.1905 – Wales	16.03.1907 – Scotland
J F Green	1	27.03.1871 – Scotland	
W R Green*	4	15.11.1997 – Australia	23.08.2003 – Wales
P B T Greening*	24	23.11.1996 – Italy	20.10.2001 – Ireland
N J J Greenstock	4	30.05.1997 – Argentina	29.11.1997 – South Africa
J H Greenwell	2	07.01.1893 – Wales	04.02.1893 – Ireland
J E Greenwood	13	08.04.1912 – France	20.03.1920 – Scotland
J R H Greenwood	5	12.02.1966 – Ireland	08.02.1969 – Ireland
W J H Greenwood*	52	15.11.1997 – Australia	27.03.2004 – France
W Greg	2	13.12.1875 – Ireland	06.03.1876 – Scotland
G G Gregory	13	14.02.1931 – Ireland	17.03.1934 – Scotland
J A Gregory	1	15.01.1949 – Wales	
D J Grewcock*	47	06.06.1997 – Argentina	27.03.2004 – France
W M Grylls	1	11.02.1905 – Ireland	
R H Guest	13	21.01.1939 – Wales	19.03.1949 – Scotland
A G Guillemard	2	27.03.1871 – Scotland	05.02.1872 – Scotland
C H A Gunamer	1	01.04.1929 – France	
C R Gunner	1	13.12.1875 – Ireland	
C Gurdon	14	30.01.1880 – Ireland	13.03.1886 – Scotland
E T Gurdon	16	04.03.1878 – Scotland	13.03.1886 – Scotland
J C Guscott*	65	13-05.1989 – Roinania	15.10.1999 – Tonga
M Haag	2	30.05.1997 – Argentina	07.06.1997 – Argentina
L Haigh	7	15.01.1910 – Wales	18.03.1911 – Scotland
P M Hale	3	20.12.1969 – South Africa	28.02.1970 – Wales

C Hall	2	09.02.1901 – Ireland	09.03.1901 – Scotland
J Hall	3	06.01.1894 – Wales	17.03.1894 – Scotland
J P Hall	21	04.02.1984 – Scotland	05.02.1994 – Scotland
N M Hall	17	18.01.1947 – Wales	12.02.1955 – Ireland
S J Halliday	23	18.01.1986 – Wales	07.03.1992 – Wales
A St G Hamersley	4	27.03.1871 – Scotland	23.02.1874 – Scotland
E A Hamilton-Hill	3	04.01.1936 – New Zealand	08.02.1936 – Ireland
R H Hamilton-Wickes	10	09.02.1924 – Ireland	15.01.1927 – Wales
E D G Hammett	8	17.01.1920 – Wales	21.01.1922 – Wales
C E L Hammond	8	18.03.1905 – Scotland	08.02.1908 – Ireland
A W Hancock	3	27.02.1965 – France	26.02.1966 – France
G E Hancock	3	21.01.1939 – Wales	18.03.1939 – Scotland
J H Hancock	2	22.01.1955 – Wales	12.02.1955 – Ireland
P F Hancock	5	02.01.1886 – Wales	15.02.1890 – Wales
P S Hancock	3	09.01.1904 – Wales	19.03.1904 v Scotland
F G Handford	4	16.01.1909 – Wales	20.03.1909 – Scotland
R H M Hands	2	03.03.1910 – France	19.03.1910 – Scotland
J Hanley	7	15.01.1927 – Wales	17.03.1928 – Scotland
S Hanley*	1	11.04.1999 – Wales	
R C Hannaford	3	16.01.1971 – Wales	27.02.1971 – France
R J Hanvey	4	16.01.1926 – Wales	20.03.1926 – Scotland
E H Harding	1	14.02.1931 – Ireland	
R M Harding	12	05.01.1985 – Romania	17.06.1988 – Fiji
V S J Harding	6	25.02.1961 – France	17.03.1962 – Scotland
P F Hardwick	8	08.02.1902 – Ireland	19.03.1904 – Scotland
R J K Hardwick	1	23.11.1996 – Italy	
E M P Hardy	3	10.02.1951 – Ireland	17.03.1951 – Scotland
W H Hare	25	16.03.1974 – Wales	09.06.1984 – South Africa
C H Harper	1	07.01.1899 – Wales	
A T Harriman	1	05.11.1988 – Australia	
S W Harris	2	14.02.1920 – Ireland	20.03.1920 – Scotland
T W Harris	2	16.03.1929 – Scotland	13.02.1932 – Ireland
A C Harrison	2	14.02.1931 – Ireland	21.03.1931 – Scotland
A L Harrison	2	14.02.1914 – Ireland	13.04.1914 – France
G Harrison	7	05.02.1877 – Ireland	07.02.1885 – Ireland
H C Harrison	4	20.03.1909 – Scotland	13.04.1914 – France
M E Harrison	15	01.06.1985 – New Zealand	06.02.1988 – Wales
B C Hartley	2	09.03.1901 – Scotland	15.03.1902 – Scotland
L W Haslett	2	13.02.1926 – Ireland	27.02.1926 – France
G W D Hastings	13	22.01.1955 – Wales	15.03.1958 – Scotland
H Havelock	3	01.01.1908 – France	08.02.1908 – Ireland
J J Hawcridge	2	03.01.1885 – Wales	07.02.1885 – Ireland
L W Hayward	1	12.02.1910 – Ireland	
D St G Hazell	4	22.01.1955 – Wales	19.03.1955 – Scotland
A S Healey*	51	15.02.1997 – Ireland	30.08.2003 – France
R D Hearn	6	26.02.1966 – France	15.04.1967 – Wales
A H Heath	1	06.03.1876 – Scotland	
J Heaton	9	19.01.1935 – Wales	19.04.1947 – France
A P Henderson	9	18.01.1947 – Wales	12.02.1949 – Ireland
R S F Henderson	5	16.12.1882 – Wales	03.01.1885 – Wales
W G Heppell	1	14.02.1903 – Ireland	
A J Herbert	6	01.03.1958 – France	21.03.1959 – Scotland
R Hesford	10	21.02.1981 – Scotland	20.04.1985 – Wales
N J Heslop	10	28.07.1990 – Argentina	07.03.1992 – Wales
J G G Hetherington	6	01.02.1958 – Australia	21.03.1959 – Scotland
E N Hewitt	3	20.01.1951 – Wales	24.02.1951 – France
W W Hewitt	4	05.02.1881 – Ireland	06.02.1882 – Ireland
J L Hickson	6	08.01.1887 – Wales	15.03.1890 – Ireland
R Higgins	13	16.01.1954 – Wales	17.01.1959 – Wales
A J Hignell	14	31.05.1975 – Australia	17.03.1979 – Wales
B A Hill	9	14.02.1903 – Ireland	12.01.1907 – Wales
R A Hill*	68	01.02.1997 – Scotland	27.03.2004 – France
R J Hill	29	02.06.1984 – South Africa	02.1 1.1991 – Australia
R J Hillard	1	03.01.1925 – New Zealand	
R Hiller	19	20.01.1968 – Wales	12.02.1972 – Ireland
A E Hind	2	02.12.1905 – New Zealand	13.01.1906 – Wales
G R Hind	2	19.03.1910 – Scotland	11.02.1911 – Ireland
R F A Hobbs	2	11.03.1899 – Scotland	10.01.1903 – Wales
R G S Hobbs	4	02.01.1932 – South Africa	19.03.1932 – Scotland
H A Hodges	2	13.01.1906 – Wales	10.02.1906 – Ireland
S D Hodgkinson	14	13.05.1989 – Romania	11.10.1991 – United States
C Hodgson	8	17.11.2001 – Romania	09.03.2003 – Italy
J McD Hodgson	7	02.01.1932 – South Africa	08.02.1936 – Ireland
S A M Hodgson	11	16.01.1960 – Wales	18.01.1964 – Wales
M B Hofineyr	3	21.01.1950 – Wales	18.03.1950 – Scotland
T B Hogarth	1	22.03.1906 – France	

G Holford	2	17.01.1920 – Wales	31.01.1920 – France
D Holland	3	20.01.1912 – Wales	16.03.1912 – Scotland
T E Holliday	7	17.03.1923 – Scotland	20.03.1926 – Scotland
C B Holmes	3	15.03.1947 – Scotland	29.03.1948 – France
E Holmes	2	01.03.1890 – Scotland	15.03.1890 – Ireland
W A Holmes	16	21.01.1950 – Wales	21.03.1953 – Scotland
W B Holmes	4	15.01.1949 – Wales	19.03.1949 – Scotland
W G Hook	3	17.03.1951 – Scotland	19.01.1952 – Wales
C A Hooper	3	06.01.1894 – Wales	17.03.1894 – Scotland
D P Hopley	3	04.06.1995 – Western Samoa	16.12.1995 – Western Samoa
F J V Hopley	3	05.01.1907 – France	08.02.1908 – Ireland
M Horack	1	22.06.2002 – Argentina	22.06.2002 – Argentina
P C Hordcrn	4	14.02.1931 – Ireland	20.01.1934 – Wales
C H Horley	1	07.02.1885 – Ireland	
A N Hornby	9	05.02.1877 – Ireland	04.03.1882 – Scotland
J P Horrocks-Taylor	9	18.01.1958 – Wales	18.01.1964 – Wales
E L Horsfall	1	15.01.1949 – Wales	
A L Horton	7	16.01.1965 – Wales	04.11-1967 – New Zealand
J P Horton	13	04.02.1978 – Wales	09.06.1984 – South Africa
N E Horton	20	08.02.1969 – Ireland	19-01.1980 – Ireland
R W Hosen	10	25.05.1963 – New Zealand	15.04.1967 – Wales
G R d'A Hosking	5	15.01.1949 – Wales	21.01.1950 – Wales
S Houghton	2	06.02.1892 – Ireland	04.01.1896 – Wales
P D Howard	8	18.01.1930 – Wales	06.04.1931 – France
G C Hubbard	3	02.01.1892 – Wales	06.02.1892 – Ireland
J C Hubbard	1	15.03.1930 – Scotland	
A Hudson	8	13.01.1906 – Wales	03.03.1910 – France
G E Hughes	1	14.03.1896 – Scotland	
P A Hull	4	04.06.1994 – South Africa	10.12.1994 – Canada
F C Hulme	4	10.01.1903 – Wales	11.02.1905 – Ireland
J T Hunt	3	06.02.1882 – Ireland	05.01.1884 – Wales
R Hunt	4	30.01.1880 – Ireland	06.02.1882 – Ireland
W H Hunt	4	06.03.1876 – Scotland	11.03.1878 – Ireland
I Hunter	7	17.10.1992 – Canada	22.06.1995 – France
R P Huntsman	2	01.06.1985 – New Zealand	08.06.1985 – New Zealand
A C B Hurst	1	17.03.1962 – Scotland	
T F Huskisson	8	16.01.1937 – Wales	18.03.1939 – Scotland
F Hutchinson	3	30.01.1909 – France	20.03.1909 – Scotland
J E Hutchinson	1	10.02.1906 – Ireland	
W C Hutchinson	2	06.03.1876 – Scotland	05.02.1877 – Ireland
W H H Hutchinson	2	15.02.1875 – Ireland	13.12.1875 – Ireland
H Huth	1	10.03.1879 – Scotland	
J P Hyde	2	25.02.1950 – France	18.03.1950 – Scotland
W B Hynes	1	08.04.1912 – France	
E D Ibbitson	4	16.01.1909 – Wales	20.03.1909 – Scotland
H M lmrie	2	02.12.1905 – New Zealand	09.02.1907 – Ireland
R E Inglis	3	02.01.1886 – Wales	13.03.1886 – Scotland
S H Irvin	1	14.01.1905 – Wales	
F W Isherwood	1	05.02.1872 – Scotland	
E J Jackett	13	02.12.1905 – New Zealand	20.03.1909 – Scotland
A H Jackson	2	11.03.1878 – Ireland	30.01.1880 – Ireland
B S Jackson	2	21.03.1970 – Scotland	18.04.1970 – France
P B Jackson	20	21.01.1956 – Wales	16.03.1963 – Scotland
W J Jackson	1	17.03.1894 – Scotland	
F Jacob	8	09.01.1897 – Wales	04.02.1899 – Ireland
H P Jacob	5	19.01.1924 – Wales	22.02.1930 – France
P G Jacob	1	05.02.1898 – Ireland	
C R Jacobs	29	21.01.1956 – Wales	21.03.1964 – Scotland
R A Jago	5	13.01.1906 – Wales	09.02.1907 – Ireland
J P A G Janion	12	16.01.1971 – Wales	31.05.1975 – Australia
J W Jarman	1	06.01.1900 – Wales	
N C Jeavons	14	21.02.1981 – Scotland	19.03.1983 – Ireland
R E G Jeeps	24	21.01.1956 – Wales	17.03.1962 – Scotland
G L Jeffery	8	02.01.1886 – Wales	05.03.1887 – Scotland
C K Jennins	3	07.01.1967 – Australia	25.02.1967 – France
J Jewitt	1	11.01.1902 – Wales	
W A Johns	7	16.01.1909 – Wales	03.03.1910 – France
M O Johnson*	84	16.01.1993 – France	22.11.2003 – Australia
B Johnston	2	22.06.2002 – Argentina	09.11.2002 – New Zealand
W R Johnston	16	15.01.1910 – Wales	13.04.1914 – France
C Jones	4	15.02.2004 – Italy	20.03.2004 – Wales
E P Jones	1	04.03.1893 – Scotland	
H A Jones	3	21.01.1950 – Wales	25.02.1950 – France
A M Jorden	7	18.04.1970 – France	15.03.1975 – Scotland
D Jowett	6	16.02.1889 – NZ Natives	07.03.1891 – Scotland
P E Judd	22	20.01.1962 – Wales	04.11.1967 – New Zealand

B J Kay	33	02.06.2001 – Canada	27.03.2004 – France
H E Kayll	1	04.03.1878 – Scotland	
J H Keeling	2	03.01.1948 – Australia	17.01.1948 – Wales
B W Keen	4	20.01.1968 – Wales	16.03.1968 – Scotland
G H Keeton	3	09.01.1904 – Wales	19.03.1904 – Scotland
G A Kelly	4	18.01.1947 – Wales	17.01.1948 – Wales
T S Kelly	12	13.01.1906 – Wales	21.03.1908 – Scotland
A T Kemble	3	03.01.1885 – Wales	05.02.1887 – Ireland
D T Kemp	1	19.01.1935 – Wales	
T A Kemp	5	16.01.1937 – Wales	17.01.1948 – Wales
P D Kendall	3	09.03.1901 – Scotland	21.03.1903 – Scotland
J M K Kendall-Carpenter	23	12.02.1949 – Ireland	10.04.1954 – France
D A Kendrew	10	18.01.1930 – Wales	08.02.1936 – Ireland
R D Kennedy	3	12.02.1949 – Ireland	19.03.1949 – Scotland
C P Kent	5	15.01.1977 – Scotland	21.01.1978 – France
T Kent	6	03.01.1891 – Wales	05.03.1892 – Scotland
C A Kershaw	16	17.01.1920 – Wales	02.04.1923 – France
E Kewley	7	23.02.1874 – Scotland	04.03.1878 – Scotland
A L Kewney	16	13.01.1906 – Wales	04.01.1913 – South Africa
A Key	2	08.02.1930 – Ireland	21.01.1933 – Wales
M Keyworth	4	03.01.1976 – Australia	06.03.1976 – Ireland
B Kilner	1	30.01.1880 – Ireland	
R S Kindersley	3	16.12.1882 – Wales	03.01.1885 – Wales
A D King*	5	06.06.1997 – Argentina	23.08.2003 – Wales
I King	3	16.01.1954 – Wales	13.02.1954 – Ireland
J A King	12	21.01.1911 – Wales	15.03.1913 – Scotland
Q E M A King	1	19.03.1921 – Scotland	
P Kingston	5	24.05.1975 – Australia	17.03.1979 – Wales
A E Kitching	1	08.02.1913 – Ireland	
H J Kittermaster	7	03.01.1925 – New Zealand	20.03.1926 – Scotland
F Knight	1	09.01.1909 – Australia	
P M Knight	3	26.02.1972 – France	03.06.1972 – South Africa
E Knowles	2	14.03.1896 – Scotland	13.03.1897 – Scotland
T C Knowles	1	21.03.1931 – Scotland	
J A Krige	1	17.01.1920 – Wales	
N A Labuschagne	5	17.01.1953 – Wales	19.03.1955 – Scotland
R O Lagden	1	18.03.1911 – Scotland	
H C C Laird	10	15.01.1927 – Wales	09.02.1929 – Ireland
D Lambert	7	05.01.1907 – France	11.02.1911 – Ireland
M S Lampkowski	4	03.01.1976 – Australia	06.03.1976 – Ireland
W N Lapage	4	01.01.1908 – France	21.03.1908 – Scotland
P J Larter	24	07.01.1967 – Australia	20.01.1973 – Wales
A F Law	1	05.03.1877 – Scotland	
D E Law	1	12.02.1927 – Ireland	
Hon H A Lawrence	4	03.03.1873 – Scotland	08.03.1875 – Scotland
P W Lawrie	2	19.03.1910 – Scotland	18.03.1911 – Scotland
R G Lawson	1	14.02.1925 – Ireland	
T M Lawson	2	07.01.1928 – Australia	21.01.1928 – Wales
M M Leadbetter	1	18.04.1970 – France	
V H Leadbetter	2	20.03.1954 – Scotland	10.04.1954 – France
W R M Leake	3	03.01.1891 – Wales	07.03.1891 – Scotland
G Leather	1	09.02.1907 – Ireland	
F H Lee	2	06.03.1876 – Scotland	05.02.1877 – Ireland
H Lee	1	05.01.1907 – France	
J Le Fleming	1	08.01.1887 – Wales	
J Leonard*	114	28.07.1990 – Argentina	15.02.2004 – Italy
F A Leslie-Jones	2	05.01.1895 – Wales	02.02.1895 – Ireland
A O Lewis	10	05.01.1952 – South Africa	10.04.1954 – France
O J Lewsey*	23	20.06.1998 – New Zealand	27.03.2004 – France
R Leyland	3	19.01.1935 – Wales	16.03.1935 – Scotland
M S Linnett	1	04.11.1989 – Fiji	
R O'H Livesay	2	02.04.1898 – Wales	07.01.1899 – Wales
L Lloyd	5	17.06.2000 – South Africa	16.06.2001 – USA
R H Lloyd	5	04.11.1967 – New Zealand	16.03.1968 – Scotland
H M Locke	12	17.03.1923 – Scotland	19.03.1927 – Scotland
R E Lockwood	14	08.01.1887 – Wales	03.02.1894 – Ireland
S H M Login	1	13.12.1875 – Ireland	
F C Lohden	1	07.01.1893 – Wales	
A E Long	3	15.11.1997 – Australia	16.06.2001 – USA
R J Longland	19	19.03.1932 – Scotland	19.03.1938 – Scotland
C N Lowe	25	04.01.1913 – South Africa	02.04.1923 – France
F W Lowrie	2	16.02.1889 – NZ Natives	15.02.1890 – Wales
W M Lowry	1	31.01.1920 – France	
R A P Lozowski	1	03.11.1984 – Australia	
W G E Luddington	13	20.01.1923 – Wales	16.01.1926 – Wales
D D Luger*	38	14.11.1998 – Holland	02.11.2003 – Wales

F Luscombe	6	05.02.1872 – Scotland	06.03.1876 – Scotland
J H Luscombe	1	27.03.1871 – Scotland	
A F C C Luxmoore	2	10.03.1900 – Scotland	05.01.1901 – Wales
H F Luya	5	17.01.1948 – Wales	15.01.1949 – Wales
A Lyon	1	27.03.1871 – Scotland	
G H D'O Lyon	2	21.03.1908 – Scotland	09.01.1909 – Australia
A H MacIlwaine	5	20.01.1912 – Wales	14.02.1920 – Ireland
O G Mackie	2	13.03.1897 – Scotland	05.02.1898 – Ireland
J E H Mackinlay	3	05.02.1872 – Scotland	15.02.1875 – Ireland
W MacLaren	1	27.03.1871 – Scotland	
R R F MacLennan	3	14.02.1925 – Ireland	13.04.1925 – France
R J P Madge	4	03.01.1948 – Australia	20.03.1948 – Scotland
F W S Malir	3	18.01.1930 – Wales	15.03.1930 – Scotland
J A Mallett	1	04.06.1995 – Western Satnoa	
J Mallinder	2	30.05.1997 – Argentina	06.06.1997 – Argentina
R H Mangles	2	09.01.1897 – Wales	06.02.1897 – Ireland
D C Manley	4	19.01.1963 – Wales	16.03.1963 – Scotland
W E Mann	3	21.01.1911 – Wales	11.02.1911 – Ireland
N D Mantell	1	24.05.1975 – Australia	
M S Maplctoft	1	06.06.1997 – Argentina	
E T Markendale	1	30.01.1880 – Ireland	
R W D Marques	23	21.01.1956 – Wales	21.01.1961 – Wales
J C Marquis	2	03.02.1900 – Ireland	10.03.1900 – Scotland
C J B Marriott	7	05.01.1884 – Wales	05.02.1887 – Ireland
E E Marriott	1	13.12.1875 – Ireland	
V R Marriott	4	25.05.1963 – New Zealand	04.01.1964 – New Zealand
G H Marsden	3	06.01.1900 – Wales	10.03.1900 – Scotland
H Marsh	1	03.03.1873 – Scotland	
J H Marsh	1	06.02.1892 – Ireland	
H Marshall	1	07.01.1893 – Wales	
M W Marshall	10	03.03.1873 – Scotland	11.03.1878 – Ireland
R M Marshall	5	12.02.1938 – Ireland	18.03.1939 – Scotland
C R Martin	4	02.02.1985 – France	20.04.1985 – Wales
N O Martin	1	26.02.1972 – France	
S A Martindale	1	01.04.1929 – France	
E J Massey	3	17.01.1925 – Wales	21.03.1925 – Scotland
B-J Mather*	1	11.04.1999 – Wales	
J L Mathias	4	14.01.1905 – Wales	02.12.1905 – New Zealand
J C Matters	1	11.03.1899 – Scotland	
J R C Matthews	10	26.02.1949 – France	05.04.1952 – France
P Maud	2	07.01.1893 – Wales	04.02.1893 – Ireland
A W Maxwell	7	24.05.1975 – Australia	21.01.1978 – France
J E Maxwell-Hyslop	3	11.02.1922 – Ireland	18.03.1922 – Scotland
A F Maynard	3	17.01.1914 – Wales	21.03.1914 – Scotland
M A McCanlis	2	17.01.1931 – Wales	14.02.1931 – Ireland
N McCarthy*	3	06.03.1999 – Ireland	18.03.2000 – Italy
C W McFadyean	11	12.02.1966 – Ireland	10.02.1968 – Ireland
N F McLeod	2	10.03.1879 – Scotland	24.03.1879 – Ireland
G W C Meikle	3	20.01.1934 – Wales	17.03.1934 – Scotland
S S C Meikle	1	16.03.1929 – Scotland	
F W Mellish	6	17.01.1920 – Wales	12.02.1921 – Ireland
N D Melville	13	03.11.1984 – Australia	19.03.1988 – Ireland
L P B Merriam	2	17.01.1920 – Wales	31.01.1920 – France
A T Michell	3	15.02.1875 – Ireland	13.12.1875 – Ireland
B B Middleton	2	06.02.1882 – Ireland	05.02.1883 – Ireland
J A Middleton	1	18.03.1922 – Scotland	
J H Miles	1	10.01.1903 – Wales	
H Millett	1	31.01.1920 – France	
F W Mills	2	05.02.1872 – Scotland	03.03.1873 – Scotland
S G F Mills	5	30.05.1981 – Argentina	03.11.1984 – Australia
W A Mills	11	13.01.1906 – Wales	18.01.1908 – Wales
D L K Milman	4	16.01.1937 – Wales	19.03.1938 – Scotland
C H Milton	1	10.02.1906 – Ireland	
J G Milton	5	09.01.1904 – Wales	09.02.1907 – Ireland
W H Milton	2	23.02.1874 – Scotland	15.02.1875 – Ireland
F Mitchell	6	05.01.1895 – Wales	14.03.1896 – Scotland
W G Mitchell	7	15.02.1890 – Wales	04.03.1893 – Scotland
E R Mobbs	7	09.01.1909 – Australia	03.03.1910 – France
W O Moberley	1	05.02.1872 – Scotland	
L W Moody	24	02.06.2001 – Canada	22.11.2003 – Australia
B C Moore	64	04.04.1987 – Scotland	22.06.1995 – France
E J Moore	2	05.02.1883 – Ireland	03.03.1883 – Scotland
NJ N H Moore	3	09.01.1904 – Wales	19.03.1904 – Scotland
P B C Moore	1	20.01.1951 – Wales	
W K T Moore	7	18.01.1947 – Wales	18.03.1950 – Scotland
R J Mordell	1	04.02.1978 – Wales	

S Morfitt	6	06.01.1894 – Wales	14.03.1896 – Scotland
J R Morgan	1	17.01.1920 – Wales	
W G D Morgan	9	16.01.1960 – Wales	18.03.1961 – Scotland
A J Morley	7	03.06.1972 – South Africa	31.05.1975 – Australia
A D W Morris	3	09.01.1909 – Australia	30.01.1909 – France
C D Morris	26	05.11.1988 – Australia	22.06.1995 – France
R Morris	2	22.02.2003 – Wales	09.03.2003 – Italy
P H Morrison	4	15.02.1890 – Wales	07.02.1891 – Ireland
S Morse	3	03.03.1873 – Scotland	08.03.1875 – Scotland
W Mortimer	1	07.01.1899 – Wales	
H J S Morton	4	13.02.1909 – Ireland	12.02.1910 – Ireland
F Moss	3	03.01.1885 – Wales	02.01.1886 – Wales
A R Mullins	1	04.11.1989 – Fiji	
J Mycock	5	18.01.1947 – Wales	03.01.1948 – Australia
E Myers	18	14.02.1920 – Ireland	13.04.1925 – France
H Myers	1	05.02.1898 – Ireland	
W M B Nanson	2	05.01.1907 – France	12.01.1907 – Wales
E H Nash	1	15.02.1875 – Ireland	
B A Neale	3	10.02.1951 – Ireland	17.03.1951 – Scotland
M E Neale	1	08.04.1912 – France	
S Neame	4	10.03.1879 – Scotland	28.02.1880 – Scotland
A Neary	43	16.01.1971 –- Wales	15.03.1980 – Scotland
B G Nelmes	6	24.05.1975 – Australia	25.11.1978 – New Zealand
C J Newbold	6	09.01.1904 – Wales	18.03.1905 – Scotland
S C Newman	3	19.04.1947 – France	17.01.1948 – Wales
A W Newton	1	16.03.1907 – Scotland	
P A Newton	1	04.03.1882 – Scotland	
J O Newton-Thompson	2	15.03.1947 – Scotland	19.04.1947 – France
W Nichol	2	02.01.1892 – Wales	05.03.1892 – Scotland
P L Nicholas	1	11.01.1902 – Wales	
B E Nicholson	2	15.01.1938 – Wales	12.02.1938 – Ireland
E S Nicholson	5	19.01.1935 – Wales	18.01.1936 – Wales
E T Nicholson	2	06.01.1900 – Wales	03.02.1900 – Ireland
T Nicholson	1	04.02.1893 – Ireland	
B F Ninnes	1	16.01.1971 – Wales	
J Noon	5	02.06.2001 – Canada	30.08.2003 – France
D J Norman	2	02.01.1932 – South Africa	16.01.1932 – Wales
E H G North	3	03.01.1891 – Wales	07.03.1891 – Scotland
S Northmore	1	06.02.1897 – Ireland	
M J Novak	3	28.02.1970 – Wales	18.04.1970 – France
A L Novis	7	16.03.1929 – Scotland	18.03.1933 – Scotland
F E Oakeley	4	15.03.1913 – Scotland	13.04.1914 – France
R F Oakes	8	09.01.1897 – Wales	11.03.1899 – Scotland
L F L Oakley	1	20.01.1951 – Wales	
A Obolensky	4	04.01.1936 – New Zealand	21.03.1936 – Scotland
S O Ojomoh*	12	19.02.1994 – Ireland	20.06.1998 – New Zealand
A G B Old	16	15.01.1972 – Wales	21.01.1978 – France
W L Oldham	2	21.03.1908 – Scotland	09.01.1909 – Australia
C J Olver	3	03.11.1990 – Argentina	17.10.1992 – Canada
A O'Neill	3	05.01.1901 – Wales	09.03.1901 – Scotland
W E Openshaw	1	24.03.1879 – Ireland	
J Orwin	14	05.01.1985 – Romania	12.06.1988 – Australia
R R Osborne	1	27.03.1871 – Scotland	
S H Osborne	1	18.03.1905 – Scotland	
C Oti	13	05.03.1988 – Scotland	08.10.1991 – Italy
B Oughtred	6	09.03.1901 – Scotland	14.02.1903 – Ireland
J E Owen	14	19.01.1963 – Wales	04.11.1967 – New Zealand
H G O Owen-Smith	10	20.01.1934 – Wales	20.03.1937 – Scotland
J J Page	5	16.01.1971 – Wales	15.03.1975 – Scotland
J N Pallant	3	11.02.1967 – Ireland	18.03.1967 – Scotland
A C Palmer	2	13.02.1909 – Ireland	20.03.1909 – Scotland
F H Palmer	1	14.01.1905 – Wales	
G V Palmer	3	11.02.1928 – Ireland	17.03.1928 – Scotland
J A Palmer	3	02.06.1984 – South Africa	01.03.1986 – Ireland
T Palmer	1	16.06.2001 – USA	16.06.2001 – USA
T A Pargetter	3	17.03.1962 – Scotland	25.05.1963 – New Zealand
G W Parker	2	12.02.1938 – Ireland	19.03.1938 – Scotland
Hon S Parker	2	23.02.1874 – Scotland	08.03.1875 – Scotland
E I Parsons	1	18.03.1939 – Scotland	
M J Parsons	4	20.01.1968 – Wales	16.03.1968 – Scotland
W M Patterson	2	07.01.1961 – South Africa	18.03.1961 – Scotland
R M Pattisson	2	05.02.1883 – Ireland	03.03.1883 – Scotland
H Paul	3	02.03.2002 – France	21.02.2004 – Scotland
J E Paul	1	08.03.1875 – Scotland	
A T Payne	2	09.02.1935 – Ireland	16.03.1935 – Scotland
C M Payne	10	08.02.1964 – Ireland	19.03.1966 – Scotland

J H Payne	7	04.03.1882 – Scotland	07.02.1885 – Ireland
G S Pearce	36	03.02.1979 – Scotland	11.10.1991 – USA
D Pears	4	28.07.1990 – Argentina	05.03.1994 – France
A W Pearson	7	15.02.1875 – Ireland	11.03.1878 – Ireland
T G A H Peart	2	22.02.1964 – France	21.03.1964 – Scotland
F E Pease	1	05.02.1887 – Ireland	
S H Penny	1	09.01.1909 – Australia	
W J Penny	3	11.03.1878 – Ireland	24.03.1879 – Ireland
L J Percival	3	07.02.1891 – Ireland	04.03.1893 – Scotland
H G Periton	21	17.01.1925 – Wales	15.03.1930 – Scotland
E S Perrott	1	15.02.1875 – Ireland	
D G Perry	15	23.02.1963 – France	26.02.1966 – France
M B Perry*	36	15.11.1997 – Australia	07.04.2001 – France
S V Perry	7	18.01.1947 – Wales	29.03.1948 – France
J Peters	5	17.03.1906 – Scotland	18.01.1908 – Wales
C Phillips	3	28.02.1880 – Scotland	19.03.1881 – Scotland
M S Phillips	25	01.02.1958 – Australia	21.03.1964 – Scotland
A S Pickering	1	09.02.1907 – Ireland	
R D A Pickering	6	11.02.1967 – Ireland	16.03.1968 – Scotland
R C W Pickles	2	11.02.1922 – Ireland	25.02.1922 – France
R Pierce	2	05.02.1898 – Ireland	21.03.1903 – Scotland
W N Pilkington	1	12.03.1898 – Scotland	
C H Pillman	18	15.01.1910 – Wales	21.03.1914 – Scotland
R L Pillman	1	13.04.1914 – France	
J Pinch	3	04.01.1896 – Wales	13.03.1897 – Scotland
W W Pinching	1	05.02.1872 – Scotland	
I J Pitman	1	18.03.1922 – Scotland	
K C Plummer	4	12.04.1969 – Wales	20.03.1976 – France
F O Poole	3	05.01.1895 – Wales	09.03.1895 – Scotland
R W Poole	1	14.03.1896 – Scotland	
R J Pool-Jones*	1	06.06.1998 – Australia	
E B Pope	3	17.01.1931 – Wales	06.04.1931 – France
G V Portus	2	01.01.1908 – France	08.02.1908 – Ireland
S Potter*	1	06.06.1998 – Australia	
R W Poulton	17	30.01.1909 – France	13.04.1914 – France
D L Powell	11	15.01.1966 – Wales	27.03.1971 – Scotland
W E Pratten	2	19.03.1927 – Scotland	02.04.1927 – France
I Preece	12	14.02.1948 – Ireland	24.02.1951 – France
P S Preece	12	03.06.1972 – South Africa	17.01.1976 – Wales
M Preedy	1	02.06.1984 – South Africa	
F D Prentice	3	11.02.1928 – Ireland	17.03.1928 – Scotland
R E Prescott	6	16.01.1937 – Wales	18.03.1939 – Scotland
N J Preston	3	24.11.1979 – New Zealand	02.02.1980 – France
H L Price	4	11.02.1922 – Ireland	10.02.1923 – Ireland
J Price	1	11.02.1961 – Ireland	
P L A Price	3	05.02.1877 – Ireland	04.03.1878 – Scotland
T W Price	6	20.03.1948 – Scotland	19.03.1949 – Scotland
J A Probyn	37	16.01.1988 – France	20.03.1993 – Ireland
D H Prout	2	20.01.1968 – Wales	10.02.1968 – Ireland
J V Pullin	42	15.01.1966 – Wales	20.03.1976 – France
S J Purdy	1	17.03.1962 – Scotland	
J Pyke	1	02.01.1892 – Wales	
J A Pym	4	20.01.1912 – Wales	08.04.1912 – France
J P Quinn	5	16.01.1954 – Wales	10.04.1954 – France
M Rafter	17	15.01.1977 – Scotland	06.06.1981 – Argentina
C W Ralston	22	27.03.1971 – Scotland	15.03.1975 – Scotland
H E Ramsden	2	12.03.1898 – Scotland	02.04.1898 – Wales
J M Ranson	7	25.05.1963 – New Zealand	21.03.1964 – Scotland
J E Raphael	9	11.01.1902 – Wales	22.03.1906 – France
J Ravenscroft	1	05.02.1881 – Ireland	
S C W Ravenscroft*	2	06.06.1998 – Australia	27.06.1998 – New Zealand
W C W Rawlinson	1	06.03.1876 – Scotland	
S Redfern	1	18.02.1984 – Ireland	
N C Redman	20	03.11.1984 – Australia	12.07.1997 – Australia
G F Redmond	1	18.04.1970 – France	
B W Redwood	2	20.01.1968 – Wales	10.02.1968 – Ireland
D L Rees*	11	15.11.1997 – Australia	26.06.1999 – Australia
G W Rees	23	09.06.1984 – South Africa	11.10.1991 – USA
J S R Reeve	8	01.04.1929 – France	21.03.1931 – Scotland
M P Regan	30	18.11.1995 – South Africa	06.03.2004 – Ireland
M Regan	12	17.01.1953 – Wales	14.04.1956 – France
P A G Rendall	28	17.03.1984 – Wales	08.10.1991 – Italy
H Rew	10	16.03.1929 – Scotland	17.03.1934 – Scotland
F J Reynolds	3	20.03.1937 – Scotland	19.03.1938 – Scotland
S Reynolds	4	06.01.1900 – Wales	09.02.1901 – Ireland
J Rhodes	3	04.01.1896 – Wales	14.03.1896 – Scotland

Name	Caps		
D Richards	48	01.03.1986 – Ireland	16.03.1996 – Ireland
E E Richards	2	16.03.1929 – Scotland	01.04.1929 – France
J Richards	3	03.01.1891 – Wales	07.03.1891 – Scotland
S B Richards	9	16.01.1965 – Wales	15.04.1967 – Wales
J V Richardson	5	07.01.1928 – Australia	17.03.1928 – Scotland
W R Richardson	1	05.02.1881 – Ireland	
C H Rickards	1	03.03.1873 – Scotland	
G Rimmer	12	15.01.1949 – Wales	20.03.1954 – Scotland
L I Rimmer	5	07.01.1961 – South Africa	18.03.1961 – Scotland
A G Ripley	24	15.01.1972 – Wales	21.02.1976 – Scotland
A B W Risrnan	8	17.01.1959 – Wales	25.02.1961 – France
J A S Ritson	8	03.03.1910 – France	15.03.1913 – Scotland
G C Rittson-Thomas	3	20.01.1951 – Wales	24.02.1951 – France
G L Robbins	2	18.01.1986 – Wales	15.02.1986 – Scotland
P G D Robbins	19	21.01.1956 – Wales	17.03.1962 – Scotland
A D Roberts	8	21-01.1911 – Wales	14.02.1914 – Ireland
E W Roberts	6	05.01.1901 – Wales	16.03.1907 – Scotland
G D Roberts	3	16.03.1907 – Scotland	18.01.1908 – Wales
J Roberts	18	16.01.1960 – Wales	04.01.1964 – New Zealand
R S Roberts	1	13.02.1932 – Ireland	
S Roberts	2	08.01.1887 – Wales	05.02.1887 – Ireland
V G Roberts	16	19.04.1947 – France	14.04.1956 – France
A R Robertshaw	5	02.01.1886 – Wales	05.03.1887 – Scotland
P Robertshaw	1	N/A – 1888 Cap	1888 Cap
A Robinson	5	16.02.1889 – NZ Natives	15.03.1890 – Ireland
E T Robinson	4	20.03.1954 – Scotland	18.03.1961 – Scotland
G C Robinson	8	06.02.1897 – Ireland	09.03.1901 – Scotland
J Robinson*	33	17.02.2001 – Italy	
J J Robinson	4	04.03.1893 – Scotland	15.03.1902 – Scotland
R A Robinson	8	12.06.1988 – Australia	18.11.1995 – South Africa
A Robson	5	19.01.1924 – Wales	16.01.1926 – Wales
M Robson	4	18.01.1930 – Wales	15.03.1930 – Scotland
T A K Rodber*	44	18.01.1992 – Scotland	11.04.1999 – Wales
D P Rogers	34	11.02.1961 – Ireland	12.04.1969 – Wales
J H Rogers	4	15.02.1890 – Wales	07.03.1891 – Scotland
W L Y Rogers	2	14.01.1905 – Wales	11.02.1905 – Ireland
D M Rollitt	11	11.02.1967 – Ireland	31.05.1975 – Australia
A D S Roncoroni	3	21.01.1933 – Wales	18.03.1933 – Scotland
W M H Rose	10	07.03.1981 – Ireland	23.05.1987 – Australia
P A Rossborough	7	16.01.1971 – Wales	01.02.1975 – France
D W A Rosser	5	16.01.1965 – Wales	15.01.1966 – Wales
Alan Rotherham	12	16.12.1882 – Wales	05.03.1887 – Scotland
Arthur Rotherham	5	12.03.1898 – Scotland	11.03.1899 – Scotland
D F K Roughley	3	17.11.1973 – Australia	16.02.1974 – Ireland
R E Rowell	2	18.01.1964 – Wales	16.01.1965 – Wales
A J Rowley	1	02.01.1932 – South Africa	
H C Rowley	9	10.03.1879 – Scotland	04.03.1882 – Scotland
G C Rowntree*	45	18.03.1995 – Scotland	30.08.2003 – France
P M R Royds	3	12.03.1898 – Scotland	07.01.1899 – Wales
A V Royle	1	16.02.1889 – NZ Natives	
E L Rudd	6	16.01.1965 – Wales	19.03.1966 – Scotland
R F Russell	1	02.12.1905 – New Zealand	
D Rutherford	14	16.01.1960 – Wales	04.11.1967 – New Zealand
H J Ryalls	2	03.01.1885 – Wales	07.02.1885 – Ireland
D Ryan	4	28.07.1990 – Argentina	22.03.1998 – Scotland
P H Ryan	2	22.01.1955 – Wales	12.02.1955 – Ireland
E H Sadler	2	11.02.1933 – Ireland	18.03.1933 – Scotland
J W Sagar	2	05.01.1901 – Wales	09.02.1901 – Ireland
J L B Salmon	12	01.06.1985 – New Zealand	08.06.1987 – Wales
C H Sample	3	04.02.1884 – Ireland	13.03.1886 – Scotland
P C Sampson*	3	04.07.1998 – South Africa	09.06.2001 – Canada
D L Sanders	9	16.01.1954 – Wales	14.04.1956 – France
F W Sanders	3	10.02.1923 – Ireland	02.04.1923 – France
A Sanderson	5	17.11.2001 – Romania	30.08.2003 – France
P H Sanderson*	6	20.06.1998 – New Zealand	16.06.2001 – USA
J R P Sandford	1	10.02.1906 – Ireland	
R D Sangwin	2	04.01.1964 – New Zealand	18.01.1964 – Wales
G F Sargent	1	07.03.1981 – Ireland	
G F Savage	13	15.01.1966 – Wales	16.03.1968 – Scotland
C M Sawyer	2	28.02.1880 – Scotland	05.02.1881 – Ireland
L E Saxby	2	02.01.1932 – South Africa	16.01.1932 – Wales
D Scarborough	1	23.08.2003 – Wales	23.08.2003 – Wales
J W Schofield	1	30.01.1880 – Ireland	
J A Scholfield	1	21.01.1911 – Wales	
R O Schwarz	3	11.03.1899 – Scotland	09.02.1901 – Ireland
E S Scorfield	1	03.03.1910 – France	

C T Scott	4	06.01.1900 – Wales	09.02.1901 – Ireland
E K Scott	5	18.01.1947 – Wales	20.03.1948 – Scotland
F S Scott	1	12.01.1907 – Wales	
H Scott	1	26.02.1955 – France	
J P Scott	34	21.01.1978 – France	09.06.1984 – South Africa
J S M Scott	1	01.03.1958 – France	
M T Scott	3	05.02.1887 – Ireland	15.03.1890 – Ireland
W M Scott	1	16.02.1889 – NZ Natives	
R L Seddon	3	08.01.1887 – Wales	05.03.1887 – Scotland
K A Sellar	7	15.01.1927 – Wales	25.02.1928 – France
H S Sever	10	04.01.1936 – New Zealand	19.03.1938 – Scotland
I R Shackleton	4	20.12.1969 – South Africa	21.03.1970 – Scotland
R A W Sharp	14	16.01.1960 – Wales	07.01.1967 – Australia
C H Shaw	6	17.03.1906 – Scotland	16.03.1907 – Scotland
F Shaw	1	05.02.1898 – Ireland	
J F Shaw	2	12.03.1898 – Scotland	02.04.1898 – Wales
S D Shaw	25	23.11.1996 – Italy	21.02.2004 – Scotland
C M A Sheasby	7	23.11.1996 – Italy	06.12.1997 – New Zealand
A Sheppard	2	17.01.1981 – Wales	20.04.1985 – Wales
C W Sherrard	2	27.03.1871 – Scotland	05.02.1872 – Scotland
G A Sherriff	3	19.03.1966 – Scotland	04.11.1967 – New Zealand
H E Shewring	10	11.02.1905 – Ireland	16.03.1907 – Scotland
J H Shooter	4	04.02.1899 – Ireland	10.03.1900 – Scotland
D W Shuttleworth	2	17.03.1951 – Scotland	21.03.1953 – Scotland
H J H Sibree	3	01.01.1908 – France	20.03.1909 – Scotland
N Silk	4	16.01.1965 – Wales	20.03.1965 – Scotland
K G Simms	15	05.01.1985 – Romania	06.02.1988 – Wales
C P Simpson	1	16.01.1965 – Wales	
P D Simpson	3	19.11.1983 – New Zealand	07.02.1987 – Ireland
T Simpson	11	15.03.1902 – Scotland	30.01.1909 – France
J Simpson-Daniel*	6	09.11.2002 – New Zealand	06.03.2004 – Ireland
D Sims*	3	20.06.1998 – New Zealand	04.07.1998 – South Africa
M G Skinner	21	16.01.1988 – France	07.03.1992 – Wales
G M Sladen	3	19.01.1929 – Wales	16.03.1929 – Scotland
J M Sleightholme	12	20.01.1996 – France	06.06.1997 – Argentina
M A C Slemen	31	06.03.1976 – Ireland	04.02.1984 – Scotland
L A N Slocock	8	05.01.1907 – France	21.03.1908 – Scotland
C F Slow	1	17.03.1934 – Scotland	
H D Small	4	21.01.1950 – Wales	18.03.1950 – Scotland
A M Smallwood	14	31.01.1920 – France	21.03.1925 – Scotland
C E Smart	17	03.03.1979 – France	19.03.1983 – Ireland
S E J Smart	12	04.01.1913 – South Africa	20.03.1920 – Scotland
R W Smeddle	4	19.01.1929 – Wales	06.04.1931 – France
C C Smith	1	05.01.1901 – Wales	
D F Smith	2	15.01.1910 – Wales	12.02.1910 – Ireland
J V Smith	4	21.01.1950 – Wales	18.03.1950 – Scotland
K Smith	4	02.03.1974 – France	15.03.1975 – Scotland
M J K Smith	1	21.01.1956 – Wales	
O Smith	3	09.03.2003 – Italy	30.08.2003 – France
S J Smith	28	10.02.1973 – Ireland	05.03.1983 – Scotland
S R Smith	5	17.01.1959 – Wales	21.03.1964 – Scotland
S T Smith	9	05.01.1985 – Romania	15.02.1986 – Scotland
T H Smith	1	20.01.1951 – Wales	
F Soane	4	04.03.1893 – Scotland	17.03.1894 – Scotland
W H Sobey	5	18.01.1930 – Wales	16.01.1932 – Wales
B Solomon	1	15.01.1910 – Wales	
R H W Sparks	9	11.02.1928 – Ireland	06.04.1931 – France
H Speed	4	06.01.1894 – Wales	14.03.1896 – Scotland
F W Spence	1	15.03.1890 – Ireland	
J Spencer	1	15.01.1966 – Wales	
J S Spencer	14	08.02.1969 – Ireland	17.04.1971 – RFU President's XV
R S Spong	8	01.04.1929 – France	16.01.1932 – Wales
R H Spooner	1	10.01.1903 – Wales	
H H Springman	2	10.03.1879 – Scotland	05.03.1887 – Scotland
A Spurling	1	06.02.1882 – Ireland	
N Spurling	4	06.02.1886 – Ireland	08.01.1887 – Wales
P J Squires	29	24.02.1973 – France	17.03.1979 – Wales
R C Stafford	4	20.01.1912 – Wales	08.04.1912 – France
W F H Stafford	1	23.02.1874 – Scotland	
E Stanbury	16	16.01.1926 – Wales	01.04.1929 – France
G Standing	2	16.12.1882 – Wales	05.02.1883 – Ireland
C F Stanger-Leathes	1	11.02.1905 – Ireland	
K J Stark	9	15.01.1927 – Wales	17.03.1928 – Scotland
A Starks	2	04.01.1896 – Wales	01.02.1896 – Ireland
N C Starmer-Smith	7	20.12.1969 – South Africa	17.04.1971 – RFU President's XV
S P Start	1	16.03.1907 – Scotland	

J H Steeds	5	26.02.1949 – France	18.03.1950 – Scotland
M R Steele-Bodger	9	18.01.1947 – Wales	29.03.1948 – France
F E Steinthal	2	18.01.1913 – Wales	25.01.1913 – France
M Stephenson	3	02.06.2001 – Canada	16.06.2001 – USA
C B Stevens	25	20.12.1969 – South Africa	15.03.1975 – Scotland
E R Still	1	03.03.1873 – Scotland	
T R G Stimpson*	19	23.11.1996 – Italy	23.11.2002 – South Africa
R V Stirling	18	20.01.1951 – Wales	10.04.1954 – France
A E Stoddart	10	03.01.1885 – Wales	04.03.1893 – Scotland
W B Stoddart	3	09.01.1897 – Wales	13.03.1897 – Scotland
F Stokes	3	27.03.1871 – Scotland	03.03.1873 – Scotland
L Stokes	12	15.02.1875 – Ireland	19.03.1881 – Scotland
F le S Stone	1	13.04.1914 – France	
A D Stoop	15	18.03.1905 – Scotland	16.03.1912 – Scotland
F M Stoop	4	19.03.1910 – Scotland	04.01.1913 – South Africa
F M Stout	14	09.01.1897 – Wales	18.03.1905 – Scotland
P W Stout	5	12.03.1898 – Scotland	11.03.1899 – Scotland
N C Stringer	5	02.01.1982 – Australia	05.01.1985 – Romania
E L Strong	3	05.01.1884 – Wales	01.03.1884 – Scotland
B Sturnham*	3	06.06.1998 – Australia	27.06.1998 – New Zealand
G E Summerscales	1	02.12.1905 – New Zealand	
J W Sutcliffe	1	16.02.1889 – NZ Natives	
D W Swarbrick	6	18.01.1947 – Wales	12.02.1949 – Ireland
D H Swayne	1	17.01.1931 – Wales	
J W R Swayne	1	19.01.1929 – Wales	
A H Swift	6	30.05.1981 – Argentina	09.06.1984 – South Africa
J P Syddall	2	06.02.1982 – Ireland	03.11.1984 – Australia
A R V Sykes	1	13.04.1914 – France	
F D Sykes	4	26.02.1955 – France	04.06.1963 – Australia
P W Sykes	7	29.03.1948 – France	28.02.1953 – France
R E Syrett	11	18.01.1958 – Wales	24.02.1962 – France
J A Tallent	5	21.03.1931 – Scotland	09.02.1935 – Ireland
C C Tanner	5	15.03.1930 – Scotland	19.03.1932 – Scotland
F N Tarr	4	09.01.1909 – Australia	15.03.1913 – Scotland
W M Tatham	7	04.03.1882 – Scotland	01.03.1884 – Scotland
A S Taylor	4	16.12.1882 – Wales	06.02.1886 – Ireland
E W Taylor	14	06.02.1892 – Ireland	04.02.1899 – Ireland
F Taylor	2	31.01.1920 – France	14.02.1920 – Ireland
F M Taylor	1	17.01.1914 – Wales	
H H Taylor	5	10.03.1879 – Scotland	04.03.1882 – Scotland
J T Taylor	11	06.02.1897 – Ireland	18.03.1905 – Scotland
P J Taylor	6	22.01.1955 – Wales	17.03.1962 – Scotland
R B Taylor	16	15.01.1966 – Wales	27.03.1971 – Scotland
W J Taylor	5	07.01.1928 – Australia	17.03.1928 – Scotland
M C Teague	27	02.02.1985 – France	20.03.1993 – Ireland
D E Teden	3	21.01.1939 – Wales	18.03.1939 – Scotland
A Teggin	6	04.02.1884 – Ireland	05.03.1887 – Scotland
T S Tetley	1	06.03.1876 – Scotland	
C Thomas	4	05.01.1895 – Wales	04.02.1899 – Ireland
P H Thompson	17	21.01.1956 – Wales	21.03.1959 – Scotland
S Thompson	29	02.02.2002 – Scotland	27.03.2004 – France
G T Thomson	9	04.03.1878 – Scotland	07.02.1885 – Ireland
W B Thomson	4	02.01.1892 – Wales	09.03.1895 – Scotland
J D Thorne	3	19.01.1963 – Wales	23.02.1963 – France
M J Tindall	35	05.02.2000 – Ireland	27.03.2004 – France
V R Tindall	4	20.01.1951 – Wales	17.03.1951 – Scotland
F Tobin	1	27.03.1871 – Scotland	
A E Todd	2	03.02.1900 – Ireland	10.03.1900 – Scotland
R Todd	1	05.03.1877 – Scotland	
H B Toft	10	21.03.1936 – Scotland	18.03.1939 – Scotland
J T Toothill	12	01.03.1890 – Scotland	03.02.1894 – Ireland
L R Tosswill	3	11.01.1902 – Wales	15.03.1902 – Scotland
C J C Touzel	2	05.02.1877 – Ireland	05.03.1877 – Scotland
A C Towell	2	29.03.1948 – France	17.03.1951 – Scotland
B H Travers	6	18.01.1947 – Wales	19.03.1949 – Scotland
W T Treadwell	3	12.02.1966 – Ireland	19.03.1966 – Scotland
D M Trick	2	19.03.1983 – Ireland	02.06.1984 – South Africa
H B Tristram	5	03.03.1883 – Scotland	05.03.1887 – Scotland
C L Troop	2	11.02.1933 – Ireland	18.03.1933 – Scotland
J S Tucker	27	21.01.1922 – Wales	17.01.1931 – Wales
W E Tucker	5	06.01.1894 – Wales	09.03.1895 – Scotland
W E Tucker	3	13.02.1926 – Ireland	08.02.1930 – Ireland
D P Turner	6	27.03.1871 – Scotland	08.03.1875 – Scotland
E B Turner	3	13.12.1875 – Ireland	11.03.1878 – Ireland
G R Turner	1	06.03.1876 – Scotland	
H J C Turner	1	27.03.1871 – Scotland	

M E Turner	2	20.03.1948 – Scotland	29.03.1948 – France
D Turquand-Young	5	07.01.1928 – Australia	01.04.1929 – France
H T Twynaru	8	24.03.1879 – Ireland	01.03.1884 – Scotland
V E Ubogu*	24	17.10.1992 – Canada	26.06.1999 – Australia
A M Underwood	5	20.01.1962 – Wales	08.02.1964 – Ireland
R Underwood	85	18.02.1984 – Ireland	16.03.1996 – Ireland
T Underwood*	27	17.10.1992 – Canada	05.12.1998 – South Africa
E J Unwin	4	20.03.1937 – Scotland	19.03.1938 – Scotland
G T Unwin	1	12.03.1898 – Scotland	
R Uren	4	14.02.1948 – Ireland	11.02.1950 – Ireland
R M Uttley	23	10.02.1973 – Ireland	15.03.1980 – Scotland
J Valentine	5	15.02.1890 – Wales	14.03.1896 – Scotland
C H R Vanderspar	1	03.03.1873 – Scotland	
C B Van Ryneveld	4	15.01.1949 – Wales	19.03.1949 – Scotland
H Varley	1	05.03.1892 – Scotland	
H Vassall	5	19.02.1881 – Wales	16.12.1882 – Wales
H H Vassall	1	08.02.1908 – Ireland	
D B Vaughan	8	03.01.1948 – Australia	21.01.1950 – Wales
A Vaughan-Jones	3	13.02.1932 – Ireland	21.01.1933 – Wales
C L Verelst	2	13.12.1875 – Ireland	11.03.1878 – Ireland
G E Vernon	5	04.03.1878 – Scotland	05.02.1881 – Ireland
G Vickery	1	11.02.1905 – Ireland	
P J Vickery*	43	21.02.1998 – Wales	27.03.2004 – France
E J Vivyan	4	05.01.1901 – Wales	19.03.1904 – Scotland
A T Voyce	27	14.02.1920 – Ireland	20.03.1926 – Scotland
T Voyce	1	16.06.2001 – USA	16.06.2001 – USA
J A S Wackett	2	17.01.1959 – Wales	14.02.1959 – Ireland
C G Wade	8	16.12.1882 – Wales	06.02.1886 – Ireland
M R Wade	3	20.01.1962 – Wales	24.02.1962 – France
D Walder	4	02.06.2001 – Canada	23.08.2003 – Wales
W W Wakefield	31	17.01.1920 – Wales	02.04.1927 – France
G A Walker	2	21.01.1939 – Wales	11.02.1939 – Ireland
H W Walker	9	18.01.1947 – Wales	29.03.1948 – France
R Walker	5	23.02.1874 – Scotland	28.02.1880 – Scotland
J N S Wallens	1	02.04.1927 – France	
E J Walton	4	05.01.1901 – Wales	15.03.1902 – Scotland
W Walton	1	17.03.1894 – Scotland	
G Ward	6	18.01.1913 – Wales	21.03.1914 – Scotland
H Ward	1	05.01.1895 – Wales	
J l Ward	2	05.02.1881 – Ireland	06.02.1882 – Ireland
J W Ward	3	04.01.1896 – Wales	14.03.1896 – Scotland
C S Wardlow	6	20.12.1969 – South Africa	27.03.1971 – Scotland
P J Warfield	6	06.01.1973 – New Zealand	15.03.1975 – Scotland
A L Warr	2	20.01.1934 – Wales	10.02.1934 – Ireland
M Warrington	3	09.01.1909 – Australia	30.01.1909 – France
F Waters	1	16.06.2001 – USA	16.06.2001 – USA
J A Watkins	7	03.06.1972 – South Africa	15.02.1975 – Wales
J K Watkins	3	21.01.1939 – Wales	18.03.1939 – Scotland
F B Watson	2	21.03.1908 – Scotland	20.03.1909 – Scotland
J H D Watson	3	17.01.1914 – Wales	13.04.1914 – France
D E J Watt	4	11.02.1967 – Ireland	15.04.1967 – Wales
C S H Webb	12	02.01.1932 – South Africa	21.03.1936 – Scotland
J M Webb	33	23.05.1987 – Australia	20.03.1993 – Ireland
J W G Webb	3	27.02.1926 – France	16.03.1929 – Scotland
R E Webb	12	18.03.1967 – Scotland	26.02.1972 – France
St L H Webb	4	17.01.1959 – Wales	21.03.1959 – Scotland
J G Webster	11	15.01.1972 – Wales	15.02.1975 – Wales
T G Wedge	2	05.01.1907 – France	16.01.1909 – Wales
R H G Weighill	4	15.03.1947 – Scotland	29.03.1948 – France
C M Wells	6	04.03.1893 – Scotland	13.03.1897 – Scotland
B R West	8	20.01.1968 – Wales	21.03.1970 – Scotland
D E West	21	07.02.1998 – France	22.11.2003 – Australia
R West	1	04.06.1995 – Western Samoa	
H T E Weston	1	09.03.1901 – Scotland	
L E Weston	2	26.02.1972 – France	18.03.1972 – Scotland
M P Weston	29	16.01.1960 – Wales	16.03.1968 – Scotland
W H Weston	16	11.02.1933 – Ireland	19.03.1938 – Scotland
A A Wheatley	5	16.01.1937 – Wales	19.03.1938 – Scotland
H F Wheatley	7	08.02.1936 – Ireland	18.03.1939 – Scotland
P J Wheeler	41	01.02.1975 – France	17.03.1984 – Wales
C White	4	19.11.1983 – New Zealand	03.03.1984 – France
D F White	14	18.01.1947 – Wales	21.03.1953 – Scotland
J White	21	17.06.2001 – South Africa	27.03.2004 – France
S White-Cooper	2	09.06.2001 – Canada	16.06.2001 – USA
E C P Whiteley	2	21.03.1931 – Scotland	06.04.1931 – France
W Whiteley	1	04.01.1896 – Wales	

H Whitley	1	19.01.1929 – Wales	
H J Wigglesworth	1	04.02.1884 – Ireland	
B J Wightman	5	17.01.1959 – Wales	04.06.1963 –Australia
D T Wilkins	13	20.01.1951 – Wales	21.03.1953 – Scotland
E Wilkinson	5	02.01.1886 – Wales	05.03.1887 – Scotland
H Wilkinson	4	19.01.1929 – Wales	22.02.1930 – France
H J Wilkinson	1	16.02.1889 – NZ Natives	
J P Wilkinson*	52	04.04.1998 – Ireland	22.11.2003 – Australia
P Wilkinson	1	05.02.1872 – Scotland	
R M Wilkinson	6	31.05.1975 – Australia	20.03.1976 – France
T J Willcocks	1	11.01.1902 – Wales	
J G Willcox	16	11.02.1961 – Ireland	21.03.1964 – Scotland
P B K W William-Powlett	1	18.03.1922 – Scotland	
C G Williams	1	20.03.1976 – France	
C S Williams	1	03.03.1910 – France	
J E Williams	9	10.04.1954 – France	16.01.1965 – Wales
J M Williams	2	10.02.1951 – Ireland	17.03.1951 – Scotland
P N Wlliams	4	04.04.1987 – Scotland	08.06.1987 – Wales
S G Williams	7	11.01.1902 – Wales	16.03.1907 – Scotland
S H Williams	4	21.01.1911 – Wales	18.03.1911 – Scotland
R H Williamson	5	18.01.1908 – Wales	30.01.1909 – France
A J Wilson	1	13.02.1909 – Ireland	
C E Wilson	1	05.02.1898 – Ireland	
C P Wilson	1	19.02.1881 – Wales	
D S Wilson	8	28.02.1953 – France	19.03.1955 – Scotland
G S Wilson	2	19.01.1929 – Wales	09.02.1929 – Ireland
K J Wilson	1	23.02.1963 – France	
R P Wilson	3	03.01.1891 – Wales	07.03.1891 – Scotland
W C Wilson	2	09.02.1907 – Ireland	16.03.1907 – Scotland
C E Winn	8	05.01.1952 – South Africa	10.04.1954 – France
P J Winterbottom	58	02.01.1982 – Australia	20.03.1993 – Ireland
T C Wintle	5	19.03.1966 – Scotland	12.04.1969 – Wales
N A Wodehouse	14	03.03.1910 – France	15.03.1913 – Scotland
A Wood	1	04.02.1884 – Ireland	
A E Wood	3	01.01.1908 – France	08.02.1908 – Ireland
G W Wood	1	17.01.1914 – Wales	
M Wood	3	02.06.2001 – Canada	16.06.2001 – USA
R Wood	1	03.02.1894 – Ireland	
R D Wood	3	09.02.1901 – Ireland	14.02.1903 – Ireland
E E Woodgate	1	19.01.1952 – Wales	
E Woodhead	1	30.01.1880 – Ireland	
T J Woodman	20	05.02.2000 – Wales	27.03.2004 – France
C G Woodruff	4	20.01.1951 – Wales	17.03.1951 – Scotland
S M J Woods	13	15.02.1890 – Wales	09.03.1895 – Scotland
Thomas Woods	1	21.03.1908 – Scotland	
Tom Woods	5	20.03.1920 – Scotland	28.03.1921 – France
Sir C R Woodward	21	19.01.1980 – Ireland	17.03.1984 – Wales
J E Woodward	15	05.01.1952 – South Africa	17.03.1956 – Scotland
C S Wooldridge	7	16.12.1882 – Wales	07.02.1885 – Ireland
A J Wordsworth	1	24.05.1975 – Australia	
J P R Worsley*	34	15.10.1999 – Tonga	27.03.2004 – France
M Worsley	1	09.03.2003 – Italy	09.03.2003 – Italy
J R B Worton	2	16.01.1926 – Wales	15.01.1927 – Wales
D F B Wrench	2	22.02.1964 – France	21.03.1964 – Scotland
C C G Wright	2	13.02.1909 – Ireland	20.03.1909 – Scotland
F T Wright	1	19.03.1881 – Scotland	
I D Wright	4	16.01.1971 – Wales	20.03.1971 – Scotland
J C Wright	1	20.01.1934 – Wales	
J F Wright	1	15.02.1890 – Wales	
T P Wright	13	16.01.1960 – Wales	17.03.1962 – Scotland
W H G Wright	2	17.01.1920 – Wales	31.01.1920 – France
D M Wyatt	1	21.02.1976 – Scotland	
P G Warranton	5	16.01.1954 – Wales	19.03.1955 – Scotland
K P Yates	2	30.05.1997 – Argentina	06.06.1997 – Argentina
W Yiend	6	16.02.1889 – NZ Natives	04.03.1893 – Scotland
A T Young	18	19.01.1924 – Wales	09.02.1929 – Ireland
J R C Young	9	08.02.1958 – Ireland	25.02.1961 – France
M Young	10	15.01.1977 – Scotland	03.02.1979 – Scotland
P D Young	9	16.01.1954 – Wales	19.03.1955 – Scotland
N G Youngs	6	19.03.1983 – Ireland	17.03.1984 – Wales

ENGLAND CAPTAINS

No.	Captain	First Match – Opponents	P	W	D	L
1	F Stokes	27.03.1871 – Scotland	3	1	1	1
2	A St G Hamersley	23.02.1874 – Scotland	1	1	0	0
3	Hon H A Lawrence	15.02.1875 – Ireland	2	1	1	0
4	F Luscombe	13.12.1875 – Ireland	2	2	0	0
5	E Kewley	05.02.1877 – Ireland	3	1	1	1
6	M W Marshall	11.03.1878 – Ireland	1	1	0	0
7	F R Adams	10.03.1879 – Scotland	2	1	1	0
8	L Stokes	30.01.1880 – Ireland	5	4	1	0
9	C Gurdon	06.02.1882 – Ireland	1	0	1	0
10	A N Hornby	04.03.1882 – Scotland	1	0	0	1
11	E T Gurdon	16.12.1882 – Wales	9	8	1	0
12	C J B Marriott	02.01.1886 – Wales	2	2	0	0
13	Alan Rotherham	08.01.1887 – Wales	3	0	2	1
14	F Bonsor	16.02.1889 – NZ Natives	1	1	0	0
15	A E Stoddart	15.02.1890 – Wales	4	1	0	3
16	J L Hickson	01.03.1890 – Scotland	1	1	0	0
17	F H R Alderson	03.01.1891 – Wales	5	4	0	1
18	S M J Woods	06.02.1892 – Ireland	5	4	0	1
19	R E Lockwood	06.01.1894 – Wales	2	1	0	1
20	E W Taylor	17.03.1894 – Scotland	6	2	0	4
21	F Mitchell	14.03.1896 – Scotland	1	0	0	1
22	J E Byrne	05.02.1898 – Ireland	3	1	1	1
23	Arthur Rotherham	07.01.1899 – Wales	3	0	0	3
24	R H B Cattell	06.01.1900 – Wales	1	0	0	1
25	J Daniell	03.02.1900 – Ireland	6	4	1	1
26	J T Taylor	05.01.1901 – Wales	1	0	0	1
27	W L Bunting	09.02.1901 – Ireland	2	0	0	2
28	H Alexander	11.01.1902 – Wales	1	0	0	1
29	B Oughtred	10.01.1903 – Wales	2	0	0	2
30	P D Kendall	21.03.1903 – Scotland	1	0	0	1
31	F M Stout	09.01.1904 – Wales	4	0	1	3
32	V H Cartwright	02.12.1905 – New Zealand	6	2	1	3
33	B A Hill	05.01.1907 – France	2	1	0	1
34	J Green	09.02.1907 – Ireland	1	0	0	1
35	E W Roberts	16.03.1907 – Scotland	1	0	0	1
36	T S Kelly	01.01.1908 – France	1	1	0	0
37	J G G Birkett	18.01.1908 – Wales	5	2	0	3
38	C E L Hammond	08.02.1908 – Ireland	1	1	0	0
39	L A N Slocock	21.03.1908 – Scotland	1	0	0	1
40	G H D'O Lyon	09.01.1909 – Australia	1	0	0	1
41	R Dibble	16.01.1909 – Wales	7	4	0	3
42	A D Stoop	15.01.1910 – Wales	2	1	1	0
43	E R Mobbs	03.03.1910 – France	1	1	0	0
44	A L H Gotley	18.03.1911 – Scotland	1	1	0	0
45	N A Wodehouse	08.04.1912 – France	6	5	0	1
46	R W Poulton	17.01.1914 – Wales	4	4	0	0
47	J E Greenwood	17.01.1920 – Wales	4	3	0	1
48	W J A Davies	15.01.1921 – Wales	11	10	1	0
49	L G Brown	21.01.1922 – Wales	1	0	0	1
50	W W Wakefield	19.01.1924 – Wales	13	7	2	4
51	L J Corbett	12.02.1927 – Ireland	4	2	0	2
52	R Cove-Smith	07.01.1928 – Australia	7	6	0	1
53	H G Periton	16.03.1929 – Scotland	4	2	0	2
54	J S Tucker	22.02.1930 – France	3	1	2	0
55	P D Howard	14.02.1931 – Ireland	1	0	0	1
56	C D Aarvold	21.03.1931 – Scotland	7	2	0	5
57	A L Novis	11.02.1933 – Ireland	2	1	0	1
58	B C Gadney	20.01.1934 – Wales	8	5	1	2
59	D A Kendrew	19.01.1935 – Wales	2	1	1	0
60	H G O Owen-Smith	16.01.1937 – Wales	3	3	0	0
61	P Cranmer	15.01.1938 – Wales	2	1	0	1
62	H B Toft	19.03.1938 – Scotland	4	2	0	2
63	J Mycock	18.01.1947 – Wales	2	1	0	1
64	J Heaton	15.03.1947 – Scotland	2	2	0	0
65	E K Scott	03.01.1948 – Australia	3	0	0	3
66	T A Kemp	17.01.1948 – Wales	1	0	1	0
67	R H G Weighill	29.03.1948 – France	1	0	0	1
68	N M Hall	15.01.1949 – Wales	13	6	2	5
69	I Preece	26.02.1949 – France	6	3	0	3
70	V G Roberts	20.01.1951 – Wales	1	0	0	1
71	J M K Kendall-Carpenter	10.02.1951 – Ireland	3	1	0	2
72	R V Stirling	16.01.1954 – Wales	5	3	0	2

73	P D Young	26.02.1955 – France	2	1	0	1
74	E Evans	21.01.1956 – Wales	13	9	2	2
75	J Butterfield	17.01.1959 – Wales	4	1	2	1
76	R E G Jeeps	16.01.1960 – Wales	13	5	4	4
77	R A W Sharp	19.01.1963 – Wales	5	3	1	1
78	M P Weston	25.05.1963 – New Zealand	5	1	0	4
79	J G Willcox	04.01.1964 – New Zealand	3	0	1	2
80	C R Jacobs	22.02.1964 – France	2	1	0	1
81	D G Perry	16.01.1965 – Wales	4	1	1	2
82	D P Rogers	15.01.1966 – Wales	7	2	1	4
83	P E Judd	11.02.1967 – Ireland	5	2	0	3
84	C W McFadyean	20.01.1968 – Wales	2	0	2	0
85	J R H Greenwood	08.02.1969 – Ireland	1	0	0	1
86	R Hiller	20.12.1969 – South Africa	7	2	1	4
87	R B Taylor	18.04.1970 – France	1	0	0	1
88	A L Bucknall	16.01.1971 – Wales	1	0	0	1
89	J S Spencer	13.02.1971 –v Ireland	4	1	0	3
90	P J Dixon	26.02.1972 – France	2	0	0	2
91	J V Pullin	03.06.1972 – South Africa	13	6	1	6
92	F E Cotton	18.01.1975 – Ireland	3	0	0	3
93	A Neary	15.03.1975 – Scotland	7	2	0	5
94	R M Uttley	08.01.1977 – Scotland	5	2	1	2
95	W B Beaumont	21.01.1978 – France	21	11	2	8
96	S J Smith	06.02.1982 – Ireland	5	2	1	2
97	J P Scott	05.03.1983 – Scotland	4	0	0	4
98	P J Wheeler	19.11.1983 – New Zealand	5	2	0	3
99	N D Melville	03.11.1984 – Australia	7	4	0	3
100	P W Dodge	05.01.1985 – Romania	7	2	1	4
101	R J Hill	07.02.1987 – Ireland	3	0	0	3
102	M E Harrison	04.04.1987 – Scotland	7	3	0	4
103	J Orwin	23.04.1988 – Ireland	3	1	0	2
104	R M Harding	17.06.1988 – Fiji	1	1	0	0
105	W D C Carling	05.11.1988 – Australia	59	44	1	14
106	C R Andrew	13.05.1989 – Romania	2	2	0	0
107	P R de Glanville	23.11.1996 – Italy	8	5	0	3
108	J Leonard	14.12.1996 – Argentina	2	2	0	0
109	L B N Dallaglio*	15.11.1997 – Australia	19	10	7	2
110	A J Diprose*	06.06.1998 – Australia	1	0	0	1
111	M J S Dawson*	20.06.1998 – New Zealand	9	4	0	5
112	M O Johnson*	14.11.1998 – Holland	39	34	0	5
113	K P P Bracken*	02.06.2001 – Canada	3	3	0	0
114	N Back*	10.11.2001 – Australia	4	4	0	0
115	P Vickery*	22.06.2002 – Argentina	2	2	0	0
116	J P Wilkinson*	09.03.2003 – Italy	1	1	0	0
117	D West*	30.08.2003 – France	1	0	0	1

MOST APPEARANCES

Player	Caps	Years
J Leonard	114	1990–2004
R Underwood	85	1984–1996
M O Johnson	84	1993–2003
W R C Carling	72	1988–1997
C R Andrew	71	1985–1997
L B N Dallaglio	70	1995–2004
R A Hill	68	1997–2004
N A Back	66	1994–2003
J C Guscott	65	1989–1999
B C Moore	64	1987–1995
M J Catt	63	1994–2004
M J S Dawson	62	1995–2004
P J Winterbottom	58	1982–1993
W A Dooley	55	1985–1993
J P Wilkinson	52	1998–2003
W J H Greenwood	52	1997–2004
A S Healey	51	1997–2003
K P P Bracken	51	1993–2003
D Richards	48	1986–1996
D J Grewcock	47	1997–2004
G C Rowntree	45	1995–2003
T A K Rodber	44	1992–1999
A Neary	43	1971–1980
P J Vickery	43	1998–2004

J V Pullin	42	1966–1976
P J Wheeler	41	1975–1984
B B Clarke	40	1992–1999
B C Cohen	40	2000–2004
D Luger	38	1998–2003
P R De Glanville	38	1992–1999
J A Probyn	37	1988–1993
M B Perry	36	1997–2001
D J Duckham	36	1969–1976
G S Pearce	36	1979–1991
M J Tindall	35	2000–2004
W B Beaumont	34	1975–1982
D P Rogers	34	1961–1969
J P Scott	34	1978–1984
J P R Worsley	34	1999–2004
B J Kay	33	2001–2004
J M Webb	33	1987–1993
J Robinson	33	2001–2004
P J Grayson	32	1995–2004
P W Dodge	32	1978–1985
M A C Slemen	31	1976–1984
W W Wakefield	31	1920–1927
F E Cotton	31	1971–1981
M C Bayfield	31	1991–1996
M Regan	30	1995–2004
E Evans	30	1948–1958
M E Corry	29	1997–2003
S Thompson	29	2002–2004
P J Squires	29	1973–1979
M P Weston	29	1960–1968
C R Jacobs	29	1956–1964
R J Hill	29	1984–1991
R Cove–Smith	29	1921–1929
P A G Rendall	28	1984–1991
S J Smith	28	1973–1983
J Butterfield	28	1953–1959
A T Voyce	27	1920–1926
J S Tucker	27	1922–1931
A Underwood	27	1992–1998
R Cockerill	27	1997–1999
M C Teague	27	1985–1993
C D Morris	26	1988–1995
J Carleton	26	1979–1984
M S Phillips	25	1958– 1964
S D Shaw	25	1996– 2004
C B Stevens	25	1969–1975
J D Currie	25	1956–1962
W H Hare	25	1974–1984
M J Colclough	25	1978–1986
D J Garforth	25	1997–2000
C N Lowe	25	1913–1923
R E G Jeeps	24	1956–1962
V E Ubogu	24	1992–1999
P B T Greening	24	1996–2001
A G Ripley	24	1972–1976
P J Larter	24	1967–1973
L W Moody	24	2001–2003
G W Rees	23	1984–1991
R W R Marques	23	1956–1961
O J Lewsey	23	1998–2004
S J Halliday	23	1986–1992
R M Uttley	23	1973–1980
J M K Kendall–Carpenter	23	1949–1954
W J A Davies	22	1913–1923
P J Ackford	22	1988–1991
P J Dixon	22	1971–1978
I R Balshaw	22	2000–2004
C W Ralston	22	1971–1975
P E Judd	22	1962–1967
G S Archer	21	1996–2000
G H Davies	21	1981–1986
D E West	21	1998–2003
H G Periton	21	1925–1930
J P Hall	21	1984–1994
M G Skinner	21	1988–1992
J White	21	2000–2004

J G G Birkett	21		1906–1912
C R Woodward	21		1980–1984
N E Horton	20		1969–1980
N C Redman	20		1984–1997
T J Woodman	20		2000–2004
P B Jackson	20		1956–1963

HIGHEST POINTS SCORERS

Player	Pts	Mat	PPM	Tr	Con	PG	DG
J P Wilkinson	817	52	15.8	5	123	161	21
P J Grayson	400	32	12.5	2	78	72	6
C R Andrew	396	71	5.57	2	33	86	21
J M Webb	296	33	8.96	4	41	66	0
W H Hare	240	25	9.60	2	14	67	1
R Underwood	210	85	2.47	49	0	0	0
S D Hodgkinson	203	14	14.50	1	35	43	0
W J H Greenwood	150	52	2.88	30	0	0	0
B C Cohen	145	40	3.65	29	0	0	0
J C Guscott	143	65	2.2	30	0	0	2
M J Catt	142	63	2.25	7	16	22	3
R B Hiller	138	19	7.26	3	12	33	2
D Luger	120	38	3.16	24	0	0	0
A G B Old	98	16	6.12	1	8	23	3
M J S Dawson	96	62	1.55	15	6	3	0
J Robinson	95	33	2.88	19	0	0	0
N A Back	83	66	1.26	16	0	0	1
W M H Rose	82	10	8.20	2	4	22	0
O J Lewsey	80	23	3.48	2	4	22	0
A S Healey	75	51	1.47	15	0	0	0
L B N Dallaglio	70	70	1	14	0	0	0
J E B Callard	69	5	13.80	0	3	21	0
A Underwood	65	27	2.40	13	0	0	0
R W Hosen	63	10	6.30	0	6	17	0
C Hodgson	59	8	7.38	2	17	5	0
C N Lowe	58	25	2.32	18	0	0	1
I R Balshaw	55	22	2.5	11	0	0	0
R A Hill	68	55	1.24	11	0	0	0
W D C Carling	54	72	0.75	12	0	0	0
M B Perry	50	36	1.39	10	0	0	0

MOST POINTS IN A MATCH

Player	Points	Opposition	Venue	Date	Result
C Hodgson	44 – 2T, 14C, 2PG	Romania	Twickenham	17.11.2001	134–0
P J Grayson	36 – 12C, 4PG	Tonga	Twickenham	15.10.1999	101–10
J P Wilkinson	35 – 1T, 9C, 4PG	Italy	Twickenham	17.02.2001	80–23
J P Wilkinson	32 – 1T, 6C, 5PG	Italy	Twickenham	02.10.1999	67–7
C R Andrew	30 – 6PG, 6C	Canada	Twickenham	10.12.1994	60–19
P J Grayson	30 – 15C	Holland	Huddersfield	14.11.1998	110–0
J P Wilkinson	30 – 1T, 5C, 4PG, 1DG	Wales	Twickenham	23.03.2002	50–10
D Walder	29 – 2T, 5C, 3PG	Canada	Vancouver	09.06.2000	59–20
C R Andrew	27 – 1T, 1DG, 5PG, 2C	South Africa	Pretoria	04.06.1994	32–15
J P Wilkinson	27 – 8PG, 1DG	South Africa	Bloemf	24.06.2000	27–22
J P Wilkinson	26 – 13C	USA	Twickenham	21.08.1999	106–8
J Lewsey	25 – 5T	Uruguay	Brisbane	02.04.2003	111–13
J M Webb	24 – 1T, 4PG, 4C	Italy	Twickenham	08.10.1991	36–6
C R Andrew	24 – 4PG, 6C	Romania	Twickenham	12.11.1994	54–3
C R Andrew	24 – 1DG, 7PG	Scotland	Twickenham	18.03.1995	24–12
C R Andrew	24 – 2DG, 6PG	Argentina	Durban	27.05.1995	24–18
J P Wilkinson	24 – 5PG, 3DG	France	Sydney	16.11.2003	24–7
S D Hodgkinson	23 – 3PG, 7C	Argentina	Twickenham	03.11.1990	51–0
P J Grayson	23 – 1DG, 6PG, 1C	Ireland	Twickenham	16.03.1996	28–15
J P Wilkinson	23 – 1C, 4PG	Fiji	Twickenham	20.10.1999	45–24
J P Wilkinson	23 – 1C, 6PG	Wales	Brisbane	09.04.2003	28–17
D Lambert	22 – 2T, 2PG, 5C	France	Twickenham	28.01.1911	37–0
J M Webb	22 – 2T, 2PG, 4C	Ireland	Twickenham	01.02.1992	38–9
J P Wilkinson	22 – 6PG, 2C	Australia	Twickenham	16.11.2002	32–31
P J Grayson	22 – 11C	Uruguay	Brisbane	02.04.2003	111–13
C R Andrew	21 – 1DG, 6PG	Wales	Twickenham	18.01.1986	21–18
S D Hodgkinson	21 – 7PG	Wales	Cardiff	19.01.1991	25–6
J E B Callard	21 – 5PG, 3C	Western Samoa	Durban	04.06.1995	44–22
P J Grayson	21 – 5PG, 3C	Scotland	Twickenham	01.02.1997	41–13
M J Catt	21 – 1T, 2PG, 5C	Argentina	Buenos Aires	30.05.1997	46–20

J P Wilkinson	21 – 7PG	France	Twickenham	20.03.1999	21–10
J P Wilkinson	21 – 3C, 5PG	Wales	Twickenham	04.03.2000	46–12
J P Wilkinson	21 – 5PG, 2DG	Australia	Twickenham	10.11.2001	21–15
J P Wilkinson	21 – 7PG	South Africa	Twickenham	24.11.2001	29 –9
J P Wilkinson	21 – 1T, 2C, 3PG, 1DG	New Zealand	Twickenham	09.11.2002	31–28
J M Webb	20 – 2PG, 7C	Japan	Sydney	30.05.1987	60–7
R Underwood	20 – 5T	Fiji	Twickenham	04.11.1989	58–23
C R Andrew	20 – 1DG, 5PG, 1C	Australia	Cape Town	17.06.1995	25–22
P J Grayson	20 – 2PG, 7C	Wales	Twickenham	21.02.1998	60–26
N A Back	20 – 4T	Holland	Huddersfield	14.11.1998	110–0
J C Guscott	20 – 4T	Holland	Huddersfield	14.11.1998	110–0
J C Guscott	20 – 4T	USA	Twickenham	21.08.1999	106–8
J Robinson	20 – 4T	Romania	Twickenham	17.11.2002	134–0
J P Wilkinson	20 – 1PG, 6C, 1T	Ireland	Twickenham	16.02.2002	45–11
J P Wilkinson	20 – 5PG, 1DG, 1C	France	Twickenham	15.02.2003	25–17
J P Wilkinson	20 – 1C, 4PG	South Africa	Perth	18.10.2003	25–6

TOP TRY SCORERS

Player	Tries	Mat	1	2	3	4	5
R Underwood	49	85	21	10	1	–	1
W Greenwood	30	52	13	7	1	–	–
J C Guscott	30	65	13	3	1	2	–
B Cohen	29	40	14	6	1	–	–
D Luger	24	38	15	3	1	–	–
J Robinson	19	33	6	3	1	1	–
C N Lowe	18	25	8	2	2	–	–
J Lewsey	16	23	5	3	–	–	1
N A Back	16	66	10	1	–	1	–
A Healey	15	51	6	3	1	–	–
M J S Dawson	15	62	11	2	–	–	–
L B N Dallaglio	14	70	12	1	–	–	–
T Underwood	13	27	7	3	–	–	–
W D C Carling	12	72	10	1	–	–	–
I Balshaw	11	22	5	3	–	–	–
R Hill	11	55	11	–	–	–	–
J C C Birkett	10	21	6	2	–	–	–
R J Duckham	10	36	6	2	–	–	–
M Perry	10	36	6	2	–	–	–
A Hudson	9	8	1	2	–	1	–
M Tindall	9	35	7	1	–	–	–
D.Lambert	8	7	1	1	–	–	1
G C Robinson	8	8	6	1	–	–	–
C Oti	8	13	1	–	1	1	–
M E Harrison	8	15	5	–	1	–	–
R W Poulton	8	17	4	–	–	1	–
C H Pillman	8	18	4	2	–	–	–
M Slemen	8	31	8	–	–	–	–
J Worsley	8	34	8	–	–	–	–
P R de Glanville	8	38	8	–	–	–	–
C G Wade	7	8	4	–	1	–	–
A M Smallwood	7	14	3	2	–	–	–
J Carleton	7	26	4	–	1	–	–
M Catt	7	63	3	2	–	–	–
H H Taylor	6	5	1	1	1	–	–
V H M Coates	6	5	1	1	1	–	–
P Greening	6	5	4	1	–	–	–
G W Burton	6	6	2	–	–	1	–
H C Catcheside	6	8	2	2	–	–	–
W N Bolton	6	11	6	–	–	–	–
J E Woodward	6	15	4	1	–	–	–
A Gomersall	6	17	2	2	–	–	–
J Roberts	6	18	4	1	–	–	–
P B Jackson	6	20	4	1	–	–	–
H G Periton	6	21	4	1	–	–	–
L Moody	6	24	4	1	–	–	–
P J Squires	6	29	6	–	–	–	–

Player							
W W Wakefield	6	31	6	–	–	–	–
D Richards	6	48	4	1	–	–	–
A D Roberts	5	8	3	1	–	–	–
J S R Reeve	5	8	1	2	–	–	–
E F Fookes	5	10	1	2	–	–	–
H C C Laird	5	10	5	–	–	–	–
H S Sever	5	10	5	–	–	–	–
R H Guest	5	13	3	1	–	–	–
R E Lockwood	5	14	3	1	–	–	–
P H Thompson	5	17	3	1	–	–	–
M S Phillips	5	25	5	–	–	–	–
C D Morris	5	26	5	–	–	–	–
A T Voyce	5	27	5	–	–	–	–
J Butterfield	5	28	5	–	–	–	–
E Evans	5	30	5	–	–	–	–
A Neary	5	43	5	–	–	–	–
T A K Rodber	5	44	5	–	–	–	–
J Wilkinson	5	52	5	–	–	–	–

MOST TRIES IN A MATCH

Player	Tries	Opposition	Venue	Date	Result
D Lambert	5	France	Richmond	05.01.1907	41–13
R Underwood	5	Fiji	Twickenham	04.11.1989	58–23
J Lewsey	5	Uruguay	Brisbane	02.11.2003	111–13
G W Burton	4	Wales	Blackheath	19.02.1881	7G 1DG 6T–0
A Hudson	4	France	Paris	22.03.1906	35–8
K W Poulton	4	France	Paris	13.04.1914	39–13
C Oti	4	Romania	Bucharest	13.05.1989	58–3
N A Back	4	Holland	Huddersfield	14.11.1998	110–0
J C Guscott	4	Holland	Huddersfield	14.11.1998	110–0
J C Guscott	4	USA	Twickenham	21.08.1999	106–8
J Robinson	4	Romania	Twickenham	17.11.2001	134–0
H H Taylor	3	Ireland	Manchester	05.02.1881	2G 2T–0
H Vassall	3	Wales	Blackheath	19.02.1881	7G 1DG 6T–0
C G Wade	3	Wales	Swansea	16.12.1882	2G 4T–0
H Marshall	3	Wales	Cardiff	07.01.1893	11–12
V H M Coates	3	France	Twickenham	25.01.1913	20–0
C N Lowe	3	Scotland	Edinburgh	21.03.1914	16–15
C N Lowe	3	France	Paris	13.04.1914	39–13
H P Jacob	3	France	Twickenham	23.02.1924	19–7
J Carleton	3	Scotland	Edinburgh	15.03.1980	30–18
M E Harrison	3	Japan	Sydney	30.05.1987	60–7
C Oti	3	Ireland	Twickenham	19.03.1988	35–3
J C Guscott	3	Romania	Bucharest	13.05.1989	58–3
R Underwood	3	Argentina	Twickenham	03.11.1990	51–0
A Healey	3	Italy	Rome	18.03.2000	59–12
W Greenwood	3	Wales	Cardiff	03.02.2001	44–15
D Luger	3	Romania	Twickenham	17.04.2001	134–0
B Cohen	3	Romania	Twickenham	17.04.2001	134–0
J Robinson	3	Italy	Rome	15.02.2004	50–9

Index